❖ The Words of War ❖

THE WORDS OF WAR

British Forces' Personal Letters and
Diaries During the Second World War

MARCUS COWPER

IMPERIAL WAR
MUSEUM

MAINSTREAM
PUBLISHING

EDINBURGH AND LONDON

Introduction and commentary
copyright © Marcus Cowper and Imperial War Museum, 2009
Images copyright © Imperial War Museum, 2009
All rights reserved
The moral rights of the authors have been asserted

First published in Great Britain in 2009 by
MAINSTREAM PUBLISHING COMPANY
(EDINBURGH) LTD
7 Albany Street
Edinburgh EH1 3UG

ISBN 9781845965310

A catalogue record for this book is available
from the British Library

Typeset in Caslon and ParmaPetit

Printed and bound in the UK by
CPI Mackays, Chatham ME5 8TD

CONTENTS

Foreword by Edward Stourton

In 1989, while I was based in Paris for the BBC, the French authorities arrested one of their country's most elusive war criminals. Paul Touvier was the Lyons head of the Vichy paramilitary police force known as the *Milice*; he worked closely with the notorious 'Butcher of Lyons', Klaus Barbie.

He was arrested in 1947 but escaped, and for long periods during the subsequent four decades he was hidden in Catholic monasteries around France. When he was finally tracked down, he was living in a convent in Nice which was loyal to the ultra-right-wing *Lefebvrist* Catholic sect.

When we interviewed the public prosecutor in the case a couple of months later, he tipped us off that a new witness had come forward. The man, a Communist resistance fighter during the German Occupation, had been picked up with seven others to be executed in reprisal for an operation by the Resistance. He was the only non-Jew in the group, and Touvier spared him at the last minute. The seven Jews were all shot, and the incident was therefore judged a crucial piece of evidence of Touvier's anti-Semitism.

We found our witness living in a slightly scruffy but comfortable farmhouse in the hills outside Lyons. At first he seemed reluctant to talk, and my heart sank when he asked whether we were in a hurry – we had in fact shoehorned him into a packed schedule. Then he explained why the interview might take some time; he had never said anything to anyone – not even his own children – about his wartime experiences, and now he wanted to unburden himself.

The stories poured out. Most moving of all was his description of the Lyons gaol the night before his execution was due. It was a custom, he explained, to keep your spirits up in such circumstances by singing – the *Marseillaise* if you were a Gaullist, the *Internationale* if you were a Communist.

One of his group revealed that he was a trained opera singer, and instead of belting out a defiant anthem he sang the aria which Cavaradossi, the hero of Puccini's *Tosca*, sings in the Castel St Angelo the night before he faces the firing squad. Even the prison guards, our witness recalled, fell silent as they listened to this poignant performance. And he said he wanted the story told so the young man would be remembered; the singer's identity was lost, and on the plaque marking the spot where the seven were shot his name is recorded simply as 'X INCONNU'.

The reticence of some of those who lived through the Second World War is understandable. Millions of people were caught up in the conflict and very many of them had extreme experiences. The extraordinary became almost commonplace. When almost everyone has a remarkable story to tell, why boast about your own?

But there is also an instinct to record and preserve events like these – and the archive which forms the basis for this book is a testimony to how powerful it can be. Reading some of the extracts from diaries and letters which Marcus Cowper has selected here gives you a strong sense of people writing in reaction against the scale of the conflict around them; they did so precisely because they wanted to assert their individuality amid the enormity of a World War, or perhaps to rescue the individuality of those, like the young Lyons opera singer, who would otherwise simply disappear beneath the juggernaut of big picture history.

Marcus Cowper has organised the material brilliantly; the links which give you the context for these vivid pieces of first-hand reporting are models of deft, disciplined storytelling. You are constantly reminded of the breadth of the theatre of war – from the chill waters of the Atlantic to the jungles of Burma and beyond – and I came away from the book with a much clearer sense of the strategic sweep of events.

Sometimes the style of the extracts made me smile, because it evoked a wartime Britain I have never quite believed in. People really did, it seems, say things like 'My hat, what bellicose, brutal, blathering bullies some Germans are'. If you described something as being 'about the size of a fairly large Oxford quadrangle', your audience, being the sort of chaps they were, immediately understood what you meant. Battle of Britain pilots really did have nicknames like 'Chubby', and if they survived being shot down in flames they could be described as 'slightly crisped but in fair working order'.

But anyone with experience of more recent wars will be struck by the echoes they find here much more than they are by the differences that separate our world from the 1940s.

One of the most terrifying aspects of the Bosnian War in the 1990s was the speed and thoroughness with which the population fractured along sectarian lines. During the siege of Sarajevo, I interviewed a group of Bosnian Muslim families who had lived in a mixed apartment block with Bosnian Serbs before the war. The Serbs had all fled from the city when the siege began, and the Muslims were simply bewildered by the way individual friends and neighbours of many years' standing had suddenly become part of a generalised, much-hated Enemy. Although almost all of them had come to loathe the Serbs with real passion – the siege was genuinely hellish, and often conducted with spiteful cruelty against the civilian population – they could not themselves quite understand the transformation that had gone on in their own minds and emotions.

There is a similar ambiguity in the attitudes to Britain's enemies revealed in these accounts. One seaman has given us a painfully honest description of his feelings as his destroyer directs furious fire at the crew of a stricken U-boat; 'in spite of my previous humanitarian ideas,' he records, 'I could summon up no feel for those men in the water. I found myself wanting, waiting to see them slaughtered in cold blood.' U-boat crews had a reputation for callousness, and when rescue boats are launched he says, 'I felt an even stronger emotion rise up. I remembered the tale of the destroyer captain who, when he received orders to pick up U-boat survivors, raised his glasses to the sky and said "I see no survivors" and steamed on.'

But equally there are glimpses of empathy and compassion, often based on a sense of shared experiences. Bomber crews who had been through the Blitz reflect on their deadly work at the height of the campaign against German cities; 'Poor Jerry. It's terrible what they are going through,' writes one Flight Engineer aboard a Halifax, 'But we enjoy doing it just the same . . . Yes, I'd much sooner be up where we are rather than down below at Jerry's end. He knows what bombing is now alright, believe me. It's mass slaughter, with Jerry at the receiving end . . .'

Whenever I return from a conflict zone – and this book is a humbling reminder that my own experiences of war have been comparatively tame – people ask whether I was frightened. It is the small details in these very personal accounts which bring to life what fear can do to people. A naval lieutenant escorting D-Day landing craft sees a ship close by being hit and sunk and recalls: 'I felt a fear of uncertainty that I'd never before known . . . for a few seconds on this occasion I couldn't get a sound from my mouth. I remember the doctor came on the bridge just then and I tried to tell him what was going on and nothing came out.' And an Anglican clergyman stationed in Malta records that during the German air raids, 'I find myself shivering as if I had the ague. Also it is necessary to use the chamber pot about every hour.'

Sometimes Marcus Cowper is able to put together several accounts of the same incident, so that you get a dramatic sense of the way a battle unfolded. There is plenty of material that evokes the sheer thrill of conflict – but just as much about its horror. And because the anecdotes are so personal – and often told in such conversational tones – I found myself getting caught up in the writers' stories almost as if I knew them. In September 1940, a young RAF pilot called Denis Wissler wrote a compelling diary entry about surviving a dogfight with a Messerschmitt. I cheered him on. After sharing his thrilling escape, it was all the more sobering to learn in the next paragraph that less than two months later he was dead.

As I read some of these stories, I found myself reflecting how delighted I would be to have them spoken into a microphone. Since I began working as a broadcast journalist in the late 1970s there has been a quiet revolution in the way wars are covered; of course we still interview the generals and the politicians, but the focus of our efforts has turned much more to recording the experience of ordinary people in extraordinary situations, and those are always the stories viewers and listeners remember.

You realise how important that is when you cannot do it. One of the most frustrating journalistic experiences I have ever had was the 2009 conflict in Gaza. From the hillsides around Gaza we had a wonderfully clear strategic view of the battlefield; we could watch the planes heading in and the missiles coming out, we could see the smoke and hear and feel the explosions. But we were unable to enter Gaza itself, so for information about what was actually happening there we had to rely on a handful of brave local journalists.

My colleague Jeremy Bowen, the BBC's Middle East editor, described the impact on our reporting like this: 'What we're not getting is some of the detail . . . For example, there were some incredibly moving pictures that I used at the end of one of my reports in the last week or so, and [one] was a man who was kissing his dead son goodbye in the hospital . . . The agency cameramen who are shooting these things are very brave and very enterprising. But if I'd been there I would have found out who that man was. I'd have gone to his house if it was still standing. I would have found out his personal story . . .'

The way history is written is also changing, so that the kind of personal stories told in this book are given greater prominence – history is, if you like, being democratised. The Imperial War Museum archive is still growing, and will continue to grow as the families of my generation clear the attics and desks of our parents and grandparents. I have no doubt at all that among my children's generation there will also be a growing appetite for an understanding of what it was like to live through that last – we hope – truly global conflict.

Edward Stourton

Introduction

Throughout the course of the Second World War, some 5.9 million men and women served in the British armed forces. The overwhelming majority, 3.8 million, served in the British Army, while 1.2 million were in the Royal Air Force and just under a million in the Royal Navy. The Department of Documents at the Imperial War Museum houses over 16,000 collections of private papers containing unpublished diaries, letters and memoirs written by servicemen and women, and by civilians in wartime, close to half of which relate to the Second World War, and these form the basis of this book.

The thousands of men and women who wrote these diaries did so in the face of official disapproval, as the keeping of personal records was seen as a threat to operational security. However, the scale and importance of the events ensured that many felt compelled to record their feelings and experiences.

Some of the diaries in this collection were written with a view to posterity, with the author consciously considering what material to include or reject. Others were scribbled down daily, or even hourly, with terse entries reflecting the immediate events affecting the writer.

The personal experiences of those who lived through the Second World War differed wildly and this is reflected in the contents of the diaries and letters. Sometimes the material contains simple lists of the author's daily routines, in other instances detailed expositions on their state of mind and feelings. The collections of the Imperial War Museum contain every possible variation of the form.

In a similar vein, every different response to the war is covered within their pages. The tumultuous events of 1939–45 elicited a huge range of responses from those who took part. Although large numbers of diaries and letters record the horror, fear and disgust at the nature of war and the cruel enemy they faced, many others also portray the Second World War as the greatest experience undertaken by the author, a time of dynamism and action when everyone had to 'do their bit'.

Perhaps most commonly they reflect the day-to-day obsessions and frustrations of the serving man and woman, irritation with the formalities and protocol of service life from those unaccustomed to its pre-war strictures; the dwelling over meals by those condemned to live on a drab, repetitive and in many cases inadequate diet. Whilst this study is structured around the major events that form the narrative of the Second World War, for the average soldier, sailor or airman, it was the detail of daily life that coloured their experience and that is what really shines through in the diaries and letters held in the collection. These reflections and recollections should not be seen as in any way definitive; in many cases their contents are contradictory and at odds with both other diaries and the official record. They should be taken for what they are, an individual response to extreme times and circumstances.

The attitudes shown in some of the material, and the language used, are also a product of a very specific time and set of events. Words and phrases that could nowadays cause offence were part of everyday usage in the 1930s and 1940s. Racial epithets such as 'Hun', 'Wop', 'Nip' and 'Wog' litter the diaries and personal correspondence of all ranks and arms of service, though it is in the material dealing with the war in the Far East that the sense of a conflict being driven by racial difference arises. In contrast, the war in Europe is seen much more in purely political terms – though this would not be the case were this study to include the war on the Eastern Front. With the war in the Far East, there is a much clearer sense of racial separation and, in some cases, a belief in superiority. It is important to note that the opinions expressed in the material are those of the individual writers, not of the author of this book or the Imperial War Museum.

In practical terms, the extracts from the personal papers held in the collections of the Imperial War Museum have been edited to correct any obvious spelling or grammatical errors, while timings and dates have been left as they were written. Where acronyms or unfamiliar words have been used, these are explained in the glossary on page 431. Apart from this the extracts are presented as written by the men and women who lived through these events and recorded them so that we can understand a little of what they went through.

1939–40

I. The Outbreak of War

Throughout the late 1930s, the threat of war in Europe gradually increased. The major European powers all started to re-arm their forces in the face of the rise of the Nazi Party and Germany's rejection of the provisions of the Versailles Treaty. Germany itself pressed aggressively forwards with territorial claims. First a union with Austria was achieved in March 1938, and then the Nazi government turned its attention to the large ethnic German population of Czechoslovakia, seeking to absorb them into Germany. This ambition provoked a major international crisis, culminating in the Munich Conference of September 1938. This crisis provoked fears of war throughout Europe, such as those of Moyra Charlton, a children's author from Takeley in Essex:

SUNDAY, 11 SEPTEMBER 1938

Home to supper and more Hitler talk – the News was full of it. I don't think it can really come to war. Apparently we are not pledged to Czechoslovakia but France is and we must stand by her. My hat, what bellicose, brutal, blathering bullies some Germans are. 'Time will show what no man knoweth' . . .

MONDAY, 12 SEPTEMBER 1938

When we got in Hitler's speech was in progress and the Cowells listening in. By missing some supper I managed to hear most of it,

17

though I only understood a word here and there. The Führer was theatrical and arresting, making the most of an emotional delivery. From what I could gather in fragments from the Cowells, he means no surrender. Sooner or later he will have Czechoslovakia; his armament and defences will be ready before the autumn is out.

In each pause a crowd of thousands cheered and roared and howled. Hearing Hitler's very words and those frenzied howls brought home without doubt the terrible significance of it. Hitler means war. His people are as mad as he is, drunk with their brutal lust for gain.

How can one man plunge Europe in to war? Thousands, millions of young lives to be spilt – and this only 20 years after last time? It can't be, God can't let it happen. But to hear those cheers made me awfully afraid.

At the end they sang 'Deutschland über Alles' with swelling grandeur and poor Mrs Cowell ran out in tears. What must it be like for her, with relations and all her friends in Germany?

Well, well. It was nothing definite, but the suspense will continue.

The Munich Conference ended with the transfer of the ethnic German region of Czechoslovakia, the Sudetenland, to Germany and peace was preserved in the short term. However, Hitler then occupied all of the country in March 1939. When Poland was threatened, the governments of Great Britain and France were resolved to act. Moyra Charlton wrote of her feelings on the impending war:

MONDAY, 28 AUGUST 1939

Nevile Henderson [the Ambassador of Great Britain to Germany from 1937 to 1939] has just flown back to Berlin. We did not hear a word of his message but if Hitler's suggestion was anything like his suggestions to the French it isn't very peaceful. He will enter into any negotiations with the provision that he gets his own way and annexes the Polish Corridor, i.e. Poland. The Mediterranean has just been closed to merchant shipping. Well, well, war it must be, it seems.

Now that the reality is so close one feels rather numb, almost indifferent. No heroics, no crusading fire at the moment, but a feeling that a very nasty job has got to be done and done thoroughly. What will come of it God alone knows, but we can't live on in this state of crisis for ever. Better put an end to it as soon as possible. All different somehow to the shock of horror and fear last September. I have had a lovely life anyhow so I can't grumble. And I once used to envy the generation who had lived through the last war!

On 1 September 1939, German troops crossed over the border into Poland and, on the 3rd, with both French and British ultimatums ignored, Britain and France declared war with Germany. Moyra Charlton once more:

Sunday, 3 September 1939

Fine and windy, with clouds.

4.30pm. England is at war with Germany. It is unbelievable but true . . .

At 11.15am Mr. Chamberlain spoke. We were all congregated in the hall, Women's Institute members, farmers, all the good solid Takeley faces, and outside the golden country spread out, with clouds over it – England. The Prime Minister spoke only in a few words. He said the HM Government had sent Hitler an ultimatum to withdraw their troops from Poland. There had been no reply and the ultimatum had expired at 11. oc. We were now at war with Germany.

He went on to say that we were fighting for the right to resist the tyranny of might alone. It brought tears to one's eyes – those grave, ruddy faces around and the golden country outside, with the church in the trees and the harvest not yet in . . .

At 6. oc the King spoke to the nation. He spoke slowly, with his slight hesitation, but forcefully. He turned the grimness of this war before us into something like a crusade. Outside the window the leaves of our sycamore trees were gold against a pale blue sky. It was a cloudless evening, the country smiling and the roses sweet in the garden, just the same as always. It was impossible to believe that we were at war . . .

The declaration of war today made one feel so sad, but now we must finish Hitlerism and win this. No one can say England went into it selfishly or blindly. I maligned Chamberlain last night, but still that delay is unaccounted for. France did not declare war till 5am today.

September 3rd 1939. I suppose history will remember it. Anyhow, thank heaven the suspense is over.

The declaration of war left both the military and the population at large unsure of what to expect, though a fear of aerial bombardment was prevalent. Jim Gray had enlisted in the Territorial Army following the Munich Agreement of 1938 and was an NCO with the 460th Battery, 70th (Sussex) Searchlight Regiment RA, in Sussex in September 1939:

SUNDAY, 3 SEPTEMBER 1939

Went to HQ at Hellingly to collect rations and was there when Chamberlain's fateful statement announced that we were at war with Germany, for the second time. Within a few moments thereafter, the now famous 'first siren' sounded and things began to get out of hand!!!

The men had been busy digging slit trenches and the order 'take cover' was given. Some men dropped into the trenches, shallow though they were, others ran about looking for shelter, officers shouted and NCOs swore. Respirators and tin helmets were worn, all to no good purpose because it soon became evident that nothing was going to happen and before long the 'all clear' was sounded. I telephoned my next-door neighbour, asking him to stop Daisy and mother from visiting me, but they decided to come and arrived in the afternoon while all hands were filling sandbags.

Troop commander had forbidden any visitors to the site 'now that we are at war', so they had to stand on one side of the hedge whilst I remained on the other side. It was mother's 64th birthday and not a very happy one.

Flight Lieutenant Cecil Flick found himself helping with the hurried preparations for war in London:

LATE AUGUST 1939

Today I turned into a labourer in the cause of ARP [Air Raid Precautions]. Been boarding up windows, filling and placing sandbags, etc.

Contractors are fully booked up and it is as much as one can hope for to get supplies of bags, sand, timber, etc., even if you are willing to go and fetch it yourself . . .

People in London to whom I have spoken seem to think there will be no war. As one commissionaire said this afternoon – ''Itler don't bugger about like this if he wants anything – he just <u>takes</u> it.'

All the same London looks very warlike. Gun and searchlight in Green Park, sentries with fixed bayonets, steel helmets and gas mask haversacks at the 'alert' position. (These last two points I think damn silly – surely it would be time to reach for the helmet and gas mask <u>after</u> war broke out – German raiders wouldn't just materialise in the air over Green Park from nowhere.) Military dispatch riders dash about on motorbikes, steel pillbox shelters erected in the courtyard of Buckingham Palace.

2. The U-Boat Threat

There was no Phoney War for the Royal Navy at the beginning of the Second World War, for at 7.39 p.m. on 3 September the outward-bound liner *Athenia* was sunk by the German U-boat *U30* with the loss of 128 passengers and crew. This act convinced the Admiralty to reintroduce the convoy system that had proved so effective in the First World War, at least in coastal waters and the Western Approaches – the major shipping lanes directly to the west of Great Britain.

Nelson Paine was steward aboard the liner the *Athlone Castle*, which was travelling back to the UK from Cape Town when war was declared:

SUNDAY, 3 SEPTEMBER 1939

Morning, and still very cold. It's strange because we have never noticed this cold wind before, and during our stay in Capetown it was quite hot. The clock went back another 45 minutes; the usual is 17 for the following days till we get to Cape Verde. We are still travelling more west than north, as our amateur navigators tell us. Everyone is looking out on board. I suppose the idea in their mind, like mine, is 'is there a submarine lurking about?' It's strange how you begin to take stock of those around you, what are they made of? It's only an emergency that brings out the best or worst in a man. I hope I shall not be lacking in the former, although I feel confident of myself, and training myself to withstand a shock that will test my nerves, so I can only wait until the time comes so that I can put my present clear thinking ideas into practice.

Church service is over, and . . . England is at war with Germany, the Captain has just announced it. What a relief. I feel almost overjoyed at the thought of it. The suspense is broken, we know exactly where we stand. Now we can prepare for the worst; it's much better than this uncertainty. News will be discontinued, but the new bulletin will be published every morning. Jokes begin to fly around – everyone seems different, looks much happier. 'Hitler, it will be the last of him.' They are saying 'Mussolini, what will he do? Germany didn't want his help yesterday, but he will be wanting it now.'

But behind all this boasting, lurks in the back of my mind, 'England still expects every man to try and get out of it'. Ah, ah, sorry, it's my little joke. It's noon and the ship is taking on a different colour, she is being painted a warship grey. Passengers are helping with the painting of it, also stewards in their time off.

On 14 September, the aircraft carrier HMS *Ark Royal* narrowly avoided being sent to the bottom by the U-boat *U39*, which was itself sunk by the carrier's escorting destroyers HMS *Foxhound*, *Faulknor*, *Firedrake* and *Eskimo*; this was the first U-boat sunk by the Royal Navy in the Second World War. Only the fact that the German torpedoes had malfunctioned saved *Ark Royal*. The lesson was not learnt, and on 17 September another of the Royal Navy's fleet carriers, HMS *Courageous*, was torpedoed three times by *U29*, sinking in fifteen minutes with the loss of 518 officers and men. Alastair Ewing was the First Lieutenant aboard HMS *Imogen*, which formed part of the escort for the aircraft carrier HMS *Hermes* during an anti-submarine sweep. Here he describes the reaction upon hearing of the loss of HMS *Courageous*:

Sunday, 17 September 1939

At 9.10pm *Ivanhoe* reported that *Courageous* had sunk at 6.20pm. Later *Impulsive* reported that she was returning to Plymouth with survivors. *Kelly* did the same later.

This was naturally staggering news and made us redouble our vigilance on *Hermes*. From various positions which we plotted out it seemed that *Courageous* can only have had *Ivanhoe* and *Impulsive* on screen while *Inglefield* and *Intrepid* were hunting a submarine. A similar situation with us and *Hermes* this afternoon.

Later I heard, with what truth I was never able to confirm or deny, that *Courageous* had a plane overdue at sunset and in their understandable concern to get it back had overlooked the submarine threat and had slowed down, switched on lights and beacon to try and help the missing plane find her . . .

Monday, 18 September 1939

After this *Hermes* made 'Ships are not to part company without orders or act on aircraft reports. Two destroyers only will be sent if prospects appear favourable.' A wise signal under the circumstances.

At 9am *Hermes* told us that 80 or more of the crew of *Courageous* had been rescued . . .

The Admiralty statement was cleverly worded to reduce the obvious importance of our loss.

'The Admiralty regret to announce that HMS *Courageous* has been lost as the result of submarine action. She was commissioned with the Reserve Fleet in August with a reduced complement of aircraft and since the opening of hostilities has been performing very good service in protecting ships of the Merchant Marine against U-boat attack.

'Survivors have been picked up by destroyers and merchant ships which are now returning to harbour. The submarine was heavily attacked by destroyers and is believed to have been sunk. HMS *Courageous* was one of our oldest aircraft carriers. She was originally built as a Cruiser in 1917 and was converted after the war.'

This was all true but most of us realised even then that aircraft carriers were extremely valuable ships whatever their age. We arrived off the breakwater at 6.40pm and zigzagged astern of *Hermes* as she entered. She made us a signal thanking us for what we had done as we passed her on our way up harbour.

The battle against the U-boats continued. Otto Steiner served as a Sub Lieutenant aboard the destroyer HMS *Ilex*, which was part of the Third Destroyer Flotilla transferred from the Mediterranean to the Western Approaches to protect Allied shipping. He describes an early encounter:

FRIDAY, 13 OCTOBER 1939

'Friday the Thirteenth' and both lucky and unlucky. We suddenly sighted the wreck of the *Emile Miguel* at 0745hrs – a big new tanker split completely in two and each half floating. As *Imogen* was sinking it by gunfire – she exploded her fuel, which made an enormous pillar of smoke – we received another SOS; this time from the *Stonepools*, one of the ships in our convoy, being attacked 105 miles from us. We accordingly shaped a course for this spot when quite unexpectedly we came up to a sinking merchantman, the French *Louisianne*, with the U-boat standing by on the surface. We opened fire at it – I don't know if we hit it – and she dived. After a long hunt with no positive success, we gave her up, very disappointed, and picked up crew. She [the *Louisianne*] had evidently been given no warning – except for a shell on her bridge! – which killed the 1st officer and three men . . .

About an hour after leaving the scene of the sinking of *Louisianne* we sighted *Stonepool* who after a five-hour fight with the U-boat had beaten her off! However, she was holed forward and we took station on either bow and escorted her in a homeward bound direction. At 1710hrs she reported that she had sighted a submarine on her port beam – no doubt the one that had previously attacked her trying to finish her off after dark.

We accordingly altered course towards her at full speed and commenced operating on arriving by plot at the position she was last seen.

We gained contact and carried out a depth charge attack – we had previously opened fire when she started to dive.

A large air bubble came up immediately after – Then nothing happened for about two minutes when the bow of the submarine appeared above water at an angle of about 20° to the vertical amidst a great cheer from the ship's company – Fire was opened immediately and she slowly levelled off and surfaced. 'Full speed ahead' to ram was ordered, but when it was seen what damage had already been done to her, full speed astern was ordered and we only rammed hard enough to pierce her engine room – we rode right over her stern.

Figures then appeared on her contact tower with a white flag and fire was checked. The survivors immediately jumped into the water and she sank like a stone.

The TI [Torpedo Instructor] fired a charge as we rode over her from the starboard thrower and this went off deep as we were picking up survivors.

She fired a torpedo at us just before we attacked but the track was seen to pass astern.

Only 18 out 43 were saved – we picked up two – and from accounts, they must have gone through absolute hell and we felt really very sorry for them. But still one more submarine gone – *U42*, one [of] Germany's latest.

One of the prime targets for Germany was the Royal Navy's fleet anchorage at Scapa Flow in Orkney, as Bessie Skea, who was a young girl on Orkney, wrote in her diary:

Tuesday, 10 October 1939

There is too little doing for my peace of mind! Hitler says he wants peace, but Britain won't give him peace, not on his terms! He is threatening to bomb every civilian town in Britain, sink every ship, and win the war! But he is NOT GOING to win. He is sure to try to bomb Kirkwall; Orkney is a dangerous place to live in. The King was in Scapa Flow and Kirkwall last week; Churchill was here the week before. There are rumours that Churchill said Orkney was not half-fortified – with the result that we are to have more coastal guns – one in Shapinsay, too.

However, on the night of 14/15 October 1939, *U47*, commanded by Günther Prien, managed to penetrate the base's defences and launch an attack on the battleship HMS *Royal Oak*, hitting her with three torpedoes and sinking her for the loss of 833 out of her company of 1,234 officers and men. Scapa Flow was also to suffer from aerial assault throughout 1939 and early 1940 until the defences were improved. Bessie Skea described one of the major raids:

THURSDAY, 11 APRIL 1940

In a few minutes firing started, fiercely. Tracer bullets climbed upwards, shells burst in an enormous barrage – a great black line in the sky. A few pale searchlights swept the sky. Great flashes from the direction of Lyness – whole batteries opening up at once. Our lighted planes scoured about, high above the shell barrage.

'There's a Jerry!' I shouted. There were three Germans over Kirkwall. As it grew darker the firing increased. The searchlights were brilliant. 'Look! A German machine-gunning!' An enemy plane, going like smoke, was rat-at-tatting with his tail gun, over Kirkwall. A shell burst right behind him. He went off, then. It eased a little, then increased – crash, bang, rattle, rat-at-tat right above us. We didn't see it, but we found out that a British plane engaged a German when that machine-gunning went. Suddenly the West Side searchlight swept across the sky – and in the beam was an enormous plane! A great bomber, flying for its life, so low down that one could easily have hit it with a shotgun! Four great engines under the wings [though there were no German four-engined aircraft]: and red fire shooting down from the tail-gun, right between Hannatoft and the Old Manse. We lost sight of it, then. Our four Shapinsay searchlights met and crossed overhead. An armed trawler, in the bay below us, fired.

A really lovely scene – searchlights playing over an almost clear sky, lighted planes humming about, shells bursting in the beams of the searchlights, tracer bullets climbing upwards, flashes from big guns to the south. Carness battery opened with a roar, a faint red light appeared at the aerodrome. A pom-pom gun went crack, crack. Planes droned – Germans! We heard the men at the Elwickbank light shouting. The officers' car went past again. More bullets – more flashes – more searchlights. The lapwings were crying, and above it all a pale, crescent moon looked down. It was weirdly beautiful.

3. The Battle of the River Plate

Towards the end of August 1939 two of Germany's three 'pocket battleships', the *Deutschland* and the *Admiral Graf Spee*, had slipped out into the North and South Atlantic respectively. Their role was to maintain a constant threat to British and Allied shipping in case of war, and to stretch Britain's naval resources by operating in a dispersed manner.

This plan worked to good effect once war broke out and, when the Admiralty realised that they were losing shipping to these two powerful German warships, eight separate hunting groups were dispatched in conjunction with the French Navy to track them down. In the event, the *Deutschland* only sank two merchant ships and captured a further one before returning to Germany on 8 November. The *Graf Spee*, under Captain Hans Langsdorff, remained at liberty in the South Atlantic and Indian Ocean, sinking nine merchant ships in the course of her cruise.

Aboard one of those merchant ships, the SS *Huntsman*, was Joseph Beazley, who was returning from Calcutta to Liverpool:

TUESDAY, 10 OCTOBER 1939

The SS *Huntsman* was in position Lat. 8½ W. approx six days south of Freetown steaming at full speed in a calm sea and fine weather. The Captain and officers were having tea in the saloon when at 5.30pm the 3rd Officer, who was on the bridge, reported sighting a warship on the horizon off the starboard bow. Capt. Brown, Chief Officer Thompson and Radio Officer McCorry immediately went to the bridge, the radio office was situated abaft the chartroom. The Chief Engineer also arose from the table and went along to the engine room leaving the 2nd Officer and myself to carry out onto the deck, as I anticipated – to see one our warships signalling to us.

The warship was now approaching at high speed. Captain Brown had altered course a few points but the warship continued directly towards us. We could see no sign of flag or ensign until she was close to and turning broadside then I saw the French ensign, a small one, being hauled down and at the same time a large German ensign was run up in its place, simultaneously the following flag signals were hoisted: 'heave to' and 'do not use your radio'. Instructed by Capt. Brown our radio officer had been sending out 'unknown warship approaching' he was now sending 'German warship approaching' and our position and managed to get it out several times in Admiralty code. (As events proved later this message was never picked up.)

Mr Thompson now ran up to the answering signal pennant and shouted to 'Sparks' to stop transmitting.

We could now see that the warship was a German pocket battleship, the bridge seemed to me to be crowded with officers all looking through glasses at us. All her guns were trained on to us, her triple forward 11-inch and four side 5.9-inch guns, and even her torpedo tubes were ready to give us a quick dispatch.

As she drew close to – perhaps 500 yards off – swinging broadside, and before she really eased down speed the amidship crane swung out and lowered a fast motor launch into the water. At this time the *Huntsman* was almost stopped with engines going full astern.

While this was taking place Capt. Brown stayed on the Bridge but sent Mr Thompson to his cabin, from there he took the specially weighted canvas bag containing the secret naval codes and instructions and these were dropped into the sea on the lee side away from the warship.

In a matter of minutes the launch was alongside. Armed officers and men with revolvers drawn rushed on board, some up the pilot ladder, which the Captain had instructed to be put over the side from the forward deck on first sighting the warship, in anticipation of more welcome visitors, others leaping over the bulwarks.

At this moment I was standing at the foot of the bridge deck ladder. A young petty officer rushed along the alleyway and with his revolver drawn asked for the radio house – 'radio house'? I pointed to the Bridge and he rushed up the ladder. Looking up a few moments later I saw 'Sparks' backing out of the wireless office with his hands up covered by the petty officer. Sparks afterwards told me that he thought his last day had come! They asked him if he had sent out our position and he said, 'Of course I have.' Lt. Hertzberg was now questioning Capt. Brown and would not let him go into his cabin, while demanding ship's papers, particulars of cargo, destination, crew, etc., while others were ransacking his room for any secret papers, ship's money, etc. The boarding party, about 40 all told, were now stationed all over the ship, including the engine room.

One of the 'hunting groups', Force G, consisting of the heavy cruiser *Exeter* and the light cruisers *Ajax* and *Achilles* under the command of Commodore Henry Harwood, intercepted the *Graf Spee* off the coast of Uruguay near the mouth of the River Plate in the early morning of 13 December. One of the bandsmen on board the *Ajax* during the action was J. Nicholls:

FRIDAY, 13 DECEMBER 1940

This calm and sunny spring morning was suddenly broken by events, which were as sudden as they were unexpected. Just as we fell out from our routine dawn action stations at 6.00am, like we have done every morning with monotonous regularity, a dramatic report was made that we had sighted that mysterious German raider believed to be the pocket battleship *Admiral Scheer*, which proved later to be the *Graf Spee*. We were some 300 miles out from the River Plate, the visibility was at its maximum, and the weather was fine, sea calm, ideal conditions for a long-range naval battle. The alarm was sounded about 6.20am and, before everyone was closed up at their action stations, the foremost turrets opened fire at a range of about 20,000 yards. We were still wondering what the 'object' was, but when the rapid fire from the foremost turrets started, we knew it was the 'real thing'. Meanwhile, the enemy had sighted us first, and her first salvo fell uncomfortably close to the *Exeter*, the rear ship, as we were closing up. It seems that she engaged *Exeter* first, being the heavier armed ship. We turned towards the enemy, and the fire was very rapid. The *Exeter* gets badly hit after some of her 8-inch had found their mark, and has to retire about 15 minutes after the commencement of the action. We close in, and divert the fire of the *Spee* to ourselves, thereby saving the *Exeter* from further damage. Continuing the fight with smokescreen, the *Achilles* and ourselves closed in to 8,000 yards, a very daring manoeuvre during which time an 11-inch shell penetrates to 'X' quarters killing seven men and injuring several more. One of the *Spee*'s 5.9s wrecks the Commodore's, Captain's and Commander's quarters, while another shot our mainmast in half, damaging one of our planes. Luckily the other plane was up and spotting for us and incidentally reported the course of six torpedoes on their way to us, three of which passed across our bows harmlessly, and three intended for *Achilles* across our foaming wake. Our torpedoes to the *Spee* also missed but we only fired five. We in the band were closed up at our action stations in the 4-inch and 6-inch transmitting stations. Although we could see nothing of the action our Captain RM in the 4-inch director gave us a running commentary on the action, through the phones with such remarks as 'Here's another one on the way' followed by 'Gosh, that was a close one!' or 'Enemy altering course.' Between some of his funny remarks, shells could be heard bursting and falling all around the ship. We also received reports from the 6-inch DS [Director Station] of casualties and damage. The action lasted about an hour and ten minutes at speeds of 32 knots, and as ammunition was running short in the foremost turrets, we opened to shadowing range. 'A' turret was reported to have fired 300 rounds, and the guns were so hot that they did not go back into place properly after recoiling. They had to be pushed back by hand and oil poured on the muzzles. Pieces of bursted shrapnel struck the ship in various places, and the 4-inch heightfinder was out of action. Due to the clever tactics of the Commodore and the skilful handling of the ship by the Captain, her superior speed, and the good gunnery, we escaped serious damage, and were able to inflict serious damage to the *Spee*. The enemy appeared also to have trouble of her own, her action was an evasive one, for apparently she was listing, and her pumps could not cope with the inrush of water from her underwater wounds. The foremost 11-inch turret was thought to have been temporarily out of action, while at one time only one of her 5.9s were firing. After the firing had stopped, an all-day high-speed chase followed in a westerly direction. It was apparent that the *Spee* was seeking refuge in the River Plate. During this period of chase and shadowing, the ammunition from damaged 'X' quarters was transferred forward, in case fire should be opened again. At dusk the *Spee* makes the River Plate, about 9.00pm, and opens fire again at the *Achilles*, to which she replies. Only a few rounds are fired at each other, with no hits. As the darkness descends, *Spee* makes her way up the River Plate from the south entrance and fires on either a Uruguayan or Argentine warship, perhaps by mistake, and then turns round to come out the northern approach to the river, and puts into Montevideo, and lands captured crews of sunk British merchant ships.

Joseph Beazley of the SS *Huntsman* was one of those housed with the captured crews from British merchant ships. He had been aboard the *Graf Spee* since his capture and lived through the entire action from his confinement on board:

WEDNESDAY, 13 DECEMBER 1939

The seaplane revved up at 5.30am as usual but had not taken off at 5.50am when the bell buzzed 'general alarm'. This was followed almost immediately by more buzzing 'action stations'. Our guard locked and screwed the door tight, the two small skylights were closed with steel cover plates on top, the whole ship was vibrating as she increased to full speed. A salvo from the heavy guns shook the ship followed by the 5.9-inch guns. We guessed by this time it was no defenceless merchant ship but at least one or more of our warships.

We could feel the ship heeling as she manoeuvred and turned at speed. Firing was continuous and at 7.30am a shell burst with a terrific crack right over our heads. There was a crash, our room deckhead was forced down about 6 inches at the centre, buckling and twisting the plating and beams; all the lights went out, the air was filled with explosive fumes, cork insulation and dust nearly choked us. Several small pieces of red-hot shell were lying about the floor, fortunately no one was injured excepting one of the three deck boys, he had received a scratch on his wrist. We afterwards found that this shell landed on the seaplane and burst into the Captain's galley, wrecking it completely and piercing our room deckhead.

In the darkness we could feel the ship was being struck elsewhere by other shells. The firing continued till about 8.45am, when there was a lull while the ship continued manoeuvring and racing at speed. We found a couple of electric globes unbroken and these we managed to fit into two sockets and so had a little light.

At 11.00am the guard shouted through a small hole in the door 'Are you all right', so we shouted back 'What about something to eat'? It was a long time since 4.30pm the day previously since we had eaten anything. About an hour later a large can of cold lime juice and three loaves of the black bread was passed in to us and the door screwed up again. Through the peep hole in the door we could see the sailors carrying their wounded along the alleyway to the hospital, and during the 'action' one our fellows saw one of the German alleyway ammunition party wounded just outside our door.

We were naturally all discussing the events of the day. Some thought this and some thought that, when, at 2.45pm the bell again buzzed 'action stations', we wondered and guessed that the *Graf Spee* could not shake them off, we also thought – How much longer was this horrible uncertainty to continue!!!

At 8.30pm still shut up with no news all day, the alarm bell again buzzed, this was followed by a few salvos from the heavy guns, and then silence.

All day long the ship had been going at speed heeling over slightly as she turned from one side to the other.

We slung our hammocks and turned in about 9.00pm. We were again shaken by a few more heavy shots from the heavy guns at 9.20pm then we fell asleep after the tension of the long day.

THURSDAY, 14 DECEMBER 1939

I was asleep and wakened by the door opening close to my hammock at approx 20 minutes past midnight, someone switched on the light as Lt. Hertzberg came in stepping carefully over those sleeping on the floor. He stood in the middle of the room and said: 'Gentlemen for you the war is over. We are now in Monte Video Harbour'. The first thing I noticed was that the engines were stopped. Hertzberg then remarked 'We will be moving into the inner harbour in the morning'.

The combined fire of the British ships had damaged the *Graf Spee* to the extent that she broke off from the action and retreated into the Uruguayan port of Montevideo. She had been damaged seriously enough to ensure that extensive repairs would be required before she could make the long passage back to Germany.

International law required that the *Graf Spee* only remain within the neutral harbour of Montevideo for 72 hours, and Langsdorff, having been deceived by the British into believing that a superior force was waiting for him out at sea, took his ship out into the River Plate and scuttled it at 6.15pm on 17 December. J. Nicholls describes his reaction to the news:

SUNDAY, 17 DECEMBER 1939

This afternoon came the surprising news that the *Spee* has transferred nearly all her ship's company to the German merchantman *Tacoma*, which has been at Montevideo since the war started. It leaves us all guessing at the time, but the move is very apparent later. Another message says that she is preparing to leave Montevideo. We move into position, and close up at action stations for another show down, as we all expect her to put up a fight. She comes out, turns to starboard and blows herself up in shallow water off Montevideo, where she burns fiercely all night. Following these dramatic events, the ships broke formation, and we 'cleared tower deck' to cheer the *Achilles* as she steamed by, and when the New Zealand flag appeared at the main, the cheering was renewed. She cheered us also. 'Hip' and our Captain 'Whimpey' also received a big 'chuck up' when they stood on the roof of the bridge. The *Cumberland* was also cheered. Thus the tension was broken and the news, when spread round was received with enthusiastic cheers. We had been instrumental in bringing her to book, and everyone breathed a sigh of relief. Now we can have a decent night's sleep, after being unable to undress and sleep properly for four nights.

4. The Norwegian Campaign

The Royal Navy was heavily involved in the next major campaign of the war, the battle for Norway. Both the Allies and the Germans were well aware of the importance of Norway as the conduit for the Swedish iron ore vital to the German war effort, and both sides sought to control the Norwegian supply routes by occupying all or part of the country. The Germans invaded Denmark and Norway by land, sea and air on 7 April 1940. The Home Fleet under Admiral Sir Charles Forbes sortied to interfere with the German invasion and found themselves confronted by the anti-shipping forces of the Luftwaffe's X Fliegerkorps, which sank the destroyer HMS *Gurkha*, damaged the cruisers *Southampton* and *Galatea*, and even hit the flagship HMS *Rodney*. Hugh Knowles was serving on the cruiser HMS *York* and witnessed the aerial assault:

TUESDAY, 9 APRIL 1940

A Dornier was shadowing the fleet, only coming within range once, to be driven off by the *Rodney*'s guns.

It was soon after three when the air raid began. From the cumulous clouds a Heinkel appeared, circled over the *Devonshire*, about eight miles off our Starboard beam, ignoring the anti-aircraft fire, and dropped two bombs. They landed close to her beam, sending a cloud of spray and smoke several hundred feet into the air. The 'plane circled round again, and banked into a dive, dropping some more bombs which fell clear of the target.

Leaving white streaks of condensed exhaust against the blue sky, another Heinkel attacked the *Berwick*, between us and the *Devonshire*. The first two bombs fell abreast her, throwing up brown columns of spray nearly five times as high as the cruiser's masts. The last lot was a salvo of four, dropped from such a height that the 'plane was invisible: yet they were so close that splinters landed on the *Devonshire*'s deck, four black masses exactly abeam of the target. The bombing was unpleasantly accurate, considering that the ships could manoeuvre as they liked, and the aircraft seemed to take no notice of the burst of gunfire through which they flew unmoved. At times it looked as though a hit must have been scored.

Our turn came next. A plane circled and set her course to attack us, upwind. Our guns' crews were working magnificently, loading and firing as though this was but a practice shoot, although they are all extremely young: while two Tribals [Tribal-class destroyers] close to us barked defiantly into the air. The two bombs fell a hundred yards off our port bow. The 'planes were over us, and our guns firing as fast as they could. We watched as our plane got into position, someone said he had seen it drop its bombs, and we took cover against the superstructure. We waited and waited, and nothing happened.

We had been zig-zagging continuously, and it was a great piece of luck which prompted the Captain to alter course so that the next pair of bombs – dropped from a machine out of sight – fell only 60 yards off our quarter as the stern swung clear. Splinters embedded themselves in the first motorboat, behind which the Fleet Air Arm [air crew] was sheltering.

It seems that the machines fired their machine guns while they were over us, as bullet holes were afterwards found below the after searchlight.

A Junkers 88 was high above the *Rodney* and *Valiant*, steaming close together. It dropped an astounding load, straddling both ships, one bomb passing through the *Rodney*'s gunroom, where it broke in half, the flash badly burning a dozen people in the vicinity, doing no material damage, thanks to the armoured deck. A terrific barrage surrounded the Junkers, and a hit was seen to register; dark smoke poured from its starboard engine, and it turned and headed for the *York*.

We watched it as it dived for us, closer and closer, machine-guns blazing, firing into the water ahead of our bows. It must have been partially out of control. It was over the forecastle our .5's raking the shining dark green fuselage, leaving a thin trail of smoke behind.

Further to the north, Vice Admiral Whitworth's force, consisting of HMS *Renown* and nine destroyers, encountered the two German battlecruisers *Scharnhorst* and *Gneisenau* off the northern coast of Norway. In the ensuing battle, the German ships were driven off, as Kenneth Wilson, who served aboard the destroyer HMS *Impulsive*, recalls:

TUESDAY, 9 APRIL 1940

Real action at last. It is over now and thank God I am still here in
one piece. At 0400hrs the fog suddenly lifted and I went on deck to
clear my head after the fug in the wireless office. At that moment we
sighted the enemy, which later proved to be a cruiser Hipper class and
a battleship Scharnhost class and some destroyers. They opened fire
first. There were brilliant orange flashes and then a noise like a flock
of wild geese passing overhead as the shells screamed over. I didn't stop
to see the second salvo, which dropped short as we altered course, but
dashed for my action station which is in the TS (Gunnery Control
Station) as the alarm bells rang. The range was very short, not more
than about 6,000 yards. We scored a direct hit on the *Scharnhost* with
our 4.7s, which seemed to start a fire. *Renown* was then hit forward.
We increased speed and zig-zagged to avoid shells dropping round
us but about 0430hrs we shipped a huge wave which tore up the
forecastle deck and flooded the forward messdecks. We had to reduce
speed and drop out of the action as the enemy passed out of range in
action with *Renown*. Three of our guns' crews collapsed with the cold
during the action. I have been drenched to the skin and my clothes
were almost frozen stiff on me. I cannot change as all my clothes are
down forward, which is flooded and the watertight doors are closed.
We are now on our own heading for Scapa Flow.

Following further naval action around Narvik, an Allied expeditionary
force was assembled and put ashore at Narvik, Namsos and Åndalsnes.
These troops rapidly came into contact with the advancing German
forces and were forced backwards, outflanked and overwhelmed by the
German aggressive tactics.

Sergeant Frank Cox served with the 8th Battalion Sherwood
Foresters, part of the 148th Brigade, which was largely destroyed in
fighting around the town of Lillehammer:

MONDAY, 22 APRIL 1940

Collected from Bn HQ after [a] couple of hours' rest and fetched by
truck to cover withdrawal of 1/5th Leicester from Ringsaker – not
many got through – managed to pull out with our motley collection

of commandeered civilian transport, as Germans in strength took crossroads.

All forces south of Lillehammer pulled back north of the town and took up positions in and around the Agricultural College.

The position was B Company Foresters to right flank, C Company Foresters left flank, one section carriers, another of HQ company personnel centre and some remaining Leicesters centre.

With my platoon officer, Lieut. C. P. C. Vallance, and approximately five others, we later took up an anti-tank position covering the roadway, with an anti-tank rifle and Bren gun.

We saw and heard the advance to our front as it hotted up. Planes set the Agricultural College on fire – mortars opened up and we could see the Germans heading northwards to the other side of the river – indicating A Company had had it. Next, in the woods to our left C Company were attacked – they counter-attacked. I heard 'fix bayonets – let's get the bastards'. We knew our force was 'puny' – not a bicycle, truck carrier or 3-inch mortar. The Germans went by on both sides . . .

Capt. Fenton returned with the news that Bn HQ had withdrawn (he didn't use those words). Our own role is decided as we hear in the direction of Lillehammer the sounds of tanks and transport.

We lit a cigarette and blew the smoke into holes in the snow. Three of us made out, and had witnessed, the form of will in our AB.64PT.1 [soldier's service book]. I looked at my wife's and son's photograph and scribbled on the back a few lines.

I seemed to feel quite steady now that we could do something.

The Bren was not to open up until the leading tank was stopped.

I got a fire order . . . but held it a while until I had a good sight on the leader of the three tanks. At the second or third shot the tank spun across the roadway and the engine stopped. (How much luck went with that second or third shot I learned in the later years when I knew the real capabilities of the Boyes anti-tank rifle.)

Brens opened up and Jerry took to a heads-down position.

We were first spotted from our right flank and came under machine-gun fire. 'Get out of it; every man for himself,' or words to that effect, were our order. As we spilled over the broad wooden fences with our weapons and equipment, the machine-gun bullets ripped through the fencing.

A few hundred yards away down the roadway was what had been Bn. HQ, a roadside house – which had had attention from mortar and aircraft. We now had a few more amongst us – Sgt. Greaves (Pioneers), fingers badly shot – another with a flesh wound in the arm. The anti-tank rifle was left behind Bn HQ and the bolt taken with us. I retained Sgt. Greaves' revolver with five rounds of .38 ammunition.

We all made for the railway track, which at this point ran through the woods, the roadway being to our right and the river Vistra [Vinstra] on our left. We had our two wounded on a builder's handcart for a time and piled our spare equipment. We felt that we were now making headway; the wounded were able to walk on while Mr Vallance and I, together with a corporal from the Leicesters, pushed the handcart down the bank and abandoned it.

Back on the track, Mr Vallance gave me a drink from his flask and had one himself and said, 'A bit of good shooting back there, Sgt. Cox'. We were not many yards further on when we heard the sound of enemy transport and motorcycles heading north. A few moments later we heard machine-gun fire close ahead of us, and saw our comrades in front take to the woods on the left – so did we.

Sergeant Cox managed to escape capture, later returning to England via the Faroe Islands. Many other members of the Allied expeditionary force were not so lucky and ended up as captives of the Germans; one such soldier was Lieutenant Walter Laing, also of 8th Battalion the Sherwood Foresters, who found his command dissolving in the face of the onslaught:

TUESDAY, 23 APRIL 1940

. . . Through field glasses we saw German tanks with supporting troops. We realised they must have broken through and that there was very little now to stop them. Their further advance was by the hill.

On our flank on one occasion we observed British troops marching along a road above us. They went into farm-buildings. The Germans had observed them too, for they soon put a shell into the farm.

It must now have been well into the afternoon. After a silent spell, firing broke out near us. Movement in a farm south of us looked like German infantry. It was our own troops withdrawing. Had it not been for the Sergeant-Major recognising them, we should have fired on them. Our two Bren guns and rifles were trained on them awaiting the order to fire. I made a fool of myself by ordering all to put on anti-gas respirators. I thought I saw German troops wearing them. It was an optical illusion.

It was now obvious from the direction in which the sound of firing came that we should soon be cut off. It was also obvious that the Germans were unlikely to use the east flank, as their attack along the main road had been completely successful. We were now being mortared from the slope west of the main road as well as being shelled. So far we had had no casualties. If we remained, casualties were certain without achieving anything. There was still a good line of withdrawal through the trees, and a good chance of joining up with forces north of Tretten. I eventually decided on withdrawal in small parties of two or three.

Shortly after the parties started leaving, a mortar-bomb came over, razing the electric wires at the side of the house in the middle of our position. It was amazing that no one was wounded. There was still a woman locked in the cellar at the bottom of the house. Every effort was made to force the door and persuade her to leave with us, but in vain.

When the last party was about 200 yards from the house, some of us turned around and were amazed to see it in flames. A mortar-bomb had landed on the roof. What happened to the poor woman? The sound of rifle-fire was coming from the area of the house. Some of our people might have withdrawn there. It was decided to observe in case we could render assistance. A man very kindly insisted on staying with me. We remained for some time in the neighbourhood. It was a great help. I was not a very cheerful person to be with; I felt that in disobeying written orders, I had deeply disgraced myself. I was wrong to allow this thought to obsess me rather than thoughts of what should be done in a most difficult situation.

Although the army had more success to the north at Narvik, the
Allied position in Norway was untenable and the decision was taken
to evacuate. Hugh Knowles of HMS *York* was involved in evacuating
the French and British troops at Namsos:

THURSDAY, 2 MAY 1940

At about 2100hrs, with the three transports, we entered the fjord
. . .

Stopping, we turned, and steamed astern towards a fire which was
burning at Namsos, silhouetting the transports as they prepared to
go alongside.

Lowered in the second motorboat with the First Lieutenant, I
towed the first whaler alongside the *Carlisle*, not realising that she
was pointing downstream. Leaving the whaler, I lay off; while the
pinnace towing another whaler went alongside, and soon afterwards
towed off both whalers to Spillum.

Leaving the *Carlisle*, my orders were to go to Namsos, and take
off the HQ staff. Steering towards the glow of the fire (a burning
coal-dump), I passed two destroyers taking troops to one of the
transports waiting in the stream. By the light of the fire I picked out
a place to go alongside the shattered jetty. The First Lieutenant and
a signalman set out to locate the Army headquarters. Standing on
what was left of the jetty, the fire lit up an unforgettable sight. The
once rich town of Namsos had been lain flat by heavy and incendiary
bombs. There was not a single wall standing within a half a mile of
me. The ground was covered with a mess of fallen planks. Dimly,
in the distance, what was left of the walls of two houses could be
seen, close to the fire, a car stove in by the impact of a bomb: two
dimmed headlights of a car as it climbed and dropped like a tank
over the debris that was once a road: Several army lorries in a group:
a continuous stream of men, great packs on their backs, carrying
skis, guns, boxes along a stone jetty to the two French troopships:
and above all glimmered the top of a church tower.

The troops already on board the transports were shouting 'Quickly!
Quickly!' to those who straggled under their enormous burdens
towards them. The stream of men seemed unending.

I returned to the *Carlisle* to collect a hand-message, coming straight back to the broken jetty. Eventually the First Lieutenant reappeared, with General Carton de Wyatt [Wiart] and his staff. It was not easy for the general, with but one eye, one arm, and a wounded leg to climb down into the boat.

The *York* was completely invisible against the black and white background, her dapple paint obscuring her completely, until we were quite close. One of the troopships had already left. It was quite light.

Meanwhile three trawlers, completely covered with branches, had come alongside the *York*, to disembark their soldiers as quickly as possible over all the brows we could produce. As they came on board, the soldiers nearly all of them French, dropped their packs on the quarterdeck or the 4-inch gun-deck, making their ways to the mess decks along organised routes. One man fell off a brow, and by a terrific stroke of luck fell onto a catamaran, letting forth a stream of French invective.

As a postscript to the campaign in Norway, this was the first time in the Second World War that German and British troops had encountered each other in the field and, as such, there was considerable interest at the highest levels of government about the equipment and personnel. Following his capture, Walter Laing was flown to Berlin for a special interview:

SATURDAY, 27 APRIL 1940

In the morning the German officer who had met us at Staaken aerodrome told me to get ready for an immediate journey. I didn't like the sound of this and I didn't want to be parted from my companions. I was taken to another room where I was glad to find that the sergeant and private soldier in our party were preparing for the same journey.

A German air force colonel came to escort us. He was the middle-aged German officer of fiction: tall, heavily built, fair, monocled, with heels ever ready to click. He didn't seem ill disposed. He took us downstairs. The taxis were hailed from the street. Guards were put

in each. I was put into the first, and the sergeant and private soldier
into the second. The air force colonel travelled with me. On the way,
he chatted in German, mentioning that a British officer's diary had
been found which proved that the British were planning to get to
Norway first (I wondered if it was mine?).

He asked if I knew where we were going? You are going to see
Hitler. Surprised, aren't you? . . .

I had little time to consider what he said. We were very soon at
the Chancellery. We drove through a carriage door into the private
garden. When we got out, the taxi-driver, who appeared surprised,
said '*Dies ist ein Ereignis*' = (This is an event) or something to that
effect. 'And also for me', said the colonel, 'I have never been in the
private garden'. (This was presumably the garden under which was
in 1945 the bunker where Hitler died.)

On three sides of the garden were buildings and on the fourth
demolitions. The garden was about the size of a fairly large Oxford
quadrangle. There was no lawn but longish grass in the continental style,
trees, shrubs, flowerbeds, and an occasional bronze animal. One of the
buildings had an arcade, another a large white bow window at ground
level, with a door. At the door were two male servants in white coats.

A lorry arrived from which was unloaded British equipment taken
in Norway. This was laid out in the arcade. We saw the German major
who had brought us from Norway and an ADC [Aide-de-Camp].
The ADC was a fine-looking man in German army uniform with
'Adolf Hitler' in silver braid on a sleeve. He asked me if we were
being well treated.

There was movement at the bow window. I was amazed to see
Hitler (or his double). I wondered what to do. Eventually I saluted. He
acknowledged my salute raising his right arm parallel to the ground.
The only person in his retinue whom I recognised was Colonel-
General (later Field Marshal) Keitel.

Hitler went straight to the arcade, where we stood in front of
him. The major, who had brought us from Norway, lectured on our
uniforms and equipment. In Norway self-confident, the major was
now like a controlled but nervous schoolboy. He stated that the British
battle-dress was good except in the lumbar regions; the British gas-
respirator good except in the lying-down position.

Hitler then made a tour of the equipment in the arcade. The anti-tank rifle interested him most. He picked up a clip of anti-tank rounds and crunched them in his hand. An item was a tin of 'bully-beef'. Did he wish it to be opened? The only time he approached a smile was in saying: 'No'. He said very little.

As far as I could see, Keitel never said a word.

When Hitler was about to leave, he was told that the officer spoke German. He asked me two questions: '*Waren Sie schon einmal in Berlin?*' (Have you been to Berlin before?) On the answer '*Nein*' he asked: '*Wo waren Sie in Deutschland?*' (Where were you in Germany?) '*Ich war in Heidelberg einige Mal,*' (I was in Heidelberg several times) I replied. He went away, saying something I could not hear and looking hostile. The air force colonel asked me if I had heard Hitler's last words as he had spoken in a low voice. His version was: '*Dieser Kreig war nicht notwendig. Sie können Ihrer Regierung dafür danken.*' (This war was not necessary. You can thank your Government for it.)

I have left Hitler's appearance to the end. He was no taller than me. He wore a round, peaked cap. It was difficult to see the eyes. He had a double-breasted khaki jacket with the Iron Cross (First Class) and Wound Badge on the left breast. His tie, trousers and shoes were black. He carried gloves at which he kept pulling. At first sight, Keitel was more impressive-looking.

5. The BEF and the Phoney War

Although Norway was the scene of the first combat between British and German troops, a far larger British force, the British Expeditionary Force (BEF), had been on the Continent for some time, occupying the 'Gort' defensive line – named after the Commander-in-Chief of the BEF, Lord Gort – in north-east France from September 1939 onwards. The period until the German attack in the west in May 1940 became known as the Phoney War, and Alec Pope, who served as a subaltern in the 1st Battalion King's Shropshire Light Infantry, wrote of the period:

OCTOBER 1939

There were plenty of cafes in the town and with an occasional concert and cinema on Saturdays everybody was very contented. Work on the area was hard and the hour fairly long. We experienced the grimness of the Flanders mud.

All the men were very keen on the defences and B Coy put up an excellent show. We were hampered by lack of materials which were not coming out from home; and at some periods we were almost brought to a stop, by lack of wine and necessary materials . . .

The weather during the month of October was fairly mild – though wet; but the continued open-air life was very healthy.

Air raid alarms were often – though only German reconnaissance planes flew over – they were soon driven off by our own fighters. These alarms became a farce as we were always obliged to take full air raid precautions, and for myself I was continually dressing up in the decontamination suits; with the rest of my recce and decontamination party.

Soon we all came to ignore these alarms, and were only ordered to take action if the enemy became hostile.

Lieutenant Pope also saw the pride of the French defences, a series of fixed fortifications along the German border known as the Maginot Line:

MONDAY, 4 DECEMBER 1939

Went on a reconnaissance to the Reserve portion of the Maginot line with Major Hunter Blair – viewed the site of an anti-tank ditch which was dug behind a position of the Maginot line. The French don't like the idea of a Reserve Line being dug as they consider the Maginot Line impenetrable. Went round a sector of the Maginot Line – whole system based on the reverse slope idea – no fire to the front. But adjacent fort supports and covers with fire the area in front of its neighbour.

Inspected their anti-tank defences – very strong – Railway Lines embedded many feet into the earth – in a concrete foundation.

This period of relative inactivity did not last forever, and on 10 May the German drive westwards began with one army group attacking the Low Countries, drawing the French and British into Belgium, while another army group advanced through the Ardennes, crossing the river Meuse on 13 May 1940 and threatening to cut the BEF off from the Channel.

6. The Fall of France

This German flanking movement by Army Group A propelled the French First Army and the BEF into retreat and, despite a partially successful counter-attack by British troops to the south of Arras on 21 May, the Germans kept hold of the initiative and pushed resolutely onwards.

Don Clark served in the 2nd/4th Battalion King's Own Yorkshire Light Infantry (KOYLI) as the battalion retreated towards St Nazaire, from where it was eventually evacuated:

MAY 1940

Movement towards the bridge and eventually crossing the river or canal quickly in the dark became something of a shambles, absolutely chaotic, tripping over the rails and sleepers despite the brilliant moonlight and the reinforcing starlight. In the red sky area behind us explosions were everywhere with shouting, casualties, the crackle of exploding ammunition, fires springing up and the noise of aircraft and the scream and detonation of the bombs. After we had crossed the bridge, now illuminated by the fires and the multiple flashes of the explosions, amid and despite all the confusion, we knew that going in the general direction away from the water was temporarily the only way to safety and the supposed rendezvous behind Abbeville.

Staying near the trains would be suicide and no use to anyone, so it was 'Go Go', get on get away.

Events in the next few hours, up to dawn, and just after, are vague to me but I do know that come daylight some 40 or 50 of us KOYLIs found ourselves lying on our groundsheets at the side of a hedge, dry, fairly comfortable but worn out as a result of the unaccustomed poor sleep and excitements we'd had in the last few days. I remember it as a small field, maybe three or four acres and there were fruit trees there, gnarled somewhat and we seemed to be behind a row of terrace houses on a road or street. A German fighter aircraft, whose Nazi crosses we could see clearly, flew low along this road but didn't see us, and we didn't move to draw his attention. We rested a few hours in total, then, without any breakfast, because we had no food except the iron rations, got to our feet and set off to attempt to get well behind the town of Abbeville on to a road in the general direction of St Pol . . .

We moved in small groups of five or six, separated by perhaps 100 feet so as to ensure we were not trapped in a bunch and got on what seemed to be a main road going north-east, judging by the sun, moving it from the rear of our field and across neighbouring fields. To our surprise we found the road was congested with refugee traffic, both civilian and military, moving south-west back in the direction from which we had just come. The road was packed, it was incredible, I have never seen anything like it. There were horse-drawn farm carts piled high with household possessions pulled by tired looking horses with children sat on wherever a space could be found and the adults pushing at the rear to help the horse. Families with smaller carts, wheelbarrows and prams taking all they could carry being pushed by other family members. It was unbelievable and we began to realise what war could really do and what war meant to civilians who had the misfortune to get in the way. There were a few cars of the wealthier people but they could only proceed at the walking speed of the multitude and then to top it all were the columns of thousands of walkers with suitcases and carrier bags. I say thousands of walkers, maybe tens of thousands or perhaps even hundreds of thousands.

It was an endless procession of misery and weariness and I found it astonishing and mind boggling to see so many people, adults and children, and animals, struggling to get away from something they obviously feared. I began to wonder what we were letting ourselves in for. It was so hot by now, even though it was only mid-morning, with that sun blazing down again out of a cloudless sky and us in our heavy uniforms and greatcoats plus a big pack on our backs. God, it was hot!

Moyra Charlton had by this point joined the Auxiliary Territorial Service (ATS) as an ambulance driver and had been posted to France, where she came face to face with the horrors of war:

FRIDAY, 7 JUNE 1940

A long wait, as usual, at the train while we all manoeuvred in turn round the platform. I had a load of six men for the Casino, five stretchers and one sitting, and the journey (some two miles) took the best part of an hour by the time we were unloaded. Bad management. (A fishing boat with sails furled and a little motor chugging is just creeping past our cove). The men had come down from the Somme and had had a hard journey. They bombed and machine-gunned the ambulances all the way to Rouen, and the man sitting beside me said they had to get out and crawl. He had a machine gun bullet in his thigh and a graze on his shoulder. His name was Robert MacSorley and he was in a well-known Highland regiment, which he said (as far as his own battn. went) had been pretty wiped out. They had followed up French tanks to attack and the tanks had outpaced them and left them to be mowed down by machine guns from the air. They had been lying flat on their stomachs for 18 hours. He said that then the rest of their battalions attacked and wiped out the Germans, disobeying the order to take prisoners. He said the Jerries could not fight as we could but their armaments were so strong now.

One of my stretcher cases was a young lad. He was a ghastly colour and had an abdominal wound, and started retching and trying to be sick. He was clearly in agony and wanted water; I did what I could for him, tumbling over the fifth stretcher in the centre. Then an RAMC [Royal Army Medical Corps] orderly looked at him and said he was very bad and that I must go over the bump to the Casino very slowly as his life depended on it. I managed to creep over it, and he was unloaded safely. Took one case on to the Hermitage, parked the ambulance and tidied it up and went back to breakfast, rather sick at our first really grim job.

The retreat became increasingly desperate, as the BEF sought to avoid the superior firepower and tactics of the advancing German forces.

John Williams's 2nd/6th Battalion of the East Surrey Regiment had already been decimated in the fighting and was now in headlong retreat towards St Nazaire:

MAY 1940

We were speeding along in the three-tonner, Lt. Hancock driving with the fifteen hundred weight behind with Lt. Gray driving. Before long we found that we were approaching Elle Boeuf, all was very quiet. The village cross roads ever getting nearer, we were almost there when explosion after explosion rent the air. We came to a stop with a shuddering jolt, bailed out of the three-tonner without even lowering the tail-board, dived for cover at the side of the road. What suckers we were – a fair ambush. Lt. Gray called for NCOs [Non-Commissioned Officers] and we armed with all available Bren guns advanced in line to the crossroads, CRASH, CRASH, down came the shells, quickly we pulled back behind cover, it was a tank ambush. I just had time to notice two blazing lorries down the right hand road and silent grotesque bodies lying around. Sgt. Cotton and Corporal Jupe, on Cotton's motorbike, had sped back down along the route we had come, obviously, they believed in every man for himself. Lt. Hancock, taking in the situation and nursing a wounded left wrist, ordered us into the three-tonner, jumped in the driver's seat, his foot down on the accelerator leaped forward taking the enemy by surprise and we were across the cross-roads before they could open fire. Just on the outskirts of the village we were waved to a stop by a *Poilu* (French soldier) who told us that German tanks controlled the whole area and that the bridge across the river two miles away was to be blown-up in three minutes.

Hell! What a fix we were in, fatal to go back and a million to one chance to cross the bridge before it was blown. The canvas canopy of our vehicle was badly ripped and we were standing grasping the frame, sweat breaking out on our foreheads and fearfully wondering what could we do. But we had not reckoned with Hancock, a pre-war Brooklands racing driver, and a three-tonner with the [engine] 'governor' removed.

Those two miles will never be forgotten. We crashed along at 60 miles an hour, swaying from side to side, careering round corners on two wheels, hanging on to the side like grim death. Soon we could see the bridge. God – would we make it? The seconds were flashing past, we stared at that seemingly never nearer bridge with baited breath, lumps in our throats and prayers on our lips.

Less than a minute to go, we couldn't make it surely and yet could we? We had turned into the last straight. Lt. Hancock seemed to urge every ounce of speed out of the hurtling truck, if we had wings we would surely have taken off.

There she was, the bridge, almost there! Another quarter of a mile! Was there still time! Past prayers now we stood transfixed, white knuckles standing out grimly as we gripped even tighter, expressions tense and rigid. The bridge!!!! The bridge!!!! We were there, we were on it, and we were across it. Thank God we made it.

As Lt. Hancock slowly eased the speed down leaving the bridge behind there was a thunderous roar as steel disintegrated and sped crazily skyward. We had made it with less than half a minute to spare. When we stopped there wasn't a man who didn't go up to Lt. Hancock to shake him by the hand and thank him. He said afterwards that he never really knew how he did it and with a wounded left wrist into the bargain.

Robin Dunn commanded a Troop of the 7th Field Regiment Royal Artillery supporting the 8th Brigade, part of General Bernard Montgomery's 3rd Division, and recorded his experiences of the retreat:

THURSDAY, 16 MAY 1940

It is time to stop mere description and try to give impressions. The first and most important impression I had was of the complete air superiority of the Germans. We seldom saw a British fighter, and when a patrol went over, it was always at a time when there were no German machines about. We usually had a Lysander overhead, but they were obviously not for defence purposes. I saw one shot down over Louvain by two Messerschmitts. It was a pathetic sight, as watching anything defenceless being attacked by greatly superior forces is apt to be.

My second impression was the terrible effect of war on a countryside. It is more vivid in town areas than in the country. One somehow associated open country with war, but towns developed for the pleasures and pursuits of peace, present a terrible picture when bombed or shelled. I remember seeing a tram hurrying down the road from Louvain to Brussels with bombs bursting all round it. Broad boulevards with shady trees built for the delight of citizens on long warm summer evenings, somehow look desolate out of all proportion to the damage done when they have been bombed or shelled. And of course the refugees with their patient faces, suffering eyes, and eternal questions '*Il y aura danger ici, monsieur?*' War is not too bad for a soldier, he has his friends and weapons with which to hit back, but it is sheer horror for civilians in the battle area.

Although Robin Dunn may not have seen much of the RAF, they were certainly there in France and still fighting. Denis Wissler flew Hurricanes as part of No. 85 Squadron, based at Seclin and Merville in France:

SUNDAY, 19 MAY 1940

We left Seclin aerodrome in a great flap, and moved about 40 miles to Merville. I flew in a lot of patrols, one an offensive . . . The aerodrome was bombed after a low flying attack by Me 109s. Once again I was about 20 yds from the bombs, sitting in my aircraft trying to start the engine. Incendiary bombs were also dropped. On landing at Merville and avoiding a DH89, which taxied across my path, I went up on my nose and smashed the prop.

MONDAY, 20 MAY 1940

All the troops but 20 were packed up in the transport vans and sent to Boulogne, plus some of the pilots. The 20 remained behind to service the a/c and one pilot for each machine also stayed. It was death or glory for us today but I missed both by going to lunch. The transport a/c arrived at 6.15 and at 7.30 I landed at England at Northolt without any of my kit, which was all left behind. We lost a further three pilots today including the CO of one day's standing.

Losses amongst RAF pilots also remained high. The Reverend Guy Mayfield was station chaplain for RAF Duxford in Cambridgeshire, and the squadrons based here were heavily involved in providing air cover for the BEF both in France and during its evacuation:

SUNDAY, 26 MAY 1940

19 Squadron have shot down ten. The Hornchurch wing has shot down 40 in all off the Belgian coast. Sinclair, Stevie, Peter and one other are missing. Too numb to feel much; all one can do is pray off and on all day. We are preparing for an invasion. 20 parachutists over Dover last night – killed before they landed. No further news of Peter and the others. They went up before breakfast towards the French coast and met about 30 Ju's. They fell for the usual German trick, for above them Me's were waiting. It's said that Peter and Michael Lyne got a German each. We are here all depressed and anxious about these casualties.

2130. Rather more hopeful news. Sinclair has landed at Manston. A Sergeant Pilot is in a French hospital. Logical Lyne is wounded and landed on Margate beach. He is at Deal Hospital. (The nurse tried to remove his trousers on the beach in order to dress his wound, but he resisted this.) Peter was last seen baling out over the Channel near the French coast; there is a chance he was picked up. Stevie was last seen flying towards Germany. Ball is wounded in the head.

This has been a black and anxious Sunday: I wish I could pray as I sleep.

What night thoughts for the twentieth century! Goodbye to Peter, returned with a smart salute from the cockpit; and last talk at dispersal about seeing Thel and having dinner next week. Tonight you don't know whether he is alive or not. It sounds so easy to say 'He bailed out over the sea'. But have you seen the inside of a Spit? Imagine bailing out of that, with the wind resistance, at 250mph at the slowest! And then – he is a good swimmer. I go on saying prayers – I do for all my friends, and he is – was – one of the most loyal; but where does the prayer reach him? Whether in the flesh or the spirit I cannot say, to adapt St Paul.

Alan Munby was a captain with the 1st Battalion Queen Victoria's Rifles, King's Royal Rifle Corps, part of 30th Brigade that was dispatched to Calais on 22 May from England in order to defend the port. He was posted to Fort Neuilly just outside the main defences of the town:

FRIDAY, 24 MAY 1940

Throughout the day casualties had mounted steadily; the fort had not been constructed to be held against modern howitzers and mortars, which lobbed HE [High Explosive] over the walls incessantly and to which the troops inside could make no reply. Under cover of their barrage the Germans had surrounded the fort and an unlucky shell on the northwest bastion knocked out both the French heavy machine guns, killing or wounding their crews. The 25mm gun sited in the flimsy iron gateway shared a similar fate and there was no means of keeping at bay the heavy German tanks which had appeared on the road outside. At this juncture I visited the French commander in his underground office. I remember the scene very well, a dead and horribly mutilated Frenchman lay across the doorway of the dugout, a handkerchief over his face. As I passed a French NCO withdrew the handkerchief to see who the dead man was and crossed himself. Inside a man trained in First Aid was attending to casualties. I went through into an inner cellar to the French HQ and had a brief conversation by flickering candlelight with the commander. He was very pale and sweating profusely – I probably looked the same to him. He said that the situation was hopeless and that the fort was being surrendered forthwith. He had already sent men to hoist the white flag and open the gates. It was obviously no time to argue about a *fait accompli*. I re-emerged into the daylight and found myself covered by a German sub-machine gun. The French captain joined me, blinking as he came out into the sunlight which he had not seen for some hours. A suitcase ready packed in each hand belied any suggestion that his surrender was an entirely unpremeditated affair. The French troops had laid down their arms and with the Germans inside the fort the British had no alternative but to follow suit. It was all indescribably inglorious and humiliating. The Germans gave a satisfied exclamation of 'Engländer' at the sight of us.

The failure of the Allied campaign in France led to recriminations not only at the highest level of government, but also at the lowest level. And relations between the French and British soldiers were severely stretched, as Alan Munby relates:

MONDAY, 27 MAY 1940

This is not an aspect of the journey that I wish to dwell on but there was sometimes present an atmosphere of ill discipline and demoralisation, a lurking suggestion that now we were German prisoners all ranks were equal, a tendency to shout down anyone who was trying to organise, say, a food or water queue. Among the troops the attitude towards our allies was rapidly becoming distrust and hatred. The French were in their own country for one thing and could scrounge much more in the way of food and comforts from the natives; the inherent meanness of so many Frenchmen, which in normal times is latent, became painfully apparent. It was not uncommon to see a Frenchman eating a chicken which a kindly farmer's wife had given him, while the English looked ravenously on. He was not above capitalising on this state of affairs and many watches and other small valuables were accepted in exchange for a leg of chicken or a small portion of bread. This was one of the more unpleasant features of the journey, but the picture could not be true if it were suppressed.

7. Operation *Dynamo*

Following the gradual collapse of the Allied armies under the relentless pressure of the German blitzkrieg, the position of the BEF in France became increasingly untenable.

Osmund Archdale served as a liaison officer between the BEF and the French 1st Group of Armies. He witnessed at first hand the increasingly desperate position of the French high command and describes a meeting between General Gaston Billotte and the Commander-in-Chief (C. in C.) of the BEF, General Lord Gort, on the night of 18/19 May:

SATURDAY, 18 MAY 1940

General Billotte met me in the Office and asked me how things were going. I replied that everything was well with us, and added, in order to get his reaction, that we were sure at GHQ [General Head Quarters] that the French would soon be able to pull themselves together and fight back.

He thereupon showed me his latest map of German order of battle, which marked in red circles, a series of German Armoured Division in front of the Allied Line. He repeated slowly '*Un panzer, deux panzers*' and so on up to '*huit panzers*' and added '*et contre ceux-la je ne peux rien faire*'.

There was only one thing to be done: arrange for him to meet the C. in C. then and there while this true mood of hopeless impotence was on him. He accepted the suggestion and the meeting was soon arranged with the help of Gregson Ellis for 11pm.

We got there to find the C. in C., the CGS [Chief of the General Staff], General Lindsell (QMG [Quartermaster General]), General Eastwood (DCGS [Deputy Chief of the General Staff]), Oliver Leese (BGS [Brigadier General Staff]), Gregson Ellis and Air Vice-Marshal Blount. The C. in C. started the conversation with a broad '*Eh Bien! Mon General qu'est-ce que vous avez á me dire*', and General Billotte then made it swiftly and abundantly clear that he had no plan, no reserves, and little hope. On the way back to Douai, he was constantly repeating: '*Je suis crevé de fatigue, crevé de fatigue*', and then pathetically, '*Et contre ces panzers je ne peux rien faire*'.

Following this meeting, Gort started to explore the possibility of withdrawing his beleaguered forces back to the coast, eventually deciding to evacuate the BEF from the port of Dunkirk. Billotte was to die four days later following a car accident on 21 May.

Captain Norman Strother Smith served with the 1st Royal Horse Artillery, who were at this point across the border in Belgium and, along with the rest of the BEF, began to fall back towards the Channel ports, notably Dunkirk. The orders for the evacuation of the BEF and Allied force in what became known as Operation *Dynamo* were given on the 26th, with the operation due to begin the following day:

MONDAY, 27 MAY 1940

At 2.30am we were woken with orders to move immediately. The transport was ready for us but there was not enough for the whole lot and two journeys were to be made. Some of the people who were due to go last had already got excited as they were afraid to travel by daylight. It certainly must be unpleasant to be caught by bombers in a convoy. There was talk of being evacuated, but no definite information. The buses took us to a place across the frontier into France again – West Cappel. Here we were met by a colonel in the Ordnance. He was all set to billet us and get us settled in. However, word came that we had to move and later it was learned that we were to go to Dunkirk to be evacuated. It meant dumping everything we couldn't carry. At the time no one understood the situation. We were all under the impression that our own Reception unit was going, perhaps to join up in rear from Le Havre or Cherbourg. We were pushed into a field to dump our stuff and so we set to sorting out all we wanted and cramming it all into haversacks or packs. The stores were being doled out to all who came and amongst them were some 20,000 cigarettes.

At 10.15 the march to Dunkirk started. Men were split into groups and each group split up over the road, one file in one ditch and the other in the other, or rather on the side of the road ready to jump. All the time we had been packing our stuff, planes had been going to and fro above us, fights had taken place and bombs dropped in neighbouring villages. It was not until we had just left our dump that they came and bombed it.

We were forever running into the ditches for shelter from aircraft, not for fear of being bombed so much as for being spotted and attacked. Hour after hour seemed to go by but in the heat and dust no track of time could be kept. We passed roadblocks manned and covered by anti-tank rifles, antiaircraft guns and all sorts of minor defence positions.

It was the hell of a march; the heat was terrific and most of us were dressed to the full, wearing greatcoats to save them and carrying blankets for the night. I had mine slung round my neck and made great use of it as a ground sheet in the ditches I jumped into and so saved my stuff from a lot of dirt.

Finally we reached the main canal at Bergues. Here we collected all the stragglers together and formed up afresh. By now my feet were quite raw and I could only hobble. The road was right on the edge of the canal bordered by trees and this gave us some protection from observation, but I am afraid it was too late by then. However we had no direct raids for some time though we saw plenty of bombers in the vicinity.

Our orders were to continue on the main road until we reached the houses on the outskirts of the town of Dunkirk. Here we were to rendezvous for further orders. As we approached the houses the air became hot with bombers and we had little peace from then on. I suppose it was 2.00pm then, though I could not be sure and I reckon we had three raids in every hour. We never met anyone to rendezvous and so a large body of us kept on down the sound into Dunkirk. All the way we were continually bombed and had to take shelter.

Dunkirk was a terrible sight. The road was covered with debris and all along one side were lorries, cars and motorbikes jettisoned, some were in the canal. Some had been blown up. In the road were two cars burnt out [and] still smouldering and in places were bodies of men covered with blankets. There was equipment, petrol and all sorts of stores destroyed. Houses were blazing furiously from recent bombs and the others were all shattered. All the time the sky was full of black smoke from oil tanks that had been blazing for some five or six days.

The air raids were something I shall never forget. The noise was something incredible.

The bombers came over in waves of three generally at least a dozen strong and the Dornier at any rate had a peculiar engine noise of its own. It had a low-pitched throb, which could be heard for miles so that a dozen of these made a roar something terrific. As they approached the AA guns would open fire. The air would be full of the cracking of heavy guns, light guns and quick-firing Bofors and each one made the same noise on bursting. The sky was full of puffs of smoke. And then the bombers would start their machine guns firing on the battery positions. It was a deafening noise; the guns and automatics and all the time the throbbing of engines. All of a sudden could be heard a screaming noise. At first one wouldn't know what it was, but after the first raid we all knew the sound well. It was the bombs.

They took some 10 to 18 seconds to fall and all the time we could hear this screaming getting louder and louder. It always sounded as if we were sure to be hit, but each one seemed to pass right over head and the sound died away and almost as soon the ground shook as the bombs hit it and the air was full of the roar of explosions or if they didn't burst the thudding of each bomb could be heard. Very frequently there was no burst.

Each wave of three planes loosed off the same attack and the noise would start again. All the time we would have our faces buried in the ground and our muscles taut, ready for any nearby explosion. The raid would last about five or ten minutes but it seemed like one hour from the moment that the planes could first be heard. After it we would get up to see what damages had been done; all expecting to see hundreds of dead and all the place shattered and blazing, but the bombs did little damage. I never saw one man hit and at the worst I saw a few cattle killed and perhaps one house shattered and smoking.

The lack of air cover over Dunkirk and the beaches was a subject much commented on by the soldiers on the ground, both at the time and afterwards, and the RAF came in for some largely undeserved criticism. Air Marshal Sir Hugh Dowding, the man in charge of the RAF's Fighter Command, had reserved the bulk of the RAF's front-line fighters for protection of Great Britain and refused to allow them to be sent to France. Much of the responsibility for the air defence of the Dunkirk pocket went to men such as Bombardier Arthur Hicks, who served with the 153rd Battery, 53rd Light Anti-Aircraft (LAA) Regiment RA:

MAY 1940

It was all very strange because we then noticed that the 25-pounders behind us began to pack up and withdraw. The tactics were that while some pulled out others kept firing and this went on until they had all gone, at which point our Troop Officer came and collected us and we proceeded back along the roads where, at intervals, there were infantry men with Bren guns lying in the verges, apparently waiting in case the enemy appeared. I often wondered whether anybody thought to pick them up. From then onwards we kept going through the same routine for no apparent reason sometimes withdrawing at night and sometimes by day.

When we passed through villages it was noticeable that the inhabitants were now pointing their thumbs in downwards direction, but at that time we had no idea that the Germans had broken through on other fronts and were threatening to encircle and cut off the BEF.

After continuing to go through very much the same process – stopping at one point to guard a bridge over a canal against possible parachutist attack and only moving on when the Royal Engineers blew it up – we were finally told that we were going to move back to the coast for evacuation and finally despite the chaos on the roads, we arrived at La Panne where we drove along the promenade with each gun dropping off onto the beach at intervals and driving over the sand until our vehicle got stuck and that's where we dropped the gun into action.

The sands were already littered with equipment left by people who had been taken off the beaches. There were boats of all shapes and sizes a little way out and shortly after we arrived so did the German Junkers 87 dive-bombers. It was our first experience of them.

We were puzzled by their actions. They were in formation out to sea and out of our range and then they appeared to be playing hide-and-seek in the clouds. What they were doing was forming up to attack and the next thing we knew they were diving one after the other, having selected the largest ship as their target and, despite quite heavy fire from our guns and other weapons from the beach, they pressed home their attack and at the end they flew away leaving the ship sinking. This was the pattern from then on – the Stukas attacked the ships and the heavy bombers concentrated on the port of Dunkirk, which was under a permanent cloud of black smoke farther along the coast.

Once on the beaches, the enormous numbers of disorganised, demoralised and confused men had to be marshalled into some state of order so that they could be evacuated by the ships of the Royal Navy and others. This task fell to men such as Harold Dibbens, who commanded 102 Provost Company (part of I Corps):

Thursday, 30 May 1940

A number of vessels out at sea were ablaze, the oil tanks in Dunkirk were belching out heavy black smoke and flames and the whole of the town and dock area was covered with a slow moving pall of depressingly dense smoke. We traversed about one third of the evacuation area but before we left the dunes we were subjected to intense strafing from German dive-bombers and, with one accord, the two of us leaping into a previously made sand crater and, by God's grace, emerged without a scratch. Almost immediately afterwards and from nowhere came a posse of horses – French or Belgian artillery horses – and as they galloped past one plainly saw they were half starved, their bones stood out like the ribs of a skeleton skiff; they were phantoms, riderless, without saddles or harness, arrived from and disappeared into space, a spectacle and a very moving experience especially as we ourselves, a couple of minutes earlier, had been very close to death.

On return to our new HQ we collected our men, returned to the beach and the dunes and gave orders to the effect that the troops were to be formed into units of around 50 – with an officer or senior NCO in charge – and stay in the dunes until called forward for embarkation. In general this order was complied with and the beach was almost cleared of troops; the stretcher wounded were taken to the nearby casualty clearing station and the walking wounded joined up with units in the dunes . . .

Having got through the morning of 30th May without any air attacks and at long last found a part answer to the loss of lives and dinghies, I felt we were not only fortunate in respect to our own lives but our efforts were meeting with success. My soaring spirits were, however, dampened down at around 1500hrs when GSO 1. (Lt. Col. – I Corps) came to me on the beach and asked for an assessment of the number of men awaiting embarkation. I told him roughly 8,000 and he replied 'We have only 12 hours to get them out'. I was stunned and could only say 'It's not possible to get them all away in that time'. The colonel just looked at me, gave a friendly smile and walked away. I did not pass on this news to my NCOs as, with the jetty then in operation and still no blitzing, we were going along like a well-oiled machine. On and through the night our small boats kept up the shuttle service and still the smoke and flames poured out of the blazing oil tanks casting shadows over the sea . . .

A number of shell-shocked troops were rescued from the sea, all of them had been blasted off their ships and most of them were in a near helpless state. Those that reacted well to first aid treatment were given 'boat priority' and the remainder were transferred to the nearby casualty clearing station.

It was impossible within the hour to give bulk numbers of the men sheltering in the dunes because there was at all times a chain of troops moving in and out. However, the transfer from shore to ship was orderly and although during the night I heard the occasional bark of a rifle or pistol no complaints were lodged which suggested the weapons had been fired with murderous or malicious intent.

The operation to take the men off the beaches was run by the Royal Navy from the dynamo room at Dover Castle, under the command of Vice Admiral Bertram Ramsay. The original naval estimate for the operation was that it would only be possible to evacuate 45,000 soldiers off the beaches before enemy action caused the operation to be shut down. However, there were nearly 400,000 men trapped in and around Dunkirk, so a greater effort had to be made.

One of the men running the operation for the Royal Navy on the beaches around Dunkirk was Commander Thomas Kerr:

1 JUNE 1940, CHARING CROSS HOTEL, LONDON

We went along the Mole at Dunkirk and landed, waiting orders. It was some time before we got them and we had many raids. There was a little house by my party, all the glass was shattered but inside it was neat, a meal laid for, just an abandoned home with the kitten being fed by my men. In due course we were marched down through the town to the beach close by and our work began. Such a terrible beach for embarking because it was practically level and nothing could come in close, not even the boats. We worked without ceasing all the dark hours, restoring order and confidence to the troops. At dawn we withdrew them to the sand dunes for an hour, and afterwards marched them into Dunkirk. Sometime during the afternoon we had

cleared that beach and we withdrew back to Dunkirk. The captain
in charge, Tennant, reorganised us and said he wanted one officer
and party to go to Bray Beach about seven miles away to embark
5,000 men. There were three of us left and so we cut for it as it was
a poor outlook by the sound of it. Richardson lost, then he said,
and quite rightly, he wanted another officer with him. I lost that
cut, so Richardson and self organised a party of 15 and started our
organisation off in a lorry along the road to get there. It took us
some time to get there by bomb-cratered road and wrong turnings
so that it was getting on for dusk when we got our party down on
to the beach. Then we gave a gasp, 5,000? Not a bit of it, there
must have been 25,000 at the very least, so we made a signal off to
the destroyer to signal the fact direct to the Admiralty. Then we got
busy. What a terrible night that was, for we had got hold of the odds
and ends of an army not the fighting soldiers. There weren't many
officers, and those there were useless, but by speech and promise of
safety and sight of our naval uniforms we got some order out of the
rabble. Pathetic the faith in the Navy, but we did our best. Some we
embarked, but by thousands we marched them off to Dunkirk. But
the sight of one little dinghy with 2,000 men waiting to get into it
was enough to make them hesitate about marching to Dunkirk. We
were always wet, anyway as far as our legs were concerned, because
we couldn't persuade the Troops it was no quicker to stand in the
water than on the dry sand. They always felt that someone would get
in front. Towards morning it blew up and beach embarkation became
impossible, so herding them and marshalling them on we marched
them towards Dunkirk. About noon, we gathered our party together,
found a lorry and made it go and went back to Dunkirk to get any
orders and fill up our water bottles . . .

The tide was nearly high in the morning and our whaler afloat.
Just before it was too late to get anyone else on board we got some
straggling British troops on board. It was blowing too hard for any
more to be got off from the beach and we told the lot they had to
make themselves warm and comfortable, and as soon as the wind
eased down they would be rescued and as a lot of small pleasure craft
and motor boats were coming they would be able to get alongside at
high water. We made them salve another whaler. In due course we

manned our whaler and even with a trained crew we barely made it, twice the seas broke over us. The destroyers had all moored off towards Dunkirk and we pulled with tired backs out to sea. Presently up came, of all things, the Margate lifeboat, and we climbed on board. We towed our whaler to the best of our judgement where it would float ashore to the others and then let go. I still feel bad about leaving those soldiers but we met the small craft and the wind did die down and I feel sure they were rescued, anyway it was their best chance. As our men landed in the lifeboat they dropped down anywhere and passed out, done to a turn. They had worked well and we hadn't lost one by desertion or casualty and I was proud of them. We landed in Margate at about 2.30 and reported ourselves to Dover.

The Panzers had halted on 24 May, held up by an order of the Führer. This order was controversial among members of the German Army's command structure at the time, and has remained so amongst historians ever since. The ground around Dunkirk was thought not to be suitable for armour, while the Panzer forces were operating at the end of lengthy supply chains and had been in continuous action for weeks. They were also needed for the further conquest of France. Whatever the exact reason, it was not until the afternoon of 26 May that the order was lifted, and the advance did not continue till the morning of the 27th. These three days enabled the bulk of the BEF to escape from Dunkirk. In the event destroyers of the Royal Navy, ably supported by vessels of the French Navy, merchant marine and the 'little ships' that have passed into popular legend, eventually succeeded in evacuating 331,226 soldiers from Dunkirk – 192,226 British and 139,000 French – by the time the operation was closed down on 4 June. Among them was Captain Strother Smith:

TUESDAY, 28 MAY 1940

And so we came down to the front. There we saw the casino. It had taken as bad a knock as any place. It was smouldering away and the houses round about were raised to the ground in some places.

And so on to the beach. Troops were wandering everywhere and the planes were forever flying over but for some reason they didn't bomb us. On the beach we found the Navy. It was a strange sight to see a party of them there then amidst all that we had seen, they were listening to jazz on a portable wireless they had. It was a very strange contrast.

Here again we were collected into groups for the march along the mole and so on to the ship. There were boats out to sea lying abandoned, one with a great rent in her side. The sea was almost as horrible a sight as the town.

Black smoke filled the sky everywhere and the bombers flew in and out, but never a bomb was dropped.

On we trudged in single file until we were on the boat. The sailors were great and what I thought was typical was the way they helped us on. We had to climb on to some planks from which they made us jump. They told us to jump clear and they would catch us, so from the middle of the planks I jumped and the weight of my kit crumpled me up on the ground but before I had landed a second I was pulled to my feet and pushed on my way with a few encouraging words from the sailors who had caught me.

I was shown downstairs and in a few minutes was having a drink. I was in a bath and then asleep on the bed in one of the two cabins.

The role of the Royal Navy in the evacuation was absolutely vital, and it was the destroyers, such as the HMS *Impulsive* on which Kenneth Wilson served, that bore the brunt of the German aerial assault on the evacuation:

28 MAY 1940, OPERATION *DYNAMO*

This has been my toughest day since the war started, a day of absolute hell, and to think that less than 48 hours ago I was sitting comfortably in our digs in Immingham with Lillian. We left Dover very early this morning, crossed the Channel and went alongside the pier at Dunkirk at 0600hrs after shooting down one dive bomber which attacked us on the way over. The whole of Dunkirk seems to be in flames and is being constantly bombed and the oil tanks are blazing only a few yards from where we were moored. They were belching black smoke, which seemed to envelop everything. Fortunately the smoke acted as a screen which hit us while we were alongside. The

BEF is being evacuated. We took onboard 1,000 troops, many of them seriously wounded by bombing, strafing and falling buildings. The pier was being bombed and shelled until a direct hit on it made it impossible to embark more troops. Soldiers then swam out to us or came in small boats. There are thousands of them on the beaches like swarms of black flies, being bombed and machine-gunned. The approaches to Dunkirk harbour are littered with wrecks of ships. Today we had 80 near misses from bombs and six of the ship's company have been killed by machine-gunning from planes. We ran out of Lewis ammunition, one of our 4.7s and our .5s were put out of action so we were a sitting target. Some of the crew, and soldiers, laid on their backs and shot at the attacking planes with .303 rifles – which seemed pretty futile. I was employed as ammunition supply party, taking shells to the remaining 4.7s when I was not wanted in the wireless office. It was no fun running the gauntlet of machine-gun fire along the upper deck with live shells in my arms. All my aerials have been shot away and the ship has as many holes as a pepper pot. I haven't eaten today, nor slept for 36 hours. Our losses today include the destroyers *Wessex*, *Wakeful*, *Grenade*, two trawlers and two French destroyers. What a day. The Army is certainly in a mess and it doesn't look as if they will be hanging washing on the Siegfried Line!

FRIDAY, 31 MAY 1940

Took troops to Dover and then back to Dunkirk early this morning and embarked another 1,000, which is as many as we can carry. We came under fire from enemy guns behind Dunkirk, on the perimeter as it is called, and had to retaliate with our 4.7s as troops came off the beach. Later this morning we were attacked by enemy fighters and machine-gunned. An able seaman was shot through the chest and dropped dead by my side on the iron deck amidships. I dragged him along the deck to cover, blood pouring from his mouth, but I guess it was a useless effort. One of the stokers, just emerging from the engine room hatch, was shot in the testicles at the same time. I have never heard such horrible screams in my life, but was too occupied with the able seaman to take much notice. This afternoon we were zig-zagging to avoid a stick of bombs and ran foul of a French destroyer which was sunk in shallow water. Our starboard propeller was dragged off at the same moment as the bombs straddled us. Generators smashed and ship plunged into darkness below decks and we listed to port. I was below decks at the time and there was a mad scramble to get out as we all thought the ship was going down. However we managed to clear the wrecked French ship and patch up damage under fire and head for Dover on one engine, being bombed and gunned all the way. I was sorry for the troops we had on board the crowded upper deck. They had had quite enough ashore without having to put up with what we caught in mid-Channel. It's been hell, but I am glad I was there. Something to recall in years to come – if there are any!

Robin Dunn also recollects his experiences on the beaches and the reaction to the defeated BEF back home:

Friday, 31 May 1940

We arrived on the beach just as dawn was breaking and marched down to the water where flat-bottomed boats were waiting. We had to wade up to our waists to get out to them, but quietly one man after another climbed in and we rowed out to the barges and small craft of all kind that were to take us back to England. I was lucky enough to be on board a destroyer, and went down to the wardroom where I dozed in a chair, drank hot tea, and did my best to dry my soaking clothes. We arrived at Dover at about 10 o'clock, were bundled into a train and by 10.30am were steaming through the Kentish countryside. We stopped at a station and were given hot tea and bread and marmalade. Never have I enjoyed a meal more. After that things became embarrassing. At every station where we stopped a mass of women appeared with cigarettes, sweet biscuits, lemonade and other delicacies. At one station a woman got into our carriage and insisted on feeding us and thanking us. I sat in my corner with 24 hours of growth on my beard longing for the train to start. It was astonishing to be treated thus, we had expected the population to turn their backs on us – a beaten army. We went on, Redhill, Ash, Wokingham, Newbury, where could we be going? We finally stopped at Shrivenham, stumbled into waiting motor cars which took us to a delightful house converted into a Mess. A charming young man took charge of me, gave me a bath, razors, socks, underclothes. He treated me like a helpless child! We returned to the Mess for dinner. As I walked into the hall, I glanced at the clock. 8.55pm. Three weeks ago to the hour, the leading gun of my Troop had passed the church in Thumesnil on our way to Belgium.

The huge numbers of men pouring across the Channel mostly passed through the port of Dover before being sent onwards. Arthur Mowbray was the head postmaster of the Dover post office and wrote of the effect of this great enterprise upon his team:

MAY/JUNE 1940

In the Telegraph Room – special arrangements had to be made on the spot; as boats of every size imaginable were emptied of their human cargoes hundreds of telegrams were handed in; 1,500 such messages were handed over in one day at a quayside office. The average daily traffic of 850 telegrams dealt with at the Head Office jumped to over 4000. No appreciable delay occurred in disposing of the traffic, due to the wholehearted co-operation of the Staff, who worked long hours at high pressure. Teleprinter speeds of 109 and 110 messages per hour were obtained; meal reliefs went by unheeded, for who could handle such messages and remain unmoved by the urgency of their appeal; the senders, somebody's fathers, somebody's sons, were indeed straight from the jaws of Hell, back from the gates of death, and the little we could do to assist them to relieve the anxiety at home was gladly undertaken . . .

I let one young fellow use my 'phone to advise his fiancée of his safe arrival, the half conversation ran like this – 'Eh kid, I'm back safe' – 'What, disappointed at not getting a letter?' – 'But I've been in <u>hell</u>' – 'You think I might have written' – 'Yes, perhaps you haven't heard for three weeks but I've been bombed and shot at on Dunkirk beaches for days' – 'No, I couldn't write, hadn't a chance: I'm lucky to be alive'. The conversation ended and he turned to me, with perspiration on his forehead – 'Poor kid' he said. 'Poor fellow' I thought, and later I was to learn that this was by no means an isolated case of misunderstanding of the issues at stake . . .

Needless to say, the Counter was thronged from morning till night and the hours of business were extended to cope with the situation. Most of the pressure was due to evacuated troops, and refugees in their hundreds who accompanied the troops. People of British, French, Belgian, Dutch, Polish and unidentifiable nationalities turned the Public Office into a Tower of Babel. Queerly clad, many wet through, tired to the point of exhaustion, dirty and wounded many were so excited at their miraculous escape, they found our currency and language a bit of a difficulty. The Counter Staff rose to the occasion, however with great patience and the use of their fingers, worked wonders in very exceptional circumstances.

By no means all the BEF returned from France unscathed. Mary Morris worked as a nurse at the Kent and Sussex Hospital in Tunbridge Wells, Kent, one of those used to treat the casualties arriving from France:

FRIDAY, 31 MAY 1940

It was about 2pm that the ambulances started to arrive. I was ordered to report to casualty sister, a 'being' who terrifies me. She looks so efficient and rustles with starch when she dashes about.

As I entered the casualty department, I was astounded to see so many wet, dirty and injured people there. Some were soldiers, (guessed they must be Dunkirk survivors), the others were civilians.

They were all laid out on stretchers on the floor, and most of our surgeons and physicians were there, assisted by several senior sisters and staff nurses. I was given the job of removing dirty wet clothing, so that they could be examined by the doctors. Several of the men had their skin flayed by oil burns, a very painful condition, others were injured by bomb splinters, and some were injured by machine-gun fire from the air as they came across the Channel. There is one badly shocked middle-aged man, a Captain Hermes, a Belgian boat owner. They were all very tired, cold, wet and hungry. All the surgical cases are now on my ward.

1 JUNE 1940, TUNBRIDGE WELLS

There is a completely different atmosphere on the ward now – more cheerful. Staff nurse chats to the BEF soldiers and has less time for making my life a misery. Capt. Hermes is still exhausted and shocked and is under sedation.

The small ward is now occupied by the burns cases. Private Brian M— is one of the most severely burned. He is about 18 years old – my age. His face and hands have been sprayed with tannic acid, which has set into a hard black cement. His arms are propped up in front of him on a pillow, the fingers extended like claws and his naked body hangs loosely on straps just clear of the bed. His eyelids are coated with a thick layer of gentian violet and we give him morphia every three hours. He was involved in an explosion on his way back from Dunkirk.

John Evans, the captain of the old *Brighton Belle*, got off lightly with a fractured tibia and fibula. His leg is in plaster and he talked to me as I helped him to have a blanket bath. He sadly misses his ship. She was certainly versatile. John told me that she used to carry holiday crowds across the Channel before the Boer War, swept mines in the Great War, and swept mines again last winter. This great old ship went over to Dunkirk to collect the soldiers, deposited one load safely on the Kent coast and went back for the second. It was on the return journey, with 400 exhausted soldiers aboard that she struck the wreck of a ship and slowly sank. John managed to transfer the soldiers to another boat and also rescued his dog Jock before the 'old *Belle*' disappeared from view.

The story of the Dunkirk rescue operation is an extraordinary one. John told me how he and his crew met up with French and Belgian fishing boats lying off Ramsgate – boats from Caen, Le Havre and Antwerp. They had all helped before at Calais and Boulogne in the preceding days at Dunkirk, but when they heard the new orders they set out again. The fishing boats were the leaders of the procession, for they were slow and with them went some Dutch 'schouts' [schuyts] stumpy little coastal vessels, commandeered at the collapse of Holland. Each little boat was flying the white ensign of the Royal Navy, and fitted with <u>one</u> Lewis gun. Next went coasters, paddle steamers and tugs. There was a car ferry and lots of yachts, large and small. There were sloops, trawlers, and rolling and pitching in a cloud of spray were open speedboats, wholly unsuited to the Channel 'chop'.

John told me as I washed his good foot that there was never such a fleet that went to war before. Some were 'tatty' with old car tyres for fenders; others were bright with new paint and chromium. It was apparently the queerest and most nondescript flotilla that ever was, and manned by all kinds of people, English, Belgian, French. There were bankers and dentists, taxi drivers, yachtsmen and fishermen, even dockers, engineers and civil servants.

8. The Channel Islands

With the evacuation of the BEF from France and the signing of the armistice between France and Germany on 22 June 1940, one part of British territory was left extremely exposed to occupation by the Germans – the Channel Islands. The British Government had decided in mid-June that there would be no attempt made to defend the islands and, on 28 June, the first bombing raids were launched, as Ella Simon of Jersey recorded:

FRIDAY, 28 JUNE 1940

When I arrived in Vauxhall two planes were fighting over my head, I swiftly went by the side door and all I could see were dense clouds of smoke and fire. I thought the harbour was destroyed but it was Holman's store . . . the Yacht Hôtel and Pomme D'or were badly damaged. I went at the manse and we stood under the stairs and the noise was terrific. I decided to return home . . . but had only arrived at Mr Rive the Baker when it started all over again. I was asked by an ARP Warden to get under shelter he said 'anywhere and now'.

The Germans eventually arrived unopposed in Guernsey on 30 June, with Jersey being occupied on 1 July. Iris Bullen wrote of her feelings on the occasion:

Monday, 1 July 1940

The most tragic time of the day was when, we were all informed that we all had to have a white flag of surrender flying from every house in the island by 7am on the Tuesday morning, the time when the Germans were to occupy the island so we were all busy making and erecting this unhappy flag. News was swirling around at great speed and we were told that if we used our wireless we could only listen to the German Stations, so most people disconnected their sets and cut down the aerials, ours were cut off too. We also thought it best to take away any pictures or photos of Royalty or military origin, as we did not know what our invaders were going to do, many papers also we burnt.

And so after a very sad day in the history of this dear island of ours we all solemnly obeyed our instruction as our Bailiff had instructed and all the family once more set off for the haven of Prospect for the night, all wishing in our hearts that the morning wouldn't come, but though we had had no official news and the Germans were not expected till next morning they had actually been arriving during this afternoon.

But God has not forsaken us, and so I know we shall rest in his care.

9. The Battle of Britain

With France conquered and the Channel Islands in German hands, Hitler's attention turned towards the main body of the British Isles. Many in both the German and British governments expected a negotiated peace, but Churchill was adamant that Britain would fight on alone and the German high command started drawing up plans for an invasion. Due in part to the overwhelming superiority in numbers of the Royal Navy over the German Navy, it was imperative that the RAF be driven from the skies over the Channel and southern England for any invasion operation to have a chance of success. The Luftwaffe would have to control the air over the Channel to protect any invasion force and prevent the Royal Navy interfering in the operation. To that end, Göring, as head of the German Air Force, instigated the campaign that became known as the Battle of Britain. From mid-July onwards, German forces began to probe the British defences and, from August onwards, they began to launch heavy attacks on the bases of Fighter Command in the south-east of England.

Jack Clark was in the 75th AA Regiment RA at Dover – right on the front line of the battle – and describes one of the early days in August:

AUGUST 1940

This morning, things started to hum at 7.15am when the alarm went, and the first all clear did not come until 1 o'clock, the 109s came over high up, but we were ready for them, and so was the RAF, with a patrol of 24 Spitfires. Between us, we drove them off, but they soon came back and managed to surprise us.

I had slipped over to the tent, some 150 yards away, when the whistle blew, and planes came in from the sea, out of the glare of the early morning sun. They were 3 109s and dropped bombs near the big wireless stations. Later I heard they missed but not by much. At the same time, they shot down a balloon. Meanwhile I was pelting back to the command post as hard as I could go, feeling very naked and unprotected without my tin-hat, and the Messerschmitt guns crackling behind me! One of the 109s was hit and came down in the sea.

The next excitement was a Dornier heralded by a vapour trail, which we saw long before the plane. In fact we may not have seen him at all, but for this. He was flying at 32,500 feet, the highest I have seen yet, and passed over us, straight inland, then turned back towards Folkestone, along the coast and out to sea again.

The Hurricanes appeared from the north-east, and the engine of one made weird noises, and conked out. The pilot made a forced landing very close to us. The fields are small, and bounded by wire fences. He just clipped the top strand of one, which twanged like a banjo string, went clean thro' the next, and finished up festooned with a triple barbed wire entanglement! His tail went up, and we thought he would turn right over but it came down again, and all was well. It was a tense few seconds, and we all cheered when it was over.

Mary Morris, based at the Kent and Sussex Hospital, was also a witness to the aerial duels that were carried out daily over the southern counties of England:

THURSDAY, 15 AUGUST 1940

The early mornings here are beautiful. I went out on to the balcony at dawn just before waking the patients. The beauty was indescribable – blue skies, the happy activity of birds, the peace and the poignant sadness which is an integral part of nature's beauty in wartime.

There is little time for philosophising these days and very little opportunity for sleep. The air raid warning usually goes off after our 'meal' at 9.30am and soon afterwards we hear the 'planes' and the ack-ack [Anti-Aircraft] guns.

Today I have been unable to sleep at all. It is so noisy. We will win this battle in the skies. People are becoming rather depressed. The papers say 'we are unprepared'. Will there be an invasion? We feel particularly vulnerable here in Kent.

This is another beautiful day – a day for happiness and gaiety. I watched another 'dogfight' this afternoon, the plane bursting into flame up there in the blue sky and the white parachute opening up like a flower and then dropping gracefully on to a field. Sometimes the parachute becomes entangled in a tree or even a church tower. All this has become a commonplace everyday event now. We switch on the wireless to listen to the BBC 9 o'clock news and wait avidly to hear about the day's 'score'. Are we killing more of theirs? Who is winning? . . .

A beautiful day – very few people on the road. The air raid siren sounded almost at once. We heard the usual 'banshee' howlings in the distance, first the 'whee' rising to an hysterical shriek and the 'oo-oo-oo' sinking to a low pitched gurgle – then sirens nearer at hand took up the lugubrious sound. Eventually the local siren burst forth and the air was filled with the sounds of souls in torment. It was almost more than nerves could stand after a hard night's work on duty.

We heard the sound of planes and the sirens were still wailing when anti-aircraft guns joined the unholy symphony.

We stopped by the roadside, and looking up saw thin vapour trails of German planes. We saw them clearly about twenty in arrow formation, looking like silver fish in the bright sunlight. There was a rattle of gunfire and we saw two Spitfires attacking a straggling Heinkel. The latter swayed dangerously and then to our horror burst into flames and plummeted straight down on to a clump of trees . . . We drove on to lunch.

The men bearing the brunt of this battle were the pilots of the RAF's Fighter Command, and in particular those of 11 Group under the command of Air Vice Marshal Keith Park based in south-east England.

One of the units that fought with 11 Group during part of the battle was No. 73 Squadron equipped with Hurricanes. Originally based at RAF Church Fenton in Yorkshire and part of 12 Group, it later transferred to RAF Debden in Essex. The squadron left a detailed diary of its action throughout the battle:

THURSDAY, 15 AUGUST 1940

Today the Squadron drew its first blood over England. 'A' flight . . . were ordered off towards Flamborough Head at 19,000 feet. The enemy were encountered and being unescorted and in wide formation 'A' flight 'went to it'. P/O Carter got two Ju 88s and a possible third. Others were shot down by Sgt Griffen, Sgt McMay, P/O [Pilot Officer] Scott and Flt/Lt Lovett. Sqn/Ldr Robinson shot up everything within sight and it is thought he must have accounted for at least three of the enemy. 'B' flight are now eagerly awaiting an opportunity to come to grips again but as the days pass it seems as if this is unlikely as long as the Squadron remains at Church Fenton.

SUNDAY, 25 AUGUST 1940

During the early hours of the morning, Sgt. Long was shot down by our own AA guns while chasing a Hun. After a fruitless attempt to reach the aerodrome he decided to bail out having come down to 4,000 feet with his aircraft on fire. Fortunately he landed safely in the middle of Beverley High Street where he was promptly arrested by the Home Guard. AA officers not too popular in the Mess these days!

Friday, 6 September 1940

Another bright day and everyone looking forward to more hunting. About 0755 all our serviceable machines, seven in all, took off on a 'scramble' by Gravesend. Contact was made near Maidstone. Blue section, led by Mike Beytagh, waded into a pile of 109. 'Chubby' Eliot unfortunately was shot down, and is now in Twickenhurst Hospital after baling out, the nature of his injuries is not known. P/O Marchand got a fairly definite 109, and gave us a bit of heart flutter when he failed to return. He landed at Tunbridge – and had a bath and a shave. 'Mike' also got a probable. Green section did not make contact being too low.

Once again at 1255 hrs nine machines, six from 'B' flight and three from 'A' flight. The order was to scramble Gravesend, and look for bandit at 36,000!! Two other squadrons were vectored on to 100 bandits. We did see a solitary EA [Enemy Aircraft] but so high that white vapour was all we could make out.

No rest for the wicked! At 1810 hours the nine machines scrambled for Chelmsford and were vectored out to sea. Nothing was seen, so Sergt. Webster is firmly convinced that there are no Hun aircraft left, he complains that he's been with us three months and hasn't seen an EA. Well, live and learn!!!

Wednesday, 11 September 1940

The weather turned out cold and bright. Activity in the morning was slight. The new machine arrived from Church Fenton safely.

Squadron took off at 1655 hrs and the 'Tally ho' was given about 1725 hours. 'A' flight attacked about 15 Me 110s, closely followed by B flight.

S/Ldr Robinson shot the tail off one, Sergt. Scott set the engine of one on fire but lost him in the cloud. F/O Smith had a crack at the last three 110s, owing to the fact that a rear gunner fired at him and made him so mad that he shot him down, attacked a second one head on and had the satisfaction of seeing pieces fall off. P/O Hobart led Sergts. Ellis and Webster in [an] . . . attack. No definite result was achieved. Sergt. Ellis returned and complained that a cannon shell had exploded amongst his feet. Examination showed that his starboard aileron control was shot away! The non arrival of Sergt. Webster caused some apprehension, but we had reassuring news that he had baled out and landed near Detling, his machine having caught fire (surely not a <u>HUN</u>!!) He is now convinced that there are Huns in the vicinity.

Throughout August and early September, losses began to mount in Fighter Command and, although the replacement of aircraft was continuing apace, the pool of trained pilots available to man those planes was getting smaller by the day:

THURSDAY, 12 SEPTEMBER 1940

F/O [Flying Officer] Smith came back from Debden this evening with the news that Chubby Eliot – having defied the whole hospital – has made good his escape and arrived at Debden slightly crisped but in fair working order. We hope to see him tomorrow. He apparently got mixed up with some He 113s, and was busy writing his initials on the Hun's backside so that he could convince the CO that it was his, when he was set on fire by some of the aforementioned Hun's boy friends. He baled out and did a delayed drop of about 15,000 before pulling 'the string'. This action is 'de rigeur' these days. However he is suffering from burns on the left leg and about the eyes, but is able to go about. He hopes to visit tomorrow.

We also received information today that F/Lt Lovett DFC had been killed and that his body has been lying in Billericay hospital. We do not know who is responsible for allowing the body to lie so long without taking any definite action, but we are all indignant about it. We shall feel the loss of this brave and gallant gentleman who has served his country and his squadron so well.

Sergt McMay must also be presumed killed as there is still no news of him, we shall miss him too, for his cheerful unassuming nature.

Although diaries such as that of No. 73 Squadron could make light of the injuries suffered, the reality for wounded pilots was often terrible. The enclosed cockpits of the fighter aircraft, proximity to the fuel tanks and the difficulty of getting out meant that burn injuries were commonplace and particularly scarring both physically and mentally. Mary Morris saw the results of this form of warfare at the Kent and Sussex Hospital:

WEDNESDAY, 14 AUGUST 1940

. . . In addition to the usual civilian surgical cases, we have several young RAF officers most of them with burns. They are Spitfire and Hurricane pilots. They usually remain with us for a few weeks' treatment prior to being transferred to Mr McIndoe's Unit at East Grinstead Hospital. Have heard a great deal about his incredible prowess in re-building faces for these young men who are so disfigured.

Dick was admitted to our ward at 1 a.m. today – a twenty-one year old Spitfire pilot. He had been picked up in the Channel having baled out after a 'dogfight' with some Messerschmitts. He is in a very bad way, blind with a fractured jaw and severe burns of the face and head. He was taken to theatre on admission and bits of bone and loose teeth were removed from the remains of his face and a stitch put through his tongue so that it could be tied to a button on his pyjama jacket – otherwise he would have choked to death.

I sat beside his bed all through the dark hours of the night. The pain and thirst were unquenchable – his mouth too burnt for even a sip of water, and the intravenous drip too slow to replace the lost fluid. I gave him morphia every three hours. In the early hours his parents came to visit him and before their arrival I placed a gauze mask over the remains of his poor face.

The grim realities of constant warfare even spread through into the war diary of No. 73 Squadron:

SATURDAY, 14 SEPTEMBER 1940

Another glorious warm day. The squadron was at 15 mins available until 1300hrs when they came to readiness. At 1530hrs they were ordered to 'scramble North Weald, Angels 15'. This turned out to be our blackest day. Twelve machines took off, seven returned in disorder. F/O Smith, supported by two others, reports that Spitfires attacked the formation and broke up the rear section. Smith followed one Spitfire right down to the ground, hence the forcefulness of his statement that they attacked our formations. Of the seven that returned, P/O Marchand was battered about a bit, having a bullet through his port main tank, one through the port aileron passing through the main spar and emerging from the landing light, and one clean through the top of the W/T mast just above his head.

F/Lt Beytagh got a bullet in his radiator and force landed at West Malling. Sergt. Marshall was shot down by an Me 109 near Dover, Sergt. Long was also shot down by one of the same tribe, near Gravesend. The CO was reported missing also Sergt. Bumble. Sergt. Buffin was shot in both legs and baled out. A pall of gloom spread over the whole unit.

However, by mid-September the crisis point of the battle passed, as the German Air Force switched the emphasis of their attacks to bombing the major British population centres, instigating what became known as the Blitz. There are a number of reasons for this: the German Air Force believed that they had ground down the RAF to such an extent that it was no longer as important to target their facilities, while they also believed that targeting London in particular could cause 'mass panic', leading to a catastrophic decline in civilian morale. There was also an element of revenge for the attacks that the RAF's Bomber Command had already carried out on Berlin. The shift of emphasis gave Fighter Command a vital period to reorganise. However, it still continued to suffer casualties, such as Pilot Officer Denis Wissler, who flew Hurricanes as part of No. 17 Squadron flying out of Tangmere and later Debden:

TUESDAY, 24 SEPTEMBER 1940

We were attacked by Me 109s and having made one attack on a 109 I was making a second at four who were well above when I realised that I should stall so I levelled off. Suddenly there was a blinding flash on my port wing and I felt a hell of a blow on my left arm, and then blood running down. I went into a hell of a dive and came back to Debden. A cannon shell had hit my wing and a bit of it had hit me just above the elbow and behind. The shell had blown away most of the port flap so I tried to land without flaps. I could not stop and crashed into a pile of stones just off the field hitting my face and cutting it in two places. I was taken to Saffron Walden General Hospital.

Denis Wissler was posted 'missing' on 11 November 1940 and he is commemorated on the Air Forces Memorial in Runnymede, Surrey.

At the end of the year, the Reverend Guy Mayfield, chaplain of RAF Duxford, looked back over the summer and autumn and reflected on the casualties of the battle:

TUESDAY, 31 DECEMBER 1940

Saw combat film – grim and exciting and it manages to convey something of what one imagines a dogfight is like and of waiting to be dived on. New Year's Eve party in the Sergeant's Mess. I only stayed an hour. I could not bear it any longer. There is nothing to sing about this year. I crept back here to sleep and to try not to think about the thunder and lightning which is threatened to come upon us very soon. I hadn't the heart to sing *Auld Lang Syne* in the bloody world as it now is. There is no time for 'old acquaintance'. Who'll be left to remember? If it is remembered next year, how much of it without bitterness and sadness, how much of it will be remembrance of times lost, of things unsaid and unshared? I can't sing when we are on the edge of an abyss once again and about to be robbed of comrades and friends as we were last summer. The summer was one of brilliant sunshine, heat, shimmering landscape; I remember walking to the Mess every day with the impression that the sky was black and heavy as lead.

10. The Beginning of the Blitz

The German Air Force had carried out raids on the urban population centres of Great Britain throughout August, but it wasn't until mid-September that the coherent policy emerged that saw a shift away from the targeting of RAF installations and airfields and a redirection of the aerial assault towards the principal cities, notably London. The first major raid consisted of 364 bombers supported by 515 fighters.

Jack Clark, manning an anti-aircraft gun in Dover, witnessed the raid going overhead:

Tuesday, 10 September 1940

The lull came to an end on Saturday, September 7th, when London suffered such enormous damage. About this I wrote: 'This evening, just after tea, the war suddenly woke up. I was off duty, and up at the huts when the alarm sounded. The raid developed well and truly, and never have I seen so many heavy bombers in the sky at the same time. There must have been literally hundreds, as they came over in formations of 30 or 40, and there were more formations than I could count. There was every type known to us, including 10 Ju 89s, giant four-engined machines. They mostly flew very high, but at the same time a few Heinkels raided the harbour probably to attract our attention. We heard several salvoes of bombs whistle down'.

That night was a real brute, and the men were out until 4.30. A continuous procession of planes went over. Next day we heard that London was their target, and that there were 2,000 casualties, and heaven knew how much damage.

Emily Riddell lived in Barnehurst in Kent and also witnessed the raid:

Saturday, 7 September 1940

One raid only so far at 4.30pm, but worst of lot. Very many (500) planes. Mrs Rowe counted 50 once. One lot came over and cleared off – heavy AA, then another lot, more than ever, came over, great deal of firing bombs dropped. Two big fires started, one over the river northwards, and the other this side, believe Dusseks. One of our Spitfires went by with torn wing. AA very heavy shrapnel dropped in garden. One airman baled out, we saw parachute. Mrs Day and I saw two bombs burst and smoke come up. Two fires very big, smoke all over along river, and black smoke billowing out other side.

Cleared off after a while and piece of shrapnel found on lawn 2 yds from shelter.

However, the principal target of the raid was not Kent but London, and specifically the Port of London. Violet Regan lived in the Isle of Dogs, home of the West India, East India and Millwall docks, and thus a major target for the German aerial armada:

7/8 SEPTEMBER 1940

Very soon we heard the ominous drone of distant aeroplanes – German aeroplanes! The drone rapidly became a roar which caused the very air to tremble, and as they drew nearer I knew there were many, many planes and they would be bombers!

I remember the rising excitement of the neighbours as they anxiously called to each other. The frantic barking of dogs – and my cat – which immediately sought shelter of his own choosing.

Shading my eyes against the sun I scanned the sky for the dread invaders – and suddenly – there they were! Silhouetted clearly against the blue of the sky flew the cream of the German Luftwaffe. They consisted of three separate flights and they were heading in our direction. They flew in what I can only describe as 'block' formation each section flying in straight lines – unlike the British 'V' formation. Altogether the three squadrons must have numbered over one hundred planes.

Suddenly the guns on the nearby gunsite opened fire. A puff of white smoke burst under the rear planes of the second squadron.

The blast caused them to be tossed about for a few seconds but they quickly regained control and flew on in perfect formation – coming ever nearer.

Fascinated, yet filled with dread, I watched this formidable enemy armada pass overhead. Then my heart seemed to stop as they suddenly banked into a great arc, retraced their course and headed straight towards us.

I watched in horror as bombs fell from the diving, screaming planes to explode on the defenceless people below, and I knew the so-called 'Bore War' was over. This time the Nazis meant business. My husband yelled at me to take cover – then he was gone – to join his colleagues at the Heavy Rescue Depot in neighbouring Millwall.

I helped to calm my terrified neighbour and her three little children who were screaming with fright and stayed with them until her parents arrived. Then I went into my own shelter.

For a very long time I sat listening to the awful bedlam going on outside. To the explosion of bombs; the clanging of firebells. During short lulls I heard the crying of terrified children and the voices of agonised parents trying to soothe them. The barking of hysterical dogs went on and on. There seemed to be no let-up or respite from the awful din . . .

What was going to happen to us? It was inevitable the thought ran through my mind. How could we possibly survive this dreadful holocaust that was raging all around us. We were literally surrounded by terrible fires and the air was too hot even to breathe.

Death was near for many this day.

When we reached the school, all of us men, women, and children were herded into a long corridor which smelt of damp cement.

This then, was to be our refuge. Refuge? With all that deadly carnage going on outside? . . .

At long last there came a lull from the bombing and during this short respite we talked quietly among ourselves exchanging our experiences of the sudden appearance of the enemy planes and ruminating bitterly on the savage bombing of helpless civilians. It helped to ease the tension for a little while.

And we forgot that night must fall . . .

With the coming of darkness the Luftwaffe resumed their attacks and all hell broke loose again. They added fuel to the already raging fires and started fresh ones. It was terribly frightening to hear the fierce crackle of flames and the constant crashing of falling masonry, so near to us, dear Lord – so near. Several times the huge building seem to rock with the impact of high explosives.

Gaping windows were all along the corridor and in my position I was sitting beneath them, facing the blank wall opposite. Fascinated, I watched the lurid reflection of the flames dancing on the opposite wall. They lit up the corridor and bathed us all in a baleful glow. It was such an eerie sensation.

We listened to the continuing sound of screaming planes and the crashing of bombs; and my heart ached for all the gallant souls who were out there fighting against such great odds – my husband among them.

The menacing drone of the enemy bombers set already badly taut nerves on edge and somebody screamed, 'What's the matter with our guns – they haven't fired a shot!' It was quite true. Apart from the solitary salvo loosed at the beginning of the raid – no gun had fired a shot in our defence – and morale by now was pretty low.

We had depended on the anti-aircraft guns, and all of us I knew, felt badly let down.

Thirst was worrying for us. Very few had had any food or drink since the afternoon; but for us water was unobtainable – the mains had burst.

This tragedy was made more poignant by the agony of mothers with tiny babies and small children who were crying with fright, hunger and thirst. Silently I wept for them. It was the awful helplessness that was hardest to bear. We felt like sitting ducks no mistake. We were all sorely tried. I thanked God my two little girls were safe in the countryside of Oxfordshire. Although sadly missed they were spared this horror.

Violet's husband, Bill Regan, worked at the Heavy Rescue Depot and was involved in the grim business of trying to find survivors and clearing the dead after the major raids:

16 SEPTEMBER 1940, DEPOT, 0800 HRS

Reported to Major Brown about the Elderlys. The night shift had been to the incident but had found nobody. I insisted that they must be somewhere about, maybe injured, so Major Brown came out with my squad to investigate. We gathered three bushel baskets of remains. I picked up two left feet. One of the men saw a body perched on the rooftop. Nobby Clark climbed up and recovered it. It was badly mutilated, it was some time before we were able to identify it as female. I had picked up two left feet, and with a right foot, Major Brown thought the three feet accounted for three people. I said that two left and one right meant two people. Some of the men were feeling queasy so rum was dished out. I was TT [teetotal] so I gave mine away, and eventually we found enough evidence to account for three people, so we came away.

At this stage of the Blitz, the anti-aircraft defences of London were not up to the task of protecting the capital, but they did what they could to put up a fight and had some occasional successes. Bill Regan again:

TUESDAY, 17 SEPTEMBER 1940

Alert about mid-day, we saw a fighter plane going across towards Essex, rather high and fast, but the Mudchute [in the Isle of Dogs] got off one shot at it, and we watched the plane suddenly explode and we were left with a clear sky.

We heard the gunners shouting their heads off. I went round to the site entrance, by the Wesleyan Chapel, and the two men on guard were grinning like gargoyles, and all I could get of them was 'One shot, one bull'.

As I came away, one of them said to me 'Wait till we get the four-fives, we'll show them'. I hope my guess is right, and that it meant 4.5 AA guns. We could do with something a bit bigger, if only to give our morale a lift. The last four nights, we have had a mobile gun on an army lorry, going round the Island, and firing a few rounds in one place, then tearing up the road, a few more rounds, then back again, 'ditto repeato', to cheer us up, or confuse the enemy. Anyhow, it's one of Churchill's better ideas.

The assault continued with the main focus of the German onslaught being London throughout September and October. Gwyneth Thomas was a nurse at the Highgate Hospital in north London and was at the forefront of the Blitz in that she had not only to put up with the constant bombing, but also to deal with the after-effects of the raids:

TUESDAY, 15 OCTOBER 1940

For many days I have not made any notes, not that each day, and certainly each night has been very hectic; in fact, that is my reason.

The remaining days of last week found me busy in the casualty ward. Outpatients were numerous, owing to the frequent bombing near us. I could tell many tragic stories, but one is enough for an example of what we meet with every day now. A bomb dropped one night on some houses near here; the occupants – man, wife (about 55 years old) and daughter (aged 17 years) were in their Anderson shelter, in which they were all buried for about four hours. The mother was admitted, rather badly hurt, the father was still in the casualty ward when I went on the following morning. There he sat, still dazed, otherwise not injured and wondering where his daughter was. He could not remember whether she was rescued or not. 9am, still no news, then at 10.30am a girl rushed into the ward; the relief on her face when she saw it was her father sitting there! I shall never forget these scenes as long as I live. Needless to say, they both broke down completely. It is difficult not to be just like them at times, and relieve my feelings with a good cry.

Last night was, I believe, the worst night. Bombs fell all around us, closer than ever. Several people were injured, one little girl of 7 was brought in dead. God knows when this will all end!

As I write this, there is yet another raid going on. The enemy planes are right overhead, our guns are crashing furiously, windows are rattling. It seems to be coming lower. The drone alone is apt to get on one's nerves. In the room where I write, there are other sisters, one sewing, one writing, four talking about patients. In the dining room next door, there are about 26 of the night nursing staff having their meal before going on to the wards for the night. So life goes on as usual. Soon the day staff should be going in to supper. I have managed to get a little sleep in this evening, having very little sleep last night and working at such a hectic pace all day, running a children's ward and then being called on to open a ward to admit some poor patients from a hospital that has been bombed.

Heavens, what a crash!

It seemed just then that the guns were just outside the window.

The constant barrage, by both night and day at this stage of the campaign, caused both physical and mental casualties amongst the defenders. Jack Clark in Dover describes the effect of the constant tension:

TUESDAY, 8 OCTOBER 1940

We had nothing to do for two days, but as things turned out, we actually did very little, had a good deal of evening leave. Discipline was even slacker than at D3.

It was not really good for us, because with so much time on our hands, and the war having slackened, many suffered from nervous reaction.

When the strain was on, all through the spring and summer, we had been too hard driven to allow it to affect us, but now that we could relax a little, I for one suffered from periods of acute mental depression, attacks of indigestion, and a general feeling of lassitude, and other men had similar troubles.

At quite early stages of the Blitz some men had a mild form of shellshock, and were quite useless on guns or instruments. They could not stand even the noise of our own guns. They were therefore put to work in the cookhouse or offices, and inevitably became objects of some contempt, but it is hardly fair to judge them too harshly, there were very few of them.

1940–41

I. The War in the Mediterranean and Africa

While the BEF had been forced from France and the RAF had been defending Britain's airspace against the German Air Force, the war went on in other parts of the world – notably around the shores of the Mediterranean.

On 10 June 1940, the Italians had declared war on France and Great Britain, as Canon Nicholls of St Paul's Anglican Cathedral on Malta wrote in his diary:

TUESDAY, 2 JULY 1940

It was on the night of June 10th that Rose Foss rang up to say that Italy was declaring war as from midnight. It was only at six o'clock that very evening that HE [His Excellency, governor of Malta] had made a short Broadcast which was not more ominous than expected. I recall that one of his points was that people should not withdraw their money from the Government Savings Bank. But there had been one particular sinister thing which made the immediate outbreak of war seem definitely certain within a few hours, viz the departure of the Italian Consul-General from the Island. In this connection an amusing thing happened. The Consul called at the best tailor's shop in Valletta and ordered a considerable amount of tweed for men's suiting. The stuff was to be delivered at his house. Unfortunately the assistant forgot to make up the parcel and send it. Next day the Consul called and asked why the goods had not been delivered. 'Is it because you think Italia go to war with you?' . . .

This entry of the Italian Government into the war seems to us peculiarly base. To wait nine months and see how the cat will jump: to let her ally take the brunt of the danger, nay all of it: and then when victory is apparently in sight, to join her, seems to an Englishman the depth of cowardice.

Immediately, the Italians launched an assault into the French Alps and planned an attack on the British in Egypt and Somaliland from their colonies in Libya and Ethiopia. The fall of France in late June also left a powerful French fleet spread throughout the Mediterranean, and the threat of this falling into German hands, combined with a British desire to emphasise to neutral powers that they were still capable of fighting on alone, provoked the first major conflict to take place in this theatre. On 3 July 1940, the British Government launched Operation *Catapult*, a plan to neutralise the French Navy. Force H of the Royal Navy under Admiral Sir James Somerville set sail from Gibraltar to deal with the powerful French fleet at Mers-el-Kebir. Somerville gave the French commander, Admiral Gensoul, four options: put to sea and join forces with the British; sail to a French West Indian port and demilitarise the ships; sail with reduced crews to any British port; scuttle the ships within six hours of receiving the ultimatum. The French refused these options and Force H attacked.

Bill Crawford served aboard the flagship of Force H, HMS *Hood*, and saw action during the engagement off Oran, Algeria:

SATURDAY, 13 JULY 1940

Dear Jim,

How are these days with you, are you still having a loaf aboard the old *Suffolk* (ahem). In my last letter I said I would have to start something so we could catch up on you after the action you were in.

Well I guess you would hear of the battle at Oran, well we were the flagship in command at that, and it sure was pretty hot there for a while. There were two other battleships with us, and altogether 150 15-inch shells went over to make the French realise we meant what we said. They opened fire on us but did not score one direct hit, and, as we were the flagship, their fire was concentrated on us.

You could see most of the shells coming, and I can tell you I did not feel so good.

Altogether we destroyed two battlecruisers, one battleship, one seaplane carrier, about three destroyers and severely damaged another battleship. Planes were sent up against us but when the old 4-inch got started they kept up top and did not drop anything. The real action lasted from about eight minutes to six until about two minutes past but we were firing at aircraft until it was dark.

A couple of days after that in the Central Med we were cruising along when we were attacked by the Ice-cream merchants, in aircraft.

The raid went on and off for about four hrs and it is reckoned that there were about 38 planes and 120 bombs dropped. They hit nothing but three of their aircraft were brought down and seven others badly damaged, four of which they don't think got back to their bases. Well after that lot I think we have done our bit (ahem).

Are you still at Auntie Jessie's, or have you got draft? We have had no mail for a while now so I have not heard from you. Well Jim I guess I will close up now so cheerio and all the best and the Ities and Gerry's bombs make holes in the sea as it doesn't cost much to fill those kind of holes in.

Your loving brother and pal,

Bill

Contrary to Bill Crawford's letter above, the overall scale of destruction was not enormous, with one battleship sunk, and one battleship and battlecruiser damaged, while another battlecruiser escaped. The French squadron at Alexandria disarmed peacefully following negotiation. However, the Royal Navy caused over 1,250 French casualties and the action soured relations between the two countries for years to come. The Royal Navy rapidly took the initiative in the Mediterranean against the Axis forces, and sought to neutralise the Italian Fleet at its base in Taranto in southern Italy. The Commander-in-Chief of the Mediterranean Fleet, Admiral Sir Andrew Cunningham, assembled a strike force based around the aircraft carriers HMS *Illustrious* and HMS *Eagle*. On 11 November 1940, the *Illustrious* alone, the

Eagle suffering from mechanical problems, launched an aerial assault on the Italian Fleet in its harbour that was to usher in a new era of naval warfare. Commander Manley Power served as Staff Officer (Operations) to Admiral Cunningham and describes the operation in a letter home to his wife:

WEDNESDAY, 13 NOVEMBER 1940

We are just on our way home now after a very pleasant spell in the briny which has had excellent results. You will have seen in the papers etc. What a crack our air boys hit the 'Wop' fleet in Taranto – while at the same time some of the light forces were beating up a convoy off Valona well in Musso's 'mare nostrum'. We are naturally delighted with the results. It was a very anxious night while it was all in progress but things got better and better next morning as the various outlying units who had been doing their stuff came rolling back under the wing of the battlefleet with their reports of successful actions.

As so much is being reported in the press I can really tell you quite a lot this time so perhaps you would like me to describe an operation.

It all starts when we get in from our last trip – things have been talked out a bit at sea and I had a rough scheme in my head and a few dirty bits of paper in my pocket. The day we put in is a busy one – threads to be picked up – all sorts of people coming on board to know this and that and all the routine of the station to be dealt with after several days cut off from normal communication by wireless silence . . .

The thing was approved in principle from my draft at about 9.30 so we go to press about 1800hrs with orders complete so as to reach the first ships who are sailing in the wee small hours next morning. Aircraft are told off to carry orders here and there about our scattered parish – and so it all goes on.

Convoys sailed for various destinations – ships rendezvous with other ships at sea – air patrols go off to quarter thousands of square miles of Mediterranean and watch the Wops in their bases. All in the orders written by your unfortunate husband. Last time I wrote was when this had all been put in train and Tom and I had been sent ashore. We sailed next morning.

Then we have days at sea, covering all the movements, wondering whether everything is going by the plan or if the weather, bombs or torpedoes are going to upset the business.

Reports come in slowly – so and so has arrived at so and so. Ships we expect to join us turn up over the horizon, sometimes late, sometimes early. The usual almost monotonous reports from the carrier come in 'shadower shot down': then the fighters come in to roost smiling all over their streamlined faces. We have a bombing attack or so – very frightened Wops, shining like silver in the sky, drop their bombs miles wide as the AA fire turns them and then the rats get at them and there is a plume or two of smoke on the horizon where they crash in flames. So it goes on for several days until the grand moment comes when all our crawling convoys are reported in and we are free to fight at last.

Ways and means have been discussed for days and now we put it into effect. CinC [Commander-in-Chief] COS [Chief of Staff] Tom and I in the chart house have a final confabulation – then off go Tom and I to write the signalled orders and work out the courses for the night. Off go the orders by flashing searchlights. Anxiety as to whether our movements are being seen and reported. It might spoil the show if they were. Fleet excitement 'shadower reported' – relief 'shadower shot down'. Signals go up from time to time 'so and so part company, proceed in execution of previous orders. Rejoin me at . . .' until we are left at nightfall with only our solemn rows of battleships plodding along in brilliant moonlight, with a ring of watchful destroyers, as a cover and rallying point for all the striking forces.

A beautiful calm night, bright moon, as still as it can be. We are near the enemy's bases now and keeping a watchful eye out for enemy ships or torpedo aircraft. We've had trouble with these last before in moonlight. Everyone at general quarters for the night. No sound except the wash of the bow waves and occasional orders as the guns train to a new look out bearing to keep the crews alive. All night wondering how things are going with the forces we've detached. We drop off for a bit of sleep in time in various corners.

Then the warm up. The carrier turns up. 'Two aircraft missing. Aircraft report three enemy battleships torpedoed and some small craft damaged, seen burning'. Mast head hoist 'manoeuvre well executed. Resume station previously ordered' and she drops into station on the fleet.

Slowly as the day wears on the other detached units come over the horizon and make their reports. A shadower or two turns up and gets shot down – one after a thrilling chase right over our heads.

Finally we are all collected and head for home full of good cheer and thinking out more schemes to confound the King's enemies and wondering if we shall find a mail when we put into harbour.

In all, the assault sank one Italian battleship and damaged two others, as well as a heavy cruiser and a number of destroyers. Most importantly, it grievously damaged the morale of the Italian Navy, giving the Royal Navy a psychological dominance that would persist throughout the campaign in the Mediterranean. The Italian Air Force, however, started a series of attacks on the island of Malta, which occupied a vitally important position in the Mediterranean, lying, as it did, on the major supply routes from Italy to North Africa. Canon Nicholls recorded them in his diary:

MONDAY, 14 OCTOBER 1940

As regards raids, we have been much less troubled lately. Up to a few weeks ago we had two raids daily – morning and evening: then it became one per day. In the week beginning Sept 22 we had four raids only. Then we had a whole week's respite, short of a few hours. On Oct 8th, with a waxing moon, two planes came over at about 8pm. They were picked up by searchlights almost immediately: one was hit and the other shot down, and many people saw it. Two men 'bailed out' – a new word to me, meaning left the plane by parachute – but were not picked up. No bombs were heard, and not a single gun fired, as our fighter plane was up. But the Rome radio said there was a tremendous A/A barrage . . . We know that they tell frightful lies about Malta, and this encourages us to believe that their other 'news' is equally unreliable. We have shot down at the very lowest computation 28 of their planes and probably many more. We have lost two fighter planes in action, and one other whose pilot, flying in formation, with no enemy planes near, suddenly broke formation, and dived straight into the sea. It may have been heart trouble, or his oxygen supply failing: no one knows, and his body was not recovered. Also two of our bombers have been hit and burnt on the ground.

By land, the Italian Army in Libya under Marshal Graziani had advanced across the border into Egypt in September, but had then settled down into a series of fortified camps in which they remained throughout the autumn. Britain's Commander-in-Chief in the region, General Archibald Wavell, planned a limited offensive to disrupt the Italian position, to be carried out by the Western Desert Force under Lieutenant-General Richard O'Connor, consisting of 7th Armoured Division, 4th Indian Division and later 6th Australian Division.

Operation *Compass* was launched on 8 December 1940 and the Italian fortified camps were rapidly surrounded and overwhelmed. The Italians regrouped around Bardia and Tobruk, which were both heavily fortified. However, Bardia fell on 5 January 1941, while Tobruk fell on the 22nd, with the Italian forces streaming back towards Tripoli.

Harry Wiles served as an NCO in 414th Battery, 104th Regiment Royal Horse Artillery (RHA), which was part of 1st Cavalry Division based in the Middle East and sent to the desert in early 1941 as reinforcements. He took part in the large assault on Bardia in January and wrote in his diary about his fears:

THURSDAY, 2 JANUARY 1941

Just a few more belated lines before the big day. Tomorrow the 'big do' for Bardia begins. I have just written a letter to Maisie and Tony, not a very cheerful one I am afraid. Let's hope that I get through this lot OK. I think that I shall be lucky. Our chances are pretty good I think. Everyone is getting very 'strung up', you can't help it. I think that the best thing is to find some work to do and try not to think, but I will not be sorry when it is all over. I keep thinking of Maisie and Tony. That's the worst of loving someone, you always have to suffer for it, but life would be terribly empty without love. Anyway,

I hope that I do my job well and that I don't let our crowd, or those I love, down. I had better not write any more as I have things to do. In case anything does happen to me, up to a month ago I had £15 in credit and I have £5.10s in notes in my A.B.64. Everything is to go to my wife.

Wiles survived the attack and the advance continued, with O'Connor sending 7th Armoured Division across the desert to cut off the Italian retreat, trapping them at Beda Fomm and destroying them by 7 February. In this campaign, over 130,000 Italian prisoners had been taken for the loss of 500 British troops killed, 1,373 wounded and 55 missing.

Jim Brooks served as a gunner in 211th Battery, 64th Medium Regiment RA, attached to the 2nd New Zealand Division, and took part in the latter stages of Operation *Compass*, which he describes in a letter to his brother written later in the war:

FRIDAY, 12 FEBRUARY 1943

I won't tell you anything about the journey out here, because it was very uneventful, I will start from the time that we arrived in Egypt. We landed from the boat on the 30th of December 1940, boarded a train of cattle trucks and after a very uncomfortable journey arrived at a camp near Cairo, we spent our New Year's Eve in Cairo and had a pretty good time. After about 10 days in Camp we got on the move, up towards the battle, we passed through all the towns and villages that we know so well now, Mersa Matruh, Sidi Barrani, Sollum, Bardia and eventually arrived at Tobruk where we knew the Italians were. We went into the gun position under cover of darkness, we could see tracer shells of all colours, going up at our aircraft, we spent most of that night and all the next day, digging and preparing ammunition. The attack started the following morning at 5.45am, with a heavy barrage, our gun alone fired approximately 200 rounds, and was she sizzling when we finished, there wasn't a bit of paint left on the piece of barrel as you could call it. We moved up in the afternoon to another position, but didn't fire, we had few shells land near us on the way and we were told afterwards that that came from a half submerged Italian cruiser in Tobruk harbour, but that was soon put out of commission. Soon afterwards we were told that the town had fallen, and did we cheer, the Ities didn't have a chance, they were nearly all caught in their beds asleep! We moved soon afterwards, to go into a bivvy area, and on the way passed thousands of prisoners trudging towards Tobruk. After a short rest we started off again, and this time cut across the desert, to try and cut the enemy off, we went into action at a small village called Giovanni Beita and it was there that we saw our first enemy aircraft, about a dozen Italian bombers circled over us, but a few rounds from a nearby Bofors gun, soon sent them scuttling for home, but not before they had dropped their load of bombs, with no damage to us. We carried on again, still over rough desert and eventually arrived at a village called Soluch. It was there that we learnt that Benghazi had fallen and that the entire Italian army had been captured. After we had been there a few hours the prisoners started rolling in, some driving their own lorries, waving white flags including the General Staff, we had a bit of a job getting these under lock and key. We garrisoned Soluch for about 10 days and during that time we had our first Jerry bombing raid, but it wasn't to be the last.

This was the German Air Force unit X Fliegerkorps, which had been posted to Sicily and southern Italy to take part in the assault on Malta and launched an attack on the aircraft carrier HMS *Illustrious*, which, having been damaged escorting a convoy, was in dry dock at Malta. Canon Nicholls witnessed what was to become known as 'The *Illustrious* Blitz'.

JANUARY 1941

In the following week, on Thursday Jan 16th the German raids began: and continued Sat and Sunday. The attack was very fierce indeed. The barrage was frightful, but many bombers got through, attacking continuously in small formations from every direction. There is a fanaticism about the German work which one cannot help admiring. They are like the Dervish troops of the Omdurman campaign, to whom death in battle is both honourable and desirable. We have heard from various sources of the fanatical state of mind of the Nazis – the Führer being addressed almost as divine. It seems that his warriors are like-minded in battle.

Many people watched the raids from a distance, or from reasonably safe places; they saw Valletta as one great cloud of smoke: the enemy planes skimmed the roof-tops as they rose out of their dives. The *Illustrious* was hit once and the Captain's cabin demolished. The *Essex*, a fine new P and O, was also hit and had about 20 killed and some injured. The DY [dockyard] is badly messed up and probably pretty well finished as a repair shop on any large scale. Senglea (I am told) is badly cut up and of course the inhabitants have wisely fled to the villages as they did in June. The noise in our crypt was just terrible. There were about 250 people huddled together, many of them crying, but many very brave. The roar was like the loudest thunder one has ever heard, but absolutely continuous, and it was not possible really to distinguish the guns from the bombs, except when one fell close to us – about 70 yards. That brought down a block of flats and five people were killed. We sat, holding hands and praying aloud. That was the only hit on Valletta. We were to have lunched with the Air-Commodore on the Sunday, but we were now excused. Monday was a quiet day except that a plane appeared and suddenly over Val. And guns burst out at the same instant as the sirens. P. and I were in the street 200 yards from our house: we hurried home, seeing the puffs of bursting shells above our heads. No bombs were dropped. But that night lone bombers hovered and cruised above the island from 0145hrs for three hours, dropping bombs every five minutes or so, and bringing down a few houses.

This was a taster of what Malta could expect throughout 1941 and 1942, as it was to become one of the most heavily bombed places on Earth during the Second World War. This commitment of German military might to the Mediterranean also saw the dispatch of the 5th Light Division, the first part of General Erwin Rommel's Afrika Korps, sent to bolster the Italian position in North Africa.

Elsewhere in Africa, the Italian position was also crumbling. Having invaded British Somaliland (part of modern Somalia) early in the war, the Italians remained on the defensive until the British launched an assault against their positions in January 1941, striking deep into Italian Eritrea.

In February, another British offensive was launched northwards into Ethiopia and Italian Somaliland from Kenya. Lieutenant D.J. Carnegie served in the East Africa Reconnaissance Squadron, the 'Recces', which had been one of the units responsible for protecting the Kenyan border against any Italian advance, and now poured forwards against their demoralised foes:

JANUARY/FEBRUARY 1941

At Jelib on the Juba River the Italian retreat – which up till then had been fairly orderly – became a rout. Outmanoeuvred, outflanked and outfought, Mussolini's legions fled panic-stricken northwards, along the coastal highway to Mogadishu.

It was a chance too good to be missed: we followed in hot pursuit, breaking all the drill-book rules in our eagerness to keep up the pressure. The gamble paid off: our lines of communication – lengthening daily – remained uncut. 'It's a good thing they're not Jerries,' growled a World War I veteran, gazing at a plume of dust on the horizon which marked the Italian rearguard. 'If they had been, they'd have cut us off by now'.

Indeed. So hurried was the withdrawal that on several occasions I was able to fill up at Italian petrol pumps along the route. It seems almost incredible that enemy demolition squads should have overlooked these filling stations, especially as it must have been obvious we were short of petrol.

We pressed on, hardly pausing even to sleep. Opposition, if it could be said to exist at all, was sporadic and ineffective. At one point a handful of gunners made a brief and heroic stand, but they were wiped out by our leading armoured cars before they had time to reload. Occasionally the Italian Air Force, greatly daring, sent a formation of bombers over our advancing column, but usually the bombs missed by a comfortable margin. Only once did they have any success – at a place called Jijiga – where they inflicted some casualties on 'B' Squadron.

Addis Ababa fell on 6 April 1941, with the restored emperor Haile Selassie making a formal entry to the city on 5 May, his country being the first to be liberated from occupation by Axis forces. Lieutenant Carnegie recorded a story he had heard about the Emperor:

JANUARY/FEBRUARY 1941

There was also a good story about the Emperor Haile Selassie, irreverently known by the troops as 'Tiger Tim'. While visiting a military hospital in Addis he came upon a South African gunner who was recovering from a painful shrapnel wound in his right buttock.

When the Emperor politely asked him how he felt the gunner glared at him and snarled: 'Go away, you little black bastard!'.

This 'Boerish' behaviour got around to Divisional Headquarters very fast, and the next day the following GRO (General Routine Order) appeared in every mess of the command:

> 'In future His Imperial Majesty Haile Selassie, King of Kings and Lion of Judah, will not, repeat not, be referred to as "that little black bastard."'

The entire Army laughed about it for days, but it was nevertheless a shocking incident. I felt quite sorry for poor little 'Tiger Tim'. He was a dignified monarch.

By 1 May, the main Italian forces under the Duke of Aosta were compelled to surrender, thus bringing the campaign to an end save for a few isolated pockets of resistance.

2. The Blitz

Having started in September 1940, the Blitz on London and the other major cities of Great Britain continued throughout the winter of 1940 and the spring of 1941.

Florence Speed lived in Brixton, South London, and describes a typical night during the Blitz in December 1940:

FRIDAY, 27 DECEMBER 1940

18.40

After three peaceful nights there goes the siren for Raid 416, the Whoo-oo ooooooo wails on and on.

18.45

Hateful buzz of engines and incendiaries dropping, now gunfire. Plane receding but audible.

19.15

Two fire engines have gone by.

19.36

HE down. The vibration shook the house . . . sounds as if it is going to be a bad night. More planes buzzing around.

20.55

Another heavy explosion. Was half asleep, but jolted awake. Norah dashed out of her bed, and flung herself on to mine. I'd have been a pancake, with her weight on top of me if anything had happened.

May still dressed, was on Ethel's end of the bed like a shot too.

21.50

All clear, after incessant activity.

23.30

Fred just popped in to tell us he is safe. Six bombs were dropped in a line in Brixton Road starting right opposite his post.

The United Navy, Christ Church, South Island Place again, Offley Road, have all been hit, people in South Island Place are still in the wreckage. A gas main at the Oval was hit and started a terrific blaze.

Stephen Woodcock served as an ARP warden based in Ladbroke Grove and describes life in the shelter he was in charge of during the Blitz:

Tuesday, 12 November 1940

A typical night in the basement shelter at 2A Stanley Crescent. After an early meal at 6.15, during which the alert sounded, I went to the shelter. The 34 'regulars' were already installed and the man from Manchester was holding forth as usual saying that Hitler didn't know what to do next and was 'fair muddled'. He assured us all that everything would soon be all right as by the spring we should have enough dive bombers and tanks to enable us to invade Belgium after devastating the coast for 30 miles inland. He was, as I expected, a believer in Mr Hore-Belisha.

A lad visiting from the country swore he could see a plane caught in the searchlights but it turned out to be a star.

The night was clear, with a full moon and occasional light clouds. Planes were about continuously overhead. By 9.15 we had heard 3 bombs dropped sufficiently close to shake the basement and start a twittering among the inmates.

About half a dozen stand talking and smoking in the area outside the basement and quickly get inside again when they hear the whistle of a bomb. Sometimes we all get jammed in the doorway if the whistle seems near by: Myself is the last in!

Most of the people sheltering stay all night as their homes have been bombed and are roofless and windowless or are of poor construction. They discuss the prospect of bunks being provided in the shelter instead of the present narrow benches and their being lucky enough to be allotted a bunk but they don't have great hopes of anything being done this side of Christmas.

They are nearly all pleasant people and the poorer ones make a joke of their troubles. One man seems to know every music hall song of the last 40 years and comes out with appropriate snatches. He and his aged friend work for a 'Vestry' and to them the councillors are still 'Vestry men'. Their language is unparliamentary and some of their words are quite staggering to hear in a mixed assembly but no offence is meant.

Some of the sheltered are educated people who get into their blankets early and have long and interesting discussions among themselves.

One couple are peevish and a nuisance. The man wears an old dressing gown and a skull cap, looking very like the old man in 'The Country Wife'. He is known as 'Poona-poona'. On one particularly noisy night when the planes seemed to be having it all their own way he asked me to telephone the Fighter Command and explain as a Warden that there was a plane overhead and would they please do something about it. The other shelterers had got so used to dropping on him that they didn't realise for once he was making a big joke.

Most of the men seem to have smoker's cough but continue smoking all the time. A young pugnacious Welshman had a row with a woman who had, he thought, encroached on his wife's bed space, and challenged everyone, Warden included to 'come outside'. I went outside and had a talk with him, without letting the others who were spoiling for a fight accompany us, and found he was a skilled tool setter who was fed up with London. We ended up amicably and he decided to apply to become a warden himself.

At 9.15 I was relieved and went back to the post to find Ward (British Museum) explaining in his precise way that the people in the Basement shelter at 123 Ladbroke Road were complaining that one of the regulars, a sluttish girl, offended their noses – most remarkable in view of the strong disinfectant which the Borough lavish on the shelters.

The raids did not lose any of their impact, as Dr Sidney Chave recorded in his diary following a major raid on South London in April:

Thursday, 17 April 1940

Last night London had the severest raid of the war. We had the Dougills in for the evening and shortly before 9 o'c the alert sounded. However, we thought little of it and continued talking. But before long planes were over and there was a good deal of gunfire. Well, we sat tight until we heard bombs falling, when we moved somewhat hurriedly into the Shelter. The disturbance awoke Jillian so Lee lay down with her in the cot, whilst we three sat on the divan. Before long, the raid became extremely heavy. There seemed to be literally hundreds of planes roaring overhead. They were flying so low that we could hear the wind rushing through the fuselage. Many bombs fell. I should think we felt over 50 shake the ground during the night.

The water supply failed before midnight and we heard baskets of incendiaries falling and bursting in the distance. I looked out of the front door and the scene was almost unbelievable. The sky was clear and starlit and bunches of flares lit the whole area like great incandescent chandeliers.

Searchlights stabbed the sky while the gun-flashes and bursts could be distinctly seen.

There were several fires – one in the Norbury district looked a great blaze. All round Croydon the greenish-white light of the incendiaries silhouetted the building against the night sky. It looked for all the world like a great fireworks gala.

Three times during the night our whistles blew indicating incendiary bombs. I turned out but the bombs invariably fell on the allotments, and just one or two landed in Waddington Way.

The Dougills were pretty scared and were glad to be with us. Seeing that they intended staying with us for the whole show, after Jillian went to sleep, the four of us turned in on the divan – and slept! At least, we dozed in between my turning out to look around when there was a lull in the bombs.

Eventually after what seemed like an age, we heard the All-Clear sounding. It was over and we were safe, thank God.

The last major attack on London took place on the night of 10 May. Mary Morris was unlucky enough to be up in London that night, staying at a hotel in the West End:

11 MAY 1941, LONDON

It is a miracle that I am still alive. There are many people dead and dying. Last night was the most frightening of my whole life. Pierre had only just left me around midnight when there was an air-raid alert. There was a momentary feeling of trepidation when I wondered whether I should go to the underground shelter, but decided that I was too tired and that it would probably be only a few bombs on the docks as usual.

I walked along the corridor to Room 101 on the second floor and went to bed. It became so noisy after a while that I decided to get up and go downstairs.

The lounge was almost in complete darkness when I entered, just a small blue light burning dimly. There were I think about twenty people there – nobody spoke to me. I looked out of a window in the darkened corridor – there were fires everywhere and the sounds of crashing glass. I went back in to the lounge and there were long sick minutes of silence that frayed the nerves and then it happened – a whining shuddering like an Express train leaving a tunnel – the air shook with a volcanic rumbling, and a marble pillar in the centre of the room cracked like a tree trunk. In the maelstrom of dust, tumbling masonry and splintering woodwork, people were screaming. I may have screamed too – I do not know, but within seconds into the room there came a Niagara stream of plaster, dust, planking and chairs. The walls seemed to burst apart raining light brackets, mirrors, clocks and chunks of ceiling. The centre of the floor where the pillar had stood burst apart and the debris thundered down to the basement. There was one terrible cry of terror from the shelterers beneath.

Suddenly I realised that I should be helping people not just standing there frozen with horror. I started by asking timidly if anybody was injured. Suddenly everybody started to talk at once. They were alright but they thought that one man had been blasted in to the kitchen. I fought my way through the rubble and broken glass, and found a middle-aged man lying unconscious in a tangle of table-clothes and cutlery. There was nothing I could do, but go to find help. I stepped out on to the street. It was like broad daylight. Mayfair and most of the West End seemed to be on fire. Suddenly there were several men there carrying blue lamps – civil defence wardens. I told them about the man in the kitchen and the trapped people in the basement.

The ambulances arrived soon afterwards to take the injured to hospital. It was nearly 1 a.m. as the last person was put in to the ambulance, the doors closed and they moved away.

I looked up at the front of the Alexandra. It was well lighted by the burning of Mayfair – and then I noticed to my astonishment that the fourth floor bedrooms stood wide open to the moonlit park.

There had obviously been a direct hit right through the hotel splitting it in two halves.

I was watching all this in horror when a policeman came by carrying a long plank and some ropes and said 'There is a family trapped up there Miss'.

2am Some more casualties from the Hotel were taken to St George's Hospital and I accompanied them to offer my services. It was utter chaos, the lighting had failed and surgeons were trying to work by torchlight. I helped with the setting up of blood transfusions and at 4.30am went outside for a breath of air. The all clear had not yet sounded, but a strange hush had fallen on the scene. Across the park the guns were silent and the only sound was the muted blaze of a gas main burning in Park Lane.

I went back to the ward. It was awful – bed nudging bed and stretchers along the full length of the Nightingale type ward. The nurses and doctors looked hollow eyed with fatigue. They were still putting up blood transfusions and saline drips. I made tea for everybody.

Following this the majority of the aircraft taking part in the Blitz were withdrawn to prepare for the German invasion of the Soviet Union due to take place in June 1941.

The RAF was the only part of the British armed forces equipped and trained to strike back at Nazi-occupied Europe and the German Reich in a substantial way. In the inter-war years, the RAF had sought to establish itself as an independent strategic bombing force, and now, with the full endorsement of Winston Churchill, they sought to carry the fight to Germany. Wing Commander Noel Clyde was the officer commanding No. 207 Squadron, a unit formed in November 1940 and equipped with the twin-engined Avro Manchester bomber, which would later be developed into the famous four-engined Avro Lancaster. Clyde wrote of his experiences in the early days of the RAF bombing campaign after the war:

On the 1st November 1940 No. 207 Sqdn was officially reformed and Sqdn Ldr Kydd & I flew L.7279 up to Waddington from Boscombe Down on November 8th. We then had almost four months in which to get our new aircraft and to train our crews . . .

Our ex-Hampden pilots had not had experience with fully-feathering airscrews before and had lots of fun feathering both airscrews and having a silent glide before unfeathering again. There was a major snag against this as Johnny Seibert was to discover. The feathering mechanism was powered by an electric battery. So, if the battery went flat – no unfeathering. This happened to Johnny, who had to force land at Bardney. He put down in the best looking field that he could see. It was not nearly big enough but, by the Grace of God, there was a low bank at the end of the field that made him airborne enough to clear a ditch and to finish his landing in the next door field. It then became the Squadron Commander's job to get it out. To dismantle & transport a large, new aircraft would have been a major undertaking so a risk had to be taken & I planned to fly her out. Every piece of equipment that could be spared was removed and fuel reduced to an absolute minimum. The best line of take off with maximum distance and freedom from obstructions was chosen. Then followed several days' waiting until the wind was from the right direction and reasonably strong, also for the ground to be hardened by frost. At last all the requirements were met and, with a sigh of relief, I cleared the far hedge to put down at Waddington fifteen minutes later.

On the 24th February 207 Sqdn carried out their first operation. The target was a Hipper class German cruiser in Brest harbour. I flew L7300 with a crew borrowed from Flt Lt French. Squadron Commanders were not established with a personal crew as they were not supposed to fly regularly on operations. I managed to do another operational sortie on 13th March. This time on the Hamburg dock area.

On the 8th April 1941 I again borrowed Flt Lt French's crew for an attack on the Kiel Dock Area. We carried 4 x 1,000 [pound] GP [General Purpose] bombs and 4 x SBC [Small Bomb Container]... My crew consisted of F/O Morgan, Sgts Wells, Buck, Budden & Hedges. All went well until we got to the target area at (I think) 20,000 ft. Here we were coned by the searchlights and received the concentrated efforts of the flak batteries. We received some damage, but nothing appeared to be serious. This was during the period when our aircraft were timed to arrive over the target at two-minute intervals in order to avoid any risk of collision. It was later found that with a concentration of aircraft over the target the collision risk was less than that of the

Flak, which had to disperse its efforts. As we were leaving the target area our starboard engine was seen to be on fire. The airscrew was feathered and the fuel cut off, but the fire continued to spread and I decided that I had better get the crew out before the fire reached the main petrol tanks in the wing. I ordered the crew to abandon aircraft. I waited a short while in the hope that the fire would subside and allow me to try flying back on one engine. However, it gave no such sign, so I followed the crew down into Schleswig Holstein, some way north of Hamburg. After arriving with a bump in a frosty field, I spent a couple of days, or rather nights, getting to Flensberg, a small Baltic port, hoping to find a Swedish ship on which I could hide. No such luck. I was picked up by the Police in Flensberg while trying to find the docks and handed over to the local Luftwaffe station.

3. The Battle of the Atlantic

Throughout late 1940 and 1941, the constant struggle between the Royal Navy and the German Navy for control of the North Atlantic continued. The Royal Navy sought to keep the vital North American supply routes open, while the German Navy, principally through its U-boats, sought to inflict unsustainable losses on the British and Allied merchant fleet.

Arthur Potts served as Third Officer on the MV *Rookley*, which was involved in both Atlantic and coastal convoys during 1941 and 1942. Here he describes how ships on convoy HX 121, bound for Great Britain from Halifax in Canada, were attacked by U-boats just south of Iceland in April 1941:

MONDAY, 28 APRIL 1941

7.30am. Three destroyers, three sub-chasers, five corvettes and a rescue ship joined us. Looked like 'Review Week' when I went on watch at 8am.

8am–Noon. Escorts darting about continuously, in fine, clear weather, with occasional showers and heavy clouds. About a score of depth charges dropped at intervals.

3pm. Tanker *Capulet*, 300 yards away on our port bow, torpedoed, her position being in centre of convoy, columns opened at Full Ahead. 'Snapped' her, in poor light, as her back was breaking. Saw one lifeboat capsize and another with only 1 occupant. Obviously the sub has been moving under and with the convoy. (*Capulet* carried crude oil.)

5pm. Convoy re-formed. Plenty of depth charge 'thumps'. *Capulet* well astern, with only stern showing.

6.30pm. Three tankers (two benzine and one aviation spirit) and the *Port Hardy* torpedoed in quick succession. All victims were in centre of convoy close to our Port beam. Scene indescribable as the tankers immediately become floating hells, while the *Port Hardy* quickly drifted into the mass of flames and smoke. Only one *Port Hardy* lifeboat got away in time and was picked up by rescue ship *Zafaran*; over 100 men must have met horrible deaths in that inferno. Watching, at close quarters, such a scene, I can only say that while it fascinated the eyes, it will always remain a ghastly memory. This isn't the 'Battle of the Atlantic', it's a 'War of Nerves'; the visible effect on those members of our crew who haven't previously sampled anything, is very obvious.

8pm–Midnight. Convoy again re-formed and proceeding zigzag. Cloudy and clear. Occasional depth charge dropping.

TUESDAY, 29 APRIL 1941

After a night of watching, waiting and wondering, everyone is very 'piano' today and yet we must be on the alert for bombers. The names of ships torpedoed yesterday are the tankers *Mirza*, *Capulet*, *San Felix Davina* and the *Port Hardy*, which carried general cargo and two bombers.

Not until after the fourth warning of 'enemy aircraft' did we sight any. They were two Dorniers, but terrific barrage from convoy made them scram damn quick without dropping any bombs.

May saw one of the most vital breakthroughs in the war against the U-boats, when the destroyer HMS *Bulldog*, part of the 3rd Escort Group, captured an intact Enigma code machine from the U-boat *U110*.

Colin Fairrie served aboard the *Bulldog* and described the capture, though he did not know the significance till later:

FRIDAY, 9 MAY 1941

Late in the morning the shock of a depth charge explosion was felt aboard the *Bulldog* – possibly dropped by accident. During [the] night a submarine had been reported near convoy – (believed to have been an Italian!) – however owing to the speed of the convoy, attack was impossible. Four depth charges were dropped by the Corvette.

1201hrs Ship noticed to be giving off white clouds of steam. Convoy moves off to port – some ships go to starboard. Smoking vessel settles low in water – bows and stern seem to be coming up to meet. Another victim of a Nazi U-boat. Another ship – larger than the other (in fact one of the largest in the convoy) is seen to be dipping her bows among the waves. The silence of the attack is eerie. *Broadway* (Yankee Destroyer [she was one of the 50 ships exchanged with the Royal Navy for bases in September 1940]) and *Aubretia* (corvette) counter-attack, three more ships in the meantime are torpedoed! The *Esmond* (the large merchant packet) is seen to have received a hit beneath the bridge. The sea is rougher today and soon bobbing black objects are seen among the waves as boats and rafts lay off. One ship blows up amid a huge mass of flame and smoke. It appears that we have run into a nest of U-boats and the convoy is broken up. Armed trawlers stand by to pick up survivors.

About 1230hrs my opposite number, the starboard lookout, suddenly sights what appears to be a conning tower – rising up out of the waves. It is! A surrounding U-boat brought up owing to damage received from *Aubretia* depth charges. At first sight I was astonished at what appeared to me to be a gasometer surfacing, and then the whole structure came into view. The starboard lookout yelled 'U-boat surfacing' before I could open my mouth! *Broadway* swings round and bears down on the U-boat. The latter's crew are pouring out of the conning tower – *Broadway* prepared to ram but at the last minute turns away, but not without damage to herself – a glancing blow on her stern which puts one of her screws out of action. She fires point blank into the conning tower. *Bulldog* turns, increases speed and prepares to ram. About 40 yds off the Captain thought better, and the *Bulldog* swung round to starb'd. Previously our 4.9s and 3-inch had opened up, but our fire fell short. Our Pom-Poms later sprayed the U-boat's decks – Tommy guns, fired from the bridge, also joined in. A man clutched his stomach and fell forward into the water. Another with face covered in blood dived from the U-boat's decks – spray and blood mingled together. A third was seen to have stopped a pom-pom bullet which took his head off; and he stood fountaining blood before pitching into the sea. Twice the crew tried to man their forward gun, but were driven back. The after deck of the U-boat was awash. By now the majority of the crew were floating about in the water – Their facial expressions were inexplicable – no sign of fear. Resigned and unquestioningly calm. One raised an arm and cried 'Kamerad!' – this was greeted by jeers and the brandishing of fists. Another Nazi was seen to be supporting a dying companion in his arms. On the side of the conning tower was a 'monogram' – a leering dog – one ear cocked another drooping; beneath this was a gaping hole in the armour plating. Two officers clung to the conning tower amid hail of murderous fire. At last they too jumped into the sea – the order 'cease fire' was given (in spite of my previous humanitarian ideas, I could summon up no feeling for those men in the water. I found myself wanting, waiting to see them slaughtered in cold blood. On a previous convoy I had witnessed oil tankers hit and the sea on fire burning survivors . . . making rescue impossible. U-boats did not wait around to pick up survivors. And when the 'cease fire' came and the boats were called to rescue survivors – I felt an even stronger emotion rise up.

I remembered the tale of the destroyer captain, who when he received orders to pick up U-boat survivors – raised his glasses to the sky and said 'I can see no survivors' and steamed on. Previously, a man believed to be the Captain (later identified as Fritz-Julius [Fritz-Julius Lemp, the man who sank the *Athenia*]), stood on the U-boat deck and semaphored to our own bridge – unintelligible. It is said that he was trying to say that his was the only U-boat operating. That for a tale!

Bulldog lowered a whaler, and with Sub Lieutenant David Balme in charge, it went alongside the U-boat. They boarded the half submerged vessel – signalled to say she was watertight below and

could be towed. The *Broadway* and the corvette stood by screening
our activities from attack . . .

Coded signal is sent to HQ 'Have Primrose in tow consider petals
to be of great value' – The following Thursday an answering signal
is received from A.V. Alexander 1st Lord – Copy of Signal from
Admiralty – To *Bulldog* – from Admiralty 'Hearty Congratulations.
The petals of your flower are of rare beauty'.

The capture of an intact Enigma and the code books that went with
it gave the code breakers of Bletchley Park a great deal of help in their
struggle to read German secure communications and thus counter
their moves. However, the U-boats were not the only weapon that the
German Navy had to use against Great Britain.

One of the principal threats to the convoy system transporting vital
supplies for Great Britain across the North Atlantic was the heavy
surface ships of the German Navy, and the most powerful of these
was the battleship *Bismarck*. On the afternoon of 18 May 1941, she
left her home port of Gotenhafen and, along with the heavy cruiser
Prinz Eugen, passed Denmark and Sweden, and headed up the coast
of Norway. Late in the evening of the 21st, the two ships set off once
more, heading out into the Arctic Ocean towards the Denmark Strait,
the patch of sea separating Iceland and Greenland.

The Royal Navy was well aware of the threat posed by the *Bismarck*
and had the 1st Cruiser Squadron, consisting of the heavy cruisers
Suffolk and *Norfolk*, patrolling the Denmark Strait, with the battlecruiser
HMS *Hood* and the newly commissioned battleship HMS *Prince of
Wales* being sent to reinforce them. This force encountered the German
ships on the evening of the 23rd. Sub Lieutenant Smith served aboard
the *Suffolk* and wrote about the encounter in his diary:

FRIDAY, 23 MAY 1941, 1922 HRS

Able Seaman N—, an AA lookout, feeling rather bored with an
empty sky, idly lowered his binoculars into his lap and cast a vacuous
eye on the horizon – there he saw two ships. But his mind being
equally vacant he reported 'Bearing Green 140° two ships'. Then his
eyes popped out of his head! (For this he will probably get a medal!)

By this time the Captain was out on the wings of the bridge; 'that's them alright' – hard aport and back with the mist we faded, with the enemy six miles away. Out went our enemy report, and I labour this point. The official version broadcast in the 9pm news of Tuesday 27th May stated that *Norfolk* first sighted the enemy – this is not correct, she was merely repeating our signal . . .

When all was ready we started off to regain contact – this we did at 2015hrs. The *Bismarck* did look huge – though she was to look even bigger later on. We just popped in and out of patches of low visibility until 2022hrs, when we saw the flash of his guns. This wasn't at all according to Cocker and we waited patiently in the end – but the bricks were going exactly away from us in *Norfolk*'s direction, who had come north in answer to our signal. *Norfolk* then sent out her first enemy report and kept her distance. Anyway the enemy showed no desire to engage us or otherwise shoot us up – but went off to the SW along the edge of the ice at high speed.

In accordance with our orders we whipped up the horses and got this (comparatively) old wagon rumbling along in pursuit. This was a chase – how long it would last and whither the enemy would lead us were very much the unknown factors. We just hoped we were going to be in on future Naval History with a story to tell our grandchildren.

Sometime during the early part of that long half light, the northern night, *Norfolk* lost contact with the enemy, but we kept them just in sight. The enemy was clearly silhouetted against a hard horizon and the advantage lay with us for the horizon to the NE was murky with the snow coming up astern. All through the twilight we tore along at 30 knots and apart from the snow slightly chilling the ardour of the personnel in exposed positions, our spirits were high. The enemy – they still stuck together (*Prinz Eugen* ahead of the *Bismarck*) – obviously had orders to avoid action if possible and my reaction was that of a naughty child playing truant.

Came what passes for dawn in those northern latitudes and there they were! We hadn't been shaken off – the Captain (Captain R. M. Ellis RN) had used skilful appreciation and judgement of the situation. So at about 5am we were able to send a further and most helpful enemy report. Shortly afterward we learnt that *Hood*, *Prince of Wales (POW)* and *Norfolk* were in a favourable position ahead to intercept the enemy.

D. Hibbit served as a telegraphist on the staff of the rear admiral commanding the 1st Cruiser Squadron, based aboard HMS *Norfolk*, and takes up the story:

FRIDAY, 23 MAY 1941

Norfolk and *Suffolk* shadowed them [*Bismarck* and *Prinz Eugen*] in a SW direction, through snow sleet and rain, until early the next morning when visibility improved. It was about this time when we were expecting the arrival of HMS *Hood* and *Prince of Wales* (0500hrs); they arrived about 0530hrs and the *Hood* opened fire on the *Bismarck* as soon as she saw her at about 13 miles range. (We were only about 10 miles from the *Bismarck* at the time.)

The *Hood* succeeded in scoring a few direct hits almost as soon as engaging but the *Bismarck* returned the fire with interest and within a couple of minutes all that could be seen of the *Hood* was a mass of orange flame followed by a terrific explosion – and the *Hood* was no more, having been blown up in no more than two minutes after opening fire. Only three survivors were afterwards picked up.

The *Prince of Wales* then opened fire, but with little or no effect, and in less time than it takes to tell, her bridge was blown away – or at least a good part of it.

The Captain of the *Prince of Wales* sent a signal to CS1 (on the *Norfolk* – Admiral Wake-Walker) requesting that she (*Prince of Wales*) return to Scapa Flow, but the Admiral would not hear of it.

The Admiral then sent a wireless message to the C in C Home Fleet informing him that we (*Norfolk*, *Suffolk* and *Prince of Wales*) intended to engage the enemy (*Bismarck* and *Prinz Eugen*). The C in C, however, decided that the risk was too great in view of what had happened to the *Hood* so we continued to shadow.

Sub Lieutenant Smith aboard the *Suffolk* was also involved in the pursuit:

FRIDAY, 23 MAY 1941

Their side still stuck together and our task in what was not very clear visibility was very simple. The only underlying thought was what if they turn to starboard and have at us? *Prince of Wales* and *Norfolk* were below the horizon to the eastward, but never the less just in sight of the enemy. So there we were – just like this and that is how we kept, until absence made the heart fonder and we realised that the enemy by putting on a spurt had left us alone in the ocean. This was about noon. We didn't like this, until a friendly Catalina flying boat came and pointed the way. When the visibility decreased and we had to get a wriggle on to 'rejoin' him – which we did at 1700hrs, sighting him still ahead (the ass) about ten miles away.

And here I must put in a good word for the Coastal Command. The Sunderlands and Catalinas were so very friendly and helpful – although we only had need to ask them the way twice! But one appreciated the immense encouragement merchant seamen must get sighting them far out in the Atlantic. Those of ours were just off the Southern end of Greenland.

From here to 1840hrs, when *Suffolk* went where angels normally fear to tred – we went slap bang at full speed into a very cunningly laid trap. That *Bismarck* wasn't expecting to see us to broad on his starboard hand as she emerged oh! So very, very large as life, out of a smoke screen (which blended beautifully with the mist) was evidenced by the fact that we were able to open fire as she did.

We could see her 15-inch shells coming at us – but they all went short. We turned and twisted under full helm made smoke and spoilt our gunnery as well as his. But subsequent analysis shows that we may well have got some hits on 'Bizzie' – not that 8-inch shells against such heavy armour is much good!

While his cruisers were shadowing the German capital ships, the commander of the Home Fleet, Admiral Tovey, assembled his forces, ordering every available ship to converge upon the *Bismarck*'s position.

Wilfred Lambert served aboard the battleship HMS *Ramillies*, which was escorting a convoy across the Atlantic, and wrote of his experience of the chase:

SATURDAY, 24 MAY 1941

Excitement. German battleship *Bismarck* and cruiser *Prinz Eugen* sighted in North Atlantic by British cruisers *Norfolk*, *Suffolk*. *Norfolk* continues to shadow enemy whilst British Ships are instructed to proceed to spot with all possible speed. *Ramillies* leaves convoy and increases speed from about 10 knots to 19 knots. Eventually, with all ship vibrating and everything red hot, speed of approx 21 knots is attained. Zig-zag course owing to submarine infested waters. Proceeding north towards coast of Greenland. *Hood* and *Renown* are pursuing *Bismarck*, *Rodney*, *King George V* and *Prince of Wales* also on the way.

Course changed so that we are racing to meet *Bismarck* head on. At present speed expect to contact at 0800hrs tomorrow.

Emergency mess arrangements made, and emergency utensils issued to galley.

News received this afternoon that HMS *Hood* received a hit in the magazine, blew up and was lost with probably all hands. *Prince of Wales* has since contacted *Bismarck* and inflicted damage, also sustained damage to her own superstructure.

All excitement, as everything is prepared for battle before turning in.

SUNDAY, 25 MAY 1941

All turn out to dawn action stations promptly, and learn that *Bismarck* has changed course, making time of possible contact with *Ramillies* 1000hrs.

Further change in course. *Bismarck* now proceeding SE and *Ramillies* making same course about 100 miles west of enemy. Many U-boats about, and zig zag course and emergency turns necessitated. One torpedo seen to cross our course a few yards astern! Apparently U-boat unable to keep up to us, as our speed is still at its maximum.

The *Ramillies* never caught up with the *Bismarck* and was forced to turn back; it was left to other forces to deal with the German ship. Guy Bolland had a unique view of the action, serving, as he did, as an RAF officer on the staff of Admiral Tovey aboard HMS *King George V* as Fleet Aviation Officer. Here he describes the pivotal role played by aviation in the search for and eventual sinking of the *Bismarck*:

MAY 1941

After the tragic loss of HMS *Hood* on the 24th May and severe damage to our sister ship the *Prince of Wales*, there was a general feeling in the staff office that the *Bismarck* was no easy customer to deal with. The *Prince of Wales* was a brand-new ship and her crew had not had time or the opportunity to work up to full efficiency. As a result naturally she had sustained substantial damage, which affected both her armament and speed. It was decided that she should do her best to keep in touch with the enemy but not to engage.

Despite the inexperience of the crews of 825 Squadron on *Victorious* the latter were asked to make a torpedo attack on the *Bismarck* with their supposedly obsolete Swordfish. This attack was carried out with great courage in bad weather and they obtained one very valuable hit on *Bismarck* which added to the previous damage done by the *Prince of Wales*, and caused a further loss of oil. This was a major factor in making the German Admiral Lutjens decide to abandon his original plan, part from *Prinz Eugen* and head for Brest . . .

The chase and hunt for *Bismarck* was now becoming critical if she were to be prevented from returning to the French coast and obtaining air cover. Help was at hand, fortunately, in the form of Force H, consisting of the renowned aircraft carrier *Ark Royal* and the cruiser *Sheffield*, which was 1,300 miles to the south-east. On the evening of the 25th May, the paths of *Bismarck* and *KGV* crossed, but of course we did not know this at the time . . .

The *Bismarck* was eventually found by a Royal Air Force Catalina, heading for Brest. The position given was 35 miles in error, considering the time the aircraft had been in the air, this was very good navigation. (When it landed, the Catalina had been in the air for 26 hours and 12 minutes.) After this sighting, aircraft from *Ark Royal* were flown off to shadow *Bismarck* and they reported the enemy about 20 miles north of her current position. At this time *KGV* was short of fuel and as we had not been able to reduce *Bismarck*'s speed we could not catch her and we would have had to return on the 26th May to re-fuel.

The *Ark Royal* was ordered to despatch a striking force of fifteen

Swordfish. Unfortunately, they had only air-to-surface radar (ASV) on the aircraft and were not certain whether the target was *Bismarck* or *Prinz Eugen*, so their torpedoes were set to detonate at 30 feet instead of 34. Due to the lack of vital information for the aircrew as to our ships' dispositions, at about 20 miles from the expected position for the enemy, they saw a ship through the cloud which they took to be the target, but she turned out to be our own HMS *Sheffield*, and eleven torpedoes were dropped. Happily, there were no hits, and with great forbearance not a shot was fired by *Sheffield* in reply! (It was fortunate that they were biplanes and easily recognisable, for normally Naval ships opened fire on every aircraft sighted, without attempting to identify them!) With great skill, the aircraft returned to *Ark Royal* in very bad weather conditions, with the deck rising and falling some fifty feet. They re-fuelled, re-armed, and carried out a second attack, this time on the *Bismarck*. Their courage cannot be praised too highly. With their old, very slow aircraft they pressed home their attacks, and these resulted in the *Bismarck* sustaining rudder damage and being reduced to 10 knots on a Northerly course that took her away from Brest. When it was confirmed that *Bismarck* had been damaged, our Admiral, Jack Tovey, decided to wait until daylight, to attack with *Rodney* from the most advantageous position. *Rodney* opened fire at 0847hrs, followed one minute later by *King George V*. The *Bismarck* reply straddled *Rodney*. I was watching the battle from the lower bridge and when I saw *Rodney* disappear in a mass of water at first I thought she had gone the same way as the *Hood*. It was a great relief when the water settled and *Rodney* was still at our side. The range between us was closing rapidly from 20,000 yards, and at mid-range the secondary armament of 5.25-inch DP guns was brought into action and after half an hour the *Bismarck* was on fire, with only one turret still in action. The range was closed to 3,300 yards, which is 'point-blank', and by 1015hrs *Bismarck* was a wreck, now without a single gun left firing. Men could be seen jumping overboard preferring death by drowning in a stormy sea to the appalling conditions caused by the gunfire. It is interesting to speculate what action our Admiral would have taken if the *Bismarck*, faced with such appalling odds, had hauled down her colours and surrendered. This would have left us in an impossible position, as we were just about in range of the

Luftwaffe and of course in danger from U-boats. Maybe a Nelsonian blind eye would have saved the day. But as it happened, she went down with her colours still flying at 1037hrs, having been sunk by torpedoes from HMS *Dorsetshire*.

One of those in at the finish was D. Hibbit aboard the *Norfolk*:

TUESDAY, 27 MAY 1941

Towards the evening the aircraft carrier *Victorious* arrived on the scene and with aerial torpedoes her aircraft managed to score a couple of hits on the *Bismarck*, causing her to leak oil fuel.

At about 3 o'clock the next morning [25 May], we discovered that we had lost the *Bismarck* and decided that she must have made her way to the West Coast of France, probably intending to seek refuge in the harbour at Brest.

So the *Suffolk* was sent back to the Denmark Straits to sink a couple of enemy oilers. The *Prince of Wales* returned to Scapa and the *Norfolk* (by herself) steamed across the Atlantic at 30 knots in the direction of Brest, in the hope of catching up with the *Bismarck*, whose speed must by this time have been considerably lessened.

Later a report came through by wireless from a British aircraft to the effect that she had sighted the *Bismarck* (the *Prinz Eugen* was not seen again).

The position of the *Bismarck* (as reported by the aircraft) proved that we were on the right track, and so we continued on our course and next day in the forenoon, we ran into her (only 12 miles away).

THIS WAS ABOUT 0800hrs, 27 May 1941.We at first thought it was the *Rodney* but a close look soon told us our mistake and we opened fire.

By this time, the *Rodney* and *King George V* had arrived on the scene and the *Bismarck* was soon put out of action.

All that remained was to sink her as the *Norfolk* (having no torpedoes left, and the *Rodney* and the *KGV* having returned to port) ordered another cruiser which had just arrived on the scene to do the easy but pleasant task of putting the disabled and abandoned *Bismarck* wreck to the bottom.

The cruiser (*Dorsetshire*) was the sister ship of the *Norfolk*: she picked up most of the few survivors from the *Bismarck*. The *Norfolk* then returned to harbour and was attacked by German aircraft on her way to Greenock but we sustained no damage in any of these engagements and when we arrived at Greenock, we found that the *Rodney* was already there and everyone was surprised that we (*Norfolk*) bore no marks of having been in action.

Over 2,000 of the German crewmen of the *Bismarck* perished, with only 109 being rescued by the *Dorsetshire* before a U-boat sighting caused her to withdraw.

4. The Greek Disaster

General Archibald Wavell's Middle East Command covered a vast area, stretching from Persia and Iraq all the way through the Middle East and Egypt to the front line in the Western Desert. One extra front opened in March 1941, when the British Government committed ground troops to support the Greek forces that were fighting off an Italian invasion, launched in October 1940. Britain was bound to support Greek independence through a declaration of 1939, while Churchill was also keen to establish a front in south-east Europe. However, for the stretched forces of the Middle East Command this was a commitment too far. Wavell sent an armoured brigade from 2nd Armoured Division, and the 6th Australian and the New Zealand Infantry Divisions. On 6 April 1941, the Germans launched Operations *Strafe* and *Marita*, the invasions of Yugoslavia and Greece, to support their Italian allies, and forced the Greek and British troops southwards.

Jim Brooks of the 64th Medium Regiment RA was part of the British force committed to the campaign:

FRIDAY, 12 FEBRUARY 1943

We managed to spend a couple of hours in Athens and found it a very interesting place. We soon moved from there, and started on our trek towards the border, we passed through a lot of towns, the name of one of them sticks in my memory, Larissa, a town devastated by earthquake and bombed by the Italians. We arrived at our position near a village called Kelly, dug gun pits and made ourselves as comfortable as was possible, incidentally this is where I received my first batch of mail from home. While we were there, Mr Eden and Sir John Dill paid us a flying visit and chatted with some of the boys. On the 6th April, Germany declared war on Yugoslavia and started marching towards Greece. On the 8th, we moved out of the position without firing a round, the Germans had started to get round us, we had rather a job getting out as it had been raining for days and the lorries and guns were bogged! We moved a few miles down the road and took up position near a village called Vivy. We fired our first rounds at the Jerry on the afternoon of the tenth, we were told to stop at the position for 48 hrs, we managed to hang on for 72 hrs, the Germans made many attacks but were pushed back each time, and we inflicted many casualties. All the time we were at Vivy it was raining and snowing, we couldn't get any sleep and we were soaked through. We only got out by the skin of our teeth, only a handful of Infantry and a couple of anti-tank guns was all that was between us and the Jerrys, and the anti-tank guns were firing at tanks which we could see coming over the hills as we were going down the road, one of the guns toppled over into a ditch and had to be blown up. But we were very lucky not to lose any men. From there we went to a position and got some sleep, we saw plenty of German planes dive-bombing the road, but never one of ours. On the 16th we went into gun positions on the Serbian [Yugoslav] frontier. The Greeks held a line here and we had come up to give them a hand. But the next day the Greeks had to throw the towel in, they were streaming along the road, most of them walking, some of them in stockinged feet, they were very poorly equipped and no match for the Germans, we had to get out of there in a hurry, and the lorries and guns were stuck in the mud again. We travelled all the next day across a plain and were bombed and machine-gunned the whole way, the road was packed tight with our vehicles and made a marvellous target for the Jerry pilots, it was here that our Colonel was killed by a bomb splinter, it was a tragic loss to us, as he was a good chap, we lost several other chaps as well. We stopped under some trees for a couple of days for a rest, and it was here that we heard that Mr Churchill had promised us air support. From there we moved up to a position near the town of Molass and dug gun pits, we had a parade there and the Major told us that the Greeks had capitulated and we had to get out, but we were going to go up and have another crack at him. We moved up under cover of darkness, and fired all the next day, we made such a nuisance of ourselves the Germans sent waves of Dive bombers after us, and as they failed to stop us firing, shelled us from all sides, you can imagine how much we looked forward to the nightfall when we knew that we were getting out for good. A truck loaded up with fags [cigarettes] tried to get to us, but was shot up by aircraft, so bang went our fag issue. When the sun did go down, we put all the guns out of action, and the whole troop or what was left of them, boarded the one lorry left, which was ours, and set off for Athens. I don't remember much of the journey, as I was asleep most of the time, but I was told afterwards that behind could be seen the headlights of the German column coming up the road.

Gunner Knight served with the 211th Battery, 64th Medium Regiment RA, and was amongst the last parties to leave Greece, being taken off the beaches outside Athens.

APRIL 1941

23. Today we learn of Greek capitulation, hence our very close at hand evacuation, also worst of all the destruction of our guns and equipment (personal equipment).

24. Moved up during the night to prepare for shelling of a 'hostile battery'. A hell of a day. Two dive-bombing attacks both of which kept us in slit trenches for over an hour. Several attacks by ME's [Messerschmitts] machine-gunning us. Two enemy batteries firing on shell control by a 'Henschel' [spotter aircraft]. Most miraculously no one was injured all day but we lost one vehicle.

We evacuated Molos at 2030hrs and made for the main road to Thebes.

25. Which we made by 0030hrs seeing anti-tank firing on enemy tanks advancing down road to Molos. We however got away without casualties and drove all night and morning and pulled in for a couple of hours in the afternoon later resuming journey though Athens and proceeded within two or three miles of Marathon Beaches. The Greeks still look up to us in spite of the position we are in.

26. 6am sees us in a 'hide' where we stayed (sleeping most of the time) until darkness when we proceeded to the 'beach' with all our kit. On arrival we were ordered to dump our packs and equipment, taking only small kit and blanket.

We get into a boat and are taken to HMS *Carlisle*, an AA cruiser. Everything carried out to a T under Navy control.

The *Carlisle* had now taken part in three evacuations (Norway, Berbera, and now Greece). Very few (about 500) in Greece now.

27. 0330hrs we left Greece, unharmed, thank God. Attacked three times during day by bombers, our ship bringing one down.

Reached Suda Bay (Crete) in the early evening, being taken ashore in a barge. On landing we received refreshments outside the town and proceeded to our destination which we did not reach owing to fatigue and slept until 0900.

28. Proceeded to our camp about two miles away and settled in, washed, shaved and bathed during the day. Learn that the Jerry entered Athens less than nine hours after our leaving.

The supposed RAF support was not noticeable and we saw only four Hurricanes whilst in Greece. Jerry used bi-planes as dive bombers and blasted away day and night.

By 30 April, all British and Commonwealth troops, some 20,000 of them, had been evacuated by the Royal Navy to the island of Crete, leaving all their heavy weaponry and equipment behind. Crete proved to be the next major target for the Germans, and air raids against the island began in earnest in early May. On 20 May, a full-scale airborne invasion – Operation *Merkur* – was launched against the island, with the paratroopers of the German 7th Flieger Division, part of XI Fliegerkorps under the German General Student. Jim Brooks had been evacuated to Crete and issued with new weaponry to confront the invasion:

FRIDAY, 12 FEBRUARY 1943

After about a fortnight we collected some 105mm Italian guns and
set out for the other end of the Island. On arrival we manhandled
the guns into position and dug ourselves in. We were told to expect
a lot of enemy air activity and we got it, at all times of the day
single planes used to come over, poodle around dropping bombs
and machine gunning and nobody to stop them. We had one old
Gladiator and that used to go up and have a go, but that was soon
written off. These went on for a couple of days, and in between air
raids we dug slit trenches, and stacked the ammunition. On the 20th
April, we sent a couple of chaps to a day's leave in Heraklion or
Candia, the capital of Crete, it is known by both names, a fairly
big town. In the afternoon the usual bombing and strafing increases
until the sky was full of planes of all sizes with dirty black crosses on
them, needless to say we were down our holes and although cramped
not worrying much, as they didn't pay much attention to us, at about
4.30 the bombing stopped and only the drone of the planes could be
heard and then somebody pointed out to sea, and we could see big
troop carriers coming in skimming the water, they were upon us in
no time and parachutists were dropping in all directions, those of us
who had rifles started to let go, and everybody was out of their holes,
either firing or cheering a solitary Bofors gun which had kept silent
all the afternoon. [It] started firing, and the troop carriers being very
slow, made a perfect target for its shells. I saw four burst into flames
and other chaps said they saw six, we could see the Germans trying
frantically to get out of the burning planes, some jumping with their
chutes in flames. One of the Jerrys landed in a cornfield near our
position, and I and a few more of our troop went after him, we soon
finished him off, but not before he had hit one of our chaps with
a burst from his Tommy gun. We couldn't go into action with our
guns as the telephone line had been cut off by the bombing, but by
evening it had been fixed up and we started firing, but by then a good
proportion of the Germans had been accounted for. We fired during
the night, and when morning came, we had time to look around, all
around us were tattered and torn parachutes, some with bodies still
hanging on them, even on a hill opposite us a troop plane crash
landed and near it a couple of burnt-out wrecks.

Bill Quinney served in the Royal Marines as a gunner and, although he was not involved in the defence of Crete on the 20th, his unit rapidly came under fire from the aerial assault:

MONDAY, 12 MAY 1941

The guns were ready for firing just in case enemy planes came overhead, but we were left in peace for the first three days, then our fun began, which was during the night. I was half asleep when I heard the drone of the planes. I saw that the searchlights had soon picked them up three at once. Suddenly the guns opened up, I almost jumped out of bed with the noise they made. After this they visited us often in the daytime . . . They began coming over in twenties and twenty fives twice a day, early in the morning and five o'clock, just about meal times. Their object was the harbour of Suda Bay, at first we always managed to split the formation up as every gun round the Bay opened up on them. Some always got through and dive-bombed the ships. One day I was fetching water from a well about a mile from the camp, I had to take cover, which was in view of the Bay, and I had the experience of seeing them diving, bombs leaving the planes, and hitting the water, I saw an oil ship hit, it blazed for three or four nights, it made a lovely target for the night bombers. Early in the morning of the twentieth May I saw paratroops landing from gliders, these soon got smashed up, some did not. From then onwards our guns were in action, so the position was not complete. One morning about nine o'clock, six fighter-bombers came over very low and we opened fire on them, but they turned round and came down bombing and machine gunning us one after the other, on this raid three of our men were badly wounded, and two died later in the day, and I was guarding the other one through the night in an old barn, and he died the next morning early. The predictor and height finder were badly damaged so therefore making the guns useless, the orders were then for the guns to be taken down to Suda Bay, where they would be more useful. Seven of us were left behind to guard the ammunition and kit bags, for which they were coming back the next night. The next night came and a ration lorry landed with two tins of bully and three packets of biscuits between seven of us and they promised that they would come for the ammunition and us the next night, but they never arrived. We remained where we were hoping they would come the next night as the driver of the lorry had told us the situation was well in hand, we had decided to wait one more night as we were beginning to feel hungry, if they did not come for the ammunition or did not bring more rations [we] were going to make our way to the beach. As we could not move during the day owing to enemy planes flying so low and bombing the place where the guns had been, because of this we moved away from the gun site under a very low bridge under the road way, here we had ample protection from the machine gun bullets. We did not get a chance to move to the beach, because about five o'clock we found ourselves surrounded by Jerrys, 26 May during that night we could not get any sleep, as they were bombing all round us, we knew then there was no hope of getting off the island. Next day the 27th May we were taken prisoner. While we were under the bridge quite a few Greeks had a chat with us, we tried to get some information from them but we could not make ourselves understood, later on in the day [a] fellow had a chat with us, and he said come out of your little house, and when we came out we found rifles and machine guns were already trained on the bridge.

Although the German airborne troops had suffered horrendous casualties during the initial assault, the invasion forces succeeded in pushing the British forces back, first towards Suda Bay and then southwards to the port of Sphakia, while those defending Heraklion retreated to the port there. Jim Brooks was one of the lucky ones who was evacuated from Heraklion:

Friday, 12 February 1943

On the 28th May, the air raids seemed a bit heavier, bombs dropping quite near to our position and we prepared for more parachutists, but they didn't come, after the raid we were told to prepare to evacuate the island. We smashed the guns up, dumped what kit we had, and as soon as it was dark marched down to Heraklion harbour where we boarded a destroyer without much hanging about. As soon as it was light, and we were on the move, the Luftwaffe was after us, and right until we were only a few miles from Alex [Alexandria], we were continually bombed and machine gunned, many boats were hit and a lot of chaps were killed, hit by a common shell. The Navy saved us again, and we got out just in time, they treated us the usual way, tea directly we were on board, and as much to eat as you wanted. We arrived in Alex on the night of the 29th, and lorries took us to a camp in town, where we got some well earned sleep, even the Ack Ack guns banging away didn't keep us awake, and they were right next door.

Many of the troops were cut off by the German advance and over 12,000 went into captivity. The job of extricating the army from this perilous position fell once more to the ships and men of the Royal Navy, and the task was made extremely difficult due to the presence of so many German aircraft over the island. Harry Speakman served as an able seaman on the cruiser HMS *Orion* and recorded lengthy observations about the evacuation in his diary:

THURSDAY, 29 MAY 1941

Over the loud speaker came the pipe 'This is your Captain speaking' – now we were about to learn the worst – 'as you will have guessed, once again we have another crisis on our hands. We, and the ships in company, are on our way to evacuate those same troops we recently landed on Crete. It is imperative that we have on board as many as humanly possible, as quickly as possible. We must be well clear before first light in the morning. The operation will be exactly as in Greece so you all know what is expected of you. Good luck; that is all'. A click and the loudspeaker went dead. So this was it again. Everyone nursed their own thoughts but the tension was so real it could almost be cut.

The look-outs didn't need any prompting to keep their eyes open, and it wasn't long before they spotted the single aircraft to starboard. We all knew it was inevitable an attack would result from this single enemy reconnaissance plane, and so it was. By the middle of the afternoon we were surrounded by splashes of 'near misses'. As usual, high-level bombers tried to draw our fire and divert attention from the Stuka dive-bombers. These came screaming out of the sun and one could see the bombs as they were released from the aircraft. After so many of these attacks, the Captain had, by this time, become an expert at altering course at just the right moment to frustrate the bomber's aim. Once again *Orion* came through this first wave without casualties, but *Ajax* was forced to break off the engagement and return to harbour with fires raging on board.

These persistent attacks ended as darkness fell with a last desperate effort by a flight of torpedo bombers. This also failed in the face of the solid wall of exploding metal which met them, and none managed to launch their load. At midnight we had reached our goal at Heraklion Bay and our boats were away to pick up the tired and hungry troops from the beach.

By 0320hrs the embarkation was complete and we sailed with approximately 1,100 extra men on board. They were stowed in every conceivable nook and cranny where they would not impair the fighting efficiency of the ship during action. Things seem to be going quite well as we entered the Caso Straits at top speed. All being well we should have cleared this hazard before first light on the 29th. But a signal from *Imperial* put paid to that idea. Her steering had jammed hard over. To give her a chance to effect repairs the whole squadron reduced speed for a short time, but when it became apparent it would take too long to rectify, it was decided to sink her. The delay in distributing her passengers and ship's company to other, already overcrowded, ships meant we were still in the narrow Straits where there was little room to manoeuvre, when dawn arrived. Being well within range of the enemy bases it didn't take them long to find us, and again the Stukas got to work, bent on our destruction.

Ammunition parties dashed to and fro from the hoists to the guns keeping up with the never-ending demand. It became very critical when the only 4-inch shells left were those in the ready use lockers on the upper deck (as it turned out later we were fortunate in this respect). Everyone was too busy to be afraid – the constant demands from the bridge to the engine room to cope with the change of speed whilst manoeuvring, kept them all busy below, and through all the noise and smoke the Admiral's instructions to the squadron kept everyone on the flag deck occupied – even some of our weary passengers had a go with their short-range weapons. They didn't do much good, but I expect they felt better for it!

With stupefying suddenness it happened. A huge column of water alongside the quarterdeck caused a shudder that was felt throughout the ship, and we knew that this time, something serious had happened. No apparent damage was visible however, and we didn't appear to be losing any speed, but when damage control reported the after magazine was flooding it meant that both the after 6-inch turrets were now useless. Of course the enemy didn't know how vulnerable this left us, especially if they attacked from astern, so they didn't try and finish us off there and then, as was their wont once they had scored a hit.

Hereward was the next to suffer. She sustained several hits. The Stukas dived on her time after time, yet still her guns kept up a barrage of sorts – God knows how. The enemy tactics seemed to change here and they started to concentrate their attacks on one ship at a time, and though the rest of us put up what firepower we could over the victim, it was inevitable they eventually got through to their target. The *Dido* was the next casualty but once again she managed to put up a terrific barrage, and still steamed on despite a direct hit.

As the light strengthened they made use of the rapidly rising sun, diving out of the glare. It was obvious that we (the *Orion*) were the next target on the list but the best they could manage were some spectacular water spouts on both sides and our luck held during their first effort. It couldn't last though because too many aircraft had us in their sights. The terrific jolt, followed by a hail of debris on the upper deck announced our first direct hit. 'A' turret had been blown to bits. The gun barrels of 'B' turret, directly above, had actually been bent upwards by the force of the explosion! We now had no 6-inch guns whatever and our 4-inch AA armament only had a few shells left. The thick column of black smoke told the pilots what they had been waiting for, and down they came to finish the job. To our surprise they only strafed the upper deck with cannon fire before breaking off the attack. It was obvious they had no bombs left. The respite gained whilst they returned to their base gave our damage control parties a chance to sort things out a bit. We were still able to do a fair rate of knots, so things could have been a lot worse, at least we were getting further and further away from the enemy bases.

As details of the damage began to circulate it became obvious there was no hope for any of 'A' guns' crew – my own best friend was amongst them, a chap I'd joined up with, trained with and gone ashore with. We also learned that the Captain, Captain Back, who had been injured on the bridge and taken down to the Sick Bay, had died. His last reported words were 'Tell the Commander to take over, and the ship's company "Well Done"' . . .

A period of quiet marked the Captain's passing, and whilst the weary gun crews rested the casualties were carried aft in an endless stream. The injured were taken care of in the makeshift sick bay set up in the Admiral's quarters. The dead were laid out on stretchers on the quarterdeck. Instead of the usual burial at sea service, a few short prayers had to suffice because we were still at first-degree readiness. I'll never forget the Padre, Reverend Gerald Ellison (later the Bishop of London) his clothing stained and dirty moving amongst the dead and giving comfort to the dying.

It was now about 1000hrs. Our speed was still quite good, but the real testing time came with the advent of a single Stuka which streaked out of the sun's glare. It was too quick for the gunners to catch in their sights, and the sudden flash followed by blackness then the eerie silence as all machinery stopped, told their own story. An armour-piercing bomb had penetrated the bridge, passed through every deck below and exploded in the 4-inch magazine. As mentioned earlier, this was empty.

The whole centre of the ship was on fire. The TS crew were no more, or at least could not be got at. The gaping hole which reached from the ship's sides down to the double bottoms, was flooded. The ship's side fuel and fresh water tanks had been breeched and their contents, plus those of the main fridge and ship's provision stores were all swilling about below. The occasional sight of a body amongst all of this, made looking down in the glare from the raging fire, like a bird's eye view of Hades.

After what seemed an eternity, the engine room department managed to restore a very limited amount of power and slowly we got underway again. All communication had been lost and the ship was being conned from the upper deck, orders being passed to the tiller flat through a human chain. And so we staggered on – outside scarred and filthy, inside broken and warped with a casualty list that was difficult to comprehend. It took some time to realise the full horror of the situation because every man on board, still alive, had lost at least one good mate. In one case, a mess of ten men was reduced to just two at the end of the day.

Slowly the hours passed, and though by this time we knew the enemy dive bombers couldn't reach us, there was always the threat from other aircraft and submarines but at last we could just make out the light house at Alexandria.

The attacks on the *Orion* caused 262 deaths, of which 112 were of the ship's company and the rest evacuated soldiers. The Royal Navy suffered severe losses in its defence and evacuation of Crete. Although over 16,000 Allied servicemen were taken back to Alexandria, three cruisers and seven destroyers were lost, with a number of other ships seriously damaged.

5. Rommel in the Desert

While General Wavell had been preoccupied with his operations in both East Africa and Greece, Erwin Rommel launched a sudden offensive on 31 March, brushing aside the British blocking positions of the 2nd Armoured Division and driving them headlong before him. Within two weeks, he had reversed almost all the gains of Richard O'Connor's earlier offensive, capturing the general himself in the process. Benghazi was once more in Axis hands, while only the vital port of Tobruk remained in Allied hands, defended by the troops of the 9th Australian Division amongst others. Having tried to take the port by storm throughout April and early May to no avail, Rommel settled his forces into siege lines around the city and attempted to force its surrender through the interdiction of supply by sea – Tobruk's lifeline.

Malta was vital for control of the central Mediterranean, and the events of April and May saw an increase in the tempo of attacks upon the island, as Canon Nicholls recorded:

APRIL 1941

The Huns have been very active here lately, and the strain is somewhat severe. At night when the siren wakes us, I find myself shivering as though I had the ague: also it is necessary to use the chamber pot about every hour. That is only at night. It is horrible to hear the drone of the enemy getting louder, and then the crumps. But what about poor London, which has just had its worst raid of the war. Last week there was a fine TBD [Torpedo Boat Destroyer] action in which four of our destroyers, which are now operating from here, sank three enemy destroyers and no less than five vessels they were convoying – the whole lot – for the loss on our side of *Mohawk* only.

FRIDAY, 9 MAY 1941

What a tragic change in the war situation! We were rejoicing at the fall of Bengazi, at the brave attitude of Jugo-Slavia and the Greeks. Now the tables are turned. The Huns have turned us out of most of Cyrenaica, the Serbians collapsed in a week, and the Greeks in a little longer. Only in Abyssinia are we still successful. Addis Ababa has been taken and Haile Selassie (descendant of King Solomon's affair with the Queen of Sheba) has returned to his capital. The enemy is now in the Mediterranean, and we are at once feeling the effects. We have had night blitzes on April 19, 22, 24, 28, 29, 30, and May 3, 6, and 7. On 22nd three big destroyers had brought us a magnificent mail – we had at least 60 letters and packets. The ships used machine guns or multiple pom-poms to shoot down flares, a horrible noise, even from our own weapons.

Daily one or two reconnaissance planes fly over the island. An Air Force officer told me that we are outnumbered by six to one. Messerschmitts get up to 35,000 feet, and are here before our Hurricanes can get above them, and so they are helpless. The parachute mines are the worst, because they do not bury their noses in the earth, and thus have a more devastating effect.

Despite being under constant attack, Malta remained a thorn in the Axis side, as its central position allowed Allied ships and aircraft to intercept the supply convoys heading for Rommel's Afrika Korps. The sinking of the *Mohawk* in such an action, mentioned by Canon Nicholls above, is described in more detail by an unknown rating below:

APRIL 1941

The destroyers HMS *Jervais*, *Janus*, *Nubian* and *Mohawk* arrived at Sliema Creek Malta on the night 19 April. They were to intercept and destroy German and Italian convoys of troops, ammunition and supplies bound for North Africa to Rommel's Africa Corps.

The Force had done two night sweeps without any success, when on the afternoon of the 15th April Sunderland aircraft reported a Tripoli-bound convoy. *Mohawk* and the other three destroyers left Malta at dusk to intercept.

As we slipped out of Sliema Creek that evening we knew that something was definitely on that night, you could sense it in the air. Excitement, fear, anticipation of impending action, I don't know but you knew this was it whatever this was. At the first 'turn of the screws' the older hands rolled their paper money carefully into thin rolls and placed them into small waterproof articles of protective clothing, which could be drawn from the sick bay before proceeding a run ashore. They did however protect your paper money if you had to swim for it. Once clear of the breakwater we close up at 'Action Stations' and tested the guns firing circuits and communications. My action station was on the bridge starboard after lookout. Everything being satisfactorily tested we lookouts were relieved every twenty minutes but had to relax in a darkened compartment away from all lights. Gallon 'Fannys' of pusser's cocoa were sent round to the guns' crews during the first (8–12 watch) and rumours of what was ahead were being spread round the ship. The 'Captain', Commander J. W. M. Eaton, eventually told us just what our objective was. It was a convoy consisting of four merchant ships escorted by three Italian destroyers. Night action ship to ship was a hell of a lot different than constant air attacks which were the normal daily war routine at sea. This was Navy against Navy and we were quite confident of the outcome. We were battle-wise having fought through Norway, Atlantic convoys, Mediterranean convoys, Calabria and Matapan. We were good and we knew it, 'Let's get at them' was the thought in everyone's mind.

At 0158hrs the enemy was sighted six miles ahead silhouetted against the moon, we closed to 2,400 yards and opened fire, the time about 0210.

All hell broke loose, *Jervais* and *Janus* engaged the first Italian destroyer, the *Lampo*, and sunk her. *Nubian* engaged the second destroyer, the *Baleno*, set her ablaze and sunk her. Meanwhile *Mohawk* and *Janus* sank the rear merchantman, which had caught fire and then blew up, we believed she was an ammunition ship. While this was going on the Italian destroyer *Luca Tarigo* tried to put herself between the sinking convoy and our destroyers. She was hit by broadsides from all four British destroyers. Although sinking and on fire she managed to fire three of her torpedoes. At about 0230hrs *Mohawk* turned hard a starboard to avoid the ramming bow of the leading merchantman and opened fire on her. Almost at the same time a torpedo struck the ship on the starboard side abreast 'Y' gun. To me it felt as if we had hit a milestone. The ship stopped dead and shuddered with the shock. I thought at first we'd hit a mine but it was definitely a torpedo, the stern had completely blown away including 'Y' gun, its crew, shell room and magazine crews and all supply parties.

'X' gun was out of action although 'A' and 'B' guns were still firing and set our target, the leading merchantman, ablaze. The engineer officer reported that the propellers and shafts seemed okay and that he would try and get the ship moving, at that moment the second torpedo struck us in No. 2 and 3 boiler room, the ship split along the centre line, the torpedo tubes crashed down in the boiler rooms killing most of the engineer staff at their posts. We started sinking by the stern and also listing heavily to Port. The Captain ordered abandon ship, my abandon ship station was the starboard whaler but she was so much firewood now. So it was over the side and swim for it. I had a lifebelt on and uninjured too, I wasn't too badly off at the moment, after a few minutes in the water I spotted a 'Carley' raft ahead of me and made for it. There were about eight of the crew onboard it, mostly, to my surprise stokers, how the hell did they get out of that flaming inferno . . .

One of the crew on the Carley craft I was on asked if anyone had a fag. A stoker passed him a waterproof tobacco pouch with the makings in it. He'd just finished rolling a fag when a voice from the water said, 'I don't think we should smoke chaps, we might give our position away to the enemy.' There was a deadly silence for a moment then howls of laughter, well with the ship sinking behind us, star shell bursting all around, guns firing like mad, an ammunition ship sending up a beautiful display of pyrotechnics, and he's worried about giving our position away to the enemy. About two hours later the fight was over and *Jervais*, *Janus* and *Nubian* turned to pick up us survivors. The Carley raft I was on bumped alongside *Nubian* and we were soon scrambling up the nets to the safety of *Nubian*'s deck. The hospitality of *Nubian*'s ship company was overwhelming, we survivors were treated like long lost brothers.

There were a dozen of us Mohawks washing each other down in *Nubian*'s ship's company bathroom. Suddenly in steps my oppo H. G. F— covered in blood and oil fuel but with his cheeky smile on his face. 'Anyone want to buy a battleship?' he asks. His smile was short lived however as when he started to strip he took off his service belt, undid the pocket on his belt to take his money out. Then with a look of horror and disbelief he held up an oily soggy mess. The pocket on his belt had been slashed by some piece of jagged metal during his escape from 'X' gun and the waterproof article of protective clothing he had put his paper money in was torn to shreds. 'I was keeping this for "Carmelita"' he said, we all howled with laughter, as his Carmelita worked in the 'Lucky Wheel' down the 'Gut' [Straight Street, Malta's 'red light' district] and she was 50 if she was a day.

However, supplies managed to reach Wavell's forces in North Africa. A convoy carrying 238 tanks, codenamed *Tiger*, reached North Africa in early May and, under intense pressure from Churchill to relieve Tobruk, Wavell launched Operation *Brevity* on 15 May. The attack succeeded in pushing Axis forces back from the vital Halfaya Pass and Fort Capuzzo but suffered heavy losses in both men and *matériel*, and the latter position was lost to an Axis counter-attack, with Halfaya Pass also being recaptured by the Germans on 27 May. Further reinforcements reached Wavell in late May, and on 15 June he launched Operation *Battleaxe*, which had the aim of destroying the Axis position in the area around Sollum and Bardia. However, in a pattern that was to become so familiar to British forces in the desert, the armour ran into strong Axis anti-tank defences and was driven off with heavy losses, being forced back to their start lines.

Harry Wiles of the 104th Regiment RHA was involved in the offensive:

FRIDAY, 13 JUNE 1941

Friday the 13th, is supposed to be unlucky, but it was my lucky day. In the evening Jerry fired some shrapnel. I was sitting on the edge of my bed pit and a piece hit me on the forehead. Not very bad, but it knocked me over. Lots of blood, some of it on the pages of this diary which I was writing at the time. The boys dressed the wound in the slit trench as Jerry was still sending a lot more over. In a break in the shelling, I walked over to the dressing station in the Wadi and had it properly cleaned and dressed. When I walked back they were still shelling and I had to take cover several times. When I got back to the gun position I found that one shell had landed in No.1 gun pit, blowing the traversing handle off the gun, but injuring no one. They were in the slit trenches at the time. The shrapnel had cut their overcoats, blankets and other items of kit to pieces. There were bits of shrapnel all over the place and we had been lucky, all I had was a slight headache.

Captain Malcolm Pleydell was the medical officer of the 3rd Battalion, Coldstream Guards, 22nd Guards Brigade, and wrote of his experiences during the battle:

MONDAY, 16 JUNE 1941

Woken up at 4am by orange flares followed by small-arms fire over us. A bit worried when I saw our men jump into trenches behind us. It seemed we might be between two fires. Went in search of company commander and on the way a plane came down to about 200ft. and dropped bombs within about 30–50 yards. Dust and stones dropping around: a bit scratched and grazed. Gathered from the company commander that it was a German patrol action and it soon stopped when our Bren-gun carriers went out. We are attacking Capuzzo on our left. Plenty of tracers flying about there, same as last night. This attack dies off about 10am. Our guns just behind are very noisy. Planes about now. They come over quite low and our AA gunners shot one down. A beautiful shot just in front of the tail. The pilot bailed out and the plane wheeled over and crashed. Soon after the pilot was brought in with fractured tibia and fibula. Very clean and German looking, better than the crying, whining Italians. Eventually evacuated them down to the Advance Dressing Station, after having given them the medical care and comfort that was available. Fairly quiet in the afternoon, apart from Jerry planes bombing Capuzzo. Our morning counter-attack failed. Early that evening we were bombed heavily. Company commander and another officer killed while returning from the cookhouse. Latter was about the best chap in the unit. Seven other casualties. During the night, flares were going up in the distance, on our right flank, on our left flank behind Capuzzo, and in our rear. Slept OK.

Tuesday, 17 June 1941

Woken by Company Sergeant-Major. Everything seemed quiet. At 10 o'clock burial service for the two officers. The company Commander always used to joke the padre when he returned from a patrol: 'Cheated you this time padre. I know you had a little grave all ready for me.' But he wasn't there to joke this time. Shortly after burial we had orders to move. Took some time to get vehicles together, and we were behind the HQ Company Cooker both looking like ammunition trucks. Some enemy tanks approached on right flank and ours went out to engage them. At the same time there was mild shelling but brisk automatic fire on our left and left front. Also a few shells away on our right and small 2lb shells dropping around, but none near us. Eventually we ran the gauntlet. Quite a number of vehicles were under small-arms fire as we dashed through the enemy pincer movement and away. Most uncomfortable hearing firing on your line of retreat, about as bad as getting shelled from behind when advancing. Went back and down Hell Fire [Halfaya] Pass to behind Buq Buq.

The failure of *Battleaxe* proved to be the final act of Wavell's command, as Churchill replaced him with General Claude Auchinleck in July 1941. The Auk's task was to create a force, Eighth Army, that would drive Rommel away from Tobruk.

6. The Siege of Tobruk and Operation *Crusader*

Inside Tobruk itself the garrison settled down to a long summer of siege while Auchinleck's attention was directed elsewhere – notably towards putting down a rebellion in Iraq and fighting the Vichy French in Syria. By the end of the summer, the largely Australian garrison was being replaced by Polish and British troops in a process that was largely complete by October.

Edward Porter served as a gunner in 192nd HAA Battery, 69th HAA Regiment, which formed part of the garrison of Tobruk from September to December 1941. Here he records in his diary his arrival by sea:

MONDAY, 22 SEPTEMBER 1941

Reveille at 3am. Breakfast at 3.45. Parade at 4.45. I volunteered to carry a box of Medical stuff (everything had to be carried by hand). At 5.30am we were en route for Alexandria in convoy. Soon we were at 14 Dock and within 15 minutes were aboard a destroyer. I had heard that destroyers were fast but when we reversed off the quay like a speedboat and swung round through the dock I only just began to believe it. When out to sea (after dipping in salute to naval vessels in the port) we fairly flew along and churned the sea to a white, milky foam. We were travelling at times at about 37 knots. I felt very sick and decided it was strategy to lie down on the deck. I felt better then except I kept getting wet whenever we shipped sea on a turn in the zigzag course. The ship was covered in spray and one big wave took away my rations and my knife, fork and spoon and almost took my greatcoat which was on the rail. An Italian reconnaissance plane dropped a bomb or two but they missed us by a quarter of a mile.

The plane was at a great height. I felt so sick I couldn't have cared if it had been a squadron of bombers. Later a squadron of Tomahawks circled overhead. There are two other ships in the convoy – a sister destroyer and an ack ack cruiser, the *Mahmoud*, reputed to be the fastest ship in the Navy. The speed is terrific, and the stern of our boat vibrates strongly. At sunset we changed course northwards and it looked as if we were really going to Malta but then we seemed to double back on our course and in darkness pulled into Tobruk. It was quiet there and soon we disembarked on a rocky hillside. An Aussie voice seemed to whisper instructions. The stone hurt our gym shod feet and we walked to a lorry with our loads of kit, hobbling over the rough ground and after a long wait when we just had no idea where we were or what was going on we were driven by a very rough route to a site in the wilds. I slept in a matador [truck] and was very tired. In the early morning the guns of the site awoke me – there was a raid on and I clambered down to terra firma shivering with cold.

The daily routine of the siege led to the troops searching for ways to keep themselves amused, often dangerous ones, as Edward Porter records:

OCTOBER/NOVEMBER 1941

Salvaging Italian equipment became a common pastime and we all had rifles and ammunitions for amusement. A favourite practice being to find a quiet wadi and blaze away at tins with Italian ammo. Another rather foolhardy game was collecting hand grenades – 'red devils' and so forth . . . One of our fellows later lost his hands through picking up an old Italian shell which everyone had kicked out of the way for weeks. He was the sanitary orderly and a quiet, harmless chap. This particular shell had lain on my route from the Wadi bivvy to the Command Post for long enough and this day the little chap picked it up and bang! He stood there with his arms still in the same position, hands shattered and a look of surprise on his face.

It was strange we had so few of these accidents considering how much ammunition and equipment was experimented with. Dave Birch once said his lorry (we were equipped with transport later on after the Relief) was the only one that had been shot up from the inside.

He and Charles Spence dismantled some Browning Machine Guns from a wrecked plane in the Desert and laid them in the lorry. As they bumped along one went off blowing a neat hole in the railboard – luckily they'd pointed the muzzle to the rear. On another occasion a Browning in a Hurricane wing let off a burst when tampered with but luckily no one was hurt.

Soapy Hudson lost all his forelock and eyebrows through dropping a cigarette on a bunch of cordite sticks and petrol burns were commonplace. In the desert the sand-petrol fire was the usual method of cooking or brewing up. Thousands of gallons of petrol were later lost every day through profligate use of the stuff as fuel, as washing and mostly because of the rough handling of the flimsy tins.

The job of re-supplying the garrison, evacuating the wounded and bringing in fresh troops fell to the Royal Navy from their bases along the North African coast. Sub Lieutenant John Carter was in command of a flotilla of lighters based at Mersa Matruh and wrote with emotion of his feelings about the conditions in North Africa and his concerns about his role:

6 OCTOBER 1941, MERSA MATRUH

I hate the desert. I hate every conceivable thing connected with it.

That is the underlying idea of my life out here, one of the governing factors, and my one great ambition is to get out of it, to get back into destroyers – but firstly to get out of it before the desert overtakes my mind, with a catastrophic crash.

I. That word is to play a great part in this diary – inevitably, as the whole idea is reactionary: it is a form of relief for the brain and mental powers, a form of exercise. For I feel that if I do not do something in the way of writing down the horrible jumble of thoughts that possess me at the present, the entire collection will reach stagnation point and I shall lose all character and individuality, which I dread.

WEDNESDAY, 8 OCTOBER 1941

Hot and dusty, and really nothing to do at all. It is fantastic keeping four officers sitting out here doing almost nothing, and paying us for it. Even the trips we do, runs to Tobruk, do not really require the services of a navigator: for if the lights are not attached to some convoy the commanding officers are all capable of reaching their destination safely. I do not mind doing the trip – or any job, however dangerous – if it is really required: but I do object to taking unnecessary risks, when heaven knows, we are subject to enough unavoidable ones. There is a war to be fought, well worn phrase, and won, and under these circumstances, I am prepared to do anything to bring that victory as soon as possible. But neither the other three navigators or myself feel that the job we are doing has a really practical value at all . . .

[The chaplain] sailed this evening in an 'A' lighter for Tobruk, George going too as navigator. I hope they are not attacked by anything: the feeling George is going through just now is, I am certain, the same that I experience every time I leave Matruh, 'I shan't be happy until I cross this boom again!' Or 'I wish it was this time tomorrow night!'. The day going up there is by far the worst, the nervous strain simply grows and grows until you have to exert all your willpower to stop yourself from appearing jittery or nervous. That is courage – the quality of being able to keep from showing your fear in the face of nervous strain: not being able to press a trigger and keep the sights on what appears to be an enormous aircraft diving into your face, bomb hurtling towards you, and the ping and splintering crunches as his bullets tear through the wood and steel around you. Enduring that is nothing in the heat of battle, behind a gun of some sort: courage is behaving calmly and normally through the period before such an attack, during the six long hours, which never seem to end, and where time seems to stop, when that sudden deadly attack may develop in a moment. Then, on top of that, the not-so-deadly anxiety one has, of not finding Tobruk by daylight, and through you, these valuable lighters and their cargoes being lost.

Throughout the summer, the Western Desert Force was steadily reinforced with troops from Britain, the Empire and Commonwealth. In recognition of this increase in size, a new unit, the famous Eighth Army, was instigated in September 1941, consisting of two corps – XXX and XIII – under the command of General Alan Cunningham. This new force was to break through Rommel's positions and relieve Tobruk in an operation codenamed *Crusader* scheduled for late November.

Reg Crimp served as an NCO with the 2nd Battalion Rifle Brigade, part of the 7th Armoured Division Support Group. In the weeks prior to the start of Operation *Crusader*, he wrote of the troops' main preoccupation in the desert:

SUNDAY, 9 NOVEMBER 1941

One thing the Quartermaster makes sure of: that we have plenty of tea, milk and sugar for brews. These desert brews are an institution, the making being almost a ritual. Half a gallon of water is poured into the brewcan and set on the fire. The fire is built of scrubwood when there's any about, with a couple of stones to support the pot, but usually consists of a cut-down biscuit tin or petrol-can, gashed in the sides for ventilation, with a few inches of neat petrol or petrol-soaked sand in the bottom, which burns fiercely for several minutes. When the pot is boiling a couple of handfuls of tea are cast upon the seething water. Then the pot's removed and the brew allowed to strengthen up. Meanwhile the section mugs are marshalled on the ground, and spoonfuls of tinned milk and sugar put in each. Then they're filled with tea, straight out of the brew-can. The result is 'Desert Char'.

Heaven knows how much petrol is used on the Blue [in the desert] for brewing-up. The whole Battalion must burn the best part of a hundred gallons daily, besides using plenty for running the vehicles and washing clothes when water's scarce. Petrol, in fact, is nearly always more plentiful than water.

Our second main comfort is tobacco. We get a buckshee issue of 50 cigarettes every week, usually of poor quality (Indian 'V'), and can buy a hundred more decent ones whenever a canteen comes up. As long as there's no lack of char or fags everyone's happy. When there's a shortage of either, morale slumps.

On 21 November the operation was launched, with XIII Corps pinning down the German forces on the frontier, whilst XXX Corps, containing most of the armour, swept through to relieve Tobruk and defeat Rommel's mobile forces. This was the plan; in reality, the British assaults were blunted by the German anti-tank screens and Rommel counter-attacked. Reg Crimp wrote of the attack going in:

FRIDAY, 21 NOVEMBER 1941

An attack goes in this morning. The 25-pounders are early putting down a barrage. From our position we get a good view of the start. At 8 o'clock two companies of infantry (our 'B' and one from another battalion in the Brigade) move off across the valley north-westwards with a dozen Bren-carriers. Strung out in open order they look pathetically exposed on the wide, flat expanse. I don't envy those poor blighters, dwindling slowly into the distance.

At last the trudging and trundling specks disappear over the horizon ridge. Shortly afterwards a burst of machine-gun fire, like a peremptory challenge, suggests they're near their objective. Then following another burst – sustained, staccato, remorseless – Brens stutter, small arms crackle, and mortar bombs crash in ragged succession like train doors slamming at Clapham Junction during the rush-hour. It all seems so remote and impersonal, but we can imagine the bitter intensity for the chaps over there in the thick of it.

Our guns in the valley now fire as fast as their crews can load them, the air is rent continuously by the blast, and, up above, the arching flight of the shells makes a wild mewing chorus. After ten minutes they slacken off, and sounds of strife over the ridge have also petered out. An hour later two carriers come back with casualties on board. They stop near us to enquire the whereabouts of the ADS [Advanced Dressing Station]. When we ask how the scrapping's gone, the sergeant says it's been tough, but the Jerry's positions are in the bag. Then mentioning a pal of his, adds bitterly: 'Poor old Smudger got his lot. But I made sure of the sod that did him. Filled his guts with this Bren, close range, the bastard!' (Smudger was a corporal, steady and serious, who came out on our draft.)

Lionel Melzer commanded the 11th Field Ambulance South African Medical Corps (SAMC), part of the 1st South African Division. His force became surrounded by Italian and German forces as Rommel counter-attacked on *Totensonntag* (the Sunday of the Dead) during the battle of Sidi Rezegh, one of the most fiercely fought encounters during Operation *Crusader*, the attempt to relieve Tobruk. Melzer had a particular fear of capture, as he was Jewish:

SUNDAY, 23 NOVEMBER 1941

I shall remember today for the rest of my life. Today I lost my unit after being its commanding officer for three days. Today we were drawn, quartered and cut to shreds. Today we saw our Waterloo. Today we fell. Today we rose higher than I had ever dared to hope . . .

The air of confusion about everything, which has existed for the past three days, seems to be intensified. Everybody is busy and tense. It seems as though the whole world is going to explode any minute from now. The very air seems charged with electricity and any word or action may be the spark which starts the conflagration. The Germans are still on all sides. Last night, we saw their planes at different times right around us. We hear strange stories. We hear from the chief actors themselves how they have driven their convoys along merrily and then suddenly found themselves in Italian or German lines. A field ambulance convoy did the same thing, and turned and made a dash for it when they realised it. They lost seven vehicles, fortunately empty at the time. Another convoy knew nothing until they actually found themselves inside an Italian camp and passing close to Italian tents. The leader kept his head and kept on moving, realising that if he stopped or turned about, the Italians would realise that something was wrong. He came to a point where the road led back to the way he had come, and he just about got clear when the alarm was raised. They then made a dash for it and were chased by motor cyclists. All but a few stragglers got away. It is true that these experiences are exciting and even, to some extent, amusing; but they are also tragically significant. They show that we are surrounded by the enemy and that our lines of communication are cut . . .

The tank battle started at about 1400hrs. We had been going flat out with medical work, and I had just completed putting on a plaster. I was in my shirt sleeves and had a waterproof apron on. Suddenly it started. It was ushered in by a sudden tremendous burst of gunfire. Again I was caught without my steel helmet. I lay on the surface of the ground next to my casualties. On my right are two German casualties. My head is towards the west, so I can see that way simply by raising my head very so slightly. I see the rear view of British tanks, not more than 400 yards west of the MDS [Main Dressing Station]. These keep up a constant north and south patrol. Their patrol is about 400 yards after which they about turn and go the other way. They keep up an intense fire the whole time. In the meantime, the shells directed at them are falling terribly close to us. The patrolling of our tanks goes on; but, to my dismay, I see that our tanks are retreating and coming closer and closer to us. Each north and south movement is nearer to us. Now they are 300 yards from us, now 200, now 100 yards. With them the shells come closer. I wonder what will happen when the tanks reach us. I know very soon as their retreat is more rapid at this stage. The tanks are immediately in front of us. They work their way between the groups of casualties lying on the ground. They are careful not to hurt anybody lying on the ground. I am certain that this embarrasses them and reduces their fighting power. They keep up this shooting the whole time, and German shells are following them. Nobody at the MDS has been hit so far. At last they have retreated past us. The next rows of British tanks soon follow them and pass us, again miraculously without damaging anybody. Now we are between the British and the German guns and tanks. This is safer because the shells are passing higher over us. In spite of this, one can just about feel the whiz of the machine gun bullets which are passing over us by the millions. I look up. On the horizon I see the front row of German tanks. They also do their patrols, and I see that these are coming closer and closer. Soon they are about 400 yards away, then they are as near as 100 yards. Soon they have reached us. I am in despair. I feel so helpless; I can do nothing for all the badly wounded on the ground beside me. I have heard all the atrocity stories about the Germans, how they ride their tanks over wounded and women and children. I shudder at what may be coming in a few moments. I can't use any more words of comfort – they sound so foolish. I tell those around me that they must do their best to get out of the way of the tanks; that it all depends on themselves. As I say these words I wonder what those with injured backs and broken thighs will do to help themselves. It is impossible for us to move them as lifting one's body one inch off the ground would mean certain death and that wouldn't help these poor lads at all. I grit my teeth and wait for the awful moment when the tanks will be on us. They come at last. To my relief, they take as much care to avoid overrunning us as the British do. The danger, however, is still terrific. British shells aimed at the German tanks are now falling near us. The first row of German tanks passes us, then the next, and so on until they have all reached east of us. At no time did they fire deliberately at anybody at the MDS, and they did not run over one person at the MDS . . .

My reactions during all this. I don't think that I thought at all. At one time, I had my mind fully occupied wondering whether any casualties lying on the ground would be run over. When this danger passed, I did have thoughts alright. I realised that I was now a prisoner of war. In a flash, all I had read and seen on pictures of what the Germans do to their captives came before my eyes. I saw myself and the other Jews singled out for 'special treatments', and I even saw myself machine-gunned or sent to some concentration camp in Germany. Somehow, this didn't worry me very much as, I think, my fatalism came to my aid. I realised that I had really nothing to complain about as I had no right to be alive at all.

Rommel pushed his mobile forces all the way through to the Egyptian frontier, leading to Cunningham calling for a withdrawal. Auchinleck replaced him with his own Chief of Staff, General Ritchie, and held his nerve, pressing on with his attacks.

David Ling was an officer in A Squadron, 44th Royal Tank Regiment, part of 4th Armoured Brigade, which suffered so heavily in the fighting against the German anti-tank guns and Panzers:

NOVEMBER 1941

Our particular spot of desert was named Zaafran while immediately in front of us was a similar area – Belhamed. Separating Zaafran from Belhamed was a small rise formed of one bank of a puny dry wadi.

It was on Belhamed that the enemy were firmly entrenched and it was our purpose to shovel him out, for beyond again were our friends holding hard to a rise called Ed Duda. They were the Tobruk forces who had battled thus far and ours was the stirring mission of relieving them. We were to join them and form a flexible corridor through a sea of shell bursts and vicious bullets. This same cold night had seen an attack on the New Zealanders on Belhamed – an attack that failed in its high hopes of sweeping clean the enemy but which succeeded in clinging to its outer defences. At dawn the infantry tanks of my regiment were to complete the task.

My troop was on the left flank and because the rise in front of us ran diagonally to our line of advance it fell to me to climb it first, to leave the reasonable safety below and confront with our massive bulk the slender barrels of anti-tank guns, dug in and out of sight but waiting. The grey dawn, icy, unfriendly, was streaked to the east with the vivid slashes of colour that only a desert awakening knows. The occasional infantryman, flattened against the damp earth, gave a roll as we clattered by, and smiled and gave an encouraging wave. Slowly I approached and climbed the gentle rise, my other two tanks a hundred yards away, to the flanks and rear. Whilst still turret down I strained through the lessening grey for a sign of the men whom I had come to kill and finding none continued cautiously into the open. I was very careful. I could see no gun flash, no tripping machine gun trace as the bullets pink and pretty, follow so close in their dainty arc. Only silence and stillness.

I was very scared. Not knowing quite what to expect, I was afraid of the unexpected. But this fright was nothing compared to the fright I was to know in later battles – fright backed by knowledge of the previous fright.

Corporal Hill, my loader operator, feared my caution. 'Don't go so slowly, Sir'. 'Keep moving, Sir.' – as I, to use my glasses with greater surety, would command the driver to slow down. His agitation became uppermost. 'For Christ's sake, keep moving, Sir.' But I must use my eyes and I had my other two tanks to protect me, to pounce on the gun who fired at me.

We were all on the ridge top now, crawling in an agonised slowness. Still no sound, only the sun in the desert distance behind us, streaking out shadows into and through the Germans in long parallel lines. No sound, no movement. Our formation was lovely to behold, of textbook exactness – we moved as one machine controlled by a single mind. The whoosh of a shell close to my head surprised me and I redoubled my efforts to find a target. There should have been a trace of the gun after firing. Dust should have been kicked up and – whoosh, whoosh. Where the hell was the damned thing. I was reporting to

Stump Gibbon, who commanded the squadron, that an invisible gun was disturbing my tranquillity when the next effort of a singularly poor enemy gun-aimer was successful and from a range of 100 yards he succeeded in hitting me on the fourth attempt.

The well was reminiscent of Alice's only it was blacker, of greater girth and infinitely deeper. In falling down it I was glad that I was not turning over and over but kept a reasonably even keel as I sped on my downward journey. I was lying on my back facing upwards and should, by all laws of nature, have seen an ever-decreasing disc of white daylight as the well's rim receded. But there was no daylight; all was blackness and I fell with an even but fast speed.

I wondered if there was a bottom and whether I would be brought up with a jolt but this did not worry me and I did not believe it would happen. Probably I would be gently slowed up. After all, to be stopped instantaneously after such a fall must kill one and that was ludicrous because one cannot be killed twice and I was already dead.

Of that there was no doubt in my mind and it was a fact, the only lucid truth I knew. I was dead, positively dead and presumably speeding to wherever dead people go. I had no knowledge of why I was dead or how I had died. I merely accepted it as a commonplace fact and one that should give rise to no excitement, speculation or regret.

I was dead and I didn't seem to mind. I was aware that this was the beginning of a new journey and I remember reflecting that death after all wasn't so bad as I had imagined and there did not seem to be any reason to be afraid of it. Fortunately the thought did not occur to me to compare the remarkable similarity between this fall and that of Lucifer from Heaven.

The humming which had started as a soft whisper grew to a gentle murmur and the moon had pushed its way through the clouds becoming faintly visible and then growing slowly to a pearly brightness. I was still falling when I became aware of a star close to the moon, that was ruby red. Its brightness drilled into me, boring away the shroud of black that encompassed me and simultaneously re-vitalising my easy death to uncomfortable life.

The star was the radio's warning light while the moon dissolved and took the shape of the illuminated turning dial.

I lay still, as clarity sanity and reality came back. I was comfortable and in no pain. I knew now that I was huddled on the floor of my tank, that we were not moving, that the engine had stopped and that my last clear memory was an urgent call on the radio that some big gun was trying to hit me. Obviously it had.

It was black inside the turret and the air was full of black smoke. With difficulty I peered across the two feet of space separating me from the face of Corporal Hill. We must have received shocks of equal intensity for he also was beginning to move. I reached to him, clutched his arm and groped his face; and he returned my grip.

'Are you all right, Hill?'

'I'm all right, Sir – are you all right?'

'Yes, I'm all right.'

I did not ask the same of Trooper B . . . my expert and lovable gunner who used always to make my biscuit burgoo and brew my char. He could impart to those warming concoctions a flavour which, like the shining efficiency of his guns, others could not match.

Now slumped across his little adjustable seat he sprawled backwards and downwards. His head, split in twain, was poised over my chest while his hot blood poured over and through me, a black glistening stream from the back of his crushed skull. His suntanned face turned half sideways was closed and white with death, shining clearly in that black murk.

I remember I struggled to get up and Hill struggled also. We were entangled and I had to move B . . . I remember I stretched up my arm to push him forward and away – and that two of my fingers went through the hole in his skull, into the warm softness within, I wiped my hand on my blood-drenched clothes.

David Ling had been wounded in the action at Belhamed, but that did not stop him being summoned by the commander of the 2nd New Zealand Division, Major-General Freyberg, later in the battle:

NOVEMBER 1941

At NZ Div HQ was General Freyberg, VC. Stump had taken all tanks fit for fighting but there must have been nearly fifteen crocks and many crew with nothing to do.

NZ infantry were pinned down flat on Belhamed and there was

no way of advancing. Seeing the tanks Freyberg told his ADC, a blond lieutenant and an All Black scrum half, to fetch the senior tank officer. That was me, in the ambulance . . .

So, without permission, but able to see with rather sore eyes, I accompanied the ADC to Freyberg. He was seated on the desert floor, his feet in a slit trench. We sat likewise on the other side. He was punching one fist into the palm of the other hand. His eyes were those of a wild man. On his head was a balaclava and by his side a Lee Enfield rifle.

I was ordered to mount a tank attack on Belhamed immediately. He would not accept my statement that the tanks he saw were crocks, and he threatened me with court martial. I asked for artillery support, which only made him angrier and I received none.

Back at the crock tanks I made a quick inspection and got verbal reports on each tank. I decided that three, a troop, could fight – their turrets were undamaged and could traverse – for other mechanical reasons they had almost broken down. I called all together and asked for volunteer crews. No problem. The response was marvellous.

We creaked, one up, to a point where I was hull down and used my glasses to survey the scene – flattened NZ infantry everywhere and little black squares about 1,000–1,500 yards away. I knew they were 'ants'.

Suddenly I heard a voice screaming at me. I looked down and there was Gen. Freyberg wearing his balaclava and waving his rifle. 'Why the hell have you stopped? Get on!' To get rid of him so I could sensibly use my glasses and make a decision, I moved the troops northward and came up again hull down. But Gen. Freyberg was there screaming again. I tried once more to shake him off by again moving northward but he had no difficulty in trotting and keeping up with my creaky Matildas and for the third time here was this extraordinary sight of a VC general, in a balaclava, red in the face, waving a rifle and screaming at the top of his voice at me.

So we came up on to Belhamed, passed the flattened NZs who gave us a wave as we went and using Besas [machine guns] on the dark square objects, to keep their crews down, we went flat out. We were only three and there were too many of them. We were repeatedly hit. My right tank radioed it had a jammed turret and could not fire. Shortly after the same happened to me.

With only one gun left, and feeling they would not pierce our armour, I told each tank to run over at least one of the ants. They were now three to four hundred yards away. My only fear was hits on the suspension or tracks. We successfully destroyed two guns. The crews flattened themselves in their slit trenches. I ordered each tank to turn and run along the slit trenches with one track in. I shall always remember my operator-loader saying 'You bloody bastard, Sir!' Later these actions bedevil you. Then, wheeling to complete a 180-degree turn, we returned safely to below the ridge and we counted hits. I had the most as lead tank – 27 – each one to two inches or so deep.

I walked to NZ Div HQ and reported to a furious Gen. Freyberg seated, as before, with his feet in the slit trench. I had no opportunity to speak. He lunged into me shouting at my cowardice and he would see me court-martialled. He just did not understand that two of the tanks were knocked out. I tried to tell him of what we had done but he would not listen. I walked back to my tank, climbed in and directed my driver to NZ HQ and Gen. Freyberg. There he was, balaclava and all, punching a fist into a palm. We drew up as close as possible. I jumped to the ground and shouted to the gunner to traverse the turret. He shouted back that he couldn't – it was jammed because of hits. I then invited Freyberg to inspect the tank and I started counting aloud and pointing to each impact in turn, the 27 hits. He just told me to go and I heard no more of the incident.

By 7 December, the German losses and lack of fuel and other supplies had become too great for Rommel to withstand and he was forced to withdraw his units, first to the Gazala Line and then beyond to El Agheila, finally raising the siege of Tobruk. Edward Porter recorded his feelings on the occasion:

WEDNESDAY, 10 DECEMBER 1941

Tobruk is now properly relieved and the enemy retreated towards Benghazi. Convoys are making short work of the vast dump of bully beef and biscuits. Soon there will be nothing left near Johnny Site rest camp.

The New Zealanders first entered Tobruk on 27th November but a counter-attack cut the Bardia road and we were more or less providing a domiciles for the relieving column until larger forces came up later, particularly the 7th Indian Division. – It was exciting seeing the new three ton trucks coming down the escarpment on the first day of our relief – all very smart compared with the strange assortment of splinter punctured vehicles we used. In the days following the relief of Tobruk we found ourselves getting hungrier – the advancing arms were taking all our food supplies and rations became less plentiful. Our small ration of bread vanished and we found ourselves on a biscuit diet – hard tack at that.

1941–42

1. The War in the Far East

Throughout the twentieth century, Japan had extended her influence throughout the Pacific, annexing Korea in 1910, occupying the former German Pacific colonies following the First World War and establishing the puppet state of Manchuko in Manchuria in 1931. This last action caused friction with the United States and led to Japan withdrawing from the League of Nations. In 1937, full-scale hostilities broke out between Japan and China with atrocities at Nanking and elsewhere hardening attitudes towards Japan in Europe and the United States.

The tensions between the US and other Western powers on one side and Japan on the other, rose following the start of the Second World War in Europe and when the US Government imposed an embargo on the sale of oil and rubber to the Japanese, as well as a freeze on Japanese assets in British, Dutch and US territories. War was all but inevitable as the Japanese, lacking their own natural resources, felt compelled to take what they needed by force.

On 7 December 1941, Japan launched a surprise attack on the US naval base of Pearl Harbor, sinking or seriously damaging six battleships and killing over 2,400 servicemen and civilians. In a coordinated assault, the Japanese landed troops in the north-east of the British colony of Malaya.

Lieutenant Stephen Abbott served with the 2nd Battalion East Surrey Regiment in the Malayan jungle and wrote of his experiences during the initial invasion and the retreat that followed:

151

WEDNESDAY, 10 DECEMBER 1941

At about 10pm on the 10th [December], a terrific barrage opens up
of every type of weapon, from 25-pounders to individual rifles. It is
raining hard at the time, and our Coy HQ is crammed into a half-dug
slit trench which is nowhere near big enough for us all. It is pitch
black, and we keep on treading over each other, and imagining forms
and shapes advancing through the trees. This deafening row goes on
for about half-an-hour continuously, and intermittently throughout
the night. A particularly disturbing LMG [Light Machine Gun] is
potting away at frequent intervals from one of our forward platoon
posts. I go out there and am informed that the Section Commander
is absolutely <u>certain</u> that there are Japs about 100 yards away! We
find, on closer investigation, that it is one of our own patrols trying
to find a way in!! Poor devils! They had had a foul time lying in
three-foot-deep padi. The whole business was a mistake anyway.
There are no Japs within two miles of us. Just panic on the part
of one platoon commander of an Indian Regiment some distance
away! Anyway, we have given away our entire position very nicely
to the enemy . . .

Then begins the frightful journey down the line to the main road
– over ten miles in distance. The fellows are done in by now, and we
stumble along the rough stone track like drunken old men. Whenever
we stop to listen, the men just fall down where they are, and have to
be lifted bodily on to their feet again. We can still hear the roar of
RA and the rattle of MGs behind us, but it seems to be slowly dying
down. The enemy hasn't arrived before us, anyway, and we reach the
main road at about 4.30am to find all quiet there.

Odds and ends of people from Bde. HQ, 'B' Echelon, and from
other Coys, have now joined us here, and in all, I suppose we number
about 90 men. We also have about 10 or 11 LMGs, but all the A/Tk.
weapons have been lost. The defence of the shops and village itself
is very well organised, with every man doing an active job, but the
enemy seems to be all round us now – even firing at us from the road
behind, and from the trees on our right and left. The trouble is that it's
so darned difficult to see the blighters. Our positions are completely
taped by now. (We find out afterwards that Fifth Column people led
the enemy round us during the night by unmarked paths.)

I am in an old wooden shop, with about ten men – including some stretcher bearers. We cut out holes in the walls so that we can see all around us, and make barricades of tables, chairs, mattresses, etc., to make the place a little more bulletproof. The atmosphere is pretty tense, but no one seems particularly frightened. Through the doorway I can see the men on the other side of the road – they are all very calm and collected. The RSM is strolling about in the road allotting positions to his troops. He is immaculately dressed, down to his highly polished boots and perfectly rolled puttees. He is carrying his ancient silver-knobbed walking stick. We have a gunner officer with us and one A/Tk. gun. His little gang are calmly sitting behind their gun, firing at odd intervals at an enemy opposite-number about 300 yards away.

This situation continues until about 9.30am when a sudden shout of 'Tanks coming' gives us a little warning of their attack. Almost simultaneously, nine dive-bombers appear overhead.

The tanks come through first – guns blazing away. The RA get the first two, but their gun is put out of action by the third. We have no weapons to use against them ourselves. I chuck a grenade at one of them, which makes no impression whatsoever, and then we just put our heads down and hope for the best.

When the tanks have passed through – five of them – the dive-bombers come down one by one and create merry hell. Our shop receives a direct hit and collapses on top of us. As I scramble from the wreckage, I hear the order shouted to get out, and collecting as many of the lads as I can find, I run out through the back entrance (or where it had been) and in the padi-field behind. The Japs seem to be everywhere, and, as we plough our way, knee-deep, through the swamp, bullets and shells whistle about all over the place and in all directions. They seem to be firing straight into their troops as well as ours – then so are we anyway – all is confusion!

Malaya was not the only Japanese target; troops had also moved into Thailand, which capitulated and later joined the war against the Allies; the Philippines; Guam, which was occupied without resistance; and Wake Island, which did not fall until 23 December. They also launched an aerial attack on the British colony of Hong Kong, as remembered by Barbara Redwood, who lived there with her family:

MONDAY, 8 DECEMBER 1941,
START OF ATTACK ON HONG KONG

Was raked out of bed this a.m. at 6.30 – to be at office at 7. At 10 to 8, Bevan said war had been declared between Britain and America and Japan, and just after 8 o'clock the air raid sirens sounded. At about 10.30 the all clear went, and it was said 1 bomb had dropped in Shamshuipo causing many casualties. At 1.30 the sirens went again and there was quite a lot of AA fire. I thought they were all bombs at first. I saw three planes high up, being chased away to Lyemoon. It's hardly worth writing diary because I can't visualise us ever getting out of this, but I want to <u>try</u> to believe in a future. Kai Tak has been bombed and I'm thinking of Arthur and Sid. Mabel is at CSO (Secretariat) and Mum at Jockey Club (Casualty Hospital). I'm home now till 7 o'clock. Scared and gloomy. I feel sure we'll have raids every night and day and in the night much worse than in the day.

On 10 December, the Japanese launched a ground attack on the British positions in the New Territories and Hong Kong itself.

Squadron Leader Donald Hill had seen his flight of aircraft destroyed on the ground at Kai Tak airfield on 8 December, and he was attached to the Winnipeg Grenadiers, a Canadian unit, as an infantryman for the remainder of the short campaign:

WEDNESDAY, 24 DECEMBER AND THURSDAY,
XMAS DAY 1941

The retirement order was a mistake and back we go to Bennetts with guns and equipment. Just as we reach the top the Japs open up on us with mortars. We have no protection and lie flat. The shells land right amongst us. Man next to me hit, also several others. Piece of shrapnel glances off my helmet and am half buried in flying debris. If we stay we shall all be killed so order the men to disperse and dash for cover and miraculously we make it. During the barrage I had noticed that one of our previous posts was still manned by Canadians who obviously had not received the order to withdraw. Cpl Blueman AC, Canadian, volunteers to go to try and get them out. We climb on our bellies through the thickest undergrowth but are fired on several times. We finally get within hailing distance and get them all into a pillbox.

We collect all the arms and equipment which we can't carry, pile them into the pillbox, and throw a couple of grenades into the pillbox. As we start back everything goes off at once and we have to duck flying bullets. Eventually we arrive intact at the AIS. No one seems to know where the Japs are so back we go to a new position guarding the bridge over Aberdeen reservoir . . .

The Canadians are badly rattled, even their officer seems to have lost control of his men. The Japs start shelling us and confusion sets in and the men start leaving their posts. A scene I never wish to see again. I am in an awkward position as I have no command over the Canadians. Just as they start moving back [up] the road, Major B— advances down the road waving a revolver and shouting to his men to get back to their posts. Some obey and some don't. The Major is highly excited and his voice rings out through the night calling his men all the names he can think of. The Japs must have a good idea of our positions. He calls his officers and men all the names under the sun and shouts for volunteers to cross the bridge.

The Canadians refuse to budge so I, more of a desire to back the Major than of any thought of heroics, go across with him. We reach the other side safely whereupon he is violently sick and I realise he is drunk. Through overwork he worked himself into a state of complete collapse and should have been relieved of his command earlier. We retire still intact. We can hear the Japs' wild animal calls and they appear to have gone another way. Most of the Canadians have disappeared and with the few left we set up a mortar which fires its first shell into a nearby tree and explodes, blowing the operator's right arm off and another man nearly loses a leg. Get the wounded into a dugout where there are some others badly wounded and try to stop their bleeding. We only have bandages and several of them are in danger of bleeding to death. Their moans are terrible and although I keep ringing for an ambulance, none arrives. What a horrible mess and I try to restore some kind of order. After a good talking to the men pull themselves together and go back to their posts.

Thank God the ambulance arrives at last, also Lts Campbell and Park.

Campbell threatens to put the Major under arrest and B— threatens
to put every Canadian under arrest. Comes the dawn and most of the
Canadians have disappeared. What an Xmas day, empty stomachs, tired
out, and heaven knows what is going on. At ten am a message arrives
saying there is a truce until midday. This news is immediately followed
by a terrific bombardment of our position. Not my idea of a truce.
More Canadians melt away leaving our line practically undefended.
I gather the few remaining men together and proceed to climb Mt
Gough hoping to join up with our main forces. When we reach the
top and strike the main road we run into several hundred Canadians
retreating from Wan Chai Gap. Wan Chai Gap is the most vital sector
of all and this means the end. We are told that the island surrendered
at 3.30 over an hour ago. The troops have no arms and are completely
worn out. A scene I will never forget with ammunition dumps going
up everywhere and the Japs pouring hundreds of shells just over our
heads into blocks of houses across the road. Finally the barrage stops
and white flags appear from all the houses.

Although the colony had fallen, a few still managed to escape into
mainland China and beyond, such as Christopher Meadows, who was
a leading telegraphist in *MTB10*, the senior officer's boat of the 2nd
Motor Torpedo Boat (MTB) Flotilla based in Hong Kong:

THURSDAY, 25 DECEMBER 1941

Japs proceeded to bomb us during the morning. Received signal
about surrender; the Official Surrender was at 1530 hrs but troops
were still fighting in isolated areas. Final preparations being made
for MTBs bid to reach 'Free China' through the Japanese lines
and thence via the 'Burma Road' to Rangoon. At about 1830 hrs
Christmas day, 1941, we were being heavily shelled from our own
base; at 2130 hrs the MTBs made a dash from Hong Kong to Mirs
Bay in 'Free China' (the troops were still fighting in isolated groups).
As we were leaving Hong Kong, I read a signal (by flashing) from
a small island asking us to take them off; I reported the signal and
was told to make 'sorry impossible'. Grim as it was, we could do
nothing to help as we had several army officers, intelligence men,
Admiral Chan Chek and other personnel besides the MTBs crews,

stores etc. As we were proceeding in a northerly direction towards Mirs Bay, searchlights suddenly came to life just over the horizon. We were at the time proceeding at high speed so they must have heard the roar of our engines; luckily, we were just over the horizon from the Japs as their searchlights indicated by hitting the horizon and then shining on the clouds.

At 0300hrs December 26th, 1941 we arrived at Mirs Bay, 'Free China' with no casualties or damage and proceeded to strip the MTBs of everything of value to the Chinese; wireless transmitters and receivers, watches, etc. Having stripped out everything of use we proceeded to a place called Nam O and sank the MTBs in deep water.

The Chinese who were helping us to get back to the UK were Chinese Guerrillas and at times used to board and pirate coastwise vessels from their motorised junks. We used to patrol this area for the prevention of piracy, but by the time we got to the area they had usually disappeared.

The Chinese Guerrillas hid us in a village during the day of 26th December and we started foot-slogging about 5pm preceded by Chinese Guerrillas; we were carrying guns, iron rations, blankets, oilskins, etc. After covering about fifteen miles we arrived at the Guerrilla Headquarters about 10pm and stayed there the night.

Other Royal Naval personnel were not so lucky. Adrian Billings served as an Engine Room Artificer (ERA) on the destroyer HMS *Thracian* and was badly wounded when the ship was attacked by aircraft some ten days before the colony's surrender to the Japanese:

SUNDAY, 1 FEBRUARY 1942

My injuries were: – shrapnel (or bomb splinters) through left biceps, severing the ulnar nerve and making a 9-inch exit hole; another piece smashed the knuckle joint of middle finger of left hand (the MOs wanted to take the knuckle and finger out); suspected fracture of lower left arm; left knee flayed – just strips of flesh left on; private parts badly bashed and some splinters there (most painful on removal later); a badly gashed chest and a lump entered my back just above left kidney.

Got bombed when we were docking ship at Aberdeen. (The Hong Kong Royal Naval Dockyard was untenable at the time.) The dockyard crowd who should have been doing the job were not available and it was thought advisable to inspect damage to see if the ship was sea-worthy. (This was before the days of aqualungs.) The Chief Engineer, Burkett RN, and Chief ERA E. Morris, and myself and some stokers were pulling the ship with rope blocks so that she would rest on the chocks on the dock.

All the others went for shelter as an air-raid siren was sounded, and bombers appeared fairly high up in bright summer sky. I remained to make fast the blocks around a bollard so that all our hard work would not be undone. The bombs were anti-personnel and none hit the ship, but struck the quayside a motor torpedo boat and another ship and the buildings.

Fortunately, I was sheltered by the bollards, over which I was blown by the first explosion, my knee being filled with fragments of steel-wire rope (and still is!) Those that took shelter paid the price of obeying orders. The Chief Engineer had severe injuries to his spine and a fractured arm. He spent the rest of his life paralysed and on his back. My Chief ERA, Ernest Morris, had his left arm severed and one stoker was killed. Seven Hong Kong Royal Naval Volunteer Reserve blokes were killed in a tug which had been hit in an earlier raid and the other stoker lost his right leg.

I crawled back into the ship which was deserted (to this day I don't know how I did it) and for the first time I lay there wondering if I was to die. Eventually First Aid came from a party at the Aberdeen Tech. who were led by a dentist (named Mason, now practising at Perth, WA). He gave me a morphine tablet, but I was too dry to make any saliva to swallow it.

My great fear at this time was that the MTBs (I think there were two), which were blazing fiercely showering small-arms ammunition all over the place, would blow up when the war-heads of their torpedoes got too hot; but they never did because the plugs fused and the TNT burned out normally.

Was terrible in RNH [Royal Naval Hospital] till Christmas Day (when Hong Kong gave in) because the Japs were shelling road junctions all day for nine days. Was praying for one to put me out.

One day, when I could just hobble, Japs drove up and gave us seven hours to vacate the hospital, bed cases and all.

2. The Channel Dash

As part of the Japanese assault on the British colonies in the Far East they had managed to sink the King George V-class battleship HMS *Prince of Wales* and the battlecruiser HMS *Repulse* by aerial assault off the coast of Malaya on 10 December. This highlighted the vulnerability of capital ships to aerial attack, especially when they were unprotected by their own naval aviation or air forces.

The German Navy was increasingly aware of the vulnerability of their ships to this sort of attack, particularly the battlecruisers *Scharnhorst* and *Gneisenau*, and the heavy cruiser *Prinz Eugen*, which had all come under regular British air attack at the French port of Brest since returning from Atlantic sorties in 1941. In early 1942, the Germans prepared an audacious plan, Operation *Cerberus*, to run the ships straight through the heavily defended Straits of Dover to the safety of German home waters.

Lieutenant Robert Butler served aboard HMS *Whitshed*, which formed part of a destroyer flotilla based at Harwich and deployed to prevent the breaking out of the German capital ships:

THURSDAY, 12 FEBRUARY 1942

Captain Mark Pizey, in *Campbell*, joined us at Harwich 4 Feb., and took command temporarily from our own Captain (D), Captain J. P. Wright (in *Mackay*). The other destroyers which attacked the *Scharnhorst* squadron were *Worcester*, *Whitshed*, *Vivacious*. All five were between 20 and 25 years old, with guns unable to elevate against aircraft, but we did have torpedoes. Indeed, we were the only remaining destroyers in the North Sea area with torpedoes – except for the Fleet destroyers at Scapa Flow, which were forbidden to come south for this operation, by order of the Admiralty . . .

In the southern North Sea the visibility was quite good until about 13.00, after which it progressively deteriorated, which made it possible to deliver our attack without being sunk before we got in range. At 15.30, when the attack developed, the visibility was about 3 or 4 kms., less in the rain squalls. I have never understood why the German destroyers, which were large, modern and fast ships, made no attempt to attack us. From the enemy point of view it was, surely, very important to detach some of those Friedrich Ihn-class destroyers to engage us before we got close enough to fire our torpedoes. Naturally I am glad they did not, but it seemed incredible to us that those German destroyers, each of them a tonnage more than three times ours – and greater speed – should just steam straight on as though we did not exist. Was the German Admiral asleep?

Admiralty sent us the position of the German squadron at 13.10, which put them on at <u>30</u> knots, and made an interception near N.W. Hinder buoy impossible. Captain Pizey immediately altered course to a little north of east, 085 degrees says my memory, which led us over our own minefield. Afterwards, at the enquiry, it was revealed that our minefield had been swept up, or had never existed, but Captain Pizey did not know that at the time of our sortie.

Air/sea recognition was a problem: we had large British markings painted on deck, but we were attacked by RAF aircraft. Just after the action, when *Worcester* had been severely damaged, with heavy casualties (27 dead and 30 or 40 wounded) an attempt was made to transfer some of the wounded to *Campbell*. At this moment an aircraft of 42 Squadron RAF lined up for a torpedo attack. Captain Pizey went 'Full Astern' and the torpedo passed only a metre or so ahead: but the huge wash from the propellers swept the wounded away. The *Worcester* was a wreck mechanically (seven hits from heavy shell), yet her Engineer Officer, Hugh Griffiths, succeeded in getting her back to Harwich under her own steam, evaporating salt water in the one usable boiler.

Flight Lieutenant Gordon Shackleton served with No. 114 Squadron RAF Bomber Command, a Blenheim Squadron based at RAF West Raynham, Norfolk. He took part in the aerial assault on the *Scharnhorst* and *Gneisenau*:

Thursday, 12 February 1942

On the 12th of February the weather was atrocious and at lunchtime we were stood down and returned to our billets. However, twenty minutes following our arrival at Weasenham Hall we were ordered to report back to the operations room where we were told that the two ships were actually half way up the Channel having slipped out of Brest unseen due to the awful weather. We were briefed to climb above the clouds and rendezvous in a formation, then if we were to find a hole in the clouds to bomb the targets or otherwise we should descend individually and attack any ships seen. There were no breaks in the clouds, so we began descending, relying purely on instruments, which due to the bumpy conditions, were all over the place. I was kept very busy keeping control, so I ordered Frank to watch the altimeter and tell me when we were below 1,000 feet then to keep on calling the height until we broke cloud which we did at 400 feet, <u>immediately over</u> one of the big ships. Fortunately Frank was too surprised to release the bombs, as at 400 feet we would have blown ourselves to Kingdom come. We were promptly set upon by two Me 109s, but within seconds we got safely back up into the freezing clouds, however after a few minutes ice began forming on the wings, chunks of it breaking off and hitting our fuselage – while to crown it all the port engine's carburettor froze and stopped. I then had no option but to drop down, when thankfully the engine restarted. Visibility was only about 400 yards and as we were very close to a German destroyer, which promptly opened fire, back into the clouds we went. By mutual agreement we decided that there was no point in hanging about to be fired at or chased by fighters, when if we did bomb from 400–500 feet, the only damage would be to us self-inflicted. Thankfully, more by luck than good judgement, we eventually found our way back to West Raynham with daylight fading and minimal visibility, having dumped our bomb load into the sea. During that operation three of our squadron were lost, mainly due to the terrible weather, combined with the inexperience of the recently arrived crews.

3. The Fall of Singapore and Burma, and the Battle of the Java Sea

In the Far East, the British troops had been forced back down through Malaya by the Japanese advance. By 31 January, they had withdrawn into the island city of Singapore. The island had been heavily fortified in the pre-war period but principally against an attack by sea; its landward defences were not impressive. The Japanese crossed the straits to Singapore on 8 February and had surrounded the city itself by the 13th.

Lieutenant Stephen Abbott had retreated throughout Malaya with his men and now found himself involved in the last-ditch defence of the city:

SATURDAY, 14 FEBRUARY 1942

The aerial and land bombardment starts, as usual, at dawn. We are getting hardened to it by now, and it does not prevent us from eating an excellent breakfast (of canned foods) without undue worry. Afterwards, I go up to the bathroom of the house, and have a wash and a shave – a great luxury in these days!

At 10am Clive tells me to make my way back to the town, try to find 'B' Echelon [the troops who man the rear area, with supply dumps, cooks, etc.], and guide a hot meal up to the Unit. I set forth a few minutes later with my Orderly, and we move cautiously along the River Valley Road, which is being shelled at the time. From here, we can see all the countryside down to the coast. This consists of a continuous ridge of hills all the way. This ridge is the last possible line of defence of the town. It is manned by all manner of troops. RE [Royal Engineers], RASC [Royal Army Service Corps], RAOC [Royal Army Ordnance Corps], etc., – nearly all untrained in Infantry warfare. There are also the remnants of the original battalions mingled with them to stiffen them up. Practically every able-bodied man they can lay their hands on had been given a rifle and attached to some unit or other. Malays are fighting shoulder to shoulder with Australians; Tommy with Ghurka; more than one party of our own unit, – unable to find the main body – has attached itself to some other force. It's the same all round the perimeter.

This defended ridge is having a bad time. Shells and bombs are piling into it from all angles. It is now almost impossible to tell whether the whistling one hears overhead is caused by our shells or theirs, because the enemy is bombarding every sector of the front from all sides of the city . . .

The city is in a shocking state. Buildings are down everywhere. It has been impossible to clear away the debris, wrecked cars, etc., because, as fast as one worked, more buildings came down and more disturbance was caused. In the end, it was given up as a hopeless task. The wounded are taken into the buildings all around, where the First Aid Posts and hospitals have been hastily established. There is no distinction between Civil and Military. British Officer lies beside Chinese coolie, Civil Servant by Indian Sepoy.

The area remaining in our hands is now so small that what remains of our superb artillery – both AA and 25-pounders – have their gun positions in Squares, on lawns, on the beaches. There is no protection whatsoever for them. Completely exposed to the air, they have no trenches or shelters in most cases. Knowing they cannot conceal themselves, they just carry on firing even when the 'planes are right above them. I pass by one battery of field guns – in position behind Raffles – and ask one of the gunners how things are going. He replies, 'Well, sir, there ain't many of our toys left, but what there is will go on until the last shell is fired.' Then, with a grin he went back to his job.

All through this war the Japs have suffered heavily under the fire of the Royal Artillery, and now they are having their revenge. Gun positions become the chief targets for all their attacks, and slowly but surely, one by one, the gallant little weapons are put out of action by sheer weight of numbers; but every one of them carries on to the end. No enemy, however superior in arms, can conquer the spirit of the men.

George Thompson was one of those gunners, serving in the 135th Field Regiment RA, part of the 18th Division that had been shipped into Singapore early in 1942 to reinforce the colony, and records his reaction to the eventual surrender:

SUNDAY, 15 FEBRUARY 1942

Shelling and bombing continued until 6.00pm, so we did not know what was going on, Ack-Ack guns still in action. Col. Toosey who had worked so hard by taking over control of all RA firing, together with Major Peacock, came to us and told us the sad news. The main reasons were the terrific loss of life amongst the civilians, only one day's ammunition left, and only 48 hours of fresh water, he then went on to say that none of the guns, vehicles or equipment had to be destroyed. He said 'I am now leaving you', he half turned and said we could go ahead and destroy them.

I should mention that the colonel also told us there was no discredit to the regiment, we had done more than our share, and if everyone else had done as much as we had, we would not perhaps be in the position we found ourselves at present. Major Peacock also spoke to us, and thanked us for our loyal support, he could not say much more, he was broken hearted.

The guns were blown up by loading the shell in the ordinary way and putting one down from the muzzle end. Instruments including signalling equipment were entirely destroyed. I am sure nobody obtained any pleasure in carrying out this work, it was a great pity that it should all end like this, but we tried to make sure that the Japanese could not use any of them again. Half an hour later word was received 'carry on fighting' but at about 6.30pm, except for an occasional shot it was now all over, and everyone is terribly depressed. When speaking to Sid and Ted we agreed that not once did it ever strike us that we would ever be a prisoner of war.

Moved into BHQ and the ammunition is being blown up, shrapnel flying everywhere. Slept on the road beside our truck, stayed there two days and regained some lost sleep.

The surrender itself took place on Sunday, 15 February, when the British commander Lieutenant-General Arthur Percival took the decision to seek a ceasefire due to the shortage of supplies. Over 100,000 Commonwealth troops had been captured during the course of the campaign. Among them was Lieutenant James Richardson, who served in the Intelligence Corps:

SUNDAY, 15 FEBRUARY 1942

Very little resistance after 1600hrs. Arms and ammo in guns spiked and destroyed before 1600hrs due to the usual and complete balls up. Our people went out to parley with Japs, white flag and all. Suggesting terms and 'cease-fire' at 1600hrs. Japs decided on 'cease-fire' at 2030hrs and let us have two bad bombing raids between 1700hrs and 1800hrs. Lots of damage below smoke and blaze of fires all over Singapore and then the deathly silence and ominous quiet after 2030hrs. A dreadful capitulation! UNCONDITIONAL SURRENDER 2030 HOURS: SUNDAY FEBRUARY 1942: SINGAPORE FALLEN.

I wonder what London and the remainder of the world think now of S'pore Fortress. Impregnable! However we did get a good sleep but I would have preferred to hear the crash of guns. The stillness was almost stupefying. The thoughts that come into one's mind are gloomy in the extreme. I never expected to see the day when we would give in to Japan. Never expected to become POW of Japs. May prove an interesting experience but would prefer to forego it.

MONDAY, 16 FEBRUARY 1942

A magnificent sunrise but there is no elation in me. Unconditional surrender! Jap troops move in lorries, our envoys have gone out to meet Japs at 0700hrs and some details were arranged. One is almost dazed by the suddenness of this capitulation. How triumphant the Japs must have felt as they entered 'impregnable Singapore'.

Once the surrender was complete the post mortems began. How could such a powerful fortress have fallen so quickly? T. Kitching was the chief surveyor of Singapore during the campaign and recorded his reasons for the fall of the city:

MONDAY, 16 FEBRUARY 1942

So the 'Fortress' of Singapore has fallen in one week! It all seems like a dream. Surely shelling the Town, and the damage to the water supply, was foreseen once they were on the Island – or even from Johore. And if we surrendered on that account, then why did Percival make that confident statement on Feb. 7, and Paterson [ADC to General Percival] on Feb. 9?

We had no 'back door' defence at all: the military pundits must have thought we could stop an attack down the Peninsula. They may have counted on Siamese help – Sir Josiah Crosby up in Bangkok was entirely deceived – but why blame the Siamese when we could achieve so little, they hadn't a hope and probably knew it . . . Military plans were certainly based on fighting in the north, I know that from the mapping programme. Our front door had marvellous defences, big guns to blow anything out of the water: mines: the most intricate system of barbed wire and other barriers, for 20 miles along the south coast, the beach, the docks, the town. Elaborate arrangements for the evacuation of the civil population from these so-called battle areas – where never a shot was fired in anger! On the Johore side absolutely nothing – so the Japanese attacked from that side. Simple.

Then, of course, a lot of the Indian troops were raw recruits and should never have been sent here. And many of our own were rushed straight into action off the ships, never having seen tropical conditions in their lives. As for the Aussies, with all the good will in the world – the less said the better. An abysmal failure . . . And above all, no air support. No one can say what the outcome might have been if we'd had that. And the effect on the morale of the troops – and the civilian population all over the Peninsula – would have been immense. You could see that on the very rare occasions our planes were visible in the sky, though I never saw a single scrap in the air in spite of constant work on the roof of the Fullerton Building, the finest vantage point in Singapore.

And as it proved, there was far too much mechanical transport – they had only to hop into lorries to 'execute a strategic withdrawal owing to infiltration'. Infiltration! How I grew to hate that word on the wireless. And I don't know yet, and never will understand, why it should be only one side which can infiltrate in a country like Malaya, where in almost any place your range of vision is restricted to a few yards.

Well, surely at any rate the surrender is not unconditional, with our Army practically intact as it appears to be. Present orders for us are to stay where we are.

Towards the end of the siege of Singapore a desperate effort was made to evacuate women and children from the colony, and Miss P. Briggs was one who left on the *Mata Hari* on 12 February, only to be intercepted by a Japanese destroyer:

SUNDAY, 15 FEBRUARY 1942

Captured by the Japanese (The day Singapore fell).

The *Mata Hari*'s maximum speed was 13 knots and her sole means of defence an obsolete gun, so the captain had no option but to surrender to the Jap destroyer. By this time we were near to the island of Banka and slowly moving into Muntok harbour, followed closely by the destroyer. Before we dropped anchor all the charts of the *Mata Hari* were thrown into the sea and the captain ordered that anyone with firearms must throw them overboard. We admired the captain, for he had been up night and day working with a scratch crew, and yet he appeared calm and polite. By the time our ship stopped we found ourselves surrounded by other Jap craft. One Dutch plane flew over us and dropped some bombs nearby, and we saw a British launch try to escape to sea. The small craft was dive-bombed by a Jap plane – it was horrible to watch – the launch zig-zagged trying to dodge the plane, but finally it got a direct hit and we saw the launch sink.

Soon after this the destroyer came alongside and our captain told all the men to go below and the women and children to come up on deck. The Jap naval officer came on board, followed by two sailors carrying swords. Our captain, wearing a spotless jacket, met the Jap officer with a salute. For a few moments there was complete silence, and there was no panic. I remember feeling icy cold in spite of the heat on deck. We heard that all the men were to be taken off the ship that morning and the women and children were to follow in the afternoon. A few of the elderly and wounded men remained with us. The Jap flag was run up, so now we were under The Rising Sun.

Kenneth Brundle, an assistant architect in the Malayan Public Works Department, was evacuated on the 13th on the SS *Kuala*, which was attacked by Japanese aircraft in the Bangka Strait on 14 February:

SATURDAY, 14 FEBRUARY 1942

Conditions on the ship were chaotic with passengers running around like disturbed red ants but they calmed down a little when it appeared that the ship was not about to sink. The ship's crew kept their heads and were throwing overboard rafts and anything which might float. I do not know how long it was before I decided to jump into the sea and swim the quarter mile to shore, but all the women and children had been taken off by lifeboat or rafts. It was after the second air attack on the nearby *Tien Kwang* when the bombs appeared to miss but caught the cliff face nearby causing casualties to those who had reached the shore. Everything that would float including rafts, had been thrown overboard to assist the passengers who had jumped from the ship which was now on fire.

Survivors, clinging to the rafts and floating boxes were at the mercy of the extremely strong current flowing from north to south and I realised that they would unlikely reach Pompong Island. In fact, very few did as most of them were swept away to other islands where they were either captured by the Japanese or rescued and taken to the Indragiri River escape route. I removed my heavy shoes and jumped into the sea – I was not a strong swimmer but took my time swimming into the strong current to maintain my course. Two flights of low flying aircraft appeared overhead and as I watched them I saw the bombs leaving the planes. I instinctively ducked under the water while the bombs were exploding between the *Kuala* and the shore but seemed to be exploding very near to me. These bombs caused many casualties among the swimmers; it occurred to me that the bombs would at least frighten away the sharks!

One could not be amused by anything in this situation but the sight of several swimmers in front of me wearing tin hats struck me as a trifle droll. Another stick of bombs hit the shore almost in front of me – some bombs fell down the face of the cliff smashing heavy pieces of rock which plunged into the sea causing splashes all around me. The shock of it stopped me swimming for a second or two during which time I saw a young RAF lad with his left arm seriously wounded with flesh hanging from the bone. He was holding his injured limb in front of him and was clambering over the rocks looking for somebody to help him.

It would seem that the bombers were aiming at the two ships the *Kuala* and *Tien Kwang* which were still afloat and not deliberately at the swimmers in the sea.

I finally staggered ashore exhausted and squeezed myself into a large fissure in the volcanic rock face having asked a lady swimmer a few feet in front of me whether she was alright. She replied 'Yes' and found somewhere to hide. I looked back to the *Kuala* and heard the cries of survivors still clinging to rafts or swimming in the sea. I think those clinging to rafts realised that they were not going to reach the shore of Pompong Island. Fortunately, there were so many other tiny islands in the Lingga Archipelago that the chances of getting ashore on one of these islands were good and so many survivors did so.

Kenneth Brundle was rescued, evacuated to Sumatra and eventually escaped to Sri Lanka, then known as Ceylon. Another who managed to get away successfully was Gladys Barnes, who left Singapore on the *Empress of Japan* (later renamed the *Empress of Scotland*) on 31 January 1942 bound for Liverpool. In her diary, she records the cramped conditions aboard:

MONDAY, 2 FEBRUARY 1942

Women in every state of undress, and every type of figure. Scene on the troop deck at night: lights shaded by dressing gowns or any suitable garment cast an eerie glow on a scene one can find few words to describe. Women of all sizes and shapes in all types of garments lying on mattresses on the floor, in every conceivable posture – feet stick out from the end of the sheet, grey heads, dark, fair and red heads lie upon the pillows – dresses, underwear, brassières, shoes, suit case, chambers etc. etc., to say nothing of children, lie or hang about the place giving the scene a queer, unreal atmosphere – tragic beyond words in spite of the humour one finds there, for nearly all these women have been used to luxury homes and the help of several servants – one's heart bleeds for them. Queerer scene in morning when all start to dress! Today I saw a brassière and petticoat hanging to dry on a rope skirting the AA gun!! Women and War!! Orchestral balcony occupied as sleeping place by some women.

Some were always going to stay behind. Lieutenant J. Wilson was part
of a group of eight volunteers who operated behind Japanese lines in
Malaya from January to July 1942. Here, in the unit diary, he describes
one of their operations against Japanese communications:

TUESDAY, 20 JANUARY 1942

It was decided to try a roadblock where the road goes over the
railway. (Point B) One tommy-gun (Hardy) with two grenade
throwers (Pelton and Morrison) were to face down the road towards
Seremban, with three tommy-guns (Berwick, Brown, and Wilson)
and a rifle (Wynne, Cubitt was sick with fever), placed on the edge
of the Estate facing the bridge and the road obliquely. A tube bomb,
containing 5lbs of gelignite was to be placed on the bridge with a
trip wire. The first tommy-gun was to open up on the lorry or car
at about 50 yards range, the grenades to be thrown when the lorry
was within range and the rest to come in as required.

Pelton and Morrison went down on the night of the 21st to find
out about Japanese patrols. They returned at midnight reporting no
patrols at all.

On Jan 22nd the party left Camp at 5.00pm, arriving on the
Estate road about 6.00pm where they waited until dusk, and then
moved down to the main road. Before everything was in position, a
car approached and Hardy opened up, but failed to stop the car, the
grenade throwers not being ready no grenades were thrown. The car
went over the bridge, fired a few revolver shots, before disappearing.
While Wynne was fixing the tube bomb, the rest had a discussion
and decided that nothing more could be done that night, Hardy and
Wynne wanted to stay and some time was lost in argument. Japanese
patrols were now approaching from each end of the road, making
owl calls to locate each other; so leaving Hardy and Wynne, the rest
of the party made off down the estate road, another Japanese patrol
was seen coming up the estate road. Waiting about 200 yards up the
path they heard intermittent Japanese rifle fire for about the next
hour, one .303 bullet went over their heads, but there was no further
tommy-gun fire. About 11.00pm it was decided to return to Camp.
Going up the gully south of the main stream, several lights were seen
moving up and down, these proved to be only the Chinese moving

their belongings down to shelters that they had dug in the side of the gully. They were told that they had seen no one, to which they agreed and the party after some difficulty returned to Camp.

The small group were later betrayed and captured by the Japanese, spending the rest of the war in prisoner-of-war camps.

Following the fall of Singapore, Japanese attention turned towards the Indonesian archipelago. By this stage, the Allies had set up a joint command, known as ABDA (American, British, Dutch, Australian) Command, and on 27 February an ABDA naval force under the command of the Dutch Admiral Karel Doorman set sail from Suribaya to attack a Japanese invasion force. Doorman's multinational fleet consisted of two heavy cruisers, HMS *Exeter* and the USS *Houston*, three light cruisers, HMAS *Perth*, HNLMS *De Ruyter* and *Java*, supported by nine destroyers. Ranged against them was a Japanese force under the command of Rear Admiral Takeo Takagi, consisting of two heavy and two light cruisers, supported by fourteen destroyers. The two sides met in the Java Sea on the night of 27/28 February, when the Japanese fleet wore down their opponents, sinking all except four US destroyers. Major Edward Barrett of the US Marine Corps served aboard the USS *Houston* during the Battle of the Java Sea:

FRIDAY, 27 FEBRUARY 1942

Early morning patrol – no contact. In afternoon, naval battle with Japanese landing force. Our forces: *Houston*, HMS *Exeter*, HMAS *Perth*, Dutch cruiser *De Ruyter* (flagship), and Dutch cruiser *Java*, also three British destroyers (*Electra*, *Jupiter* and *Encounter*), two Dutch destroyers, and four US destroyers. Action lasted from about 3.00pm to 6.00pm. We receive two eight-inch shell hits – one of which went through my room and my bunk. *Exeter* badly damaged, *Electra* sunk (broken in two) and one Dutch destroyer sunk. As action ends, at least one Jap heavy cruiser is burning from stem to stern. In the evening, we return (minus *Exeter*) to attempt an attack on the transports. We walk into a submarine and destroyer trap and the *De Ruyter*, *Java* and *Jupiter* are torpedoed and burning fiercely still as we go out of sight.

No hits on us or on *Perth*. Japs used very novel lights on water and plane flares to keep our striking force marked. During day we fired about 600 rounds of 8-inch ammunition.

SATURDAY, 28 FEBRUARY 1942

Entered Batavia Harbor about 4.00pm – Repaired hole in bow and refuelled for dash through Sunda Straits and Indian Ocean. Left Batavia about 7.30pm and ran into Jap landing force at entrance to Sunda Straits about 11.00pm. Fired first shot at 11.10pm. Fired all remaining 5-inch amm. including star shells, and got off about 30 salvos of 8-inch shells. About 11.40pm we get an 8-inch hit on turret No. 2. 'Abandon ship' passes and then retracted. At second passing of 'abandon ship' and the sounding by bugles, I make ready to go over the side. Shell salvo lands between me and water line as Jap destroyers with searchlights glaring close in. I go over the side and join one of the life raft parties. Ship rolls over to starboard and sinks about 12.35am. This is the climax of a month of pure hell and constant fighting for the USS *Houston*. Japs later told us we sank one aircraft carrier, four cruisers, nine destroyers, three transports, and one hospital supply ship that night.

SUNDAY, 1 MARCH 1942

Picked up by Japanese landing boat about 8.00am, after about eight hours in the water. About an hour of this time we were swimming in fuel oil. Commander Galbraith, Ensign J. B. Nelson, and Ensign J. M. Hamill are other officers that came ashore with me. Marines included Sgt. Pryor and PFC Charles. Made to work by Japanese soldiers all day unloading and carrying heavy bundles of landing equipment and supplies. Finally fed by them at evening a snack of hard-tack. Sun burned everyone badly during day because of fuel oil. Officers loaded into troop truck about midnight and driven to town of Serang, Java.

Elsewhere in the Far East the Japanese had invaded the British colony of Burma in December and reinforced this effort towards the end of January, capturing Rangoon on 7 March as the British Burma Army pulled back towards the Indian border. There followed a hellish route march, as the British struggled northwards.

Bombardier Alan Perry served in the 9th Anti-Tank Regiment RA and was caught up in the retreat:

FRIDAY, 31 JULY 1942

Eventually we got everything off and in a week we got slung up to the front. From then on it was a tale of misery and woe. Fortunately for us the Japs had very few tanks at the beginning but this was more than discounted by the lack of RAF. In fact formations of 40 or 50 Jap bombers became fairly common. The RAF were rotten – they allowed themselves to be bombed out of one place after another and at Magwe we passed 22 of our planes burnt out on the ground. After we were driven out of Prome we never saw one of our planes again.

One night we put a road block on and the first vehicle up was a tank. Alf Rowe and Charlie Woodley immediately knocked it for 6 but very shortly afterwards they had to move back as the Jap infantry were creeping up in the trees. George Beddard and Hepplestone were captured but got away when Alf Rowe opened fire again as all the Japs lay down. 'Hep' suffered from shock and we have not seen him since. A day or two later Alf Rowe was killed and Tom Range got a lump of shrapnel in his back from a bomb, but he is back with us again. Since, whom you may remember was the first casualty in the old 73rd in the desert, was killed and Freddie Kirkham on Johnny Davies' gun was killed too. Eventually we got pushed right back to the river Chindwin and when we went to cross it early in the morning the Japs were there. Major Mackintosh nearly caught a basinful but got away with it. When night fell we did a forced march over the mountains after destroying all the tanks and guns etc and crossed higher up.

After that it was just a case of sticking it. We had about 200 miles to go into India which we did by marching and riding. It was very hot, food was bad as was the water and everybody was ill with malaria, cholera, dysentery or enteric. At length we reached a point known as dysentery hill and there I went sick with dysentery after reaching the fine total of 22 shits in 18 hours – not bad.

4. Commando Raids

Although the British were suffering catastrophes in their attempts to keep control of their colonies in the Far East in the face of the Japanese onslaught, back in Europe they were having more success at carrying out raids on occupied Europe. Ever since they had been driven from the Continent in 1940, British Commandos and other units had carried out numerous raids against German installations and positions. The first was Operation *Collar* on the night of 24/25 June 1940, a poorly executed seaborne raid on Boulogne.

In March 1941, two Special Service Battalions carried out Operation *Claymore*, a large-scale attack on the Lofoten Islands off the coast of Norway. Robert Meadows was a chief petty officer in the Landing Ship Infantry (Medium) HMS *Princess Beatrix*, which was one of the vessels used to carry the Commandos to the operation:

SATURDAY, 1 MARCH 1941

Officer i/c No.3 Unit Brigadier Durnford-Slater. He told our skipper (Joe Brunton) he was very seasick on our first day at sea. Joe told him to drink a bottle of beer each morning plus cheese and pickled onions which apparently proved very effective!

We rolled heavily during the first part of our journey north but after passing into the Arctic Circle it was quite warm for the time of the year. We arrived at Stamsund at 4am March 4th and passed a number of fishing boats leaving harbour. When they realised we were British they gave us a cheer of welcome and hoisted Norwegian flags on their boats. Destroyer *Somali* sighted an armed German trawler which she promptly sunk by gunfire. When the Commandos landed ashore they found no German soldiers in the town but some Gestapo and German businessmen. Several of the former were rounded up and sent back to the ship as prisoners. A Sub. Lieut. went into the local post office and despatched the following telegram to Hitler – 'You said in your last speech that German troops would meet the English wherever they landed (stop) Where are your troops?' Result of this first raid on enemy occupied territory was highly successful, 18 factories being destroyed, 20 thousand tons of shipping destroyed and nearly one million tons of oil and petrol went up in smoke. In addition 216 prisoners plus 60 Quislings were taken. Also maps, code systems and valuable documents seized. Before we left on our return trip home some 300 loyal Norwegians volunteered to leave with us to carry on their country's fight against the common enemy. The journey back to Scapa Flow was uneventful except that shortly after leaving the Islands an enemy recon. plane passed overhead but no attack developed. Eventually we reached Gourock in the Firth of Clyde safely. On our arrival Sir Roger Keyes greeted both ships and expressed his delight with the whole successful operation, after which the Commandos left the ship together with the Norwegian volunteers and prisoners.

Emboldened by the success of such operations, the raids became organised on a larger scale, none more so than the attack on the port facilities at St Nazaire in March 1942. The dock here was the only one outside Germany large enough to accommodate the German battleship *Tirpitz*, so it was vital that it was put out of action. Operation *Chariot* saw a flotilla of small ships loaded with Commandos storm the port, with the explosive-filled HMS *Campbeltown* putting the dry dock out of operation for the remainder of the war. Buster Woodiwiss served as a corporal with No. 2 Commando during the raid:

Thursday, 26 March 1942

On 26th March 1942, before sunrise, we were aboard the old American destroyer USS *Buchanan* now renamed as HMS *Campbeltown*. Our troop of Commandos had their heads down as we tore up the river Loire with the German shore and ship guns pouring shell and shot into us and into the flimsy wooden-hulled motor gun boats which accompanied us. In spite of heavy hits and fires onboard, we hit the great dock gates at St Nazaire at full speed, embedding the bows into and over the gates. The concrete reinforced bows hid a secret. They concealed 24 depth charges containing 8,500 pounds of high explosive placed into a steel tank and set over the fuel tanks aft of the forward gun turret.

I was the first man ashore with my comrades close behind.

Specialist demolition units fanned out to place explosives in the winding house and pump houses which controlled the great caissons and the water levels in the dry dock which had been for the *Normandie* [a French ocean liner] and was capable of taking the German pocket battleships. My job was to keep the defending German forces off the demolition teams then after the charges had been placed, we carried out the next part of our operation which was to get out of the battle zone.

With most of the motor boats damaged or sunk, we aimed to walk out to Spain but at the town outskirts, we were beset by superior numbers of German forces and in the end, out of ammunition we had to surrender. By now, the demolition charges had all gone off and put the dockside engine houses out of action, for a long time as it happened. Eight hours later, there was a terrific explosion as the *Cambeltown* blew up killing hundreds of German military and technical personnel who were examining the ship and inflicting severe damage to the great dock gates which remained inoperative for the rest of the war.

Special forces of various sorts also flourished in the Western Desert, and none proved more successful than the Long Range Desert Group (LRDG), whose vehicles patrolled the desert to the flank of the Allied and Axis armies, reporting enemy movement and carrying out raids as required.

Major Jean Caneri, a Frenchman, served with the LRDG and then in No. 1 Demolition Squadron (which was known as Popski's Private Army after its commander, a Belgian emigré of Russian extraction called Vladimir Peniakoff) throughout North Africa and Italy. Here he records the measures taken when spotted by enemy aircraft:

ANTI-AIRCRAFT MEASURES

When an enemy aircraft is spotted – the patrol did not stop – She continues to advance as if all was OK – When the enemy plane is over their head they even wave with the hand.

If the bad boy dropped bombs they scattered at once.

If he dive bombs them, the man who is in the back of the truck give orders to the driver 'right' 'left' – The car is turning right angle of full speed – with that procedure the LRDG had avoid till now a direct hit.

If the ground is suitable and if the C/O thinks that they have seen the plane before having been spotted they stopped and hid themselves.

Cyril Richardson served in G1 Patrol of the LRDG, while on attachment from the 3rd Battalion Coldstream Guards, and describes being under aerial assault while on patrol in the desert:

DECEMBER 1941

On checking up our course the navigator found we had come to within three or four miles of Msus, a fort in the hands of the Italians. But it was too late then, for just at that moment we spotted a Italian plane coming in our direction from the fort. He spotted us, and bombed and machine-gunned us for a few minutes, but it was rather a big plane and could not manoeuvre about enough to do us any harm. And as soon as we opened up on him he flew off. Actually I think he was hit but as we did not bring him down we cannot say. When we had collected together again we continued on our way. But not for long: About four o'clock we had stopped to check our course again when from our right we saw diving straight for us another plane. The recognition signal for our planes was at the time that they should fly with their wheels down. Well we were happy this one had its wheels down alright. They were almost touching the ground, but we soon learnt it was not one of our own but a Ju 87 out for a bit of fun. We split up as soon as he opened up on us, going in all directions. Being the leading truck he gave us all his attention for about ten minutes, the longest ten minutes I have ever spent in my life. We twisted and turned all over the desert dodging his bursts of lead. I got a few shots off at him before the gun mounting broke and my Vickers went flying over the side of the truck. He then left us alone and concentrated on the rest, dive bombing at his leisure. He kept us busy for at least half an hour and when he had gone it took us nearly two hours to find each other. We carried on until about nine o'clock that night, and it was dark when we arrived at our meeting place . . .

The next day we had quite a few planes flying around but they failed to spot us. It was just after four o'clock when we left the wadi the next night bound this time for a spot in the road further south. The sun had just set when we pulled up behind a little hillock no more than twenty five yards from the road. We could hear the drivers singing we were that close. We decided this time on a ground action. So we mounted the guns along the top of the ridge and waited for a suitable target. The vehicles tonight were even at further intervals than the previous night. So we picked on a big oil tanker and trailer and let him have it good. We waited for a while hoping for another customer but all traffic stopped. They must have heard or seen the firing because nothing else came our way. So we once more did a flit into the night.

5. British Disaster at Gazala

Following the *Crusader* offensive in late 1941, the British drove Rommel and his forces as far back as El Agheila. However, he did not stop there for long, and by the end of January 1942 he was on the attack once more, driving the British back past Benghazi and Derna to a position known as the Gazala Line, stretching from Gazala on the coast to Bir Hacheim in the desert, where the British were grouped in defensive strongpoints known as boxes. At this point both sides settled down into fixed positions and built up their strength for the offensive to come. In the event, Rommel managed to launch his offensive first, sending a diversionary attack to the north of the British line while leading the bulk of the Panzerarmee Afrika to the south of the British position.

Peter Lovett was a signalman attached to 50th Division, part of XIII Corps, holding positions towards the northern end of the Gazala Line. Here he records his impression of the early days of the attack launched by Rommel on 26 May:

WEDNESDAY, 27 MAY 1942

50 Div 'flaps'! Heavy bombing and some machine-gunning overnight – the prelude to a Jerry attack. Away about 12 in desert convoy

pushing back well behind El Adem towards the east. Literally hundreds of lorries were all streaking back across the desert, and in the opposite direction the huge tanks of 7 Armoured Division came charging forward to the attack. The big American tanks look as though nothing could stop them; a large gun points to the fore and I gather they are driven by a 1,200hp radial aero-engine. Settle down for the night somewhere in the blue and hear that a German attack with 250 tanks had been made since this morning. When we beat it from Div position they were only two miles away, over the escarpment! What will tomorrow hold? The small smoking 'bomblets' which had been dropping on the escarpment just above us were tank mortars according to griff [rumour]. Enjoyed driving the new truck.

THURSDAY, 28 MAY 1942

Up at 5 – heavy bombing and machine-gunning in the distance all night – vehicles lined up ready for moving off at 'first light'. By the light of a lugubrious morning sun we pushed slowly eastward for about two hours and halted at a new position on a flat part of the desert somewhere towards Gambut aerodrome. I become a busy man on these 'do's' – batteries run down on continuous watch almost as soon as they can be charged – and the truck is badly in need of maintenance. We hear of a big tank-battle going on about Bir Hacheim south of Sidi Rezegh and not far from our old position – some of our chaps who dropped out of convoy or got lost are believed to be captured.

Rommel was able to move his armoured units to the centre of the British line and, having beaten off a number of British counter-attacks, finally managed to reduce the Free French 'box' of Bir Hacheim to the south following a week of heavy fighting.

Reg Crimp was serving with the 2nd Battalion Rifle Brigade and witnessed the end of the Free French position:

WEDNESDAY, 10 JUNE 1942

Tonight is the end of Bir Hacheim.

At a conference before sunset the Company Commander tells us we're going to give covering fire, during the following hours of darkness, to the Free French forces breaking out. The operation will be extremely tricky, as the Free French have decided to bring out all their guns and transport of several hundred vehicles. The whole garrison, many thousands strong, will evacuate their positions in stages throughout the night. There's no alternative, as the Box has become untenable.

Immediately after dark the Company moves a few miles west and takes up position to the southwest for the Bir. Already white star-shells are being thrown up by the enemy. Apparently there's one exit from the Box and Jerry's placed himself right across it. The night is clear, but with no moon.

Soon after ten o'clock the sharp rattle of an M/G burst is heard, and from now on it's bedlam: rat-tatting of machine-guns, crashing of mortars, hoarse rumbling of shells, white, red and green lights climbing at all angles into the sky, streams of white and yellow tracer playing over the horizon, sprouting red glows, and all the while the drone and surge of vehicle engines. Cabbett and I, on listening-post a short distance forward of the section position, lie on our bellies and think what an inferno the Frenchmen are going through. Now and then we hear a truck approaching, but the sound invariably recedes. Sometimes we imagine we can hear voices, and once Cabbett leaps up to report the footfalls of a patrol coming nearer. But whoever it is, Frenchmen or Jerry or English, they give us the go-by. It's only in the heavy mist before dawn that the commotion dies down.

THURSDAY, 11 JUNE 1942

When there's sufficient light, single men and small bands approach furtively, and recognising, join us. They're haggard, unshaven, tattered and tired, but one after another, on the instinct of discipline, gripping weapons and equipment, they fall into rank. Some are quite young, others hardened old legionnaires. One youth, numb with fatigue, begs his warrant-officer for permission to go back for his rifle which he lost when his truck got hit.

When the mist clears, shells begin falling near by. As we move to quieter quarters, out of the patches of scrub rise groups of Frenchmen who clamber aboard our trucks. We take them back to a batch of 3-tonners, which appear to be waiting for them. Their warrant-officer thanks us politely for our help.

With his right flank secure to the south, Rommel resumed his advance in the centre, leading to a massed armoured battle on 12/13 June in which the British armoured divisions and brigades were decisively defeated. Robin Dunn wrote in his diary of his experiences of his role in the battle, where he served with 11th Honourable Artillery Company, part of 2nd Armoured Brigade Group:

WEDNESDAY, 27 MAY 1942

It seemed that nothing could live in that mass corruption, but still the tracer shell came flying from the enemy position. We seemed to be irresistible. On every side the tanks were moving forward. Behind us our own guns barked and the shells whistled overhead. The tracer flying among us seemed to have no effect. We were filled with a feeling of invulnerability and I had to reprimand my crew for opening the front visor to get a better view. By now several lorries were burning on the enemy position and the general mass of transport was hurrying away from us. Suddenly a few figures appeared out of the smoke with their hands up and their helmets off. We were then about 800 yards from the guns. The squadron I was with were ordered to go in among the guns. Off we went, the BESA machine guns stuttering and chattering as the cruisers raced for the guns. They went straight through them and then away in a right handed semi-circle among the transport behind, while the Grants halted on the position and began to fire at the guns behind. The German gunners now left their guns and slit trenches and came shambling through our tanks with their hands up and their shoulders bent looking furtively about them. I was struck by how old many of them were and how pale faced. They could not have been long in the desert sun. Meanwhile we were being met by an accurate fire from a second position behind the first, and I could see the Boche gunners feverishly serving their guns. I at once ranged my gun on to them, but they were very determined and continued to hold up any further advance. By this time the Grants had run out of ammunition and were withdrawn behind a small ridge to replenish. I found myself alone on the captured enemy position, but was so engrossed in shooting at the enemy guns and transport which were wonderful targets, that I did not realise that I was being sniped by an anti-tank gun until two rounds fell just in front of the tank. I ordered the driver to reverse a few yards and lock over so as to avoid the next round, but it was too late. The round hit the tank, penetrated the front armour and wounded my wireless operator in the face. I accordingly asked permission to withdraw and took him back to the nearest troop of guns, which had been moved close up behind us. We lifted him out, poor lad, he was unconscious and bleeding a lot, but I gather is now all right. I split a couple of bottles of beer with the other two members of the crew and we went back again to the firing line.

The destruction of the Allied armour left the infantry in their isolated defensive boxes exposed and liable to be defeated in detail by Rommel's armoured forces. Laurie Phillips served with 1st Battalion The Rifle Brigade, an anti-tank gun unit, and recalls trying to hold off the German armour during the retreat:

FRIDAY, 12 JUNE 1942

Next day we tried to help the Guards withstand heavy attacks on their box, but by evening our three armoured brigades had lost 105 tanks in two days, and had only 50 left between them. The following morning about 20 German tanks arrived with breakfast, but instead of coming close enough for us to open up, they sat back and engaged us with HE and machine guns, and we had another very sticky withdrawal – one of our portees had a direct hit, but they managed to get the gun away with a three-tonner. We moved north to the minefield running north from Acroma, here we had to make a 'last stand' because beyond the minefield and below the escarpment was the coast road, along which the 1st South African Division were streaming, having been ordered (much to their disgust, as they had hardly been engaged during the past three weeks) to evacuate the Gazala position and withdraw through Tobruk to the Egyptian frontier, and they needed the rest of the day and the night to get clear. Our platoon was very lucky here, because the German attack just missed us and fell on the rest of the Company. Half of the 6 and the whole of 7 and 8 Platoons, having first knocked out a few tanks, were overrun and lost all ten guns. A handful of the 60–70 in the crews got away on two portees but the rest were missing – most of them captured. That night we were able to start getting away, but there was a problem. Apart from having to gap the minefield behind us, the escarpment was negotiable for vehicles only in one or two places. Eventually a way was found, and by morning we had made our way down to the road, where we joined a nose-to-tail procession with the South Africans – luckily we were only bombed once, and only a few shells came over.

This retreat rapidly risked turning into a rout, as Eighth Army poured back from the now-shattered Gazala Line towards the Egyptian border. Peter Lovett captures some of the flavour of the retreat in his diary:

Sunday, 14 June 1942

We moved off later in the morning, our wireless-truck following the major in his staff-car; he tore hell-for-leather along the track and climbed the escarpment by a fearfully steep and rocky way. The Div was finally planted right by the harbour in Tobruk, well positioned for bombing and shrapnel from the heavy AA fire, we thought of sleeping under the over-turned chassis of a wrecked lorry, but after a brief stay of three hours only – we were out! The road out of Tobruk and the desert on either side were packed tight with vehicles of every kind, tanks, Bren-carriers, Scammell transporters, big trucks, worming among themselves in attempt to get away while harassed Redcaps tried to regulate them. It was a mass exodus from Tobruk, so we concluded that the battle round Bir Hacheim and El Adem was not going so well. We pushed on nose-to-tail for miles and then plunged across the blue, through evening, through twilight and well into darkness right till 11.30pm. By then we estimated we were east of Gambut. Driving blindly forward following the dark shape of the truck in front across unknown ground was a ghastly experience – then I stalled the engine negotiating a steep embankment over the railway and it wouldn't re-start for some time. We sank down worn out for a kip till 5am.

Monday, 15 June 1942

Off once again as soon as glum dawn broke over the desert. The character of the land has changed vastly, there are now long bald stretches of stony sand level enough for speeding, and before long we were passing through Gap H over the 'wire' and were once more in Egypt.

We hear on the wireless of the fall of Tobruk . . . A dismal reflection that the position is now worse than it has ever been. Why? Have we no genii like Rommel or can't we get the men and materials up fast enough? 50 Division is now sadly depleted, hardly a brigade is anything like up to strength, vehicles are in a shockingly unreliable state (the petrol-truck goes up in flames tonight, so that's one less). Discovered I had lost all my army kit in my kit-bag which must have fallen off the truck in that hell-for-leather ride.

Again, in the absence of the armour it was left to the anti-tank guns of units such as Sergeant Hwyel 'Stalky' Francis's 95th Anti-Tank Regiment to hold up the German advance and allow the Eighth Army to retreat:

Wednesday, 17 June 1942

Taking up our task to protect any escaping British Troops, we occasionally tossed round over to our parallel ridge and supported our lads escaping . . . We went forward a couple of miles until we saw a couple of tanks on our parallel ridge. The enemy tossed a round or two towards Atherton's portee . . . I yelled for absolutely no movement. We were playing 'cowboys and Indians' and did nothing but skulk and watch for the movement on the ridge on the other side. Some time later some one hissed that 'they' were on the other side. I had been looking carefully at the ridge upon which we were and prepared our possible safe withdrawal. An enemy column were moving and were fairly clear that they were several dozen troops and lorries.

'Two anti tank guns. Stand to. One thousand, lay on right gun. Fire. <u>Up four hundred. Left ten degrees. Repeat.</u>' Our few shots landed in the general area and one lorry burst into fire. I yelled out, 'Drive left and go like hell'. It appeared that the gun crew and the three Murattees dropped on to the gun platform. The jumping portee swung and raced like hell but within a few hundred yards the driver screamed that the portee was punctured. Naturally I directed to my driver to carry out my order and drive me home. In spite of my oaths and threats the driver said the portee was dead. It seemed the only hope was to yell, so I yelled, 'Action left'.

The old portee wheezed around until the gun faced the enemy. I hollered for the crew and guests to slip to the floor and keep quiet. I told the crew to help the driver to change the wheel. Meanwhile I lay down and spied at the enemy on the other ridge. I realised that the enemy had opened up on a wreck a couple of hundred yards away from us. We were of course covered by the blinding sun. I realised the enemy thought that the old wrecked ambulance was really us and tossed all sorts of nastiness towards the poor old ambulance. I yelled out enthusiasm for the wheel changing. A general peon [sic] of thanks arose from the crew etc and especially from me.

The problem now puts me in my usual position to consider whether to stay or to move. I have considered on many moments that the best thing to do at any dangerous time, is to leave the spot in which I am in danger. I have no doubts whatsoever. That is exactly what I will do. I nearly whispered that the crew must move very slowly so that no obvious movement will be noticed by me or the enemy. The driver was ordered to slip into our trustworthy portee. The layer was told to lay on the last flash we noticed at 1,500yds, and when I order, fire five rounds within five seconds. I hissed get the ammo in and out in five secs. Leave where our spare wheel is. Murattees to lie flat on top. Move like mice.

'Go'. Everyone was up and silent. I called out clearly 'Fire. Start. Two, three, four, fire, Move.' Like a dream, the portee hummed like a swan and we took off. Each undulation of the ground was like a fairground experience. Looking back in every direction I was sure to be safe. 'OK ease off a little.' In due course we met up with the other portee and the OP who gave no friendly call.

By the 17th, Panzerarmee Afrika had surrounded the port of Tobruk. There was to be no long siege this time. The defences had been allowed to fall into disrepair and the defenders were off balance. On the 20th, the Afrika Korps achieved a breakthrough and the South African commander surrendered Tobruk on 21 June with 35,000 soldiers, mostly South African, going into captivity. With the port in his hands, Rommel urged his troops onwards to the border with Egypt.

By this stage in the battle, Auchinleck had relieved Eighth Army's commander, General Ritchie, and taken direct control of the battle himself, ordering Eighth Army to make a stand in the Mersa Matruh defensive position on the Egyptian border. Jim Brooks of the 211th Battery, 64th Medium Regiment RA, wrote of this time:

FRIDAY, 12 FEBRUARY 1943

On the 22nd we cleared out and only just in time too, we were nearly cut off then. From there we went to a gun position in Mersa Matruh on the coast, but we were only there a day, we moved up again, then back, and eventually arrived at a position the other side of Mersa on the 28th. By now we realised the Germans were all around us, we were firing due east, and that was the way back, anyway we fired all day and got plenty back, sustaining a couple of casualties. As soon as it got dark we moved out, and formed up into a column. There was a brilliant moon up and it was as light as day, and so we started off. What a nightmare ride that was, shelling and machine gunning from all sides, trucks blowing up all around us, when we eventually got clear and stopped for a breather, there was only three guns and a small truck left, we didn't know what had happened to the others. We carried on all through that night dodging Jerry tanks and patrols, we met one of our officers and he brought us to the Regiment's rendezvous. We were the first of the Regiment to arrive, and we began to wonder where the rest were. During this withdrawal or should I say stampede, we lived like lords . . . Service Corps food dumps were left and we simply went and helped ourselves, consequently every lorry was loaded up with beer, tinned fruit, fags, and sweets, the Jerrys must have done well out of us. I won't tell you how many men, trucks and guns we lost, I doubt whether the censor would pass it. It was a big loss anyway.

With the Matruh position given up by the 28th, there were few positions left to hold on to before the major Egyptian population centres of Alexandria and Cairo came under threat. Auchinleck again ordered Eighth Army to consolidate in the last of these positions, around a small railway station called El Alamein. Bert Fisher served in the 83rd Battery, 16th LAA Regiment RA, providing air defence for RAF bases, and wrote of this final retreat:

SUNDAY, 28 JUNE 1942

At about 10am on the 28th June (Sunday) we were told to pack up and be ready to leave in ten minutes. Well we loaded up, but not exactly in ten minutes. At roughly 2pm we were about to move off, so we left behind fires all over the place of what we had to leave behind. We then proceeded to the road, but, much to our surprise, instead of going East, we turned West. However, we only went two miles to one of our Troops, and waited. Our role, apparently, was to guard the Landing Grounds [LG] until the last plane had left. Later, we were informed we would not leave Daba until the following day. That night the Germans came over and dropped many land-flares and bombs, but at a distance from us. Reports came through that the tanks had reached Fuka (about 23 miles west of Daba), then they were supposed to be only seven miles away, whilst others were to the south of us. The Troops were then ordered up the road to take up anti-tank positions. We did not see them again that night. Meanwhile, we were in slit trenches with loaded rifles (God knows what we would have done had Fritz turned up in tanks)! Our feelings were rather mixed, and I really cannot express them, but we were going to get a few Germans before they got us (perhaps). In the middle of all this we had a good laugh at the expense of the driver of 'Q' lorry. Several Bren Gun Carriers came along the road from

Daba, and stopped on the road near where we were. Of course, we
didn't know who they were, and they were in a similar position. It
so happened that the driver of Q's lorry was in the cabin when the
Bren Gun Carriers decided to deploy, and one of them came alongside
his vehicle and asked whether anyone was there. This driver of ours
happened to have an attack of nerves then, so jumped out of the
opposite side door and took about two leaps and landed in our slit
trench, his rifle preceding him. It was several minutes before we could
get anything out of him (he naturally stutters), but when we did, he
said he thought they were Germans speaking good English. They
turned out to be New Zealanders looking for an Officer to take them
up and meet the Germans. It was a good laugh and we felt okay,
having got some rum out of the stores that were left behind. The
next morning (29th June 1942) we were just going to have a cup of
tea and a sausage, when we were told we had to move, so we got our
tea and sausage as we passed the cook's lorry. In the meantime, there
was a terrific explosion and machine-gunning on the LG. On this
particular morning there was a heavy mist which made it impossible
to see more than a few yards. Of course, for the moment we thought
Jerry had arrived, but it so happened that they were blowing up the
crashed aircraft however, we didn't go far, only to the railway line,
and then stopped. Suddenly, through the mist, we heard a very heavy
tank coming towards us which eventually stopped on the other side
of the railway line. This turned out to be one of ours. It was evident
that the occupants had been in the desert for some time, as one of
them came out of the turret, and, although his face was covered in
a thick layer of dust, he still had a cheery smile. Shortly afterwards
we shifted to the roadside and then waited several hours. At about
3pm the guns turned up again, and we then formed a Regimental
convoy and proceeded in the direction of Alamein at about 3.30pm.
Really, a convoy such as ours was a grand target for enemy aircraft,
but none came over. After travelling 23 miles east, a chap from a
wireless truck yelled for us from the roadside that the Germans had
just then made contact with the road at El Daba – about an hour had
elapsed – so we were lucky. It was a wonderful sight, and gave us a
queer feeling, to see the stuff at Alamein as we crossed through into
our lines, and as we did, there was General Auchinleck, sat upon a

truck and he gave us a cheerful smile and wave. We came through without the loss of a gun or vehicle.

Gazala had been a profound defeat for the British, and especially their armoured forces. Robin Dunn reflected after the battle on the reasons for the Germans' superiority:

FRIDAY, 12 JUNE 1942

Such was the battle of Point 69, June 12th. Before it we had all been hopeful of destroying the enemy's armour and thereby regaining the initiative. Thereafter it seemed to all of us that only a miracle could prevent a withdrawal to the wire. We had suffered heavy losses, the enemy's had been comparatively light and we were in danger of being completely surrounded.

Our tank crews had for two years been fighting an enemy better equipped than themselves in tanks better armoured and, more importantly, with longer range guns. This inequality was too much for even the finest units. The first time they met the Germans they would go in with tremendous dash and courage, and very few of them would come out. One by one the morale of these proud regiments was broken. The Army Tank Brigade when they were thrown against 88 millimetres in the frontal attack on Halfaya in June 1941. The 4th Armoured Brigade in the ding dong battle of Sidi Rezegh, the 22nd Armoured Brigade at El Gubi and Agedabia. The 2nd Armoured Brigade after their mishandling in January 1942 and at the first battle of Knightsbridge. It was more than flesh and blood and nerves could stand, always to be asked to fight at such fearful odds. And whatever Ministers may say they were fearful odds. So they had lost their dash. The tanks, designed to be used offensively and to seize the initiative, were allowed to sit inactive in Battle Positions while the enemy manoeuvred around them and retained the initiative.

Cruiser tanks were allowed to sit out of range without firing a shot, instead of being used as destroyers in a Naval battle. That is the first and most important reason why we lost the battle.

Second was the amazing adaptability of the Germans. The Grant, although not the complete answer to the Mark III–Mark IV combination, was a very fine tank. It dominated the battlefield in the first few days. At once the Germans devised a means of beating this tank which was so much more formidable than anything they had had to face before. They used their 88 millimetres offensively in close co-operation with their tanks, which by their superior range could drive back the Grants. They even mounted some of their 88 millimetres on tanks. Compare this with the British government which allows the bulk of its Armoured Corps to be equipped with tanks mounting 2-pounder guns in June 1942, whereas in June 1940 the 10th Hussars had reported that 2-pounders had not pierced the armour of Mark III tanks.

Finally compare the leadership of the two armies. Compare the vacillation and hesitation before the attack on Aslag with Rommel's brilliant move to the south after that attack had gone in, which cut off almost all the attacking force. British soldiers will fight today as well as they fought at Agincourt or Blenheim or Waterloo or Ypres, provided they are well led. But without inspired leadership, personal leadership on the field of battle, they are useless. That inspired leadership was sadly lacking in the 8th Army in June 1942.

When I am asked why the great tank battle on June 12th was lost I say 'Because the enemy had higher morale, and was in better tanks better handled'. Surely adequate reason.

6. The Convoy Battles

One of the reasons that Rommel was able to launch his offensive on the British position at Gazala was that he was getting increasingly regular supply convoys through to him due to increased pressure on the island of Malta by the aircraft of the Italian and German air forces, which greatly reduced its effectiveness as an offensive base against German shipping. It was vital that the Royal Navy force convoys through to the island, not only to re-equip it with the fighters and ammunition it needed to defend itself and conduct operations, but also to provide the vital food and fuel supplies to keep the population going. The largest and most important of these convoys was codenamed *Pedestal* and was launched on 13 August 1942 on a vast scale, with the escort group consisting of two battleships, three aircraft carriers with seventy-two aircraft, seven cruisers and thirty-one destroyers. All these naval vessels were there to escort 14 merchant ships.

George Blundell was the executive officer of the battleship HMS *Nelson*, which was the flagship of Force H in the Mediterranean and formed part of the escort for the convoy:

MONDAY, 3 AUGUST 1942

At 1000hrs on Monday 3rd August we rendezvoused with our convoy of 14 ships, some of them old friends, *Empire Hope, Dorset, Waimarama, Brisbane Star,* with the Commodore in *Port Chalmers, Almeira Lykers, Santa Eliza, Wairanga, Rochester Castle,* the tanker *Ohio, Clan Ferguson* and *Glenorchy. Nigeria* and *Kenya* are with them, and *Nigeria* flies the flag of C.S.10 who is H. M. Burrough. *Kenya* is painted pink! . . .

I read the orders for the operation which is called 'Pedestal', or for short 'Ped'. It makes me sweat reading the bit about the poor convoy getting through the last bit. Otherwise it is just one of our usual club runs through the Med, leaving the poor blighters at the Skerki Channel. The last party that tried it got rather badly beaten up, and, I suppose, this time we are doubling our stakes for we have two battleships and three aircraft carriers, and a host of destroyers, not to mention the 14 merchantmen.

SUNDAY, 9 AUGUST 1942

We looked quite a formidable force today and had the inspiring sight of five aircraft carriers together, something I've never seen at sea before: *Eagle, Argus, Furious, Indomitable* and *Victorious. Argus,* the smallest and oldest is always affectionately called 'The Ditty Box'. All the forenoon they carried out 'Fighter Direction' and at 1700hrs they did dummy attacks on us, after which a 'recognition' fly past to show us the types. There were 'Albacores', 'Martlets', 'Hurricanes', 'Fulmars', and one 'Hudson' from Gib. Our fighters have a yellow front to their wings and the tail fin is painted yellow.

TUESDAY 11, WEDNESDAY 12, THURSDAY 13, FRIDAY 14 . . .

So much happened during these days and the Commander's life in a ship like this is so busy that it is impossible to do much writing. And what a tragic failure the convoy has been! Nine ships out of the fourteen lost and great damage and loss to warships. The first terrible happening occurred about 1315hrs on Tuesday. A submarine got inside the screen and the first anyone knew about it was to see the *Eagle* listing over to starboard as far as her upper, or flight, deck. No noise, nothing was heard. One moment there was a serene blue sea with peaceful ships and hardly a cloud in the sky or on one's mind. Next moment there were some billows of smoke from *Eagle*, mostly funnel gas, I thought, and she had 'gone' in 8 minutes. I've never before seen such a thing. It makes one tremble. If anyone took a good film of it, it should be shown throughout the Country and especially to the Director of Naval Construction and his department. She rolled over bottom up and left her bow momentarily jutting up into the air, before plunging. One couldn't believe that was the *Eagle*, or had been the *Eagle*. We felt there would be few survivors. I remember thinking of the trapped men. I saw Skinner, the constructor, looking like a man who'd seen a horrible nightmare; he was sweating and white and I heard him say 'They couldn't have had anything closed' . . .

That night I was planning to give a final 'pep' talk to the ship's company, but it was not to be, for at 2030hrs we sounded off 'The Alarm to Arms', followed shortly by the alarm rattlers. Then followed two of the most exciting hours of my life. At about 2100hrs we were missed by two torpedoes as near as any ship can ever have been; one passed for'ard – its bubble track actually went under us – and the other passed aft. The track seemed to give a cant towards the stern about 500 yards off and it can hardly have missed us by more than a few feet. Bombs fell all over the place, and after one 'blue' turn to port, a big bomb fell dead between *Rodney* and ourselves. When it got darkish about 2115hrs or 2100hrs, the barrage put up by the fleet and its screen was aesthetically one of the weirdest and most wonderful and beautiful I have even seen. People who had been up on the SP deck and seen it all had a look on their faces as if they'd seen a vision – the sort of look a man would have on his face just after he'd looked on the Almighty.

It was the purple sea and the black sky, and the Red in the West, and the pearls and rubies of the tracer necklaces, and the lurid bursts in the sky, and the dark little ships putting up this miracle display . . .

Just after 7 . . . there was fierce air attack. I counted about 13 torpedo planes coming in on the starbd. bow, but they were beaten off by our 16-inch barrage. This action plainly shows that accurate barrage fire is <u>the</u> answer to the Italian methods of delivering torpedo plane attacks. But just after 7 about 14 Stukas caught the *Indomitable* just at the wrong angle, coming down on her out of the sun.

Indomitable completely disappeared, for all we saw of her for minutes was just columns of spray. Finally the maelstrom subsided and there was *Indom*. Still there, but blazing both for'ard and aft of the monkey island with great columns of smoke pouring from her flight deck.

Nelson and *Rodney* were ordered to leave the convoy and turn back to shield her as the Admiral feared torpedo planes would try to finish her off. So we said 'goodbye' to the convoy and shortly after we left them they got beaten up badly – it's a pity we couldn't have stayed on a little longer.

Edward Venn served as a telegraphist in the *Indomitable* that was so badly damaged during Operation *Pedestal*:

Wednesday, 12 August 1942

Raiders about. Submarine depth charged by destroyer. Sub came up and was shelled and rammed by destroyer. Quiet in afternoon but our fighters were very busy breaking up raids. Big raid by torpedo and dive bombers at 1850hrs. Ship hit by three bombs, three near misses. Pretty extensive damage. One on A turret killing most of crew. Destroyed forward lift and big mass of side of ship. Hole big enough to drive double decker bus through. Another bomb put aft lift out of action. Destroyed and set fire to stores and cabins aft. Third struck ward room. Fires were soon under control.

Everyone prayed for nightfall. Luckily engines were unaffected so we were able to get out of sight of land by morning in company with *Nelson* and *Rodney*. Destroyers and cruisers escort. Afraid convoy were badly mauled after we left them.

HMS *Manchester* sunk also *Cairo*, *Kenya* mined.
Arrived at Gibraltar. Aug 14th.

Christopher Gould served aboard the destroyer HMS *Lightning* and witnessed the loss of the *Eagle* and the damage to *Indomitable*. He describes the action in a letter to his fiancée:

WEDNESDAY, 12 AUGUST 1942

I'm just about all in, they just about gave us 12 hours of it today. I've had no dinner, tea or supper – I'm sure glad to be alive sweet. They started on us at about eight this morning (10.30pm now) but the morning was quiet compared with the rest of the day. We ran into more U-boats and got rid of two. We were next on the list for dinner at 12.30 when they really started coming at us, that lasted till 2.00. They bombed us, a 1000lbr but as I'm writing this you can see it missed – 20 feet away – they tried a torpedo, but the captain was too good for them and dodged it; he made a good show of dodging bombs, as they sorted us out in the screen of destroyers. We were in a very bad position, also the light was with them. It was a beautiful day but just hazy, so they flew very low and you just couldn't see them till they were on top of you. The last attack was made with Stuka dive-bombers. Two came forward for us and about six went for the *Indomitable* and got two on her, one aft and one forward. The for'd one knocked out her port gun position, two twin turrets they just blew up. She looked bad at first, but she is OK and they say she will be OK tomorrow for flying off aircraft again. Only one merchant ship was damaged by near misses so they opened her seacocks and scuttled her. It seemed funny out of 50 ships they tried for us so many times! The convoy has gone on with about 15 destroyers and some cruisers. We are with the aircraft carriers *Rodney* and *Nelson* and a couple of cruisers. We have nine destroyers. I'm writing this at action stations as we are remaining at them all night. What I would like is a nice bath and go to bed! We picked up one of our pilots and he said he was fighting the Stukas and caught one of our Pom Pom shells. That was just before they turned in to dive on the *Indomitable* he was above them. He is an *Indomitable* pilot of the 13th squadron. He said he got one of the Stukas and we got one of the two that attacked us. Our Pom Pom claims two planes and one probable! Not bad darling. Our ammo is very low, we could just about stand four or five attacks but no more. The state of our guns are bad, one of the 4-inch HA is useless worn out and the left gun of 'A' turret is worn out also it could almost take a 5-inch shell now. My eyes are very sore darling so I'll say goodnight to you my precious.

SATURDAY, 15 AUGUST 1942

The believed official information is that one cruiser sank, two hit by torpedoes, one of them is returning, the other is carrying on. One destroyer was damaged and is also returning. Apparently they had a net of U-boats waiting for them. They also had a dusk raid just after nine last night. The *Indomitable* commit their dead to the sea at dusk tonight, killed six officers, 60 ratings, wounded 55. Five of the convoy were sunk too so that was a very costly convoy altogether, but as Malta is our base off Libya I suppose we'll have to expect to do it. The captain said we were attacked as we were because our gunnery was bad! Maybe!

We claim three and a probable. I've just heard on the news that you had bombs in the Greater London area and some people were killed. I'm wondering if they will say anything about the convoy to Malta! 9 o'clock news *Eagle* sunk. They made light of it, just as though it were nothing. I'd like to have some of those people on one of these trips in my magazine. I'd like to see 'em change colour as we do when each bomb drops.

I've had a nice bath and shave and am in my pyjamas. I feel very tired though. I hadn't had anything to eat for two days except for two sandwiches. I had a cup of water but the tanks had a good shake up by the gun fire so the water was lousy so I put some Andrews in it, boy did it do things to me. I was glad we weren't at action! We had a good dinner tonight. Well sweet I must stop now as my eyes are too tired. Goodnight dearest.

Well dearest they have arrived all four out of fourteen convoy. One still in two that might get there. Our losses *Eagle* and *Manchester* they announced on the news. The *Cairo* and *Foresight* we sank ourselves as they were damaged and we couldn't keep off the air

attack on them as the escorting vessels ran out of ammo. We are all
on our way to Gib and there is a U-boat concentration waiting for us
along the coast somewhere. I haven't time to write anymore darling
as I'm on at eight. Goodnight sweet. The wireless is playing. You and
the night and music.

Although only five of the fourteen merchant ships reached their
destination, whilst the Royal Navy had lost the aircraft carrier HMS
Eagle, as well as the cruisers *Manchester* and *Cairo* and the destroyer
HMS *Foresight*, *Pedestal* supplied Malta with enough to keep fighting
for a further ten weeks, enabling the island to act as a base for Royal
Air Force and Royal Naval forces to attack the convoys supplying
Rommel's desert forces.

Malta was not the only destination of Allied convoys in the
summer of 1942. Ever since the entry of the Soviet Union into
the war in June 1941, huge amounts of supplies had been sent to
Russia, both from Britain and North America. Approximately 20
per cent of these supplies were sent via the Arctic route, going from
Iceland or the British Isles to the ports of Murmansk or Archangel.
These convoys were protected against the German aerial and naval
threat by an escort force consisting of destroyers, corvettes, frigates
and minesweepers, to fight off the constant U-boat attacks, while
there were generally two further covering forces: a close support
(cruiser) force and distant cover made up of battleships, cruisers and
sometimes aircraft carriers.

Perhaps the most famous of these Arctic convoys was PQ17, which
was forced to scatter in July 1942 following the threat of intervention
by German capital ships. D. Hibbit by now served on the County-
class heavy cruiser HMS *London* and was part of the close escort for
the ill-fated PQ17:

THURSDAY, 2 JULY 1942

The convoy (for which we are acting as a covering force) is attacked
by waves of Torpedo-Bombers. A couple get shot down by one of
the nine destroyers which, together with about 10 or more trawlers
etc. form the escort of the 40 or so merchant ships. We suffered no

losses in this encounter, and in the ones which followed that day not one ship was hit.

The following day however, one of the four cruisers (the US Ship *Tuscaloosa*) was attacked by a U-boat and three torpedoes were expended on her, all of which missed their mark. All the day and the day following, the convoy was being attacked by wave after wave of German Torpedo – carrying aircraft and also an occasional U-boat. The final outcome was that we lost four merchant ships of the convoy.

Later in the day it was reported that enemy surface units were known to be in our close proximity, among them the much talked of *Tirpitz*.

This enemy fleet was superior to our own force (greatly so) and thus it would have been folly to attempt to engage them. They also had the great advantage of air protection – we had none and so after ordering the ships of the convoy (Negative destroyers) to proceed independently to Archangel (we were about 75ºN, 28ºE) we turned 'homeward'.

Later the following day reports were received to the effect that several more of the Convoy had been torpedoed and sunk.

Walter Edgley was an able seaman in the auxiliary anti-aircraft vessel HMS *Pozarica* (a converted banana boat), which served as part of the escort for PQ17, and describes the intensity of the air attacks on the convoy prior to its scattering:

SATURDAY, 4 JULY 1942

Middle Watch, at 0200hrs some He 115s came in and dropped torpedoes. One merchant ship was hit and had to be sunk later by one of our subs. Action Stations again at 0630hrs. Afternoon Watch. At 1500hrs Action Stations. Several Ju 88s were about and bombed convoy. There was low mist and the planes were only occasionally seen although they could be heard. Fell out at 1700hrs but closed up almost at once when a dozen He 115s appeared. They circled round and I saw torpedoes dropped (one at a corvette) but planes did not press home their attack. Then at 1900hrs a large formation of the He 111s came in. They split up into smaller formations and approached the convoy at different angles, and dropped torpedoes. The leader of the first formation flew right down low between the lines of the convoy, swerved to drop his torpedo at a large merchant ship, then banked away across our bows. This plane flew through a terrific barrage and our pom-pom shells could be seen bursting on the sides of the merchant ships! The leader was hit by our starboard pom-pom as he banked and a small fire started just in front of his tail, this fire rapidly grew as he crossed our bows, and then it crashed in flames off our port bow. Terrific barrages put up, particularly by our pom-poms. Captain told us that seven aircraft were definitely destroyed and more damaged. 28 aircraft attacked but only eight pressed home their attack fully. Two merchant ships were hit and abandoned. One Russian oil-tanker was set on fire, but the crew got it under control and joined convoy again.

Lieutenant Richard Walker served on board the destroyer HMS *Ledbury*, again part of the escort to PQ17, and describes his reactions to the order to scatter and the aftermath:

SUNDAY, 5 JULY 1942

The most appalling and ignominious thing has happened – defeat is perhaps the word. We were shadowed all the forenoon by our friends the B & V [Blohm and Voss, a German reconnaissance aircraft]. CS1 had already arrived earlier in the morning – *London*, *Norfolk*, *Wichita*, *Tuscaloosa*, with destroyer escort, *Somali*, *Rowan*, *Wainwright*, and were steaming hull down on the horizon. During the afternoon two Ju 88s turned up and later the convoy was half-heartedly attacked by He 115s who never approached within range. Then about twenty-five He 111Ks came up over the horizon and pressed home a most determined attack, zigzagging through the barrage and torpedoing two merchant ships. Several were brought down, one probably by one of our 4-inch guns and another by our Oerlikon [20 mm Swiss-made anti-aircraft gun] fire. It was flat calm and a clear day. We should have had more. The sea seemed to be littered with rafts, floats, ship's boats, and wrecked planes. The attack was wildly exhilarating, guns firing in every direction, planes flashing in the sun like swallows as they turned and twisted to attack, shells bursting just above the water (none of the aircraft flew higher than 50 feet above the sea), torpedoes dropping everywhere, tracer bullets, the Captain directing fire over the loud hailer: control, control, control, barrage, barrage, barrage, all the thrill of battle. I was staggered by the beauty and excitement of it all. There was no time to be afraid. It was a matter of engaging aircraft all over the place. At times they came so close that we could see the expression on the pilots' faces.

At last it was over and we could look around and see the damage – two merchant ships only were slowly sinking, a Russian tanker (*Azerbaijan*) and an American cargo ship. They had dropped astern and were being attended to by the rescue ships. Poor devils on board; at least they do not have to endure survival, or non-survival, in these freezing waters. We steamed off to the beam and picked up four Nazi airmen from a yellow rubber float, one seriously wounded by shrapnel, one slightly hurt, the other two undamaged. I was able to take some quite good photographs, of the float alongside and of the pilot and navigator on our bridge – very brave but rather arrogant young men and not specially grateful for being rescued. I think they had expected the Blohm & Voss shadower to pick them up anyway. We handed them over to the sailors who made them scrub decks and other harsh chores.

Then came disaster. A cipher arrives from the Admiralty telling CS1 and destroyers to leave the convoy and proceed west immediately, superior enemy forces in the vicinity. At first we thought this was fine and we were to have a fleet action with *Tirpitz*, *Scheer*, *Hipper* and escorting German destroyers. We were still at action stations, table now to low angle, SAP [armour piercing] ammunition at the guns – all set for a big engagement. Then the most desolate signal came through by R/T from *London*:

'General. From CS1 ('Turtle' Hamilton). I know you will all be feeling as distressed as I am at having to leave that fine collection of ships to find their own way to harbour. The enemy, under cover of haze and shore-based aircraft, has succeeded in concentrating a far superior force in the area. We were therefore ordered to withdraw. We are all sorry that the good work of the close escort could not be completed. I hope we shall all have a chance of settling this score with Hun soon. 0115B/5.'

Agonising words from a brave naval officer. We are deserting the convoy to carry on to Archangel (Murmansk has been demolished by German bombers) unprotected except for two escort vessels (*Salamander* and *Britomart*), two AA ships (*Palomares* and *Pozarica*), two corvettes (*La Malouine* and *Poppy*), three trawlers (*Lord Austin, Lord Middleton*, and *Northern Gem*) and two submarines. They were to sail across 600 more miles of Arctic Ocean infested with torpedo bombers, dive bombers, U-boats, and of course *Tirpitz, Hipper* and destroyers.

Meanwhile, two American cruisers, two English cruisers and nine destroyers (with *Duke of York, Washington, Victorious, Cumberland* and *Ligeria*, somewhere in the vicinity) were steaming at 25 knots up to Spizbergen and the ice, and then away to safety. As the Chief Yeoman of Signals remarked, we should all be having spaghetti and Italian Vermouth for supper tonight. The whole affair seems like some fantastic nightmare. Perhaps we shall wake up to find ourselves on the starboard quarter of PQ17 again, defending them from gleaming twisting He 111s and weird booted He sea-planes.

MONDAY, 6 JULY 1942

There must be something more behind all this that we know nothing about. None of [us] can believe that all these ships have run off just because we are near Norway and a couple of big German battle cruisers are somewhere in the area. All sorts of fantastic tales and excuses fly around – the invasion of England, peace has been declared, *Tirpitz* and *Hipper* have been sunk by Coastal Command, we are off to a German base in Norway. It is hard to believe that we have really run away. Our flotilla leader, Jackie Broome in *Keppel*, volunteered to rejoin the convoy, but CS1 turned him down; orders from Admiralty are sacrosanct. To add irony to the situation a cipher has come through from a Russian submarine claiming two torpedo hits on *Tirpitz* . . .

TUESDAY, 7 JULY 1942

Fleeing westwards.

WEDNESDAY, 8 JULY 1942

Just before sighting the Orkneys we took part in a dummy A/C torpedo attack, with the big ships and destroyers all altering course to take avoiding action at the same time. Swordfish and Albacores were the 'enemy'. They seemed amazingly slow after the Heinkels and offered many easy shots.

On arrival in Scapa, the Captain mustered all hands on the foc's'le and made a most excellent speech, the gist being that he was unbearably disappointed to have to leave the convoy to the mercy of the Hun, and it was difficult, without being disloyal to superior officers, to understand exactly what happened. It appeared that someone in the Admiralty had lost his head and made a complete cock up – 'balzup' was the actual word.

SUNDAY, 12 JULY 1942

It turns out that as soon as we received CS1's signal that we were to leave the convoy for home (0115B/5), *Keppel* volunteered to return taking the close screen with him. CS1 refused. When the fog cleared *Keppel* volunteered again, but it was too late and CS1 refused again. If we had been allowed to rejoin the convoy, which of course we were never supposed to leave, we should be in Archangel by now. We all feel strongly that that sort of decision should have been made by the men on the spot, not by the Admiralty with theoretical information in London.

RA(D), Admiral Burnett said to Alistair Ewing, the captain of *Offa* 'Of course, it was difficult for you to disobey orders, but the Nelson touch . . . etc.' as though it were possible for a junior destroyer captain, when told to join up with the First Cruiser Squadron, to pipe up and say, I won't.

Only 11 out of the 37 ships of PQ17 reached their destination and arguments continue to rage over this controversial convoy battle.

7. The Dieppe Raid

In August 1942, the first major assault on occupied Europe was undertaken by a mixed force of Canadians and Commandos under the auspices of Lord Louis Mountbatten's Combined Operations Headquarters. The aim of Operation *Jubilee*, as it became known, was to carry out a reconnaissance in force on the fortified Channel port of Dieppe. Robert Meadows was carrying the Commandos once more, on their way to subdue the coastal batteries to the flanks of the main Dieppe operation:

AUGUST 1942

No. 3 & 4 Commandos were allocated to the many ships and landing craft lying off the harbour. At the same time a large number of Canadian troops were detailed to make a frontal attack on the port. Our passage across the Channel was uneventful until we were a few miles from the French coast. Obviously our approach was reported to the authorities ashore as almost immediately firing started and the night was lit up by star shells. The attack pressed on towards Dieppe but as the German forces ashore were now fully aware of the imminent attempted landing the troops who eventually landed had a very hostile reception and as a consequence a great many, mostly Canadians, were either killed, wounded or taken as prisoner. This attempted attack on a defended port proved totally unsuccessful and we had to beat a fairly hasty retreat. In doing so we had a slight collision with another ship of the force and as a consequence we sustained some damage to our port side davits. We were ordered to proceed towards Southampton for repairs to be carried out.

Captain Turner was a Bombardment Liaison Officer (BLO) positioned on board the destroyer HMS *Garth* off the coast of Dieppe, responsible for supporting the infantry as they landed on the enemy beaches. He recorded his experiences in a diary written after the event:

WEDNESDAY, 19 AUGUST 1942

About 5.30am the doctor came in and said that one could see large flashes ahead – our bombers laying their eggs on the French Coast. I collected my equipment and went up to the bridge. It was pitch dark but not at all cold. Ahead I saw great and sudden flashes light up the sky. It gave one a horrid feeling inside to think that when those bombs were bursting, our enemies were probably running about in streets – in French streets, not knowing (we hoped) that 5,000 Canadians and British were about to surprise them from the sea.

It was extremely dark as we sailed in doing about 10 knots and I stood near the front of the bridge peering though my glasses and then searching with my naked eye, trying to distinguish the coast line from the gloom. The Captain sounded rather excited when he ordered, 'Now everyone keep an eye out for the coast: keep your bloody eyes fixed for the coast'! And then every now and again he shouted, 'Anyone see anything?' I could see nothing but darkness. Then something happened on our port beam. I saw tracer fire at sea level, about a mile to port. I reported it to the Captain, who grunted and looked again for the coast. It had become just a little less dark – dawn was approaching – and we could definitely define a vague outline in the sky ahead, with a gap in the middle of it (it was 0540 hrs). The captain yelled, 'Can anyone see the town? Is that the town'? And then, as if I was his navigator, he turned round and said, 'Come on soldier, you're the man for this job. Is that Dieppe ahead?' It could have been a cloud bank for all I could make out through my glasses just at that moment, but it did <u>look</u> like where Dieppe should be, and I was having a last look before answering when, thank God, the town's anti-aircraft barrage opened up, and left me in no doubt. 'Yes Sir, that's certainly Dieppe ahead,' I replied – with a great deal of relief!

We made straight for it. The time was 0545 hrs and zero hour for the landings was in five minutes time. The light rapidly improved and slowly I could make out the haze over the town – the smoke from bombs. I spoke to George Conran in the 'director' and asked him if he saw his targets. He said he did. The captain said 'Turner, are you ready?' I was on the telephone to the signalling office and couldn't answer him. He said again, 'Turner, are you ready?' I said 'Ready,

Sir' and he said 'Right, open-fire'. I shouted down my phone to the
gunnery transmitting-station and to George, 'Open Fire!' There was
the sound of the warning gong followed immediately by the flash
and hot dusty blast and the noise of the guns. The battle was on.
I put my glasses up and watched half through them and half with
my naked eyes for the 'splashes' of our two-gun salvo. I could see
Tank Landing Craft ahead, and near in to shore (we were a mile
off shore) but I couldn't see our shells burst. This worried me and I
gave 'up 100'. Other destroyers started firing now and squadrons of
our planes flew overhead firing their guns. Could I see our shells? I
gave again, 'Up 100', and we fired again. We fired at the left hand
side of the town for eight minutes, as hard as we could go, and
although we closed in very close to shore I never saw one of our
bursts – in the dim light of dawn. The sea was calm, and I remember
seeing and marvelling at the other destroyers throwing out smoke
and flame. But in the excitement of the moment one never noticed
the tremendous noise which was going on . . .

We went on firing and then suddenly my line to the TS went
'dead'. Someone cried, 'TS direct hit' and someone else said, 'TS
knocked out'. 'What d'you mean, "knocked out", go and tell me
what's happened', said the Captain and the second man with the
voice ran from the bridge to investigate. We fired from the gun
mountings.

Within a few moments, a rating came up to the bridge to tell
the Captain than an unexploded shell had lodged in the safe in
the wheel-house, just below the bridge. I heard someone say that
it had no fuse in it. It was then that we realised what the enemy
were doing.

They must have over-estimated the thickness of our armour and
were firing unfused rounds as armour piercing shot, but as our sides
were not thick enough to prevent a bullet going in one side of the ship
and out the other, their shells were doing the same, without exploding.
It was fully a further quarter of an hour before they changed their
tactics and fired air bursting rounds above the ship. (The casualties
in the TS were now replaced by relief hands.)

These air bursts of the enemy were hellish – bursting about 15 feet
above us with a sharp crack and then the whine and 'whirr' of flying

shell, fragments and then nothing but little puffs of smoke were left hanging in the air above us.

I could see some aircraft now and every now and again a bomb threw up the sea near some ships – none near us yet.

A Messerschmitt 110 dived to sea level off our port bow followed closely by a Mustang, firing her guns for all she was worth and making the sea boil and froth. The enemy's shells began bursting all round the bridge – there were some casualties below somewhere. The Captain ordered 'make smoke!' and soon – but it seemed ages – we were able to dodge behind our own screen and the enemy's fire immediately lost its accuracy. Things were getting hotter. A message from HQ Ship said that it would be impossible to take casualties off from Blue Beach in the near future . . .

The Hun's shells began bursting all around us again and we ran behind our screen again and I signalled to George to say that we could accept no more targets as we had to 'shoot up' the coast guns. Our ammunition was beginning to become a bit short, but we had to go on firing. We poked our bows through the screen again firing as we went. The enemy got our range straight away and then for a minute seemed to wander. I offered a Squadron Leader, who was standing beside me, a cigarette and we both lit up.

A shell burst very close and the blast blew my papers from the roof of the bridge shelter; the captain yelled, 'make smoke'. Thick black smoke gushed from the funnel but to our horror, it went straight up in the air. The captain ordered Chemical Smoke to be made from the stern. It takes much longer and this time it took too long. Pieces of shells whistled all round us. I felt an extraordinary numb bang on my fingers on my left hand and heard the loudest noise I've ever heard – a short sharp scream of metal. I looked at my fingers, my index finger was hanging mainly off and I felt no pain. I then felt the back of my right leg with my right hand and felt nothing but hot rawness but again, no pain.

I could not stand. I lay down on the bridge. I cannot say that I was frightened – if anything, the shock made me feel very collected and natural and I spoke to the signaller and several other people.

I held my finger between my centre finger and thumb. I saw the side of the bridge was splattered with blood and there was a piece of meat about the size of a large mouthful sticking to some woodwork and slipping down. I looked round to see if anyone else had been hit – they hadn't – and that meat was a bit of me!

I heard the Captain shout down a voice pipe 'Doctor to the bridge!'

The Doctor came very quickly but to me it seemed a long time.

On the beaches in front of Dieppe, the supporting armour became trapped and the infantry pinned down, never managing to break out. The attack had failed and the Canadians were withdrawn, having suffered heavy casualties, some of whom ended up in the Kent and Sussex Hospital under the care of Mary Morris:

21 AUGUST 1942, TUNBRIDGE WELLS

Matron has asked me to go on night duty to 'Special'. Four Canadian soldiers in a small surgical side ward. They were transferred here yesterday and are reputed to be tough and uncooperative. Am feeling more than a little nervous. Their presence here is very hush-hush and must not be discussed outside the hospital.

Went on duty at 8pm. The Sergeant, Mc—, presumably of Scottish descent, is in his early thirties, the three private soldiers are in their twenties, and seem to be in a state of severe shock.

Mc— is in severe pain from shrapnel wounds of the left thigh. He is on Me B693 in an effort to prevent and combat infection. He is to go down to theatre tomorrow to have the deep-seated shrapnel removed.

His first words to me as I entered the ward were . . . 'where is my bloody morphia?' I gave it to him without comment and he gradually relaxed as the pain decreased. I made him as comfortable as possible and introduced myself to the other patients. They were in a state of complete exhaustion and shock – too tired to talk. They just lay there looking at the ceiling. Their physical injuries are not very serious, but I have never seen such total exhaustion as this. They are all Commandos, and the Sergeant said over and over again . . . 'It was bloody murder' and then fell asleep.

Had to awaken Sgt. Mc— at 2am for his M and B tablets, they

have to be administered four hourly and I feared his wrath at being disturbed. He took his tablets and then asked for a glass of beer. There wasn't any beer but he settled for a cup of tea instead. He was not too keen on the tea but he obviously wanted to talk.

I listened for nearly two hours whilst he told me about the incredible daylight raid on Dieppe. He told me about the dawn landing and the annihilation of practically the whole of the Canadian Commandos. He said . . . 'We managed to negotiate safely through the enemy minefields and then came face to face with a gun battery. They mowed us down and as we retreated to the beach we ran into E. boats and flak ships.'

Sgt. Mc— needed more morphia by now but he carried on talking and talking. It seemed to help him. He called the Dieppe raid the . . . 'most murderously suicidal operation of the war so far'. His anger was very great and he is sad too for his dead comrades and for the mental horror that has been inflicted on 'his' young soldiers.

This volatile and brave Canadian was sleeping like a baby when I came off duty. The other young men were quiet – too quiet.

8. The Battles for El Alamein

Following the British retreat to the Alamein Line, Rommel immediately tried to bounce Eighth Army out of the position using his tired troops between 1 July and 3 July. However this failed, and throughout July both sides sought to gain the upper hand through a series of attacks and counter-attacks in what became known as the First Battle of El Alamein.

Laurie Phillips of 1st Battalion The Rifle Brigade was involved in the early battles to hold off Rommel's Panzers:

THURSDAY, 2 JULY 1942

We moved straight on to the Ruweisat Ridge and dug in, but because of the shortage of tanks they decided to use us as 'armour'; with the guns up 'on portee' [mounted on the bed of a lorry] we reversed into action alongside the tanks. Because there was a lot of soft

sand in the area where we were operating, south of Ruweisat, we
had Honey tanks standing by to tow us out if we got stuck, and
Crusaders to bring us up ammunition and petrol. We put in an attack
in the afternoon and met the 21st Panzer Division head on as it
advanced to attack us; we fired over 100 rounds with our gun (we
had to pull back for more after we had used the 70 we carried) and
it got pretty hot. We can hardly claim to have done a comparable
amount of damage – we claimed five tanks between us – but we
must have given them a few frights with the high velocity shells
whistling past their ears. We weren't very anxious to close the range
too much, being stuck up on the portee with machine-gun as well
as shellfire to cope with. That night in leaguer the tanks' crews said
they were 'very glad to have us with them', which we though a bit
rich, considering they were sitting behind several inches of armour.
(On the other hand a solid shot which would devastate them if it
penetrated their armour would just whistle through or past our portee
without a great deal of risk.) Next morning, 3rd July, we repeated
the process, but our platoon did not get a shoot, just got shot at.
Unluckily a stray shell, the last of the day, just as we were moving
into leaguer, killed one of our chaps and took the arm off another.
It was one of the ironies that we could go through two days under
direct fire almost the whole of the time without a casualty, and then
get caught by a random shell. We got our own back next morning,
however. As we opened out from leaguer on Ruweisat Ridge, at dawn,
we peeped over the ridge and found a big column of tanks and trucks
leaguered in the wadi below. We blazed away with everything – even
our Bren gunner managed to get off over 1,000 rounds – and hit a
number of tanks before the survivors withdrew in disorder. We had
one or two casualties from small arms fire and one of my old friends
Dicky Dyer, was hit by shrapnel (he recovered, but was later killed
at Caen). In the afternoon we pushed along the ridge and our guns
knocked out two more German tanks. Rommel was forced to give
up for the time being, and our Regimental History says 'It was the
1st Battalion who played as large a part as any one unit in halting
the Afrika Korps.'

Following a visit by Winston Churchill and General Sir Alan Brooke, Chief of the Imperial General Staff, in early August, General Auchinleck was removed as Commander in Chief Middle East, to be replaced by General Sir Harold Alexander, with General Bernard Montgomery as commander of Eighth Army. Following his arrival on 12 August, he set about building up the army's defensive position, notably around the Alam Halfa Ridge. At the end of August Rommel attacked once more and ran straight into these newly strengthened defences, which once more included Laurie Phillips of 1st Battalion The Rifle Brigade:

TUESDAY, 25 AUGUST 1942

We set off back on the morning of the 25th, reaching the Company next morning, where we found them still waiting on the top line for Rommel's push. This finally came on August 31st, when he came through the minefields at the southern end, delayed by our 2nd and 7th Battalions in the 7th Motor Brigade. Looking south from our positions we watched the 4th Light Armoured Brigade withdrawing eastwards, firing over the back of their tanks as they went, with the Afrika Korps following. When they came level with us, our tanks were ordered to show themselves, so they moved forward and fired a few shots, whereupon the German tanks turned and headed for us on the forward slopes of the Alam Halfa Ridge. This was a crucial battle, because it was Rommel's last chance to reach the Delta, and our Brigade, known as the 'ELH Brigade' (Egypt's Last Hope!), because it held nearly all the remaining tanks, was the force mainly relied on to stop him. We were dug in on the forward slopes with a squadron of Grants of the CLY (County of London Yeomanry) behind us. As the German tanks – about 80 of them – approached, their artillery opened up a heavy barrage on our positions, and the Stukas made a rare appearance, but concentrated on the gun and transport lines behind us. When they had got to within about 1,000 yards, [tanks on] both sides had been knocked out, a number of them in flames. The damage was due mainly to a new German tank – the Mark IV Special, which had a new long-barrelled 75mm gun which was able to penetrate the frontal armour of the Grants; luckily the one nearest to us (about 10

yards), although hit, with two of the crew killed, did not brew up, or
we would have had a very warm time. We did not fire a shot from
our gun, as nothing came within our arc of fire . . . But the Company
was said to have knocked out 19 tanks in all, including five credited
to an old friend of mine from Farnham days, Lance-Sergeant Norman
Griffiths, who was awarded the DCM [Distinguished Conduct
Medal] (he was later commissioned and returned to the Company as
an officer at Homs). Two of our platoons – 7 and 8 – were overrun,
and two chaps were killed when a grenade was thrown into their
gunpit from a tank, and another was killed whilst getting away on a
truck. Most crews were told to start walking back towards the German
positions, but their infantry were not following up closely, and when
our chaps had gone a short way, most of them dived into convenient
slit-trenches and made their way back to us after dark! I think we
had 11 missing in the end. We were able to recover the guns during
the night. One chap was crouching in his slit trench when a German
tank stopped right beside him, and the tank commander tapped his
wrist and shouted '*Uhr*'. The chap replied 'Half past six', whereupon
the Jerry showed every sign of rage and shouted '*Nein, nein, geben Sie
mir*', so he reluctantly surrendered his watch. (For some reason, the
first thing anyone did with a prisoner, on both sides, was to pinch his
watch, almost before he had been disarmed; there must have been a
great shortage of watches in the POW camps.) The German tanks
were gradually edging closer, from a direction in which we could
not fire at them, and I was anxiously calculating how long it would
be before the sun went down, and how near the tanks would be by
then, when there was a rumble, and over the ridge behind us roared
the Grant squadrons of the Royal Scots Greys, the Brigade's reserve
armoured regiment. Apparently they had been a bit slow-moving, and
the Brigadier had urged them over the air 'Come on, Greys, get the
whip out.' Anyway it was a marvellous sight to see 30 Grants come
roaring down and open fire simultaneously – one of them stopped
only a few yards behind us, and the blast deafened us; when we made
our presence known, the tank commander said 'Good God, I didn't
know anyone was still alive down there.' The arrival of the Greys was
too much for the Germans, who had already suffered considerable
losses, and they decided they had had enough for one day and pulled

back. As dusk fell it was a relief to be able to stand up and stretch our legs again. We then had a somewhat nervous night, fearing that the Germans might send their infantry in to knock out the anti-tank guns, and as we had no infantry with us, it was somewhat lonely with no one else around except another of our guns about 200 yards away. But in the end all was quiet except for the RAF busily bombing the German leaguers.

The following day, Jerry made a half-hearted attack to the left of us, but got nowhere. For the next two days there was a lot of artillery activity and plenty of bombing – we used to take great delight in watching the Bostons dropping their loads on the Afrika Korps with great regularity (ten times in a day), the Imperturbable Eighteen, we used to call them, and our night bombers were also very active. The Luftwaffe was also over, but the RAF got amongst them, and we saw a number of Ju 88s and Stukas brought down. By then Rommel decided he had had enough; he had lost nearly half his tanks and was very short of petrol, so he started pulling back again to the minefield.

One of the reasons for the British success was the ability of the Desert Air Force to overcome their German rivals and disrupt the German attacking forces, as witnessed by Arthur Hicks:

THURSDAY, 3 SEPTEMBER 1942

25s [25-pounder field guns] started to open up just as I started my letter to Pam, some Hurri-bombers were in the distance dive bombing a Jerry column who were throwing hundreds of shells up at them and what with that and planes coming over, listening and looking for them – (they're a devil of a job to spot out here) I couldn't settle down very well, anyway nothing really happened in our district that evening and we settled down to see what morning brought forth. 25s having a real go shelling Jerry MT [Motor Transport] about 6 miles away, our Regiment and others behind, I'd hate to be at the receiving end when they get going properly, lots of planes about, several lots of our bombers going over with fighter escort. Some MEs and Hurricanes had a 'do' right over us and the Hs seemed to deliberately draw them down to us and then made off. We all had a go and they sheered off pretty pronto and then the Hs had a do at them going away. Half way this morning moved forward with 25s to have a closer do at G. position between two ridges right on top of a hill between. Lord knows how many 25s, also a number of 6-pounder ATs 25s got cracking in real style and we began to get used to the crack of them. Our turn came when 50 Stukas came over with fighter escort and us 12 Bofors gave them all we'd got. Didn't fetch any down and they didn't dive as they used to in France but just a shallow one and then away without touching any of the guns or crews, a few answering shells came back (don't like them) and a B Troop gun was unlucky enough to catch one, knocking out five of the team, two seriously, several anti-tank shells came whistling over. One just missed a truck and another bit the ground a few yards from a 25 and then rolled along the ground to another. A Do 17 came over on Rec. and we had a do at it but it was rather high and made off. 70–80 tanks reported around somewhere. Ours have had one do at them and we were told by the Field Officer that we had lost 12 to 14. Did a guard, we each do an hour a piece as a rule but had a double that night and were expecting lots of trouble in the morning. Stukas over first thing once more they did a shallow dive and made straight off, killed two or three chaps but otherwise did little damage. Didn't hit any but once again I think we shook 'em a bit. Later on, three Mes. came diving out of the sun. Hell of a job to see them but managed to get a few rounds off at them. Were expecting lots more Stukas and artillery fire but none came. Which was puzzling. What a queer war. From the top of our ridge we could see hundreds of enemy vehicles like flies on the desert about five to six miles away and our 25s and bombers were giving them hell. Tanks were about four miles away and we could watch our planes bombing them and shells dropping among them. They halted and still nothing came back except a few planes. Skirmishes in the sky all over the place. Two MEs forced a H down just near us and we had a bang at them as they made off. One Kittyhawk came down straight and it hit the ground bursting into flames right out of the sun. The pilot baled out, REs exploded some delayed action bombs dropped by the Stukas.

The German attack stalled and what became known as the Battle of Alam Halfa was abandoned the following day, with the initiative passing to the British forces.

Montgomery spent the next two months training Eighth Army for the task of breaking frontally through the defensive positions now occupied by Rommel's Axis forces. These positions were surrounded by numerous minefields, which would have to be breached and the front-line trenches taken before the armour could be poured through to complete the breakthrough and win the desert war decisively.

On 23 October, Montgomery launched Operation *Lightfoot*, preceded by an enormous artillery barrage, with four infantry divisions of XXX Corps attacking the north of the German line while the armour of X Corps broke through two corridors in the German minefields.

As part of the 64th Medium Regiment RA, Jim Brooks was among those responsible for creating the largest artillery barrage of the war as a preliminary to the infantry advance:

SUNDAY, 3 OCTOBER 1943

On Oct 23rd 1942, our second in command, told us that the long awaited attack started that night and at 20 mins to ten we started firing, the infantry went in at ten o'clock. We were firing continuously for over five hours, and we started again at 6am the following morning. During the day both air forces went to town, and we saw our first Stuka for many months, plenty were shot down. We continued firing night and day until Nov 4th when the Jerries started clearing out.

J. Green served with the military police during the battle and was responsible for control of movement through one of the tracks through the minefields:

FRIDAY, 23 OCTOBER 1942

1600hrs take position, my position West of Quatara Track, which means I am in front of our own artillery.

1730hrs L/C Newton reports to me track all ready and lit nothing to do now only wait.

App. 2140hrs British Barrage goes over, it is like hell let loose, shells are screaming over my head by the thousand. I don't think anybody ever experienced any thing like this before. It is terrific. The push is on.

0000hrs Tanks are using my track now hundreds of them nose to tail they are going in, it is going to be a terrific battle. I am choked with dust and deafened by the noise of the guns.

SATURDAY, 24 OCTOBER 1942

0200hrs MT & tanks ease up on tracks to allow the stuff to get clear that went in front.

Our bombers roaring overhead in one continuous stream & bombing Jerry's position. They are never going to stop. Barrage eased off about 0200hrs.

0300hrs Traffic starts again Tanks, MT & Infantry going in 0400hrs. Barrage bursts out again plastering Jerry with Shells. This continues until 0600hrs. All night our planes have been blasting Jerry's lines.

0730hrs I am relieved for breakfast & what a relief. Everybody is full of high spirits. The main topic is the barrage. Every one was impressed by the intensity of it, I should think the people most impressed are the Germans.

Laurie Phillips was located to the south of the line carrying out diversionary attacks on the Axis lines:

FRIDAY, 23 OCTOBER 1942

Although they did not tell us at the time, the main attack was to be made up north, near the coast, and our attack in the south was only a diversion to keep the 21st Panzer Division occupied. The 1st and 10th Armoured Divisions had been completely re-equipped with Sherman tanks, self-propelled field guns, etc, and were to form a Corps de Chasse, which would break out and chase the Afrika Korps out of Libya. The 7th Armoured, however, was given no new equipment – our armoured regiments had only Grants and Crusaders (with fewer Grants than the others had Shermans) and our carriers were barely battleworthy. Whereas in the north the break-in was to be made by the infantry divisions, in the south we had to make our own, and we were told that this was our job – in the words of our Brigadier 'If they ask us to go beyond Matruh we shall have to walk, because none of the vehicles will make it!' In the event things didn't work out like that. We were feeling fairly confident of the outcome of the battle, not because of the presence of Montgomery, but because we had six fully equipped armoured brigades, twice as many as we'd ever had before, and all the new tanks and other equipment, with two new infantry divisions from England – the Home Counties and the Highland – and complete superiority in the air.

The gaps in the minefield were to be made by the sappers, covered by the carriers of the 44th Recce Regiment, with the new Scorpion flail tanks to help them lift the mines. Our Company was to go through the two left-hand gaps, and 'A' Company the two on the right, to form a bridgehead on the far side through which the armour could advance; the rest of the Brigade would follow. Having dealt with the first minefield (January) in this way, the second (February) would be similarly penetrated. I cannot believe that this was the best way to do it. The whole of the Brigade's vehicles were lined up nose to tail in four columns stretching from the German minefield back across no-man's-land, through the gaps in our own minefield and beyond. It has been described as being like 'Epsom High Street on Derby Day' and 'The car park at Cheltenham races'. (They used the same method in the attack in the north.) The troops facing us were an Italian parachute division – the Folgore – a fairly tough lot. As soon as they realised where the gaps were being made, their guns, machine-guns and mortars opened up; some vehicles were set on fire, lighting up the scene like daylight and making it even easier for them. Our company had a difficult time getting through, and when they finally got through January they had to knock out a number of machine-gun nests and anti-tank guns; they had quite a lot of casualties with the company commander and two other officers wounded, and two of the sergeants in our platoon killed.

The initial attacks failed to break through the German lines decisively and Operation *Lightfoot* descended into a bitter slogging match, with Rommel even counter-attacking 1st Armoured Division around Kidney Ridge on 27 October. Eric Laker was a private in the 4th Battalion Royal Sussex Regiment, part of 1st Armoured Division, and was caught up in this German counter-attack:

TUESDAY, 27 OCTOBER 1942

At 1830hrs on Tuesday 27th October we moved off from our place of rest – the start of the night attack. From the back of my closed truck we appeared to move most of the way through dense traffic, and the sandy dust was rising in thick clouds. Almost from the start the manoeuvre was a fiasco – unfortunately for us! We arrived at the appointed starting line at approximately 2215hrs, apparently 45 minutes late, for the preliminary barrage by the Corps Artillery had ceased at 2115hrs. Another barrage had started and been cut short again because we were still not there. Absolute chaos reigned. Officers were dashing here, there, and all over the place, trying to put their men 'in the picture' but owing to the rush instructions were perforce of a very much abridged nature.

At 2230hrs the barrage came down again and we had to be ready to go in at 2300hrs when the guns ceased fire. For that 30 minutes one had to shout to be heard, and to add to the din Jerry returned a fraction of our fire with his mortars. One shell landed on one side of a carrier while I was approaching the other side and about five yards away. It rendered hors de combat one of the carrier crew and the blast sent me reeling. When we were due to start the IO [Intelligence Officer], who should have led the battalion, could not be found. Finally we went off and with such a devil of a rush that I was sure lots of people never started. Anyway our little party of Company HQ and about eight signallers trailed along behind a line of trucks as we had been told, until we found it was the wrong line! We rectified this and made another start. Going steadily forward someone was blessed with the bright idea of fixing bayonets, so with a sinking heart I drew my 'tin opener' and affixed it to the end of my rifle in the approved manner. The fact that for a time we were mixed up with our 'A' company and then with the 2nd battalion, our reserve battalion, was a mere nothing. However we eventually got more or less sorted out.

At this point I may as well give the object of the attack. The Rifle Brigade was supposed to have taken the position which was classed as a strongpoint. Apparently they had not done so, and the 88mm guns there were proving an obstacle to our tanks. We were to go in with the design of putting out the 88s, hold the position until dawn, when our tanks would go through us and we would withdraw, our job done. That was what it was on paper!

A hundred yards from the starting point we were at right angles through a long line of 'Swallows' and 'Crusaders'. Comforting sight. 'Don't be late in the morning' someone shouted to one of the crews. 'We'll be there about five – don't worry' came the answer.

On still more, and in the distance I could see a bright glow which as we approached turned out to be one of our English 3-tonners. It was the ration truck of the Gordon Highlanders, set on fire by our forward companies. Apparently the chaps had not been told to expect any of our own troops in front of them, in fact they had been told to shoot up anyone they came across. Consequently when they came up to a company of the Gordons they opened fire on them and inflicted severe casualties until the error was realised. All this while the 88's were cracking away in front of us and their tracer shells were singing overhead. Mortar and artillery fire was dropping among us as we went forward. Eventually we halted and dug shallow trenches for shelter from small arms fire which was now whistling over. We got down in them and I even had a fairly respectable sleep. We were awakened by the Company Commander shouting that we were going forward. Forward again, passing a derelict tank out of which I got a grand little automatic. We then came to some Italian trenches and stopped there. It was now about dawn and we heard the tanks warming up in the distance.

WEDNESDAY, 28 OCTOBER 1942

We then saw a couple of Crusaders come up and lay a perfect smoke screen, but when it had cleared all our tanks had WITHDRAWN under cover of it. We did not worry unduly however, thinking they were perhaps going through in a different place, but concentrated on keeping well down as the stuff was now coming over thick and fast. MG fire was singing about in goodly quantities also.

At about 0900hrs we received the shock of our lives. We were contentedly playing with our automatics when I looked up and saw some of our fellows climbing out of their slit trenches with their hands up! One even had a white handkerchief tied to his rifle. I blinked and then looked round. I saw a tank that had come over the ridge with others on the right of it. A fellow was sitting on the top with a nasty looking LMG which he was waving around in a most unfriendly manner, and walking beside the tank was another chap with a revolver. He was waving his hands around him indicating to our fellows that they were to come to him and surrender. Then to my horror I saw a black cross on the front of the tank. I am convinced that no man living can put into words what my feelings were at that moment. What had happened? Had our tanks been beaten back? Impossible! Had Jerry made a counter-attack and broken through our companies? Question after question flashed through my mind as we sat seemingly frozen. Prisoners of war – horrible thought! Stories that I had heard of the gruesome camps and treatment of the last war that I had forgotten long since came streaming back to me with fearsome clarity. I tried to think straight, but the truth was that we were all a little dazed with the pounding we had received during the night and that morning. Slightly bomb-happy if you like. Well the three of us climb out of the trench, first putting on our small packs, (and how glad I was of that later), and went over and joined the crowd of our fellows that were now beginning to stream towards the German lines. The fact that we had to walk through a barrage from our own guns did not exactly help matters but we went steadily forwards – or was it backwards?

While moving behind the Hun lines I could not help but notice how well his tanks were dug in, and being used as MG nests. Transport etc. was very well dispersed, but at the same time there was very little of it – in fact very little of anything at all and I think our tanks could have gone through as a knife through butter. But of course that is only my opinion from what I saw. We walked for what must have been about miles. During that walk we were stopped first and asked for compasses, then a roughneck stopped us and took most of our fellows' cigarettes, and made us take off and dump our equipment but I managed to hang on to my haversack with washing tackle etc in it. Then we went again, incidentally all this time with no escort, finally being brought to a halt by an Italian officer. Here we were searched again and I was relieved of my knife, fork, spoon and tin opener, but luckily I had just put my watch down my sock. This time we were bundled into trucks and taken on, being dumped in the middle of nowhere by what I imagined to be some sort of HQ. We squatted here for some time, and were very agreeably surprised when our captors produced biscuits and Italian bully for us.

During the afternoon we several times saw Bostons come over in formation and bomb objectives. Again we hung about until dusk, and it was during this time that the full realisation of what had happened came over me. I nearly cried in my misery, if I had been alone I think I would have done so. I hoped desperately that our troops were still pushing and might catch up with us before the wops could get us away. But it was a vain hope.

J. Green's unit was also beginning to feel the strain of the constant operations:

THURSDAY, 29 OCTOBER 1942

All these days are nearly alike busy all day & getting as much sleep as Jerry allows at night. I am used it by now. We hear Jerry is retreating – slowly but surely although the din he makes doesn't seem much like it, but things are going in our favour.

FRIDAY, 30 OCTOBER 1942

Bombed again during last night at frequent intervals. Detailed for a special job I take six L/Cpls with me. I have to go forward as far as the second German minefield and light the gaps for our armour to [go] through at night. This takes me right into the forward zone about 4 miles west of Quatara Rd. The Germans were here only a few hours ago. All my past experiences were nothing compared to this. We are right amongst it.

SATURDAY, 31 OCTOBER 1942

We had bacon, beans & Stukas for breakfast. 21 of them dive bombing. Lucky we have each got a good dug out. We are shelled for two hours. Our artillery are behind us & are replying. We are shelled again in the afternoon. Jerry seems to have taken a personal dislike to us.

We spend most of the day in our holes. At night our dug outs are one continuous boom, owing to the guns. After a while you get used to it & find you can sleep without difficulty. We light up the gap tonight. The NZs go through the gap 'Good Luck to Them'.

SUNDAY, 1 NOVEMBER 1942

Plenty of air raids 1st night also Jerry dropped his shells around us. It is a hot spot here. L/Cpl. S looks like cracking up. He takes hold of himself fairly well. All day is the same as yesterday. Lighting the gap again tonight.

MONDAY, 2 NOVEMBER 1942

Two German planes are shot down quite near us. We see seven shot down altogether. S. is definitely 'Bomb Happy' – he has been much worse today and I have taken him off duty tonight & do his duty myself – the gap lighting is pretty sticky when within range of enemy guns.

TUESDAY, 3 NOVEMBER 1942

More air raids last night. We have had them every night since the push started we are shelled again at intervals Jerry is definitely being pushed back. More prisoners pass us today. Shelling is worst this afternoon. 3pm DR brings message. I have to hand over to S. African police at 4pm. We are all pleased to leave this joint. We pack our kit and make ready to move – Jerry is shelling again (as we) pull out. My dug out has got hit. Lucky I got out.

We go back to Alamein & dig in once again.

WEDNESDAY, 4 NOVEMBER 1942

More bombing last night flares by the thousand. I am informed that the whole company is moving forward. We move west of Quatara Rd on the coast Rd at 9am. At 11.30 I am detailed along with my section to lengthen Diamond Track, running it two miles nearer Jerry's lines, Jerry is shelling the track all the time. At 5.00pm Hopkinson is killed . . . At 5.15 Varley dies. Power has about 11 wounds. We get our job finished about 6pm, from 12.00 to 7 pm we were shelled, straffed & Stuka-ed continuously. It has been a trying day. Young Hopkinson has only been out here three weeks & Varley has a baby he hasn't seen. It shook me a bit today to see my own blokes get wiped out.

However, a further attack by Eighth Army, known as Operation *Supercharge*, had been launched on 2 November and had broken through the German lines, and by the 4th Rommel's army was in full retreat with the British in pursuit.

Harold White of the 2nd Derbyshire Yeomanry was one of those leading the pursuit in his armoured car:

FRIDAY, 23 OCTOBER 1942

On the night of 23rd. October the Battle of Alamein started. 2DY was given the job of policing two minefield gaps until relieved by the Household Cavalry Regiment, when, on the 4th November we led the Brigade through the enemy lines heading for Fuka.

We shot up lots of enemy transport and I was asked to go to the assistance of our No. 1 Troop and knock out a German disabled tank with my 2-pounder gun.

My gunner hit it with his second shot but Jerry turned nasty and shot back with an explosive shell which just missed us – we retreated smartly, my driver didn't need telling! Shortly after this we came under fire and my Troop Leader, Lt. Fowke, was badly wounded in the head, after evacuating him I took over as Troop Leader and remained so for the rest of the campaign. Next morning before first light the advance was resumed, we shot up and captured lots of Italians, but as we got nearer to Fuka, the heavens opened and it poured with rain, in no time the desert became a quagmire, even tanks became bogged down and the pursuit came to a halt while the Germans escaped along the coast road. We spent a miserable wet night huddled in our cars, the ground was too wet to lie on. Next morning it soon dried up and we pushed on west towards the Libyan border. During the day I was shot at by 20mm gun fire which didn't penetrate the armour but didn't do our rations much good, they were in tin-plate boxes on the outside of the car. It was about this point that I got left behind as three of our tyres were punctured, we could carry on for a few miles on our 'Runflats' but only at a much slower rate. Fortunately we came across an abandoned Daimler which wouldn't start. Its tyres WERE sound so we changed three and took one as a spare, this took long enough for us to lose contact with the squadron until we reached a few miles west of Tobruk, I'd lost the second car of my troop, way back with a worn-out engine!

1942–43

I. Operation *Torch* and the End in North Africa

On 8 November 1942, a joint Anglo-American expeditionary force under the command of General Eisenhower landed in Vichy French Morocco and Algeria in an operation codenamed *Torch*.

Lieutenant Freer Roger served with the 8th Battalion Argyll and Sutherland Highlanders during the landings in North Africa (10 November 1942) and the fighting in Tunisia:

SATURDAY, 7 NOVEMBER 1942

We passed through the Straits at midnight. The lights of Tangiers twinkling close on the starboard beam, and the little Moorish Felukkas could be seen dodging in and out of the convoy in the starlight. Next day we sailed close to the Spanish coast, the snows of the Sierra Nevada sparkling white in the sunshine. The CO addressed all officers, and we were told our destination – N. Africa. It appeared that one convoy had left us at Gibraltar, and was making for Casablanca – mostly Americans, while another was going to Oran. We were to be furthest east – making for Algiers, a combined British and American force. Sheafs of intelligence reports, maps and detailed air photographs were issued, and orders were given out. Speculation as to whether the French would or would not fight was rife. Meanwhile we had been spotted by enemy recc. planes, and the 'flak' ships went into action for the first time.

SUNDAY, 8 NOVEMBER 1942

Before dawn we lay off Algiers, the convoy having turned hard a starboard during the night. We could see the twinkling lights of the city straight ahead. Even as the first ALCs left for the shore we heard President Roosevelt's speech to the French nation. As dawn came up we were close in-shore about four miles west of Algiers, and the first troops were ashore, having met with little or no opposition, except a Commando who had landed off a destroyer in Algiers harbour itself, and had been fired upon. However, within a very few hours all resistance had ceased and we heard that Admiral Darlan had been captured by the Americans. Within six hours our Spitfires were flying from Maison Blanche aerodrome and that evening, when a flight of 15 Ju 88s came over, ten of them were shot down, with no loss to ourselves. Meanwhile, 36 Bde. were floating reserve, and that evening our ship docked at Algiers to unload other units who were going ashore. It was an impressive night watching our MT ships unloading. One American ship was unloading 'Jeeps' at the rate of one every 37 secs., and were being driven away by their drivers at top speed. That evening the Jerries came over again but were met with such a hail of AA that they veered off and dropped their bombs in the sea. We remained at Algiers all the next day without going ashore, and that evening put to sea again. The following morning we were to land at Boujie – 100 miles east of Algiers. We were told that the landing would be opposed. Our drill had been rehearsed again and again, and only last minute inspections and orders remained. After a short sleep we were awakened by the sound of the anchor dropping.

WEDNESDAY, 11 NOVEMBER 1942

We sat between decks in full equipment waiting for the landing officer to call out our Serial Nos. through the loudspeaker. A Coy was the first company to go, and at about 3am we made our way down the gangways in the dark to the waiting ALCs. I was in No. 13 – as Squire Webb, who was with me, was kind enough to point out: Dawn was breaking when the first 'flight' had assembled, and then we were off – going hard for the shore three miles away. Behind a magnificent range of mountains about 8,000 feet high the first streaks of dawn

Evening newspaper placards in London announce the news of Germany's invasion of Poland on 1 September 1939. 'Now that the reality is so close one feels rather numb, almost indifferent. No heroics, no crusading fire at the moment, but a feeling that a very nasty job has got to be done and done thoroughly.' Moyra Charlton (IWM HU5517)

The German pocket battleship *Admiral Graf Spee* in flames after being scuttled in the River Plate estuary off Montevideo, Uruguay. 'We move into position, and close up at action stations for another show down, as we all expect her to put up a fight. She comes out, turns to starboard and blows herself up in shallow water off Montevideo, where she burns fiercely all night.' J. Nicholls, HMS *Ajax* (IWM A6)

British soldiers wade out to a waiting destroyer off Dunkirk during Operation *Dynamo*. 'Soldiers then swam out to us or came in small boats. There are thousands of them on the beaches like swarms of black flies, being bombed and machine-gunned.' Kenneth Wilson, Royal Navy (IWM HU41240)

Fighter pilots of No. 610 Squadron, Royal Air Force, relaxing between sorties at Hawkinge, Kent. Each man wears his life jacket to save time when the call to scramble comes. 'The summer was one of brilliant sunshine, heat, shimmering landscape; I remember walking to the Mess every day with the impression that the sky was black and heavy as lead.' Reverend Guy Mayfield, Chaplain, RAF Duxford (IWM HU1062)

Members of the London Fire Brigade train their hoses on burning buildings after the last and heaviest major raid mounted on the capital during the Blitz, 10–11 May 1941. 'The air shook with a volcanic rumbling, and a marble pillar in the centre of the room cracked like a tree trunk. In the maelstrom of dust, tumbling masonry and splintering woodwork, people were screaming.' Mary Morris (IWM HU1129)

Field Marshal Erwin Rommel (left) with his Chief of Staff, Fritz Bayerlein, in the North African desert. British soldiers constantly compared Rommel with their own commanders. 'Have we no genii like Rommel?' Peter Lovett, 50th (Northumberland) Division (IWM HU5628)

The German battleship *Bismarck* firing at HMS *Hood* during the action in the Denmark Strait. 'The *Hood* succeeded in scoring a few direct hits almost as soon as engaging but the *Bismarck* returned the fire with interest and within a couple of minutes all that could be seen of the *Hood* was a mass of orange flame followed by a terrific explosion – and the *Hood* was no more.' D. Hibbit, HMS *Norfolk* (IWM HU381)

A Japanese landing party charges into Hong Kong in early 1942. 'The troops . . . are completely worn out. A scene I will never forget with ammunition dumps going up everywhere and the Japs pouring hundreds of shells just over our heads into blocks of houses across the road. Finally the barrage stops and white flags appear from all the houses.' Squadron Leader Donald Hill (IWM HU2780)

British Crusader tanks in the desert, 1942: '. . . our tank crews had for two years been fighting an enemy better equipped than themselves in tanks better armoured and, more importantly, with longer range guns. This inequality was too much for even the finest units.' Robin Dunn, 11th Honourable Artillery Company (IWM E18642)

An American soldier having returned from Dieppe; fifty American Rangers took part in the raid, as the first US troops to see action in Europe. 'We managed to negotiate safely through the enemy minefields and then came face to face with a gun battery. They mowed us down and as we retreated to the beach we ran into E. boats and flak ships.' Sergeant Mc—, Canadian Army (IWM H22580)

An Avro Lancaster silhouetted above Hamburg during a raid. 'One minute the place is peaceful and then in about 30 mins it's a mass of blazing ruins, on fire from end to end. Flames and smoke thousands of feet high. I could still see the fires burning, when we were 200 miles away, and that's not exaggerating.' Harold Wakefield, No. 51 Squadron, RAF (IWM C3371)

British troops and vehicles are unloaded onto the beaches of Salerno. 'The noise was deafening and wave after wave of hot air struck me with considerable force. I stood tightly clutching the boat rail gazing with fatal fascination at a scene of utter horror, chilling my whole body.' John Williams, Royal Artillery (IWM NA6630)

Gun crews of HMS *Duke of York* after the sinking of the German warship *Scharnhorst* on 26 December 1943. 'It is astonishing what a drug and intoxicant action is. One barely noticed the shattering thud of recoils as the guns kept running back, and we did not feel or notice as their shells hit and fell around us. It was all so exciting that everyone almost automatically did their jobs correctly with clear heads.' Alan Tyler, HMS *Norfolk* (IWM A21168)

A Sherman tank and jeep of the 4th Brigade entering the ruins of Cassino. '"Wiped off the face of the earth." "Razed to the ground." Such phrases are seldom justified, here they are an understatement. Stormed repeatedly, blasted by the very breath of hell, Cassino is only a name.' Patrick Burns, Royal Engineers (IWM NA15079)

Chindits with their mules, carrying supplies, make their way through the jungle. 'Sometimes the nature of the country was such that we only covered a mile or two during the day's march. Where the track was impassable to a loaded mule, the loads were removed and carried by the men.' N. Aylen, 5th Reconnaissance Regiment (IWM SE7910)

Troops of 11th East African Division on the road to Kalewa, Burma, during the Chindwin River crossing. 'Throw your heart over and your body will surely follow.' General Messervy (IWM SE1884)

Troops crouch down on Sword Beach as they await the signal to advance. 'We had a grandstand view of the first landings at seven thirty as we ceased fire; we watched the bitter fighting and the masses of material being landed and the tanks getting ashore and fighting in the fields above the beaches.' Lieutenant John Pelly, HMS *Tyrian* (IWM B5090)

POWs at Stalag IIB at Fallingbostel welcome their liberators, 16 April 1945. (IWM BU3661)

The British commander and Indian crew of a Sherman tank encounter a newly liberated elephant on the road to Meiktila, 29 March 1945. 'I remember flying over the area and seeing the devastation below and thinking how glad I was that I was in the Air Force and not the Army.' Bob Court, No. 194 Squadron, RAF (IWM SE3640)

German SS guards at Belsen forced to lie face down in one of the empty mass graves. 'Never will I forget what I had seen that day and never, never will I forgive the race, who produced men capable of such cold blooded misery and death to the thousands who were driven into Belsen Camp.' Robert Daniell, Royal Artillery (IWM BU4094)

were casting their reflection over the bay, and tinting the peaks with rosy light. The distant boom of the surf rose above the noise of the engine. Men gripped their rifles and fixed bayonets peering over the cowlings. A wide expanse of golden sand with gradually sloping vineyards and sheer cliffs to the right could be seen. I was with rear A Coy. HQ, and supposed to be second last to land, but old No. 13 was showing a pretty turn of knots – too pretty I thought – and sure enough we were first ashore, carried in on the crest of a breaker. We rushed up the beach expecting bullets, but none came and we pushed on to the rendezvous at a farm, without seeing any sign of life.

Having overwhelmed the limited French resistance, the Allied forces in Algeria began a drive across the border and into Tunisia, before the offensive ground to a halt following a German counter-attack on 1 December and the onset of winter. Following its victory over Rommel, Eighth Army was also advancing westwards and on 4 February crossed the border into Tunisia, heading for Tunis.

The Reverend Geoffrey Druitt was the senior chaplain of the 6th Armoured Division and found himself attached to the 16/5th Lancers for much of the Tunisian campaign. Here he describes being under air attack:

SUNDAY, 11 APRIL 1943

The CO summoned squadron leaders for an 'Orders Group' before moving off (MO [Medical Officer] and CF [Chaplain to the Forces] also attended). We were sitting on the ground in the shade of the CO's tank when three Stukas came diving out of the blue. 'Maps' yelled the CO, a tell tale mark for the Boche pilots, but it was too late. Looking up I saw the planes coming at us in a vicious, wheeling dive. I flattened; the screaming whistles and then an ear splitting, shattering explosions, ('70 yards'); another in quick succession from another direction shook and thundered ('50 yards'); after that, something happened which lifted us off the ground and seemed to kill all life for some seconds; all was still; dreadfully still! I sat up, mentally feeling myself all over. I remember saying rather foolishly, 'I reckon that is near enough for this morning.' 'Everybody alright?' came the CO's voice; and there he was spitting grass and wild flowers from his mouth! Then we all scattered to see what damage the other 'eggs' had done. Several bodies and men with blood streaming from wounds were visible as soon as we stood up. 'The ammo!' the cry went up, and then I saw the blasted lorry blazing. Men started to pull off the load of ammunition but I went with David to deal with the wounded. Some were pretty bad and very near the burning ammo. I took one end of a stretcher and was glad to find myself 100 yards away behind a friendly Sherman. Then came one of those horrible moments when the instinct of self preservation struggled against duty; for I saw David, alone with one wounded man, close beside that dam' lorry. I suppose it was only a second before I was yanking another stretcher off the MO's truck, but it seemed an age. The ammo was beginning to go up nicely as we placed the man on the stretcher and started to carry him away. I remember making jocular remarks about his bare and bloody bottom as we made our way towards that Sherman. Willie Nicholson strolled coolly over to meet us and added his quota of wit concerning the 'school girl complexion' of those nether regions. But I'm sure no one was as frightened as I was!!

The German Army in Tunisia had been strongly reinforced, with over 150,000 men shipped over to form the new Fifth Panzer Army. Amongst the new equipment was the formidable Tiger tank. This ensured that the Allied progress was hard fought, and the Reverend Druitt describes a tank skirmish by the 16/5th Lancers and its aftermath:

SUNDAY, 11 APRIL 1943

The Regt had weathered one very sticky patch. They had run straight into trouble. A huge cactus plantation had been ahead of them, (about one mile away), hills on their left and the plain on the right. Within a few seconds the Boche plan was obvious. Twenty tanks were reported approaching from the right, SP guns and more tanks appeared like magic from the hills on the left and at the same time it was realised that the cactus ahead was stiff with guns! They were in a trap!! The CO thundered over the air 'It's life or death; at the cactus, charge!' And more than 50 Shermans, with flaming guns, charged at 40mph. Dust rose to 200ft and hid the main body from the eyes of German gunners. One terrific concentration of fire came from them, but the dust had them 'foxed'. Then the Shermans reached that cactus. Five of our tanks were left burning on the plain but not a German escaped. Then wheeling left, our chaps knocked out five SP 88mms and four tanks before the Boche flanking party retreated. Meanwhile the Brigadier had whistled up the 17/21 to deal with the 20 tanks on the right.

The Boche had reckoned without realising that Regts who were responsible for the Charge of the Light Brigade and the Charge of the Battle of Omdurman, had still the same spirit. Every tank bore scars of battle at the end of that day . . .

TUESDAY, 13 APRIL 1943

After breakfast I went over to the enemy tanks knocked out during the battle two days ago. Three Italians were lying dead there and stinking to high Heaven. One was lying outside on the ground; another was badly shot up, lying over the controls; a third had been hit as he baled out, one foot was caught so that the body was half suspended in a spread-eagled position. Several men were inspecting the tanks but doing nothing about the bodies. Much against their will, they helped me to extricate these relics of victory and we dumped them in a nearby slit trench and I read the short Service as laid down for the burial of enemy dead. No marks of identification were on them and so nothing else could be done. I find it very difficult to feel any kind of regret or feeling regarding enemy dead. The Service part therefore is difficult and makes me feel something of a hypocrite. However it consists only of the Lord's Prayer and the Committal; the difficult part is to say 'as we forgive them that trespass against us'.

I returned to the Regt and asked for a party of men to form a burial party to dispose of the charred remains of our chaps in the tanks knocked out during the charge of the cactus. Half an hour later we were 'dumped' alongside the first tank and left to it.

First of all, we looked inside all the tanks and, by means of enquiry from men specially chosen for the purpose, identified all the bodies by their position in their particular tank. I carefully noted names etc. on Graves Registration labels. As I finished writing these out, two of the men came to me and said 'We're very sorry, Sir, but we can't touch them.' I was horrified! It is not a jolly prospect to have all the work in five tanks, as hot as ovens, with bodies burnt, or partly burnt, having been there for two days. After a moment's pause I said, 'I understand, chaps. It is a rotten thing to have to do, but it is the least we can do for our friends. Between us we are going to bury them here and now. I will do the job inside the tank, but someone will have to be on top, to take the remains from me as I pass them through the hatch.' (It is always the driver and co driver who have not time to get out, and a small hatch like a port hole is the only exit as far as extricating their bodies goes.)

And so I started. In every case it meant removing scrap iron and shell cases to be pulled out of the way. It is complete chaos inside a burnt out tank. Then came the task of gathering whatever remained. Sometimes it was very little; just dust and usually a block of burnt bone vaguely recognisable as the hip joints. But of others, much more was to be found; and always that terrible, torpid stench of burnt flesh. It is a different smell from any other I know. It seems to hang in one's nostrils for days. Again and again one detects it as one passes some burning vehicle during a battle.

So the morning was spent performing this gruesome task. While the majority of our little party were digging the graves, I was silently passing up charred bones; the blackened skull; black and brittle arms; half the shoulders with a few powdering ribs below. Again and again I had to 'come up for air' to prevent me retching up my breakfast . . .

We buried those remains wrapped in gas capes and canvas coverings. I walked back to the Regt alone, leaving that pathetic line of upturned shell cases, marking the cost of a gallant charge that saved the day.

The Tunisian campaign saw the first commitment of the British parachute regiments to battle on a large scale, normally as infantry, and Alan Clements, an officer of the 1st Battalion The Parachute Regiment, describes an action fought to clear the position of Djebel Mansour in February 1943:

TUESDAY, 2 FEBRUARY 1943

A few minutes before five we were standing-to and at five o'clock we crossed the starting line as one man. We had only advanced a few paces, when the firing started, sporadic at first but swelling in volume. It was machine-gun fire and all tracer. The crash of a mortar bomb occasionally varied the high staccato of this fusillade. These bursts of fire described coloured parabolas across the darkness.

Now I was sufficiently composed to note a significant fact, and that was that most of this fire was either wild or on a fixed line. Consequently it did not need alarm one unduly if one kept cool. The streams of fire that went rocketing away into the ether were of course negligible but one could even avoid the low lines by taking advantage of the ground or passing between the bursts. The ground assisted our advance no end. The moral protection which tall shrubs afforded was supported by the more solid protection of fissures and dips in the ground. I very soon lost touch with my platoon, but every so often my cries of '9 Platoon' elicited the answer of some familiar sergeant. Curtis was up with me, but I did not hear much of Thornton or Osborne. The reason for this was the exceptional difficulty of keeping contact and direction quite apart from the daunting effect of the fire. I think I must have been well ahead of my platoon, all by myself occasionally I saw or passed other individuals but they belonged to different platoons. Because of this I could only keep climbing and hope that I struck the summit among my company. The Germans continually sent up white Verey lights which I had read about in stories of the Great War. These shed an unearthly light for about thirty seconds, flickered, and then went out. They rooted me to the same spot and their illuminations always redoubled the volume of fire. At last I reached the top. En route I had encountered no enemy, but I had seen a machine-gun firing close by at my side. I gave it two rounds from my pistol firing at the flash. I very much fear it was a Bren gun. I can now distinguish a Bren and Solothurn even in the dark, but was less experienced then. Whichever it was it continued to fire despite my intervention! The first thing that happened on top was the taking of two Italian prisoners. Wretched, shivering little boys they seemed. They were in a slit trench just under the crest. I gave orders for them to be conducted to the rear and endeavoured to find my company . . .

We began the sweep of the summit. We made a steady advance. Major Bull was well up in front and I was to his right side. We kept contact by shouting and I did this to keep my platoon together as well. It's difficult to describe all that happened, for it was still dark. It must have been about six o'clock. The top of the hill was sown with small entrenchments some of which were occupied, some abandoned. It was while approaching one that I was first wounded. Grenades were banging all round and suddenly I felt a sharp pain in my left shoulder which brought me to my knees. I said rather foolishly 'I'm hit' and those immediately around me stopped for a moment. I remember Corporal Meadow's prudence. He had the sense to relieve me of a grenade from which I had extracted the pin and to toss it down the mountain side. Bull asked me if I was alright and as I felt perfectly [OK] I carried on . . .

Then followed a very exciting incident. Bowmer, an intrepid 'Bren' gunner, and I were rushing along when we saw a tall parachutist emerge from some bushes in front of us with rifle and bayonet. There was a burst and he went down screaming. Then just behind him Bowmer and I saw four cream coloured helmets at ground level. Bowmer let them have a whole magazine firing from the hip and I contributed with my pistol. Then we charged and we found three Germans cowering in a veritable spasm of terror at the bottom of the trench and a fourth already passing out. Other parachutists who had come up and seen the fire burst thirsted for their blood. Words passed, our fellows saying 'Comrade' and pointing to the body, but I ordered them to be taken to the rear. I then continued. I rather think the Germans were shot. I have never before seen such abject terror on men's faces. I too tried my hand at booty and said, 'Pistol' to the three, they replied '*Nein, Nein,*' I picked up my Mauser and cartridges for I was already beginning to find my pistol a little useless. We were now approaching the summit of Alliliga from which there was a lot of fire.

This summit is a bare scalp and so a difficult position to assault. Our men seemed to be more numerous all of a sudden (our front had contracted) and again I saw Rickey and Bull. The former's face was covered in blood and he looked a bit shakey. Bull serene as ever, seemed to imply by his deportment 'I hate this very much but I've got to do it'. Then bursts of machine-gun fire came in our direction. I lay down quickly choosing a rotten old tree stump. Beside me was Sergeant Osborne. This was the first time I was alarmed, I had only been exhilarated before. The bullets 'tore through' that log. How they missed me I don't know. At any rate I do not exaggerate when I say they fanned my face and body. Osborne at my side got one through the helmet and head. He began moaning 'Oh sir, Oh sir!' I was myself too frightened to move until those devilish bursts had ceased. I then found that he was not dying and told him to roll away to better cover.

Rommel still had enough men and materiel to launch an offensive, this time against the inexperienced American troops around Kasserine Pass, and British armoured troops were heavily involved in the fighting.

Eddie Parkinson was a driver in the 1st Derbyshire Yeomanry, the armoured car regiment of the 6th Armoured Division, and was sent to reinforce the Americans following the German breakthrough at Kasserine:

Saturday, 27 February 1943

We were detailed to go to a place called Kasserine (just our own troop) to work with the Americans. We drove all day and most of the night and reached Kasserine about nine o'clock. We managed to find a farm that had been evacuated by French people and put our cars under cover of some trees. The next day we spent in finding an observation post and that night went to bed thinking we were alright for a good nights sleep. About midnight the guard heard a car coming up the drive. It was a scout car sent by Regt Headquarters to tell us we had to move out as the Germans were pushing on. You never saw anybody get ready quicker in your life. Again we drove all night and stopped about six again for a couple of hours. Even then we had not finished but were sent to an OP out on a plain just on the borders of Tunisia and Algeria. We found out that during the night the Germans had taken Kasserine. We stayed out on the plain that night and I had to go to HQ for rations.

The next day we saw four eight-wheeled German cars come out of the pass at the far end of the plain. They fired at us and we moved back. They went back into the pass and again we slept on the plain. The next day our jeep and a scout car went out to an OP to watch for the enemy. We saw them coming and got ready to move. Evidently they saw us and gave chase. The scout car and my jeep took to the hills. You should have seen us go. They did not fire at us. Why I do not know, because we were within easy range. When we got back to the other end of the plain we found some Yankee support coming up. There were three tank busters and three Honey tanks. Were we glad to see them. They got into position and the enemy cars fled back into the pass.

The next day my corporal and I were sent on a reconnaissance into the hills to see if we could find anything about the pass. We took the jeep as far as we could and then set off on foot. We walked over the hills for about four hours and eventually got within sight of the pass. We could not see right down into it but could see a few men. No cars or tanks. We came back and the CO of the regiment came to find out what we had seen. We told him and he congratulated us on our information. The next day the Americans launched an attack on the pass. They took it without any difficulty. They found plenty of mines and one of our scout cars sent out to give them wireless support ran over one and both men in it broke their legs. They were lucky at that. They might have been killed. We kept watch on that pass for three more days and then were taken out for a rest and a few days maintenance. That is where we are just at present.

Captain Jones, the medical officer attached to the 16th Battalion Durham Light Infantry, also wrote of the battle:

THURSDAY, 25 FEBRUARY 1943

Sudden message to prepare to move. Rommel had attacked further down at Kasserine pass. Company commanders move forward as an advance guard.

FRIDAY, 26 FEBRUARY 1943

Order to remove early next day. I am in charge of an ambulance with the DLI. On the way to them we see a French Algerian soldier, who shouted at us 'Le Boche', 'ou est the Boche' and he pointed to a hill a short distance away. The DLI get ready to occupy these hills, and many casualties. I was told to fetch them with some stretcher bearers. We find a German wounded, who told us he was from the Rhineland. He was a well-built lad of eighteen and had a severe leg wound. He was heavy to carry back to the advance dressing station, which had been established at the tunnel at Sedjenane.

Peter Pettit was an officer with 17th Field Regiment RA, attached at various times to 78th Infantry Division and 6th Armoured Division during the Tunisian campaign. Here he describes the preparations for the final large-scale attack against the German positions in Tunisia:

THURSDAY, 22 APRIL 1943

The stage is all set for the final battle of the Tunisian Campaign, Eighth Army started two mornings ago. The Hun attacked 1 Div. yesterday with three Battalions or more and over 50 tanks; he was beaten off with the loss of 27 tanks and 500 prisoners. By the sound of gunfire from the south for several hours this morning 9 Corps have attacked at Bou Arada.

78 Division is concentrated in the mountains north of Medjez having been in the line since April 7th when the preliminary attack from Oued Zarga to Chaouach and Kelbine began. The infantry are tired and in many cases well below strength; they have already put up a magnificent show in capturing these mountains and have received the congratulations of the Army Commander and General Alexander. As one good fighter in 5 Buffs told his CO 'I do not feel so brave. If I had had a week's rest I should feel as fine as ever'.

Preliminary moves of Artillery and Infantry took place last night: infantry move into forming up areas after dark tonight. All day the Boche has shelled our HQ area intermittently – there is a track behind us in full view which has been used at various times by Mules, Vehicles and Infantry and even Anti Tank Guns, it is the only one.

No damage as far as we know except my windscreen starred. He has also shelled and mortared OP areas as usual, unfortunately killing Tom Farr who was up for the day to release a Tp Commander before tonight's battle; very bad luck and we lost a promising officer. We lost an OP assistant in a similar way yesterday.

The RAF have sent over several sorties of bombers, Mitchells and a similar machine with one tail fin about which we have had a lot of argument! All ranks have enjoyed the sight and sound of our own bombers at work on the defences of Longstop. Not a single enemy aircraft has been seen all day.

The Army Commander said 'Never before has a British Army gone into battle with such overwhelming superiority', six to one in the air, command of the sea, almost ten to one in tanks, more men and very heavy odds on in guns.

There are thunder clouds and lightning in the sky, a haze and a darkness over the view. It looks as though the elements will join in the night's noise with real thunder and perhaps more rain.

Gunners are completing gun pits and slits. Command posts are working out the gun programmes for two separate attacks, firing from 1945hrs to 0219hrs with some breaks and then by observation in moonlight and by day. OP parties are preparing to join their Battalions by daylight ready to advance with them carrying their 21 sets [radios] and gear in the initial advance. Mules are laid on for supplies and reliefs tomorrow evening.

There is a general air of battle and preparation about, almost a tension, and this is added to by the weather which threatens. You wonder whether there is anything which is not properly buttoned up. You go round the regiment, the gunners are tired after a night move and digging but full of fight and eager to shoot all night if it will help. The valley is full of ammunition over 400rpg [rounds per gun] most of which will be used tonight. Hardly any vehicles remain in the area. They have gone back to our previous position for cover and to save congestion.

John Windeatt was the Brigade Major in the 36th Brigade, part of the 78th Division, which saw a great deal of action during the campaign in Tunisia. Here he describes his reaction to the capture of Longstop Hill, a tactically vital position close to Tunis:

MONDAY, 26 APRIL 1943

A great day for the Bde. The Buffs attacked early this morning and with very few casualties they captured Dj Rha, so Longstop is ours. The tanks were magnificent and were largely responsible for the success of the show. We took about 300 prisoners who were herded into a barn close by. The Boche must have seen them, for six shells, 88 mm I think, arrived with great suddenness all around Bde. HQ. Only one came right into us, and that practically wrecked the Office Truck, its usual occupants having departed into a slit trench fortunately, and the only unfortunate chap was Townsend-Rose, a Sapper subaltern who had been visiting us. He was hit in the leg but not badly. David Dawnay nearly came to blows with a Boche officer prisoner after he had brought the Churchills [tanks] down from Longstop. This bloke refused to obey an order from one of the escorts so David seized him by the collar and shook him! The Boche in good English said 'That's not fair'! I had listened to the battle on the tank net, it was like a running commentary from Twickenham. The Boche commander said that he was prepared to hold the position against two British Bdes or 10,000 Americans but had never expected tanks to get on top!

The city of Tunis fell on 7 May, with Fifth Panzer Army surrendering two days later and the remaining Axis forces following suit on the 12th.

The end of the campaign was a time for reflection for men such as the Reverend Druitt, who describes his feelings at the final surrender of German troops in North Africa:

THURSDAY, 13 MAY 1943

Yesterday was an historic occasion; this campaign finished . . .

There now remained a few hundred of the 90th Light Division. Proud of being the last Boche Division still holding out, they thought they would hold us up or cause great losses to us. But Willie Nicholson suggested the course which was followed. The enemy had asked for surrender with battle honours. Our reply was immediate and unconditional surrender. Failing that we would blow them out . . .

It was given out over the Regt wireless that a 'party had been arranged'. It soon came. Droning was heard and the first flight of 18 bombers approached, each carrying a full capacity of loads. With the falling of the first bomb every gun opened up; hundreds of them (including 150 from 8th Army). 'How was that?' came the query from the air. 'Splendid. Right on the target.' The second flight approached and again every bomb devastated part of the target area. Still the guns thundered and roared. The third flight of 18 heavy bombers circled and again the deadly accuracy was repeated. When the last bomb dropped, the guns ceased. There was a deathly stillness. The world was dead. Life had been blasted and detonated. The earth had trembled and shaken. But now everything was dead. Humans had been in the midst of that inferno. Nothing could be seen. Earth and sky were blotted out by huge rolling clouds of smoke and dust. 'O God!' said a British lad, 'Poor buggers!' And the Colonel said, 'It nearly made me sick to watch it; and I suggested it.'

Gradually the clouds of smoke and fume and dust lifted. Our tanks crept forward cautiously. But there was no need for caution. With every few yards of vision clearing, white flags became visible. (Mostly mosquito netting). Presently, the whole area could be seen studded with white flags.

'Be careful!' came the Colonel's voice, 'Be ready for dirty tricks. Direct all prisoners to the road. Tell 'em to walk towards Bon Ficha.'

A squadron leader called the Colonel, 'I can see some guns in the cactus, not pointing this way, but the crews are making no sign of surrender.' 'OK, give them a few rounds with your Browning.'

Prisoners began to pour in from the hills and from holes dug in behind the A/tk ditches. Men who had lived through the hell of shell and bomb. Somehow they seemed amazingly unshaken as a whole but all of them singularly relieved. That was the atmosphere I caught as about 150 passed me.

The tanks rumbled on. One Troop of the 16/5 then made history. Advancing on the left by the beach, these lads actually met and joined up with some 8th Army armour; and so the moment came when the Mediterranean coast from Turkey to Casablanca was in British hands. The Eighth and First Armies had really completed their job and the whole north coast of Africa was freed from Hitler's grip.

At this point David and I reached the Colonel's tank. On our way, cheery greetings came from nearby tanks' crews. Everyone was in great form, including the prisoners who were still rolling up.

A colonel of one of our gunner Regts joined us after a few minutes. As we stood talking, the RA Colonel gave an exclamation and bending down picked up a sparrow, apparently killed by blast. 'Oh, look at this!' he said with regret in his voice, 'And never a sparrow shall fall' he quoted softly and laid it carefully on the grass. How queer men are! A few moments before, his whole Regt. had been contributing to that blasting inferno thrown down on brother men.

Just then four prisoners were advancing towards us. Passing a dead German on the road, they stood round the body for a moment and then came on. I suggested that we might bury the body with their help. So three of us took them back and they carried the body of their comrade to a slit trench. British and German removed their caps and I read the Service. The Germans then asked whether I would take a Service over the grave of their friend, a few hundred yards further on. I agreed and together we walked up the road.

I shall not forget that second Service. The 8th Army had come north and the 1st Army had met them but on this main road they were separated by a blown bridge. Elements of each Army stood facing each other while RE were already arriving to deal with the gap. Our General and General Freyberg and several other brass hats were grouped there. A Press correspondent had also rolled up, and the German grave was between the two Armies. Two Germans and I stood bare headed round that grave as the RE bulldozers rumbled to and fro making the road passable. It was a symbol; the meeting of the two Armies had meant death to Germany in North Africa.

2. The First Chindit Expedition

In the Far East, the British were making their first attempts at offensive action against the Japanese in Burma. The 77th Indian Infantry Brigade, popularly known as the Chindits, was organised by

Brigadier Orde Wingate and dispatched across the river Chindwin in
February 1943 to disrupt Japanese communications.

Captain Wilding served with the 3rd Gurkha Rifles and was attached
as the Cypher Officer to the Headquarters of 77th Indian Infantry
Brigade. Here he records his impressions of the commanding officer:

APRIL 1943

As the Brigadier was, and is, a controversial figure, it is perhaps
proper that I should air my opinion.

He was, most certainly, a great man. A lot of little men have done
their best to denigrate him. They would have been better employed
trying to help him.

He had great physical and moral courage and possessed a will of
iron. I have been fortunate in that I have spent most of my life in
the company of very intelligent people so I am some sort of judge
of intelligence. His was a blazing intelligence.

He was a great reader of the Old Testament, I suppose he was,
possibly, the last of the 'Sword of Bible Generals'.

Of course he had his faults; he could not or would not suffer fools
gladly, he could be rather rude and he was ruthless.

When he emerged from Burma after the 1943 expedition his
report, to put it mildly, pulled no punches. To be frank it was libellous.
But if you are writing a report which may well influence the conduct
of a campaign there is not much point in covering up the deficiencies
of people. I think he was right to write as he did but the authorities
re-called the copies, expurgated the Report and re-issued it. I was
shown one of the originals. I am not sure how it avoided the shredder!
It was quite something. It is gratifying that in the Report he paid
tribute to Ken and me.

Ruthlessness is, I fear, something that all commanders must have.
He steered a car well, but he regarded it as something to get him
from A to B. He had no thought for the engine's well being. He
steered a horse well but was ready to ride one to death if he <u>had</u> to
reach his destination quickly.

He never threw a life away, but you always felt that he realised
that his life and the life of each of us was expendable if it was
necessary.

I remember, when things were very bad, sitting under a bush with my sergeant trying to decipher a more than usually corrupt signal and hearing him ask the MO, 'How long can Wilding last?' The MO said, 'About a week I think.' The Brigadier's reply, 'I only want him for another two days.' Of course neither of them knew I was within ear-shot and were taken aback by my not very respectful interjection, 'After that I suppose you will have me shot like the bloody mules.'

At this time we were, I think, in the neighbourhood of the Heythin Chaung about 40 miles from where we had crossed the Irrawaddy.

We marched those 40 miles in 24 hours and arrived in the vicinity of Inywa early in the morning.

The march stays in my memory – we were very hungry and very tired but we had jettisoned a great deal of kit and our mules had been decimated by Anthrax and this made the going easier. Also our packs were lighter as we carried no food. So our customary 80 lb load was much reduced. Against this we were, frankly, lousy!

Almost as soon as we arrived at the river, I was told to take my ciphers, my sergeant and a transmitter across the river and to be ready to encipher and send a message to the RAF for help if our crossing was interrupted. As the only canoe immediately available held but three and the paddlers, we decided to take one of the bomber dinghies which I had acquired at Argatala and tow it. I put the transmitter in the dinghy.

To my horror we were fired on from the West bank. I much regretted the dinghy which was bright yellow! It is a very odd feeling when you, personally, are fired at – especially for the first time. Also the noise made by bullets ricocheting off water is a bit intimidating.

The paddlers, who were locals, knew that the Japs would kill them but were pretty sure that in spite of my lurid threats, I would not, so they turned back and we regained the East bank. Very sadly Sergeant Crawford of the Royal Signals was killed. It was rotten bad luck – he was hit by a bullet which had ricocheted off the water and, going sideways, hit him in the throat killing him instantly.

I reported with some apprehension to the Brigadier who, fortunately, had seen it all.

We withdrew from the bank and rested.

Wilding was later captured by the Japanese, which was the fate of
many on the First Chindit Expedition. Harassed by the Japanese,
Wingate ordered the columns to disperse and make their way back
to India on 24 March 1943. Only two-thirds of them made it back.
One who didn't was RAF officer F/Lt Ken W . . . whose capture,
imprisonment and death were recorded by his friend and colleague
Flight Lieutenant Edmonds in a fragmentary diary:

APRIL–AUGUST 1943

Both Ken & myself & Col. Alexander wounded – Col A. seriously
wounded in thigh . . . & bleeding badly – Ken has slight wound in
hip & two bullets thro stomach. We managed to carry Col A several
hundred yards, but we were too weak to go further – Col A died
– We hid in some long grass, intending to make our getaway after
dark . . . Our wounds stiffened up – neither of us could walk – very
thirsty – Japs are searching for us – Ken says his mother will know
he is wounded – Japs pass within 10 ft of us – our chances look very
slim – Ken appears unconscious – had [or have] no hat – sun very
hot – would give anything for a drink – shots being fired near & a
good deal of . . .

Japs plug our wounds & give us water and food – they are very
young & fanatical – Ken is capable of walking but is in pain – Mynya.
Interrogated 3 times . . .

5 days in cattle truck – Japs more hostile – Am still unable to walk
– Ken much better – Kalaw. Midnight interrogation by candlelight
. . . Food very poor – Ken much better – still unable to walk myself
– guards rough . . .

Maymo am being taken to Rangoon tomorrow. Rangoon. Am – in
cell No 82 – filthy conditions somebody died last night of dysentery
– unable to get any medical treatment or a wash . . . – Cell searched
& Ken's wallet and photos taken – I made complaint & said photo
was picture of my wife & got it back (hope Ken's sister won't mind!!)
Several prisoners very sick with dysentery. Ken arrives from Maymo.
Has recovered from wounds. Has frequent doses of Malaria – no
Quinine. Was experimented on by Japs with fever. Aug 20. Ken very
bad with high fever – Unable to get any quinine – Unconscious . . .

rambling in speech – Talks of his family – appears to think he is in France. Seems to recognise me at times – unconscious again & I do not think he will live tonight – Aug 21 Ken died – one of the Bravest chaps that I have seen In this war – buried in Rangoon.

Lieutenant Denis Gudgeon of the 3rd Battalion 2nd Gurkha Rifles was luckier and survived in captivity till the end of the war. On his release in 1945, he wrote in a letter of his capture in April 1943:

TUESDAY, 30 APRIL 1945

WHOOPEE, WHOOPEE, WHOOPEE. I AM FREE SAFE AND WELL IN BRITISH HANDS. I feel absolutely overjoyed. I hope to be flown out to India very soon. I will probably be put in hospital first, as the Japs did not treat me very well. I lived on a bowl of rice 3 times a day for 2 years and 8 days of captivity. I was captured on April 20th, 1943, and was in Major-General Wingate's Brigade. I very nearly got back to India, in fact I reached the banks of the Chindwin river, only to be betrayed by Burmese civilians to the Japs. I was absolutely on my last legs, suffering from thirst, hunger, and exhaustion. I don't think I could have gone another day. I had a rather unpleasant time being interrogated, as I refused to talk at first, just giving my name, rank and no. They threatened to cut my head off with a sword, and all the time during my questioning, this Jap officer had his sword pointed at my throat. On April 26th I arrived at the Central Gaol, Rangoon, and was immediately put in solitary confinement for 35 days.

3. The Battle of the Atlantic

The period from late 1942 through to May 1943 was the decisive period for the Battle of the Atlantic. Allied technological and tactical advances during the first half of the war had seen losses to U-boat attack gradually decrease, though the entry of America into the war had seen a spike in losses as the U-boats targeted the American ships travelling up and down the American East Coast in a period that became known as the second 'happy time' to U-boat crews. The lack of an established convoy system combined with the absence of coastal blackout ensured that there were plenty of easy targets for the U-boats. The first half of 1943 saw a renewed assault on British shipping in the Atlantic, with increasing numbers of U-boats available and the use of pack tactics to concentrate the U-boats on particular convoys. More shipping was lost in March 1943 than in any other month of the war.

George Treadaway was a seaman aboard the merchant ship *Empire Bunting* and wrote of his experiences during the convoy SC121, when his ship struggled during a hard-fought passage from Newfoundland back to Great Britain:

TUESDAY NIGHT, 10 MARCH 1943

All hell breaks out starting at 8pm, a ship on the starboard column is torpedoed, I was on lookout when I saw the flash and saw rockets. The wind was blowing and heavy sea running. I pitied the men aboard her.

Just about 8 bells midnight. I was lying in my bunk when another went. I went on deck the sky was alight with star shells sent up by the escort; in no time [at] all the starboard column had gone. The blasties were in the centre of the column evidently.

Some more bangs. I went onto the poop and saw in the light of the shells a ship just heeling over off our quarter. Another on the beam. The rest of the convoy continued at the same speed and same course. I returned to the Foc'sle and half an hour later our steering gear broke again, we were drifting helpless across the convoy. A big ship barely missed our stern. As the convoy continued I felt a tear at my heart, and yet a curious feeling of jubilation to leave the convoy, the U-boats had it marked. The wind was drifting us in an easterly direction. Our only hope was to fix up emergency steering which we set about right away tho this operation took us till daylight.

It was nearly dark when I saw a light moving in the gloom, my first thought was it may be a sub, but presently a corvette looking for survivors [HMCS *Trillium*]. To see its welcome form was a mighty relief. The corvette promised to stand by. We fixed up the relieving tackle, but as the engines got under way . . . wires were broke in no time.

My heart gave a twinge, I felt helpless, the thought of our cargo (explosives) gave me no peace of mind.

As daylight came, so did the wind and sea, we were beam on, and taking them over her.

We set to work on the steering gear again and this time made a more strong job. The corvette was getting anxious and wanted to join the convoy. But the skipper would not get under way owing to the weather. Several of the crew asked the old man to have a try at her but he declined to give the temporary gear a test. Another night drew on, we heard that twelve ships had been hit.

12 out of 36.

Originally the convoy had consisted of over 60 ships, all heavily laden, half of this number had lost the convoy due to bad weather perhaps fortunately for them.

The corvette signalled to us he was short of fuel and as our chances were better if he was with us we offered to refuel him if he could come along side.

Six hours we wasted endeavouring to get him alongside. Once we got his line but it snapped like a carrot.

He tried a dozen times to do it, but in the end he asked us to get cracking. The corvette was *K172*. A message came through another ship out of the convoy near us had got it. A tanker the *Rosewood* was 50 miles away sinking and all her boats and rafts swept away by seas. I hope they were rescued in time the weather was terrible. Rumours were all round the ship; one was we were 200 miles from the nearest point of Scotland, actually we were 600 miles. Fortunately we had drifted about 70 odd miles nearer home. Another night of nervous waiting came and went, the steering gear, with a bit of attention was holding though we was steering an erratic course.

We met an American cutter who relieved our corvette, who signalled the bridge a good luck message and with just enough fuel, set out for Glasgow. How we cheered that night when we had first seen him, while we was helpless, a guy on the escort kept taking pictures of us. I'd like to have one, may be it would show the different expressions on our faces as we tried desperately to get her ropes aboard, our minds dwelling all the time on the TNT below decks.

About 9 o'clock in the evening the submarine warning flag went up on the escort, I felt my heart beat at twice as fast for a time but after a couple of hours it eased up. Any case we left it behind.

Off the coast of Ireland a tug was waiting for us. We sighted her about dark, she had several fruitless attempts to tie us up. I could have sworn, because in trying to get her line aboard she fired rockets.

I heard one guy say if he got out of this one OK, he'd kiss the pavement. They were my sentiments, too.

Sunday morning we were off the Mull of Kintyre, the most welcome sight ever. We still continued our queer steering up the Clyde and home to anchor in Loch Long. The cargo is estimated at a million pounds, rice, copper and high explosive.

Charles Matthews served as a leading signalman aboard HMS *Fame*, operating from Liverpool and St Johns and Argentia in Newfoundland with B6 Escort Group on North Atlantic convoys. His destroyer saw constant action during this period, even including ramming a U-boat, which he describes below:

WEDNESDAY, 14 OCTOBER 1942

U-boats attacking all last night and we lost ten ships. We couldn't do a thing about it. I think that a U-boat must have got into the convoy and just picked off the ships until he ran out of torpedoes.

THURSDAY, 15 OCTOBER 1942

All daylight hours spent chasing U-boats that we can see on the horizon following the convoy. We go after them at full speed, sometimes firing our 4.7-inch guns to make them dive, then drop a few depth charges to send them as deep as we can, then rush back to our position on the screen. Our sister destroyer, HMS *Viscount*, managed to catch one on the surface and rammed it at full speed. This drastic action knocked the *Viscount's* bows back a bit and she requested permission to make for home as she was in a sinking condition. Permission was granted and she disappeared over the horizon like a speed boat, at least that is how it appeared to me.

Chased U-boats all day, they seem to be all over the place. Every ship in the escort group was doing its stuff.

FRIDAY, 16 OCTOBER 1942

On the go all last night fighting off the U-boats. The sky all around the convoy was alight with star shells from the escort ships, gunfire and the dull thud of exploding depth charges.

Following this, I had the forenoon watch (0800 to 1230hrs); it was teeming with rain, having no sleep and soaked to the skin everyone on the bridge was very bad tempered. We were in station ahead of the convoy and towards the end of this miserable watch we got an asdic [sonar] contact and attacked with depth charges.

As the sea astern shivered, flattened and then rose in great fountains, the black bow of a U-boat rose into the air. As we turned, she levelled out and was probably going to dive again. The skipper gave the order, 'stand by to ram', this was shouted over the ship and we went at the U-boat full ahead. We hit her a glancing blow, just forward of her conning tower. She slewed round and her conning tower scraped down our starboard side tearing a hole in our ship's side.

The U-boat was almost as big as we were and after rolling under our stern she levelled onto an even keel on the surface. As we came round again some of the Jerries came out of the conning tower and made a run for the gun on her forward deck. Every gun we had opened fire at her and everyone aboard was cheering like mad. Jerries then came tumbling out of the conning tower and jumping into the drink.

In the meantime, ships of the convoy had caught us up and as the lines of ships passed through the mists of the rain they saw the U-boat and they opened up. Shells were whistling all over the place. We lowered a boat and our navigator Lt. Jones went aboard the U-boat. He came out of the conning tower and stepped into our boat as the U-boat sank. He was a very brave man.

While this was going on, we were hove-to and picking up the Jerry crew helped by the *Potentilla*. There were about 40 of them. They were stripped re-clothed and distributed around the ship. We had 17 on our mess to look after.

Whilst this activity was going on, the engine room was flooded and we were slowly sinking. The gash in our side was blocked off by dropping hair mats over the side, the ship was trimmed to list and raise the hole as far as possible out of the water; and then the pumps became effective and were able to compete with the water coming inboard. We were stationary for about four hours with one corvette circling us until we could get under way again. It was a highly dangerous situation with so many U-boats about.

LATER

We eventually got back to Liverpool where a Marine Band and the Commander-in-Chief Western Approaches, Admiral Sir Max Horton turned out to give us a civic reception of welcome. Unfortunately there was a delay as they got the welcome party ready. This nearly proved to be disastrous as the skipper said that it would be undignified to enter harbour with a list to starboard and so had trimmed the ship to put us on an even keel. During the delay we sat in the river in a sinking condition with the skipper biting his nails and saying 'Wouldn't it be awful if we sank'.

The prisoners were taken off the ship and I just caught one of them walking off wearing my best boots. There are limits to love for your fellow men and I was just in time to recover them.

Charles Matthews describes another convoy later in the year:

SATURDAY, 5 DECEMBER 1942

Have had some pretty foul weather that has slowed the convoy but things are calming down a bit and we are making better headway.

We have U-boats with us. Sighted one on the horizon and made a run at him but all we could do was put him down. One popped up this morning and had a look at us.

It's a black night and snowing but the weather is not too bad. During the last few days of gales life has been lousy. The mess deck is right up in the bows of the ship under the fo'c'sle and when the ship is pitching, life is hell. The ship climbs up the side of a wave and falls on the top of it. You can feel yourself flying downwards. You land with a terrible crash and the noise of the sea crashing over the bows of the ship is deafening. What a racket! Why did I join the Navy?

It's impossible to imagine what it's like to get a meal. You have to keep picking yourself and your dinner off the deck. Everything flies around – it's chronic.

The weather is OK now. It's snowing of course but the wind is behind us so it's not so cold.

We are escorting a fast convoy, 10 knots, so if we can dodge the subs we ought to be home by next Sunday.

SUNDAY, 6 DECEMBER 1942

Middle watch. Midnight till 0400hrs . . . I have the afternoon watch, 1230 till 1600hrs, and then from midnight till 0400hrs and on again at 0800 till 1230hrs tomorrow. It doesn't give a bloke much time to sleep.

I must go and have a bath and shave. My beard is quite long.

We have pork chops (American) and apple sauce for dinner.

Sunday Evening. I didn't get my bath or shave. It's been a lovely day, sunshine between the snow and between the showers excellent visibility.

We saw a U-boat on the surface and together with another destroyer set off in chase. After he had dived we saw another one and have been hunting them all day. We kept them below surface while the convoy altered course and got miles out of sight. We then joined the convoy hoping that they would have lost us, but hopes were soon dashed. When we got to the convoy another sub came up and gave our position away again.

It's a lovely night and you can see for miles.

MONDAY, 7 DECEMBER 1942

Surprisingly a fairly quiet night. A long range attack was made on the convoy but no ships were hit. It's been a grand day today, sunshine with just enough bite in the air to make things lively and an occasional snow-storm.

Chased another U-boat today but again as the skipper says, 'The buggers dive too quick for us'.

There are several U-boats around us tonight and I think this night is going to be critical. Am on duty at 0400 till 0800hrs.

TUESDAY, 8 DECEMBER 1942

No sleep last night. It was a grand starlit night with the whole sky ablaze with the Northern Lights. You could see for miles. We chase and attack U-boats continually, with depth charges and gunfire. Four times we went 'full ahead, hard a-starboard/port' to dodge torpedoes aimed at us. We lost one tanker. She was loaded with aircraft fuel and the sea was a sheet of flame. The miracle was that most of her crew were picked up. She was hit just after 2300hrs and the sky was still lit up astern at 0600hrs.

The commodore of the convoy complimented the escort on the grand fight they had put up, here's one fellow who was glad to see the dawn.

WEDNESDAY, 9 DECEMBER 1942

The weather worsened during last night and today there is a fairly rough sea and continual heavy hail and rain storms.

We are still surrounded with U-boats and made several attacks on them before midnight. The *Potentilla* got a probable.

I came off watch at midnight without much hope of getting any sleep.

THURSDAY, 10 DECEMBER 1942

Climbed into my hammock last night and slept until 0800hrs this morning. I felt a lot better for it but am still a bit bleary eyed. The skipper took pity on us and didn't sound Action Stations although the convoy was attacked.

We lost another tanker at about 0600hrs this morning. I understand that she sank in about four minutes. I don't know if any of her crew have been saved.*

(*Learned later that there was no survivors).

The sea is very rough today and the ship is rolling and tossing about just to make things more unpleasant. U-boats are still with us. I go on watch at 1230hrs and again at midnight.

Awful night – pouring with rain. There are U-boats all around us again so we can expect another bad night; these blokes are fresh ones, we believe, as the others must have used nearly all of their torpedoes at this time.

This is a valuable convoy and the Jerries know it. We had expected to have got past the danger area by now. It isn't very often that they follow us as far east as this. Tonight we are 26 East, so it won't be long before we reach England. Saturday or Sunday I suppose. But I'm chocker with these nights. I suppose that I'm feeling the loss of sleep.

I need a haircut badly and the first thing I do when I arrive in port is a hair cut then a bath.

Hectic night. No sleep for anyone. The battle started just after dark and lasted without stop until dawn. Gunfire, starshells and tracers and depth charges all night. We are greatly outnumbered by U-boats but didn't lose a ship.

The commodore said this morning, 'I am lost in admiration at the skill of your escort. You have made escort history.'

FRIDAY, 11 DECEMBER 1942

Made a good attack on a sub and probably got him.

We have had aircraft over today and one of them sank a sub near us. The pilot said 'Will we go and pick up survivors who were in the water', but the skipper said that we couldn't afford to send a ship. It's rotten to think of those Jerries waiting to die but that's war and their pals would only like to weaken the escort.

We saw distress signals over the horizon and one of the Corvettes went to investigate and found that one of the aircraft has crashed. He could find no survivors.

SATURDAY, 12 DECEMBER 1942

Our friends have left us, anyway we had a quiet night. The weather was perfectly lousy – maybe that was why we had no attacks. Today it has been congratulations all round.

Although we lost two ships we can say it was a victory to us.

Tonight we have left the convoy and are making for Liverpool at 20 knots. We will see England tomorrow.

Charles Matthews' entry for 12 December highlights the growing role of air power in the war against the U-boats. Once the convoy came in range of land-based aircraft, the U-boats withdrew in the face of the aerial threat. It was in the area of the Atlantic that air power could not cover, the mid-Atlantic 'air gap', that most of the submarine attacks occurred.

The entry of the USA into the war had opened another front for the U-boats along the North American East Coast and in the Caribbean. Arthur Potts of the MV *Rookley* describes being under attack by a U-boat in the waters off Trinidad in August 1942:

SUNDAY, 2 AUGUST 1942

7.15pm alarm bell rang, when Bill Davidson sighted sub ¼ mile away on starboard bow. First torpedo passed close astern, exploding about 100yds further away. Torpedo number 2 seemed certain to hit us near No 1 hold, but we watched it pass under the bow and explode very close. Torpedo number 3 we never saw. It must have been fired from greater depth, but the explosion seemed to be right under our bows and gave us a nasty jarring. Our surface speed soon took us out of his sight before moon rise at 11pm but it is an anxious night . . .

MONDAY, 3 AUGUST 1942

At 2am an American patrol plane began circling us for a while. Possibly sent out to see if we were still afloat as we haven't sent any further message since our 'SSSS' last night.

Daylight at 5am was very welcome for everyone is very tired and some of us are 'sore eyed' too.

I think everyone aboard is still rather dazed and wondering how we managed to get out of such a 'mess'.

It is extremely difficult to write about my own feeling, for the hissing white wake of the torpedo that I saw is still too vivid in my mind's eye yet and it will be a while before our latest 'escape' is properly settled in its proper place in my memory. Actually, I think I'm still feeling a little scared. The tension of running an almost continuous gauntlet plays havoc with one's nerves – or is it that I'm getting old and can't take it.

How is it possible for a sub to miss a ship from less than 500 yards range? Being a light ship, we must have looked huge to him.

THURSDAY, 13 AUGUST 1942

Awake at 3.50am by explosion followed by alarm bell. *Delmundo* torpedoed, right alongside, on our port hand. Just reached bridge when the *Eversleigh*, under Latvian flag, got it amidships. As we were the nearest ship to both, Eversleigh being right astern to us, – we fired the rockets as signal to escorts.

Delmundo began sinking by the stern, slowly, while boats were being lowered, but the Latvian went down like a stone – iron ore!

And so the careers of two more ships – and definitely a number of lives – ended, while planes and escorts searched and we 'waited for it'.

The fact of no depth charges being used was proof enough that the sub had dived under the convoy; the beat of the props helping him to keep under shelter.

Daylight at 6am brought relief to us after more nasty tension.

The now inevitable jokes about the '*Rookley* luck' were made, but to me they leave a nasty taste in the mouth and by the look on the 'OM's' face he doesn't appear to be amused any more. After all, he and I have been living on that 'luck' for 2 yrs now.

FRIDAY, 14 AUGUST 1942

Terrific explosion at 6.15am was the prelude to more fun – again on our port hand.

First a tanker, who broke apart, leaving her bow portion afloat. Then the *Michael Jebson*, loaded with sugar, got it in the engine room, capsized and sank in seven minutes. The third and last explosion was the loudest. A British tanker had her bows blasted wide open, but did her damnedest to keep in station abaft our port beam. Her crew accommodation was in the bows, so there will be a sorry mess aboard her.

Escorts did plenty of blasting, while the crippled tanker edged towards the rear centre of the convoy.

At noon she signalled 'lower flags, funeral at 1pm', again at 4.30pm she lowered some more of her crew over the side for good.

Course set at 6pm to take us through the Bahama Channel.

'Uncle Sam' has a full-time job on his hands to clear this infested area.

⚜

4. The RAF's Strategic Bombing Campaign

The year 1942–43 also saw the RAF undertake a major effort to 'de-house' German workers and run down German industrial capacity. Sir Arthur Harris, the head of Bomber Command, had fought hard to maintain the position of his force as a war-winning weapon, notably through the 1,000-bomber raids on Cologne in the first half of 1942. However, by the end of the year his bomber force increasingly consisted of four-engined 'heavy' bombers such as the Halifax and the Lancaster and he felt confident enough to launch a major campaign.

Ken Handley was a British flight engineer on the Halifax bombers of No. 466 Squadron Royal Australian Air Force (RAAF) during the campaign and describes his feelings on making his first operational sortie:

TUESDAY, 15 FEBRUARY 1944

1,300 Miles, 'Berlin'

Bombload. 4,500 lbs incendiaries. A.M.P.G. [air miles per gallon]: 81. 7 hrs 30 mins.

An uneventful trip with no searchlights owing to ten tenths cloud base 2000 tops 6,000 over target. Bombing height 22,300ft. Out of target, 24,000. Light Flak below us + numerous fighter flares around target + on return trip. Evasive action taken but no combats with fighters. Aircraft lost 2 missing. 1 crashed on return near Scarborough. Wireless account 45 missing. 1758 gals used.

Reaction

Not so frightening as I had expected. A little fear at the bottom of it all. Tense last half hour when tank 4 iced up + no joy with it for 10 minutes. Returned just tired – after eggs and bacon slept well.

Re: a tense 'last half hour' in notes across page – The resultant tenseness was due to arriving over our coast with literally NO FUEL showing on the gauges – Jack asked permission to land immediately without any 'stacking'. This we did expecting the engines to cut at any moment. What a relief to be taxiing along the runway and perimeter track.

It was not until the following morning that the ground crew said that they could not get any fuel into the bomb bay tank – it was still full – I had forgotten to pump (230 gals) into tanks 1 & 3 after leaving the target area. Hence the apparent use of all the fuel as read by the gauges.

The lure of Berlin as a target, the 'Big City', as it became known, is apparent from many of the diaries of the flight crew of Bomber Command, such as Charles Owen, a Lancaster pilot with No. 97 Squadron RAF:

FRIDAY, 26 NOVEMBER 1943

First trip with my own crew, and the Big City at that. Usual flares and aircraft shot down on the way in. Target was clear, and we could see fires burning from an attack on the previous night. Hundreds of searchlights and very heavy flak, firing mainly into the cones. Flew over HANNOVER by mistake on return journey and was coned for seven minutes. Lost height from 20,000 to 13,000ft during evasive action from intense heavy flak. Several holes in starboard wing and roof of cockpit, and the bomb aimer was wounded slightly in the leg. Also attacked by fighter when coned, but only damage was 6 ins. knocked off one blade of the starboard outer prop.

Charles Owen was not so lucky on another trip to Berlin early in 1944:

SUNDAY, 2 JANUARY 1944

New Year but same target. Very quiet on way in, and 10/10 cloud over target. Flak was moderate. Got jumped badly by fighter on way home across France. Both gunners were wounded, the rear gunner seriously, and the starboard outer engine caught fire. Found it impossible either to extinguish fire or feather prop., and had to have rudder tied by engineer to maintain straight flight, as the rudder trimmers had been shot away. Limped into Tangmere and swung off runway on landing, due to starboard tyre being holed by cannon shell. End of V-VICTOR I.

Robert Raymond was an American volunteer who originally served in an American Ambulance Unit in France in 1940, before travelling via Spain and Portugal to the UK, where he served as a Sergeant Pilot in the RAF. He wrote home to America describing his exploits in the air:

Monday, 18 January 1943

On January 16 we were briefed for Berlin. We all knew that sooner or later during this winter we should go there. Any raid on that city has tremendous propaganda value and is good for morale. Nevertheless, although it was not entirely unexpected and everyone wanted to have it on a line in his Log Book, I felt rather weak in the knees when I walked into the Briefing Room and saw that name on the big board. Price, my Wireless Operator, said, 'I'd rather go to Essen than Berlin, and I hate Essen as a target.'

We took off about dusk and never saw the ground after leaving Base until we were over Berlin, which fortunately was in a clear area. Just heavy flak and lots of it over the target, no tracers from light guns, which only reach up to about 8,000 feet, no balloons, no searchlights or night fighters, etc. They knew what height we were and put up a box barrage all around us. We were straight and level for two minutes for the bombing run, and every second seemed like a year. The whole of northern Europe is covered with snow, and the moon being nearly full, the ground detail was clearly visible. The only colourful parts of the target were a half dozen flares and the great glowing mushrooms from our four thousand pounders. We carried one 4000lb. bomb and nearly a thousand incendiaries and got a fairly good photo of our results. Since Carter has been AWOL [Absent Without Leave] for three weeks, we took another Rear Gunner. It was his first Operational flight, and he was so excited before, during and after the trip that he wasn't worth much. Much of our report on the trip depends on his accurate observations over the target where he has a better view than anyone else. Before take off he looked up into the bomb bay and asked if that big cylindrical object was a spare petrol tank. It was the 4000lb cookie [blockbuster bomb], and he had never seen one before.

Cloud over Base when we returned was less than 1000 feet and I did a short cross-country flight until most of the others had landed. I don't like being stacked up on a circuit in cloud at 500-foot intervals with a dozen other tired pilots.

Had eight hours sleep, and all crews that had serviceable planes were briefed for Berlin again. Climbed up through layers of cloud over the North Sea that were tinted with the red glow of the setting sun. In the clear air between them it looked like some of those dreamy cloudland shots in *Lost Horizon*. Just a space without a horizon except for the banded cloud of soft greys, mauve, purple, and grey blues, and with George flying I had plenty of time to think – odd thoughts as mine always are – how scared I had been in a nearby town two nights ago when sitting in a café during an Air Raid Alert. Several enemy planes bombed from low level, and one bomb demolished the building across the street. The blast effect even from that small effort was considerable and made me appreciate what we were doing to the enemy targets with our forces and weight-carrying capacity. Verily it is better to send than to receive in this racket.

Then I thought about the message from the Chief of Bomber Command which had been addressed to us tonight and read out at Briefing, 'Go to it, Chaps, and show them the red rose of Lancaster in full bloom.' Someone behind a desk had given an order to a great organization, and here we were a few hours later, one of the pawns in the game, sitting up over the North Sea with the temperature at minus 30 degrees Centigrade, wondering if we would ever see England again.

Vapour condensation trails were plainly visible in the clear moonlight above cloud, showing that many other planes were a few minutes ahead on the same track. They are always a curious phenomenon and form at the trailing edge of your wings, due to the decrease in pressure there. Out over the sea we pay no attention to them, but over enemy territory they always result in attacks by night fighters. Conditions over the target about the same as the previous night, except the visibility was even better. Several members of the crew heard shrapnel from spent bursts bounce off our fuselage, and the Rear Gunner saw five members of a crew bail out and go down on their white silk umbrellas. We passed quite close to them. Flak was more accurate than the previous night, and several times I saw the black smoke puffs indicating shell bursts right in front of us as we were leaving the target area.

Collected some ice on the return trip, but I have no fear of that now, having studied diligently and knowing why, when and how it occurs. It is only necessary to be able to recognise the type of cloud, the frontal weather conditions, and have an accurate thermometer to avoid its cumulative effects. Each time I climbed to lower temperatures or descended to clearer areas, and we went through it confidently although I have reason to believe that it accounted for some that are missing.

Impossible to land at base, and we were diverted nearly 200 miles, by which time we were running on the fumes that came from the last drops of petrol that Griffiths was squeezing out of the tanks.

Came back to base today and found many missing and the rest scattered over England in various ways. More and more I find that knowledge is a more valued asset than courage. Each member of the Crew is still learning. Griffiths has found the best speeds to fly and rates of climb for most economical fuel consumption. We keep our own charts and are improving steadily.

Two consecutive nights to Berlin leaves me with but one thought when I have finished this letter. To sleep for at least 12 hours. And my stomach reminds me that I haven't seen an egg for nearly a month, and our food is very poor.

Harold Wakefield served on the Halifaxes of No. 51 Squadron RAF as a Flight Engineer, and wrote to his parents describing his dangerous early operations with the enthusiasm and excitement typical of such a young man:

FRIDAY, 24 SEPTEMBER 1943

Well I am quite fit and well and glad to hear you are both OK. Now I have something to tell you which will probably surprise you. I didn't really know whether to tell you or not. But you're not scared to know, and you always like to know what I'm doing. Well I've done two ops. It was grand, really grand. Talk about fun and excitement. I was on

Wed night 22nd. We went to Hanover. You've probably read about it by now. Then I was on again last night Thursday 23rd, this time to Mannheim.

Two in two nights, it's not often that happens. We do on average two or three a week.

I enjoyed every minute of it, and believe me there's not much of those two cities left. Jerry's certainly going through it. One minute the place is peaceful and then in about 30 mins it's a mass of blazing ruins, on fire from end to end. Flames and smoke thousands of feet high. They're just swamped. I could still see the fires burning, the glow in the sky, when we were 200 miles away, and that's not exaggerating. Plane after plane, one after the other, just shoving 'em down. Poor Jerry. It's terrible what they're going through. But we enjoy doing it just the same. Their defences aren't bad, but just bewildered. We're all in and out so quickly that they don't have time to get going. Their flak doesn't seem to be able to reach us. But it explodes underneath us and shakes us a bit, it's quite a pleasant sensation though. They rely chiefly on their night fighters. But they're not so hot. Nothing we can't deal with, and if we see them coming first they don't stand a earthly because there are eight belching machine guns waiting for 'em, and I've seen more than one Jerry fighter going down in flames, bless 'em. Yes I'd much sooner be up where we are than down below at Jerry's end. He knows what bombing is now alright, believe me. It's mass slaughter, with Jerry at the receiving end, and he won't be able to stand it much longer. Hanover and Mannheim are heaps of rubble now, and I'll bet those fires will burn for days. I think the Jerry firemen are the hardest worked blokes of the war.

We've had no trouble at all yet, and I've done my job to the satisfaction of everyone.

Johnny our pilot is wonderful. He can throw our kite about like an Austin seven. A searchlight picked us up over Hanover but Johnny was out of that in about 2 seconds. A fighter got on our tail but Jock had him spotted, and told Johnny, a couple of twists and turns and that fighter was soon disposed of, he lost us altogether. Poor old Jock was mad though because he didn't have a burst at it. There's no need for guns on our kite because Johnny can lose 'em in two shakes. It's a piece of cake.

The first trip on Wed. night to Hanover we weren't nervous, more excited. The only time we were scared, was when we arrived a little way off the target. When we saw the fires, searchlights and ack-ack, we did feel nervous for a second but it passed over. Johnny said, 'OK blokes, I'm not stopping here long, it ain't healthy, let's get back for the eggs and bacon'. So he turned in, opened up the engines, put the nose down for extra speed, and we dived over Hanover at about 250, dropped the goods and were out again, all in about 2 mins. One of the lads said over the intercom, 'Coo, ain't it pretty'. Another said, 'Blimey, it's just like Blackpool illuminations'. Some of the things they say are really funny. Last night I wasn't the slightest bit nervous or excited, honestly. It's rather boring.

We have egg and bacon before we go, and again as soon as we get back. It's worth it to get two lots of egg and bacon.

We've got a rest for two or three nights now, to catch up on our sleep. I don't feel any different. My nerves are better, if anything. It's nice on the way back home, when we get well away from the target and get the coffee out, and the chocolates. It makes me hungry.

Well, I thought you'd want to know, because you've always liked to know what I'm doing, and I thought you'd be getting suspicious if I didn't tell you soon. But there's no reason at all for you to worry, because I know I'm going to be OK and I've always got my parachute handy . . .

SATURDAY, 25 SEPTEMBER 1943

The other thing I've got to tell you about is very exciting. I've baled out! and made a successful descent by parachute. Mon. night as you know we went to Berlin, Tues and Wed nights we had off. Thursday we took off at 11.30pm for Frankfurt. We flew down England and turned towards the coast at Reading. As we neared the coast before we knew what had happened another Halifax hit us. It sort of side-slipped across the top of us. There was a terrific crunching etc. But Johnny kept control all the time. But it was very hard to fly and we were losing height. Half the tailplane and one rudder was torn off. Two feet of the port wing was ripped off, one of the props was shattered consequently we only had three engines and they had been knocked about a bit and any minute we expected the rest of the tailplane to fall off. But we held on while we crossed the coast and jettisoned our bomb in the sea. Then we turned back over land again, and Johnny gave orders to 'abandon aircraft'. He said he'd stay a bit and see if he could land it by himself, but if necessary he'd bale out himself. So we clipped on our 'chutes and said a little prayer (at least I did) and baled out one after another. We were all a bit nervous, but I was pretty excited myself. Anyway I went out head first and was battered and banged about by the slipstream, I turned several somersaults and dropped several hundred feet. Then there was a colossal jerk as if I'd been torn in half and I knew my 'chute had opened OK. I jumped at 10,000 feet but there was no wind hardly and I drifted down, it was a lovely sensation floating down, but it only took me about seven mins before I hit the ground with a bit of a thud, my knees buckled up and I landed on my <u>bum</u>. On the way down I crashed through a tree but luckily didn't get stuck although I did get a slight scratch across my cheek. I landed in a field. So I rolled my 'chute up and slung it over my shoulder and started walking over fields and hedges until I came to a road, after about 2 hrs walking I came to a small village. I went to the house and knocked them up (by this time it was 3 o clock Friday morning as I baled out about 1 o clock). They took me in (it was a young man and his wife) and were very good.

They wanted to give me a bath, whisky etc. But I had a cup of tea. They rang the nearest RAF 'drome up and gave them all the particulars. The 'drome was only about 10 miles away and someone was sent immediately in a car to pick me up.

Not all escapes by parachute occurred over friendly territory. Geoffrey Hall, an RAF sergeant navigator with 427 Squadron RCAF, a Canadian Wellington bomber squadron, had to bail out during his first operation, a raid on Ludwigshafen in April 1943:

16/17 APRIL 1943

Much has happened since the 13th. On the afternoon of the 16th. we were briefed to attack AG Farben Industrie on the banks of the Rhine at Ludwigshafen.

We took off at dusk and headed south-east, climbing on course. My last glimpse of England was the fading grey arm of Flamborough Head. We passed through the French coastal barrage uneventfully and soon after that the Gee set [radar] became useless, the Germans jamming it with waving streamers of 'grass'. From then on the navigation was dead reckoning only.

Ostaficiuk startled us once by giving a night-fighter false alarm and firing his guns at the planet Jupiter. Then it was a tedious but suspenseful journey. We saw flak going up in streams in the moonlit haze many miles to starboard and I identified it as Saarbrucken.

Soon after we were approaching the target and the first Pathfinder marker flares were going down. Because of inexperience we made a mess of our first bombing run and went round and tried again. The bombs went but we were held in a powerful blue searchlight. I heard Bill shouting over the intercom, 'Get weaving, skipper, for Christ's sake.'

There was a dull thump like someone hitting a wall with his fist and the port engine stopped dead. The Wimpey [Wellington bomber] lurched, hung in the sky for a moment, then dropped like a stone. She went down so fast that I left my seat and remained suspended in mid air for a few seconds. Also floating near my nose were my dividers, ruler and pencil. Through my headphones I could hear the crew shouting at Steve and above all Ostaficiuk screaming, 'We gotta get out. She's going down.' Then the aircraft must have righted itself because I suddenly hit the floor violently and immediately was very sick. I heard Steve asking me for a course to steer and collecting my charts together gave him a direction pointing to the nearest part of France.

By this time the starboard engine was making a noise like an old lawnmower and we were not doing much more than gliding west. It was obvious that we would never make the French border. However we had bombed from twenty-one thousand feet and despite our momentary loss of altitude during the stall we were still at a considerable height.

While Steve held the Wimpey in a steep glide, Albert and Tony, the W/Op AG [Wireless Operator Air Gunner], worked frantically at the balance cocks which changed our fuel tanks over. They wondered whether the engines were starved of petrol by fuel lines being cut. But it was useless and presently Steve, probably thinking he couldn't hold the Wimpey much longer, gave us the order to bale out. I clipped my chute on the two harness rings on my chest, pressed a button to blow up the still secret Gee set, and made my way forward to the front escape hatch. Only an hour or two ago I had entered the hatch so confidently at the beginning of my career with Bomber Command and the Navigation Officer saying, 'Good luck, see you at breakfast.' No chance of that now.

Ostaficiuk swung his turret and dropped out backwards. Tony and Albert went out of the front hatch and I paused a moment on the brink, looking down. The moonlight picked out a great river in the black landscape. Steve was still in his seat, holding the plane steady. He jerked his thumb down and the next moment I was gone. The black shape of the aircraft was silhouetted for a second against the silver backcloth of the clouds then it too disappeared.

I pulled the ripcord and was momentarily horrified by the sound of tearing stitches as the heavy leather straps broke away to be stopped by the steel bands on the shoulders. Unaware of the principle, I believed that the chute had torn itself away from me. But no, after a tremendous jerk on the shoulders, I was floating gently peacefully down and saying over and over again, 'Oh, my poor mother, my poor Jo', and thinking about them receiving a 'missing' telegram in the morning.

I still could not see the kind of terrain in which I was going to land but over on the right a fire was burning fiercely where the bomber had crashed and I could hear crisp popping as thousands of rounds of ammunition exploded. Then the ground came up swiftly, soft, ploughed earth, but even so I bit my tongue with the impact.

Undulating countryside, no noise but a faint, pervasive scent that was new to me. Magnolias? It was easy to bury the parachute in the soft earth. I then ripped off the button from the shoulder of my battledress and unscrewed the escape compass. The tiny, luminous needle flickered to the north and I began to walk west towards the big river I had seen in the moonlight, towards France. Overhead a very lonely sound as bombers from some other raid droned home.

I was dressed in blue battledress tunic and trousers, a white aircrew issue roll-neck-collar pullover and brown suede leather flying boots with rubber soles. On my battledress tunic was a whistle to summon other members of the crew if down in the drink and three lucky charms – a Land Army brooch my girl had given me and two tiny toy dogs from my future mother-in-law. In my pocket was a slim box called an escape kit which contained essentials for this kind of emergency. I was in enemy country with no clear idea of exactly where I had landed but I knew that I was hundreds of miles from England.

Geoffrey Hall landed safely, was captured and spent the rest of the war in German prisoner of war camps.

Thoughts of mortality occupied the minds of many of the flight personnel of Bomber Command. Sergeant Reg Fayers flew as a navigator on Halifax bombers with No. 76 Squadron RAF, based at RAF Holme-on-Spalding Moor in Lincolnshire. In an unsent letter to his wife, he explains his reasons for flying and fighting in the war in general:

SUMMER 1943

From Sergt. R. J. Fayers, Sergeants Mess,

RAF HOLME ON SPALDING MOOR

To Mistress Phyl Fayers, Ploughlane Dairy, SUDBURY, SFK.

(Not posted).

Darling, I've occasionally felt lately that should I not come home on leave next week, you would think it rather inconsiderate of me not to say a farewell and an excuse, so herewith both. (It's a grey evening and I've nothing to do but write and read, and I've already read.)

Lately in letters I've mentioned that I've flown by night and that I've been tired by day, but I haven't said that I can now claim battle honours – Krefeld, Muhlheim, Gelsenkirchen, Wuppertal and Cologne. I suppose I've been fighting in the Battle of the Ruhr.

But it hasn't felt like that. It doesn't seem like fighting to climb aboard an aircraft with your friends and climb to a space where the sunset seems infinite; to sit in a small space, and on the engine-noise background hear the everyday commonplaces spoken to you while you juggle with figures and lines to find God's intentions in the winds; to sit for a few hours at 20,000 feet working hard so that when Tom eventually says 'Bombs gone, photograph taken. OK Steve, fly away,' it doesn't seem anything more than part of the job, and a fresh course to be steered, this time for home. It's aloof and impersonal, this air war. One has no time to think of hell happening below to a set of people who are the same as you except that their thinking has gone a bit haywire. It's a fair assumption that when Tom dropped our bombs the other night, women and boys and girls were killed and cathedrals damaged. It must have been so. Were it more personal, I should be more regretting, I suppose. But I sit up there with my charts and pencils and I don't see a thing. I never look out. In five raids all I've seen is a cone of searchlights up by Amsterdam, with the southern coast of the Zuider Zee – where poor Ben Dove was found – and a few stars. And as far as humanity is concerned, I can't definitely regret that I've helped to kill German people.

The only thought that comes from the outside is when occasionally Gillie, the mid-upper gunner, says 'Turn to starboard, go . . .' It might mean that out there in the darkness which you cannot even see, somewhere there is a night fighter with a German boy in it; and he may kill you. When Gillie or Reuben says 'Turn to starboard, go . . .', that quick weakening thought comes in – 'May be this is It'. But you never can believe it. It doesn't seem possible that what is so orderly and efficient a machine one second can become, within the next minute, a falling killing thing, with us throwing ourselves from it into a startling world of surprised chaos. But it can happen, and, I suppose, does happen to a lot of us. So far we've had two small holes in 'H' for 'Harry' and nothing more. We have been very lucky. We have flown straight and high, dropped our bombs and come home to bacon and eggs, or maybe only beans on toast. But, so far, we have come home.

Should you ever read this, I suppose it will mean that I haven't. I can't imagine that. If I really could imagine it, I suppose I wouldn't fly. Or would I?

I really don't know.

But, darling, I could never live easy with the thought inside me that a struggle is going on in the world without me helping good old Right against the things so wrong that have got into our system. This world is a swell sort of place even now; there's so much beauty in it, such thrilling beauty. If a thing is really beautiful, through and through beautiful, it seems to me it is good. And it could be so much more so. I suppose really that is why I sit on our bombs and fly with them until we come to one more of Jerry's cities. Instinctively it seems I've come to help, first in destroying the bad old things, and then in rebuilding.

If you read this, I suppose there'll be no Simon in this world. But for those other worlds that will come, there will be Simon. And there will be other worlds, darling; there will be Simon. For them, I suppose, it is that I fly. That must be the answer, I guess. I struggle instinctively to be with you, walking so quietly by Brundon fields and Barnardiston hedges, eating enough lettuce hearts so clean and green for the two of us, being together in the excitement of our love, and in the quiet moonlit night when one wonders about God. That is the beginning of my new world, of all my new worlds.

The most real and living thing in the life that I've had has been you, Phyl Kirby. I have loved you so that I haven't words left to say. And I believe it's so much in the soul of me that it will always stay with me. I don't know what heaven I'll go to (the immodesty of the man) but I fancy something simple, with a river, and lots of green. And I know you'll be there. If there be a god – and there must be – and if there be a heaven – and there must be – then, too, there must be us. I'm afraid I really believe that, darling. I hope it doesn't sound too mystic or anything, but I do believe in always having you, and in new worlds.

I suppose that is why I have no personal fear of dying. It would be darned interesting, were it not that it might mean breaking an early date with you. And I'd rather take leave next week than the alternative, of course. Life is sweet, too; I'll have as much as I can.

So, if you ever read this, darling, I'm sorry if I had to break a date. It means keeping the next one the more certainly. And please don't be too sad. Together we've had more out of living than most people can reasonably expect. And if we had to stop sharing those wonderful things, perhaps it was better that it ended when our love was so strong and firm and young, and while we both had our own teeth. If I have to go to heaven, I'd rather go attractively, and still be able to play soccer.

Love me till then, darling,

Toujours a vous,

Reg

Reg Fayers was shot down in November 1943, but luckily survived and spent the rest of the war in Stalag Luft 1.

5. The Invasions of Italy and Sicily

Having defeated the German forces in North Africa, the Allied forces under Eisenhower now turned their attention towards the southern part of Europe itself, notably the Italian island of Sicily. The choice of Sicily was fiercely argued, with the British favouring increased involvement in the Mediterranean while the American senior commanders saw the theatre as more of a sideshow, preferring to focus on a more direct attack across the English Channel. The Casablanca Conference of January 1943 resolved the issue, with the decision taken that Sicily should be invaded.

The American Seventh Army under General George Patton and the British Eighth Army under General Bernard Montgomery were shipped over from North Africa in the ships of the Royal Navy under the control of Admiral Bertram Ramsay, the organiser of the Dunkirk evacuation. Launched on the night of 8/9 July 1943, the invasion of Sicily was codenamed Operation *Husky*.

The first act of the invasion was an airborne assault by British and American paratroopers. Alan Clements of the 1st Parachute Battalion took part in the action and wrote home about it:

WEDNESDAY, 28 JULY 1943

I hope you received my last letter in which I hinted I might be off to a new sphere. I was – the next night, and I expect with the British and enemy news blaring at you, you have been wondering how I have been faring. A day or two ago an intrepid Press representative visited us and noted down our doings and told us that what we had told him would appear in the British Press on July 19th, so a reference to the papers on that day will give you the picture. I must add that I was one of the fortunate ones to be in the melee from start to finish and at the hub, as it were, i.e. the bridge party – not miles away.

My trip to Sicily was an unforgettable one. Usually flying over the sea is boring; the element looks flat and uninteresting, different from what it does from an undulating ship. But soon it became dusk and was quite dark by 9.30. I sat near the door, through which a waxing moon was shedding a brilliant light. I felt quite composed and when the time came to stand up I felt I was spectator rather than a player in some drama. And dramatic indeed was my first sight of the island. Immense red fires were burning all over the plain; streams of coloured tracer bullets were pouring up into the air and forming curves and cascades, etc. – very pretty were they not lethal and aimed at our heavily-laden and low-flying carriers! Every now and then a great searchlight would sweep the sky. Well, we had struck land at an angle and now the pilot made a great circle to effect a proper landfall – the mouth of the river Simento. The land receded, we banked steeply, almost skimming the water. Then suddenly the land re-appeared, fires and all, and we turned in. The engines roared at full throttle and we climbed. I caught a glimpse of a long, straight road, then a serpentine river. The red light went on green, and out we went. A few twists and jerks and I hit the ground – a comfortable point of impact – a corn stook! The jump was easy, but I can only describe the period of alertness at the door as eerie!

George Blundell, the executive officer of the battleship HMS *Nelson*, recalled supporting the invasion off the coast of Sicily:

SATURDAY, 10 JULY 1943

About a month ago I believe Musso [Mussolini] ordered that everybody on the Sicilian coasts and Southern Italian coasts was to be evacuated by 10th July. If true, he guessed well.

There is absolutely no sign of a move by the Italian Fleet, and 'intelligence' reports that one of the battleships at Taranto has gone into dry dock.

I believe all these Continental countries are scared of the sea and have an inferiority complex about the Royal Navy. Anyhow there was not a smell of enemy activity of any sort near us during the night.

At 0430hrs we went to full action stations. There was no enemy reports and no RDF contacts. RDF is now called Radar to conform with the Yanks. So, after we had closed up, closed 'Y' armoured hatches and test communications, we had a cocoa party in the Upper Conning Tower!

Later on, very brief reports started to come through; the Commandos had captured their beaches, 44 beach was captured, Amber and Red beaches were captured, destroyers and cruisers were called on to fire at annoying shore batteries, and, in the main, things seem to be going well, but the captain says that those on the spot tend to be over-optimistic in their early reports, and tho' a beach may be reported as captured, one may get stopped later, as at Dieppe . . .

At 0230hrs, 11th July, we saw quite a firework display in the direction of Syracuse and, by broad daylight at 0630, most of the beaches were reported to be in our hands, and that the Canadians had got ashore and had joined up with the Highland Division. Where the Royal Marines are, in 'Sugar' area, 2,400 prisoners have been captured. The Americans seem to have got ashore without much trouble.

At dawn we had a splendid view of Etna, 92 miles away and also to the North we could see the toe of Italy. It was a simply wonderful golden morning.

Ken Oakley was an able seaman with 'Fox' RN Commando, one of the units responsible for controlling the traffic on the beaches, at the landing at Avola in Sicily:

FRIDAY, 9 JULY 1943

At midnight on the 9th July we lay at anchor eight miles from Avola, our immediate objective. After a good meal we donned our equipment and manned the assault boats. I was sitting right in the stern of the boat and spent some time making myself comfortable. At last the order came 'Lower Boats' and we were away, the sea was rough and our boat was thrown against the parent ship. 'Crash', away went the two-inch mortar, swept over the side by the hook of the boat's falls. 'It's time they supplied us with umbrellas', said one soldier, as another great sea swept over us.

Now came that very trying time between the ship and shore when one wonders if he will survive the unknown that lies ahead. The boats were tossed all over the ocean and all the soldiers were sea-sick but they had cardboard boxes to vomit into and this helped them a lot.

Suddenly a flare burst above us and surprise was lost, when we still have about a mile to go. The formations split up and began to make for their own landing places, with fire from enemy machine guns passing over them.

Tat-Tat-Tat-Tat, Bren guns began to speak and then 'Crunch', 'Down Door' and we were there. A sapper began to cry, plead and cling to the floor-boards, swearing he would not move. We left him (his nerve was gone) and dived into about three feet of water to wade fifty yards to the shore. The shrill whine of bullets speeded us on and at last we went to earth at the water's edge. Bren guns engaged the enemy machine-guns and we began to take our bearings. We had landed in almost exactly the right place and so it did not take us long to set up our lights and call in the second flight. We then waded out along the length of the beach, to find the best landing places. These were marked and the Assistant Beach Master and myself proceeded to find the Beach Master . . .

No other B Commandos had landed and the BM had not appeared so we did our best getting the craft in and directing the avalanche of men ashore. It was about this time, nearly an hour after H. hour, that a battery on the hills began to shell us. A landing craft carrying about 250 men was the target. It was beached and the men were pouring off down two ladders, but near misses and one hit were making things hot. I waded out and told the men to jump for it as the water was not very deep. A few jumped and I steadied them as they fell and then it came. A terrific explosion and I felt myself fading away into oblivion. I came to under the water. I felt numb and shocked: had I been wounded? Or maybe some limbs were missing? I could not tell and then I felt someone clutch my legs and drag me down again. I lost my reason and kicked like mad until I was free and shot to the surface. A body floated by, its limbs still kicking, it must have been the man who clutched me. The water had become a sea of blood and limbs, remains of once grand fighting men who would never be identified.

I staggered through all this to the water's edge and then looked dazedly around. My comrades were fleeing for cover and in the water were men crying for help. I went in the water again to fetch a man whose arm was hanging on by a few bits of cloth and flesh. He cried, 'My arm! Look, it's hit me'. I said nothing, but managed to get him to the beach and lay him down. I then collapsed, exhausted and still those shells came down far too close for comfort. I rose again to see a man sitting on the ladder of the Landing Craft crying 'Help me, oh help'. I went and goodness knows how I got him to the beach. He was hit all over his body and was a dead weight with shattered legs dragging in the water. I shall never forget how he thanked me as I lay there almost sobbing at such terrible sights; so this was War!

Behind the beach parties the forces of the British Eighth Army and the US Seventh Army, part of 15th Army Group, were waiting to land. Amongst them was B. Christy of 368 Battery, 92nd Field Regiment RA, part of the 5th Infantry Division:

FRIDAY, 9 JULY 1943

July 9th was an unbearably long day. At its slow, steady pace the convoy of invasion craft, all our town type 'LSTs' [Landing Ship Tank] ploughed and rolled onward. The wind had mounted steadily in clear sky, and the blue waves were capped with 'white horses', our vessel was towing a long steel pontoon of some kind which bucked & shuddered at the end of its steel hawser and seemed in imminent danger of breaking free. All around, the sea and sky were empty. We might have been hundreds of miles from enemy coasts.

As the greyness of evening came, bringing with it a chill feeling
of loneliness and the grimness of our position, we came up with
another convoy of big merchant vessels hove to. Their presence was
comforting . . .

As I ran on deck for the first glimpse of enemy-occupied Europe
the cone of Mount Etna and the distant shore of Sicily were visible
through a thin veil of haze. The convoy was ploughing steadily ahead.
A few Spitfires patrolled the sky high overhead, their wings touched
by the first morning rays of the sun. We were expected to land about
eight o-clock, but as the beach crept ever more slowly nearer it became
plain that it would be later.

For about eight hours we lay only a mile or so from shore. It was
an amazing experience. Every detail of the coast could be seen – the
yellow sandy beaches alternating with low cliffs, the restful greenness
of the olive trees and orange groves, which seemed to form one huge
continuous orchard. It was all so good to look upon after the desert
countries of the East. But what was most amazing was the absence of
the sights and sounds of battle. A whole fleet of big ships was unloading
troops into small craft to our right and they were continually being
ferried ashore. Just a few Spitfires appearing from time to time high
up in the brilliant sky . . . a wrecked plane or glider lying on its back
in the water (was it 'ours' or 'theirs'?) . . . columns of smoke rising
far inland. The coast, with small houses standing here & there, was
deserted. It was just like a Sunday morning at home when everybody
had slept late! . . .

'Stand by your vehicles' had come the order as at last our LST was
signalled to the beach, and slowly she slid forward to the absurdly
small stretch of yellow sand. Trucks were started up and their roar
filled the great space of the hold. The chains holding them secure
were released. As the big door in the bows was lowered we crowded
forward between the line of Sherman tanks, which were to go off
before us, to watch the final phase in the Navy's part of the operations.
Slowly the LST's bows slipped down the coast within yards of land.
The sand shelved steeply and looked soft and treacherous. Would
the vehicles make it? At last we grounded and held firm. There
was a bare stretch of twenty yards between the lowered prow door
and where small waves lapped the beach. The first of the Shermans

rumbled out of the hold, through the water with a great cloud of steam and fumes and, without pausing, clambered up the beach and was away. The other followed with almost clockwork precision. It gave one a grand feeling to watch them rumble off into action. The first of our vehicles followed, but it could not make the beach. A tractor hauled it out in no time. Soon came 'Y's turn, but we, like the others, stuck and had to be hauled out.

A sailor's helping hand was held out, but it was not needed; the warm water reached only to the thighs of my khaki drill trousers, and I squelched ashore. The Command Post truck was soon started again, & with quickly spoken instructions from the beach party and a cheery farewell, we were on our way. 'Mind the mines & keep to the taped track,' they said. We lurched up and down steep slopes in the finely churned dust of an olive orchard, sardined under the truck's canopy or clinging to the back and ducking with gritted teeth as boughs scraped the roof. Dusty-faced comrades from the Battery, out of another invasion craft, greeted us at the assembly area, after we had done the essential 'de-water-proofing', and now it was a wide straight stretch of tarmac road.

The two armies landed safely and advanced towards their key target, the town of Messina. Despite staunch resistance from German units such as the Hermann Göring Division, by early August the Axis troops had withdrawn to a defensive position called the Etna Line and started to withdraw to the Italian mainland. The Germans managed to withdraw in secret and got their entire force away intact to fight on in Italy. Messina fell on 17 August, precipitating the fall of Mussolini and the withdrawal of Italy from the Axis forces.

With Sicily secured, attention turned towards the Italian mainland and a series of landings was planned. The continued involvement in the Mediterranean remained a sore point for senior American commanders, but in the absence of a cross-Channel invasion in 1943 they realised that Allied forces needed to be committed to fighting the Axis on the ground in Europe, and Italy was the only realistic option. Two British divisions attacked Reggio di Calabria on 3 September as a prelude to the bulk of the Allied forces landing further north around Salerno.

The Italian Government formally surrendered on 8 September, and British troops immediately occupied the port of Taranto. The following day, the 9th, the main invasion force launched Operation *Avalanche*, the amphibious assault on Salerno.

George Blundell once more found himself covering the invasion from his position aboard the battleship HMS *Nelson*:

WEDNESDAY, 8 SEPTEMBER 1943

Our covering force consists of *Illustrious*, *Formidable*, *Nelson*, *Rodney*, *Warspite*, *Valiant* and 18 destroyers, which include two froggies *Terrible* and *Fantasque* . . .

The talk in the Wardroom is that there must be a lot of 5th column stuff in Italy and that we are doing this landing with the connivance of high up Italians who wish to be freed from the Germans. I feel there must be truth in this because there are tremendously weak threads in our plan.

At 1835hrs I was rung up from the bridge to say 'Italy has surrendered unconditionally'.

Five minutes later the BBC announced it.

I imagine we shall still go on with our expedition as the Germans won't leave Italy without trouble.

THURSDAY, 9 SEPTEMBER 1943

We have gone on with the landings which started at 0300hrs this morning. The only alteration has been to stop the airborne and paratroops doing the diversion on the coast north of Naples.

We had a terrific night. Torpedo planes, we believe were ordered to attack the transports, came at us instead, and one of them came down our port side in a mass of flame. Later in the day we took some prisoners from two rubber dinghies from Heinkel IIIs. The prisoners said that from 20 to 30 planes had attacked us. We shot down several by blind barrages.

Actually we only had about 2 big air attacks during the night although it was my impression that several came in and sniffed at us once or twice.

Much of the stuff we fired at were undoubtedly friendly aircraft not showing IFF [Identification Friend or Foe]. We are in a restricted flying area, so friendly aircraft shouldn't be in our area, unless they are night fighters.

We fired about 300 rounds of 4.7-inch alone during the night, not to mention other stuff. We only have six 4.7 guns, but numbers of Oerlikons, pom-poms, half-inch and 6-inch blind barrage.

The Italian Fleet has been ordered to put to sea and surrender to us. Those at Spezia and Genoa are going to Bone or Bizerta on their way to Malta and those at Taranto to Malta, direct. *Warspite* and *Valiant* have been detailed to look after the three Littorios, *Howe* and *K.G.V.*, the Cavours from Taranto. We shan't see them: it is a great disappointment.

Most of the military seem to have got ashore, they are landing on the beaches near and south of Salerno, the first objective being to capture the big airfield about three miles inland. Then the idea is for the British 10th Corps to push on to Naples and for the US 6th Corps to hold the south and east flanks.

It has been reported that Musso has fled to Sardinia.

FRIDAY, 10 SEPTEMBER 1943

We didn't have such a bad night as last night, only opening fire about five or six times. During the day we spotted some Lightnings carrying out recce on us, and it seems the Germans are using captured ones for this purpose.

The three Littorios coming down the West coast of Corsica turned to pass through the Straits of Bonifacio and were bombed by German planes. The *Roma*, their latest and the flagship, was hit by one bomb (I heard it went down her funnel) and sank in 20 minutes drowning the Italian C-in-C.

The *Roma* was in fact destroyed by a new kind of radio-guided bomb developed by the Germans called the Fritz X. The Germans had considerable success with this new weapon off the coast of Italy, hitting the US light cruiser *Savannah*, the British light cruiser HMS *Uganda* and the battleship HMS *Warspite*, as Captain Vere Wight-Boycott, who commanded the destroyer HMS *Ilex*, describes:

FRIDAY, 17 SEPTEMBER 1943

Warspite has 'had it'. She was hit yesterday afternoon by two 'glider/ bombs' – the latest German secret weapon, and a very dangerous one too. One cruiser (*Orion*) has already been disabled by one. It seems to be a small wireless-controlled aircraft with a wing span of about seven feet, controlled by the parent aircraft up to a distance of about six miles. It is thought to be propelled by rocket apparatus, and can be directed by w/t on to its target.

Warspite is in tow of two tugs and nine destroyers and two cruisers are circling round her to give AA and a/s protection. She is making about three knots and at this rate will take two days to reach Malta. Her boiler rooms are flooded and she has no steam. Otherwise she is said to be all right, on an even keel, and in no danger of sinking.

This casualty will lend weight to the (to my mind very mistaken) view that Admiral Cunningham needlessly exposes his ships to unreasonable hazards. It is difficult, I admit, to see what a battleship's bombarding can effect that cannot be equally well done by the monitors mounting 15-inch guns. We watched *Warspite*'s first bombardment and it was almost entirely on gun salvos, so that having 8 guns to the monitor's two did not seem any great advantage, but I am ready to suppose the C in C knows more about it than I. Still there has been this talk. I heard it first after Crete, strangely enough from FAA [Fleet Air Arm] Officers from *Illustrious*. More recently we heard the same kind of thing in *Aurora*. There is no doubt that the C in C's view is that there is no point in having ships unless they do something useful, and it is logical to conclude from that any job however small its value and however disproportionately high its risk is better than no job. If not expressed better than that it is easy to see that some may think their lives are being needlessly exposed. It is probably true that the C in C is no psychologist so far as his own service is concerned. Having a complete disregard of danger himself he cannot allow for it in others of his own kind (though he may assess the enemy's morale very astutely).

Kenneth Wilson served aboard the escort carrier HMS *Attacker*, which, along with the other escort carriers *Hunter*, *Unicorn*, *Stalker* and *Battler*, was tasked with providing air cover for the forces landing on the beaches:

THURSDAY, 9 SEPTEMBER 1943

Zero hour, 0300hrs passed quietly but the day started at dawn, 0500hrs when our first sortie took off. All day our fighter planes have been flying off and landing on. We (*Attacker*) have lost four planes. Sub Lieutenant Prentice was killed this morning while landing on after combat over the beaches. Total losses from all carriers today are 15 planes and several pilots. The sea is dead calm and there is no wind, which makes landing on our short flight deck very tricky. One plane crashed this evening with its cannon firing. I was on deck seeing to the aerials and cannon shells hit the bulkhead very close to me, a near do. Things are going fairly well ashore but we are not getting things all our own way and have withdrawn from one beachhead, so I hear [this was only a rumour]. We are getting short of fighters and air crews as several air crews have been smashed on landing. More troops are landing this evening. It is now 24 hours since I had any sleep and no wash or meal since leaving Malta. Living on coffee and sandwiches.

FRIDAY, 10 SEPTEMBER 1943

We captured an airfield last night but it is not yet serviceable. Our first sortie flew off at 0615hrs and kept at it all day. *Unicorn*'s fighters shot down four enemy planes and one of our fighters downed an Me 109 this afternoon. Several enemy planes flew over and we opened fire with our HA [High Angle] guns. Five of our planes were damaged landing on the flight deck. We started the operation with 110 Seafires between us but now only 38 are serviceable. *Attacker* can still put up 10 of our original 19. Most losses are on landing – through lack of wind, and not by enemy action. One of our flight deck crew was killed at 0800hrs when he walked into a Seafire propeller. He was more or less chopped to pieces. We buried him over the side at 1100hrs. I managed a short sleep today but still no wash or meal. Salerno has fallen to us but Naples and Rome still held by the enemy. Rommel has taken command of the enemy forces.

SATURDAY, 11 SEPTEMBER 1943

The day started at 0500hrs with an enemy attack, which did not last very long. Our first sortie flew off at 0600hrs. By this evening we only had five serviceable aircraft. The airfield ashore is now in use for emergency landings. The 8th Army south of us is driving northwards to join our forces at Salerno. We are now pushing eastwards and north towards Naples. Altogether we have landed about 100,000 troops. We are now landing more tanks and guns and are being opposed by the 15th Panzer Division. 120 sorties have so far been flown from *Attacker*. Two of our escort left this evening to go to Palermo to refuel. 17 Italian ships, including two battleships and seven cruisers have arrived and have surrendered in Malta. Another battleship was sunk by German air attack on the way. 10 more Italian ships have arrived at Palma. Managed to get a wash today, and a little more sleep.

SUNDAY, 12 SEPTEMBER 1943

It is still pretty tough going ashore. Sub Lieutenant Sturgess is missing after a sortie this morning and another of our pilots has been taken prisoner after landing on an airstrip which is still in enemy hands. 10,000 more troops landed by air this morning. 8th Army captured Brindisi. We anchored at Palermo at 2000hrs and refuelled some of the destroyers. We were attacked by a U-boat en-route near Stromboli.

Following his experiences in France in 1940, John Williams had been commissioned into the Queen's Royal Regiment and his battalion had been converted into the 99th LAA Regiment RA. Here he recalls the anxious moments before the landing at Salerno:

THURSDAY, 9 SEPTEMBER 1943

0315hrs, 15 minutes before H-hour, absolute hell let loose on the beaches of 46 and 56 Divisions. A terrifying bombardment until H-hour from cruisers, destroyers, LCGs [Landing Craft Gun, a support vessel] and rocket ships trained and firing on pre-selected targets along the landing areas, and they were subjected to a terrific hammering. Then the barrage switched to hedgerows and possible defensive areas. The noise was deafening and wave after wave of hot air struck me with considerable force. I stood tightly clutching the boat rail gazing with fatal fascination at a scene of utter horror, chilling my whole body. The very air was charged with expectancy with as it were a final hate. The coast was split with whizzing, exploding rockets and the barrage lifted inland for it was H-Hour.

At 0330hrs the first waves of the assault Rangers and Commandos landed in their small craft to be followed by waves of LCVP [Landing Craft Vehicle Personnel], LCIs and LCTs. As the initial infantry wave made contact so the fog of war clouded the picture and it was difficult to know how the landing was going. It seemed from the explosions, tracers, machine gun and rifle fire, along with flares and Verey lights exploding overhead that some opposition was being encountered. Sometime after 0400hrs four German artillery shells fell into the water close to the pontoon which had formed the causeway. Shrapnel fragments fell over the causeway and pounded against some of the LST. Warrant Officer Dick Look and 22 of the Seabees were already astride the pontoons and were fully exposed to the fire but fortunately no one was hit. At 0430hrs the ship's klaxon horn thundered out, its suddenness chilled me to the very bone. It was the signal for the troops to unshackle the guns and vehicles and start them up for the one test before beaching. 0515hrs it was obvious that considerable opposition was being met and there was the possibility that our landing would be held up. Meanwhile a hefty air raid was taking place and the entire bay was illuminated as if it were day by countless parachute flares; all the ships were busy pumping up shells at the attacking aircraft . . .

Batteries of German 88s and mortars were ranging onto the beach and they kept the shelling up throughout the whole of the day. The beach was one hell of a shambles. What few guns and vehicles that had landed from earlier LCIs were hopelessly stuck in the soft sand. A self-propelled gun was burning furiously whilst other vehicles were badly damaged by machine gun fire and exploding shells. On the beach and all around us an intense barrage from the Germans was creating havoc. What personnel remained alive on the beach had burrowed into the sand except for a few soldiers with light machine guns who were firing from the top of the beach, whilst a handful of sappers were gallantly trying to lay down army track. It was not many minutes before our craft was included in the barrage and life became exceedingly unpleasant especially as I was standing on the ramp. How much shrapnel missed me and my chaps I do not know but the situation was suicidal for we were sitting targets for almost half an hour and the boat received eight direct hits.

The landings at Salerno were fiercely contested by the Germans, with the 16th Panzer Division being strongly reinforced by three Panzergrenadier divisions. Senior commanders even considered withdrawing from the beachhead on 14 September. However, the power of the naval offshore battery force broke up many of the German attacks and, with Eighth Army advancing from the south and the German Tenth Army withdrawing, Allied forces at Salerno were able to break out of the beachhead and take Naples on 1 October 1943.

6. Prisoners of War

In the first three years of the war large numbers of British servicemen had been captured as prisoners of war. In the 1940 campaign in France alone over 40,000 had gone into captivity, while a similar number were captured in the North African campaign. The increased number of RAF raids over occupied Europe also led to a large number of aircrew falling into German hands. Those captured by the Germans or Italians could usually expect reasonable treatment according to the Geneva convention. Those captured by the Japanese – over 130,000 during the Malayan campaign – endured years of suffering.

Following his capture at the fall of Singapore, Bombardier Thompson spent the following three years in Changi camp, which housed some 50,000 Allied prisoners:

SUNDAY, 1 APRIL 1945

We all had a day off. The Nips were celebrating the anniversary of someone who had died many years ago. We only wish that they had a few more celebrations. We were busy all day getting our camp in order. We are working for ten days, then we have one day off. We worked from dawn to dusk and some of the lads are feeling the strain. We all in turn get roughed up a bit, some more than others. It seems a long time before the tenth day arrives.

The majority of the lads do not bother to shave every day but wait until we have a day off. On our day off we cook some tap root which we have managed to steal and get into the camp. I have been in charge of the food orderlies. We draw the food from the cookhouse for every meal and I have to make sure that everyone receives his rightful share.

The rations vary from day to day and it also depends upon the quality of the rice and how it is cooked. It varies from a packed pint mug to a slack mug of rice.

When you collect the dixies of rice you have to make a quick calculation of how much rice each man will get. It is difficult at times to keep the peace, because everyone is watching each other to make sure that no one receives more rice than anyone else. There is always the same small crowd who watch and wait and they are always the last to be served and they never vary their routine.

It is quite common for one or more feeding points to run out of rice before everyone has been served. When this happens you have to run round to one of the other feeding points and hope that they have some rice. You may want about five to ten pint mugs of rice, so if you are lucky the first thing you have to do the following day is to return that quantity before you start serving your own lads.

So, to be on the safe side, you try and make sure that you have a little left over after completing the serving, then you start a *leggi* (second helping) and a strict check is kept and the names are ticked off on a sheet which we keep, so that we know where to start next time.

Jimmy Parry was also held within Changi camp before being transferred to camps in Thailand and eventually back to Japan itself, travelling there in July/August 1944 on the *Hakasoka Maru* in cramped conditions; these ships became known as 'hell ships':

SUNDAY, 3 JULY 1944

On the dockside, it was now 1500hrs. We were marched single file into a large warehouse, and given a large hunk of raw rubber shaped like an attaché case, complete with handles. 'Lifebelts' grinned a guard. We thought it was just another racket to get more rubber to

Japan, even if it had to take up more of our living space. When one
chap dropped one into the dock, and it promptly sank, we gathered
our guesses were better than the guard's – who remarked as he saw
it sink – '*Hu-lifebeet – damedan*' (no good).

Then the fun started. The only entrances, and incidentally exits,
into and out of the holds, were two wooden stairs with built up stairs,
roofs, and doors, it was impossible for more than one man and his
kit to get down a staircase at a time. The Japs wanted at least four;
the more they yelled, the slower we went, and soon the yells and
whacks of flat bayonets echoed far over the still waters. In the hold
pandemonium reigned, the sight had to be seen to be believed, and
will live with us always. The Japs were ramming our fellows into the
shelves round the hold's sides, when two men, and their kit were
huddled in, one lane, as it were – was filled completely.

In each bay there was about room for 20 men, one now at the
bulkheads, and the other on the outside. When all the bays were full,
the rest stood or sat on the lower hatch cover.

Then Tiger arrived, his famous roar shot everyone into action.
The guard started to lash out at anyone who was not in a bay,
considering there were at least three hundred so placed, one can
guess what happened.

We all thought we would have to travel like this, it was not a
happy thought, but eventually after many of us had sore posteriors
things got organised. Our bales of rubber were stored in the centre
of the hold, on the hatch cover, along with what kit we had, less our
small kit & mess tins; actually our mess tin and towel more or less
was our small kit, which did make things a little easier, but we were
grossly overcrowded, and more cramped than in the train. After dark,
somehow we managed to settle down, and hope for the best.

Tam Innes-Ker was also kept in Changi camp, but he was moved
to form part of F Force, a group of Allied prisoners of war used to
build the infamous 'Death Railway', constructed by the Japanese to
link Burma and Thailand. Here he describes his arrival at a new camp
and the conditions there:

JUNE 1943

What a nightmare – how we did it I can't say and many fell by the wayside. Arrived here completely out and like skeletons. Bobby Thomson, my pal, nearly died and for three days was like a corpse – he is still weak six weeks later. This camp, built by Burmans, houses 1400 of us, all British troops, Norfolks, Suffolks, Manchesters, RAOC, RASC, Volunteers and RAMC. The huts, huge bamboo structures, are very rickety – breaking up already. The country, barren bamboo filled jungle, not a village for 50 miles as far as we know. Most desolate and wet – rain every day and for 5 days we had no roofs to the huts. Dysentery broke out immediately and that dread of the country, cholera. In a week 50 were dead, medical supplies practically nil, roads more or less impassable and the Nips roaring for us to set to work. This work is railway construction, to join Moulmein and Bangkok. In two weeks our dead were 100 and panic not far off – work or any attempt at it ceased – how could we? Out of 1,400, 200 [sic] were dead and over 1,000 sick with dysentery and exhaustion. Rations practically only rice. Now after four weeks our dead are 180 – mostly cholera. Many friends amongst them.

FRIDAY, 18 JUNE 1943

God what a place this is – no one knows its name. Sanitation foul – open shit pits with shit not only inside but all around as well, where dozens of poor fellows couldn't make it. Everyone has festering sores – which are covered in flies – we have no more bandages and little antiseptic.

Flies are terrible. Rain and ankle deep mud for weeks – no one has any socks left and many no boots. We are not allowed to bathe in the river and of course all drinking water must be boiled – we have to carry it 200–300 yards up a slippery slope. To feed 1,200 men we have 20 buckets so feed in relays – some get breakfast at 5.30am and some at 11! Ditto for supper. Rations are now reduced as trucks cannot get through to us either way from Burma or Thai. We actually draw from Burma and now every other day 100 men have to drag bullockless wagons through knee deep mud to another camp five kilos away for rice and beans. Takes them all day and exhausts them and this before the monsoon has really started! Cholera is said to be a little better and total deaths now 206 – out of 1,400. The next camp (Aussies) has 190 out of 700. It's sheer bloody murder – I imagine that out of some 7,000 troops on this section of the road there can only be 1,000 working and 5,000 of the rest sick. No exaggeration. How long we can endure I don't know. Two parties already have beat it but nothing further is known of them. An Aussie camp some 60 kilos away has been bombed by our planes and some lads killed – also some Nips!

Bill Leaney, who also worked on the Burma–Thailand railway, provides a vivid picture of the conditions inside his camp, Tonchan:

WEDNESDAY, 6 JANUARY 1943

I thought that sufficient time had elapsed since my last death entry and true enough we were told of two deaths this morning. This makes 31 deaths here now. Both of these chaps were sergeant-majors and they say that one of them has been putting up a magnificent fight now for weeks and he was winning it too, everybody thought, even on this food. But out he went this morning. A loud cheer rent the air last evening about 6 o'clock when two bullocks were driven into the camp. Thus giving some colour to the Nips' promises about food. I am writing this in the tiffin [tea] break and they haven't as yet killed these bullocks so I don't know when we are to have them. It's funny here how nothing ever seems to work out so that we get more food, for instance yesterday the Nips in an endeavour to augment our food organised a fish gathering party. They collected a dozen or so good swimmers from our chaps and then threw a hand-grenade into the river. A highly successful business many dead fish came floating to the surface and the swimmers were able to grab them and quite a lot were collected. In the cookhouse they said they'd make a fish stew, save on the 'veg' make a better stew in the evening. Well we had the fish stew and it was absolutely bloody awful – not the vestige or trace of fish or, of course, veg either, and I'm sure we have no more 'veg' in our stew in the evening, so the fish, to us consumers at least, was an absolute dead loss.

Saturday, 9 January 1943

The climate here is really quite good really, it's hot in the daytime and quite cool in the night and morning. We are up in the hills and thusly are up in the clouds somewhat. When I read this in the future I want to try to recapture this all if I can. Pity I am not a little better with a pen (or rather a pencil). We struggle down the side of this hill to our breakfast just as dawn is breaking. It's quite a risky trip too, for you can't see the undulations at your feet. To see dawn breaking over the hill and thro' the mist – pinkish very nice but one would appreciate it much more on a decent breakfast – a spoonful of sugar and rice doesn't really make one ready to appreciate beauty in any form. I suppose all of us now would say that the most beautiful sight in the world would be a big plateful of English food – say steak and onions.

Bill Leaney was one of the many Allied prisoners of war who would lose their lives when the unmarked Japanese prison ship on which he was travelling was sunk by Allied action en route to Japan in September 1944.

Conditions for those captured by the Japanese were considerably worse than those for prisoners of the other Axis powers, although with food scarce in Europe the lives of the latter were still very hard. Lawrence Bains of the Middlesex Yeomanry was captured by the Germans at the Battle of Gazala in June 1942 and passed into Italian hands. He spent time in various POW camps in North Africa before being transferred to Capua on the Italian mainland:

July 1943

Tarhuma stands out in my memory as the worst example of corruption I have ever seen. As rations were at the best, scarce, it was essential we should get everything to which we were entitled, but the cookhouse staff, some of whom had been there several months, took an undue proportion of all the best. Every day they had lovely fried steaks, plenty of thick rice or macaroni rich with tomato purée, quite a bit of buckshee bread, large issues of cheese and sweet coffee, whilst everyone else had very meagre and plain rations and could do nothing about it. Fellows got very discontented, but lacking leaders or authority had to be content with what the cooks gave them; when the bread ration was cut from two small loaves to one and a third, the situation was aggravated, but the cooks got on well with the Italians and nothing could be done.

The way in which food was issued was ridiculous – everyone was crowded into a wire enclosure at one end of the camp and the dixies were brought into the adjacent section, which led to the cookhouse. At the given signal 70 per cent of the fellows rushed for the gate and as the sgts on duty only allowed two through at a time, the result was the usual scrum. The advantage of being among the first was that you stood a chance at some buckshees. Against this was the actual system of issue – the front part of the queue would usually get 1½ ladles, the middle might be cut down to one, and the last got anything from one to two; the big advantage of being at the bottom of the dixie, where the rice was thickest, also caused fellows to push forwards and backwards to secure an advantageous position. It may seem ridiculous for all this struggling over a little rice or macaroni, but when it is remembered that apart from two or 1⅓ loaves (approx 4 ozs) this rice and a very thin soup was all we had, and we had not yet become accustomed to small rations, I think it is a wonder that we did not raid the cookhouse. We were beginning to feel the effects of under-feeding and food became the dominant thought in everyone's mind. All conversations tended to revert to this topic, and we all related excellent meals we had had this last February and March at Sidi Bish and Beni Yussef, and also many of our favourite dishes at home.

Despite their conditions, Allied POWs realised that some prisoners of the Axis were considerably worse off than they were, notably the millions of Russians captured during the great German advances of 1941 and 1942, and most particularly the mainly Jewish inmates of the concentration camps. Maurice Newey, captured at the surrender of Tobruk in June 1942, describes his experiences of these prisoners at Lamsdorf in Germany:

EARLY SEPTEMBER 1943

We were soon put to work. They had us digging a huge pit. We were told that it was for a swimming pool. Here we met a few Russian prisoners, mostly Ukranians. Conversing by sign language, we learned that the Jerries gave them a rough time, giving them very little food to eat. There were no Geneva Conventions to safeguard them. They seemed to be a tough lot though.

The story went round that, if a Russian died (and many did), his comrades would not report his death to the Germans, but kept taking him out to roll-call, propping him up between themselves, until the stench of his body could no longer fool the Germans. They did this in order to keep drawing his rations for as long as possible. It made me glad that I was an Englishman . . .

The fortunate state that we were in didn't blind us to the fact that there were a lot of people suffering from worse conditions than what we had to endure in Italy. The Germans treated the Jews as if they were vermin. Even the normal decent German had been so brainwashed that he could hold no sympathy for them. They just turned their faces away as if they didn't exist.

They would trudge down to the baustelle, dressed in a flimsy, white and blue striped pyjama suit, with a big Star of David emblazoned on the back, proclaiming to the world that he was a Jew. They were starved, humiliated and made to work until they dropped. When this happened, the Jews told us, and he was no more use to the Reich, he would be despatched to the gas chamber. They would half carry one another if they were sick, for if he was left in the camp, that would be the last they saw of him.

Every morning, even in the coldest weather, they would be halted by the main admin. block. A huge SS man would ride down on this large sit-up-and-beg bicycle to search them. He would order, 'hands up and trousers down'. Putting on a pair of immaculate white gloves, he would perform the distasteful task, of actually having to touch these 'vermin'. Woe betide anyone found with as much as a saccharine on his person. A savage, scientific beating up would be his reward as a salutary lesson to the others. They would just stand there and watch numbly as this was going on. The Jews would be standing there, their sex exposed for all the world to see and the

German workers, including female typists and office staff, would just walk by, unseeing.

To alleviate their suffering a little, we used to cut off the crust of the bread and smuggle it to them. They were most grateful for these crusts and made extravagant promises to us, as to how they would repay us after the war. One told me that he had been a leading diamond merchant in Amsterdam before the war, but I always took these tales with a pinch of salt. I never saw him as our whispered conversation was through a grille. We gave them hope by telling them the best war news we had heard, and prophesied the opening of the second front in 1944.

All Allied prisoners of war had a duty to attempt to escape from captivity although there were far more opportunities for officers, who under the terms of the Geneva Convention could not be put to work, than there were for other ranks. Arguably the most famous escape attempt was the 'Great Escape', when 76 Allied air force officers escaped from Stalag Luft III on the night of 24/25 March 1944. Flight Lieutenant Tony Bethell was one of those involved in the escape attempt:

MARCH 1944

The Escape Committee had given me two jobs to do – the first was to go down the tunnel to Leicester Square (the 2nd 'halfway' house) take over from the person there (Hank Birkland) and pull 20 people through my section of the tunnel; and, being relieved by the twentieth (65 down the tunnel) go on down the tunnel and out. Once out, my second job was to lie behind 'the tree' in the woods near the tunnel exit and wait for the nine following escapees to crawl out and join me. Once my party of ten was complete, the next man (Larry Reavell-Carter – 75 out of the tunnel) was to relieve me, and I was to lead my party into the woods and out to open country, where we would split up into parties of two, each pair going its own way.

The briefing for travelling to and lying in Leicester Square was pretty simple – when ordered, get on the trolley, lying down, at the foot of the entrance shaft and signal 'ready' by giving a tug on the rope attached to the front of the trolley ahead, tug on the rope, and be hauled up to Leicester Square, and relieve the man on duty there (Hank Birkland). Facing the rear, in a coffin, about seven feet long and open at either end, and to be lit electrically – the job was to turn and pull back the trolley that had gone down the tunnel to the escape shaft, keeping a feel on the rope attached to the trolley that had returned to Piccadilly Circus; and on feeling a tug, to pull that trolley with its human cargo up to Leicester Square.

The twentieth man I pulled up (Ken Rees) would relieve me. In the event, I suppose I had pulled through about a dozen people when the rope went dead – no pulls to signal another human being to haul down the line – the continuing reminder that one was connected to the outside world and one was temporarily isolated from it.

With one's 'lifeline' gone dead, the realisation bore in quickly that anything might have happened, and that one's little airspace, 30 feet below ground, could indeed be a permanent coffin. Claustrophobia took over and I sweated with fear – for about 45 minutes I believe – though it seemed like an eternity. Since that night, I think I can truly say that I have understood the condition and feelings of trapped miners – and the heroic (I use the word advisedly) efforts of their fellow miners to reach them.

At first I tried shouting – in both directions until I realised that sound didn't travel too far in a confined space and fear that resonance might cause a collapse in the tunnel. A desire to get on the trolley to freedom was indeed strong. Eventually, a tug did come on the rope and I hauled the next man up to Leicester Square – he told me as he crawled past me that an escapee had stuck in the tunnel and with difficulty had been pulled out backwards by his legs – the operation causing a collapse in the tunnel that had to be repaired . . .

I hauled through my relief and I got on to a trolley to the escape shaft – up the ladder – a tug on the rope signalling 'okay to proceed' from a controller watching the sentries – crawl quickly to 'the tree' through the snow – watch ten men disappear in the trees behind me.

The briefing on job 2 – leading my group of ten to open country from 'the tree' – was roughly as follows. In the woods a couple of hundred yards to the northwest of the tunnel exit was an electrical transformer station, said to be guarded by dogs. To the west of us was the American compound and beyond it a French and Russian compound. To the north lay the railway line with the station, and, beyond it, the town of Sagan. The route to open country lay between the Russian compound and the railway line running southwest out of the station. Anticipated congestion around the railway station (to be avoided by the hard-arsers) and the location of the transformer station required that the hard-arser group (of ten) go north for 200/300 yards – and then west – then slightly south to get to open country – about a mile away.

Again, what was proposed and what happened were at variance. I had led my group about a 100 yards north into the woods when a shot rang out behind us – the tunnel had been discovered – with that, I and my group bolted – north and then west (I thought). I never saw the transformer station, but suddenly we were kicking cans (garbage?) and looking at the perimeter wire of, I think, the Russian camp – we scampered back into the woods in a northwesterly and then westerly direction and fortunately soon came to open country, where we dispersed. Cookie Long and I were alone. My discharge of job 2 was hardly a model of navigation or of execution.

It was getting light quickly and, knowing that the tunnel had been discovered, Cookie and I agreed that the hunt would now be on and that we must find hiding for the first day. No barns were visible but we came to a fir tree plantation – young trees about 6 to 8 ft. tall with their foliage growing down to the ground – ideal for hiding though, with 6 inches of snow on the ground, not the best shelter. We pushed our way into the young trees for about 50 yards and then made ourselves comfortable as we could with branches from the trees underneath and around us. With good boots on and warm clothing we were in reasonable shape for a daylight wait . . .

Cookie and I had originally intended to make for Czechoslovakia – only some 65 kilometres to the south, but the snow and flooding rivers caused us to opt for a walk up the railway line towards Frankfurt-on-Oder and Berlin, with the purpose of catching a lift on a freight train – and an end objective of Stettin and Sweden . . .

As dusk fell we pushed out of the young trees and headed along a path that ran beside the plantation to the north-northwest. It was not too long before we hit the railway line – and we walked along it – no snow on the sleepers and rail bed – to the northwest (towards Frankfurt).

As the sky began to lighten we saw a barn with no other buildings near it, and made for it, let ourselves in, noting a loft full of hay. We climbed up, took off our outer clothing, boots and socks, to dry them out; covered ourselves with hay and were soon asleep. During the day someone came into the barn, seemingly to look for something below – otherwise we were not disturbed. We ate some dry porridge, some D-bar (chocolate) and some raisins – much the same as the previous day . . .

Since leaving the tunnel area, the temperature had gone up and much of the snow had melted – the ground outside looked and was very soggy. However, warm and dry, we decided to return to the railway track and move on up it, hoping to pick up a slow freight train – we had seen three or four freight trains from the barn during the day, though none of them slow enough to jump aboard. Walking along the track after dark we had to crouch down in bushes (wet) beside the track, a couple of times, to watch trains go by us in the right direction but too fast.

An hour or so after we had arrived at the track we got to what was obviously, from its lights, a small town (we discovered its name was Benau) with a signal box and lighted railway yard immediately ahead of us. The town seemed to lie mostly to the north of the railway but other buildings (including a railway station) lay ahead of us. South of the track appeared to be farm land – so we decided to strike out across this land to walk around the town area and get back on the tracks on the other side of town. Almost immediately we found ourselves in ploughed fields – all heavy soggy mud. Each foot step required effort and we were getting nowhere fast. We were all getting very, very wet and dirty.

Some while later we recognised that we were achieving nothing except the prospect of a soaked fatigue by daylight with shelter possibilities unknown. Retracing, muddy step by muddy step, our way back down the railway track, as dawn broke, we saw 'our barn' again. It was not long before we were back in the loft drying out. Throughout the day we observed little movement near our barn but thought that we could see enough unploughed field in the general direction we wished to go that should allow us to get around Benau and back to the railway line. So, at dusk, we left the barn.

That night turned into a virtual repetition of the night before – and dawn saw us back where we started – wet and miserable and now convinced that we must break our rule and walk, for this occasion at any rate, by daylight.

At mid-day (lunch time for the goons, was our rationale) on 28th March, therefore, we left our shelter and struck out into some woods to the west of us. These woods on a ridge running north took us safely around Benau leaving us half a mile or so of clear path down across fields back to the railway line. There was no sign of life so we set off down the path for a couple of hundred yards when a shout rang out behind us from the edge of the woods we'd just left – 'halt'! We looked round to see two *Feldpolizei*, pointing rifles and advancing towards us. Apart from keeping their rifles pointed at us they were not particularly hostile, but firmly steered us on down a path across the railway line and into Benau. At that moment, a freight train steamed slowly past us! It was not our day!

Of the 76 who got out through the tunnel, 73 were recaptured by the Germans and 50 of them were selected to be shot, amongst them Flight Lieutenant Bethell's fellow escapee, Cookie Long.

7. The Special Operations Executive

Prisoners of war were not the only Allied personnel behind enemy lines in occupied Europe and Asia. The Special Operations Executive (SOE) had been formed in July 1940 on the express orders of Winston Churchill to 'set Europe ablaze'. This organisation was to carry out sabotage operations in occupied territory and support local resistance groups in their efforts against the Axis occupiers.

Major Richard Tolson served with SOE in northern Italy, liaising with the guerrillas in the Veneto region. In his diary, he records the constant threat posed by German patrols:

SATURDAY, 28 OCTOBER 1944

Our situation here is pleasant. To the south the plains, as far as the
eye can see, with the Tagliamento and Meduna running straight down
from the hills to an eventual junction. To the north is Mt Rosso,
not yet snow covered but rising sheer and forbidding from our little
valley: To the west Mt Ciaurlec and to the east Mt Pala, which
is occupied by an Osoppo [Partisan] Bde. One kilometre south is
Clauzetto, our metropolis. The other half of the 'Unified' command
resides in Campone, a village north of Mt Ciaurlec, and distant about
10km from here . . .

Sudden interruption – Enemy Cossack Tps are reported to be in
S. Francesco which is 10km away, and held by Garibaldini. We have
packed up the radio and all our kit, and are ready, if necessary, to flit.
The old woman in whose house I have a room is nearly in tears and
thinks it will be burned to the ground. But we will leave no trace of
our lodgement. I don't particularly like the idea of running tonight,
it's started to rain again, and the radio makes it no joke. Oh for arms
and ammo. However, it may not be as bad as we think.

These patrols could turn into fully fledged operations to drive the
guerrillas out, as Captain Paul Brietsche found from his position in the
Monte Grappa massif, also in the Veneto. He describes the German
operation in his official report:

4. The first signs of the gathering storm started about the 18th,
but I rather stupidly ignored it. There were a few alarms and troop
movements around the foot of the mountain, but I believed at the time
that it would be impossible for anything other than an enormous force
to attack the partisan positions. I was unfortunately wrong . . .

6. At 0300hrs on the morning of 21 September, the fun started.
I was woken up by Longo, who informed me that the Germans had
surrounded the mountain in large numbers, blocked all the villages,
placing mobile artillery, road blocks and sentries every 50m on the
roads surrounding Grappa, and that we should be prepared for what
might happen at daybreak.

7. We packed all kit, destroyed all superfluous W/T kit and burnt all incriminating papers. At dawn, the enemy opened shell and mortar fire from all directions. The first bad news arrived when a messenger informed me that the whole of the Italia Libera Brigade, commanded by Major Pirotti, had deserted overnight, leaving their arms behind them. They had apparently all got into civilian clothes and fled. This completely exposed our south-east and eastern flanks. On arrival at their area, we discovered an enormous dump of arms of all descriptions, including four heavy machine guns and ninety thousand rounds of ammunition. I instructed Longo to collect a few stout-hearted men, and to endeavour to hold the position, at least until dusk. He accordingly did so, raising half a dozen British ex-prisoners of war, a few ex-Caribinieri, along with a sprinkling from each other brigade. They took up their positions along the ridge, and as things turned out, did magnificently, holding off five enemy attacks during the course of the day, before withdrawing at night . . .

10. News came through that the Georgio Italia Libera had been surrounded, many being killed and the rest captured. The British company fighting with them under Hilary (I do not remember the other name) had fought magnificently. Hilary himself had been killed in action, and the rest surrounded. The Germans had commenced stringing up prisoners to the nearest trees.

11. Thus with only the Garibaldini left, the Mission moved to a position overlooking Schivinin, where we were at nightfall.

12. The following morning found us in the bush overlooking Val Di Seren. The first enemy elements had passed through us overnight, but at about 1100hrs, a company of enemy were seen approaching our position. Then started the final Garibaldini panic. They threw away what arms they had left, and started to vanish in all directions. I was forced to hide my radio, the batteries had long since been discarded as too heavy to run around with, and with my four companions, took to the bush independently. That was the last I saw of the partisans. From then until 2 October life was a matter of hide and seek around the mountain. The enemy traced my presence and seemed determined to catch us somehow. This they tried to achieve by watching all water holes and stopping us

from getting down to the villages for food. It was impossible to get out right away, as Grappa is geographically an island, and the place was entirely surrounded. We found some nuts and managed to get some water at nights, and eventually got over to Tomatica into a small house which had not been burnt. Unfortunately they traced our presence there, and we had to move once again, and made our way to Croce. It was then that, according to my belief, the enemy gave up the hunt for us, considering we had either all been killed in their blitz, or succeeded to cross the Piave or Brenta.

13. I retrieved my radio from its hiding place and managed to obtain a car battery only partly charged. Message No. 910 was sent, and we received eight messages from Base, the majority of which were rumours for dissemination and a loud complaint that I had received a sortie during the *rastrellamento* [sweep]. The car battery was then flat again, but I managed to contact three rather scared partisans who promised to get me another. I was trying until the 12th to regain contact with partisan leaders, but it was quite impossible. All had completely disappeared, and the local civilians would give us no information owing to the fact that they suspected we were Germans . . .

14. On Friday, 13 October, at approximately 1130hrs, I happened to glance through the door of the Malga in which we were hiding, and spotted approximately 100m away, a large German patrol coming uphill with their heads down and a civilian guide leading them. It was a hot day and they were sweating. To get away from the Malga entailed coming out through the front door in full sight of the enemy, and going up an open bank at the back for about sixty yards before being able to disappear out of sight behind it. There was no time to grab anything, but we managed to get away as no enemy managed to glance up. Their guide spotted us, but just grinned and winked and said nothing. The Malga was burned. I lost my radio for good, and the enemy once more discovered that the British Mission was still in the vicinity.

Elsewhere in the Mediterranean, SOE was carrying out operations in Greece and the Aegean. Lieutenant Bill Heppell was attached to the Greek partisan group EDES based in north-east Greece and describes a sabotage operation along the Jannina–Arta road in August 1944:

WEDNESDAY, 9 AUGUST 1944

Arrived Papastathi Bridge 8.00 after much trouble with guides. Nearly shot one. Harry passed at 9.00am. Slept until 3.00pm. Captured EDES deserter brought to me weeping; boots taken from him. Sent him to Yerakari; will probably be shot. Went to village to buy food; only got four eggs; they wanted soap for more. Message at 9.30pm from Harry.

THURSDAY, 10 AUGUST 1944

Up 4.00am. Left 5.00 with Andarte guide for Monastery. Waded river three times. 3 hrs march. Ordered sheep for lunch, eggs, bread, tomatoes, cheese, milk, melons and cucumber. Arthus and Sam arrived. Harry came with Constantinides.

Discussed plan of attack on bridge.

Chickens for tea and hot bread and milk.

10.15 recce of bridge. Foul journey across country. Walked down road for a kilometre. 150 Huns at Baldouma. Walk until dawn.

FRIDAY, 11 AUGUST 1944

Arrived Monastery at 6.00am after 8 hr walk. Breakfast from Bruno then bed until 3.00pm. Ordered another sheep and more food. Prepared charge for bridge – 100 lbs of 808 plastic explosive.

Moved off at 7.30 with 100 Andartes and Constantinides to bridge. On to road when lorries had passed. Spent one hour digging road across bridge with pick; blisters on hands. Put charge in and also on telegraph pole. Andartes on road covering us. One with Bren and no magazine. Fixed trip wire then retired to hill above. Andartes with 17 light machine guns and 1 mmg on hills already.

4.00am. 25 lorries in convoy came; first hit trip wire and detonated charge. First two lorries blown for six. Other lorries all pulled up nose to tail. Perfect target. Looked round for Andartes to open fire with all they had. Prospect of bags of loot! Alas!! Andartes had flown. Constantinides exhorted us to flee too. Harry in fluent Greek cursed him for a coward. Absolutely disgusted we left. ¾ hour away we found Andartes resting after strenuous exercise. Only 100 rounds of mmg fired and that 15 mins after explosion. Returned to base at dawn.

Perhaps the most famous of SOE's exploits in the Mediterranean was the capture of the German General Heinrich Kriepe on the island of Crete. The SOE team was led by Major Patrick Leigh-Fermor and assisted by Captain Bill Moss, who later wrote of their exploits in the book *Ill Met by Moonlight*. Here Bill describes his arrival on Crete:

9 APRIL 1943, CRETE

Hooray! At long last!

This is my fourth day in Crete, and Paddy has just left me with Manoli, George, and one or two henchmen, while he goes with a good man named Mihale to do a reconnaissance in Heraklion. So now I have plenty of time to write of the events of the past few days.

The morning of 4th had been fine and the sea, with a long swell running, as pleasant as one could expect.

Brian Cowley was in high spirits and confident in the weather.

We all sat up on the bridge, drinking tea, eating bacon sandwiches. At noon we passed a large convoy bound for the Far East, and later British planes flew overhead.

A short nap between tea and dusk, then some final arrangements of kit and a segregation of packs, rucksacks and arms. At 10 o'clock a sailor came below and told us that we were very close to Crete, so we took all our things up on deck and then joined Cowley on the bridge.

We were three miles off shore, but in the light of the half-moon the mountains loomed up large and misty-white so that it seemed that we were much, much closer. The sea had become miraculously calm, and the noise of the ship's engines had cut down by half. We were apparently running East, parallel to the coast. All eyes towards the shore, and those who knew the landmarks were speculating as to how far we were from our pin-point.

'It must be pretty near here', one suggested, and it was agreed to sail closer inshore to see if we could spot any signals from the land.

They were dropping a line now, testing for depth, and Cowley ordered a man to the very forefront of the boat to keep an eye open for rocks.

A chubby, cheerful young sailor, whom I noticed was called 'Blondie' by his fellows, was sitting up beside me.

Suddenly he called, 'A light flashing, sir.'

All eyes strained.

The moon shimmering on the water and the whispery sea-mist.

'There it goes again.'

Yes – it was like a sudden pin-prick in a huge mountainous back-cloth.

The engines cut down and we started moving in towards the light. A call now and then from the man who was watching for rocks, and the depth shouted up every so often from those who were sounding.

The light was flashing more regularly now, and became brighter and brighter. Looking through a pair of binoculars I could see the high rocks that surrounded the little beach, and on the water's edge some blurry shapes moving to and fro'. As we drew nearer, the shapes became the figures of men, running, walking, clustering and bunching.

'Five fathoms.'

We kept moving slowly in. The engines were making more noise now.

I remember thinking to myself how much more thrilling this approach was in comparison to that by aeroplane. One could feel all the drama of the situation because one saw everything, heard everything – whereas in an aeroplane one sees nothing and all one hears is the roaring of the engines. Even so, I still prefer the idea of infiltration by air – it is more attractive in so many other ways.

We were very close to the shore now. I could plainly see the frothy rim of surf on the beach, and the light seemed as big as a head-lamp, and the little figures disentangled themselves from the clumps of shadows and became real men.

Fifty yards from the beach Cowley gave the order to stop. The engines ceased to turn, and all we heard now were the lapping of the waves, the surf on the beach, and the muffled sound of voices. The ship's Third Officer was scrambling down into the dinghy, and a moment later was being rowed ashore with the tow-lines for two rubber dinghies.

Jim Herratt and I had decided to land first, and so, upon a signal to say that the Third Officer had reached the beach, we clambered down the rope ladders into the rubber dinghies, piled them high with kit, and then, having shouted a few goodbyes to those on board, found ourselves being pulled swiftly through the water towards the light. A large party of men, reminiscent of Nikita Balieff's interpretation of the Song of the Volga Boatmen, were gathered together, some waist-deep in water, hauling in the tow lines. And in a moment we seemed to be among them, being heaved up out of the surf, and a score of hands were grabbing at the kit-bags and containers and pulling them out and away on to the dry sand. My first impressions were extraordinary – dark faces, heavy moustaches, turbaned heads, black and shabby clothes, tall boots, a hundred voices, and, above all, a strange smell that I presumed must come from unwashed bodies and dirty clothes (and which, no doubt, is by now as much a part of one!)

'Hullo Bill.'

I looked about me, at all those black piratical faces, to see who had spoken. But my guess was as good as the moon's.

'You don't know me. Paddy will be along in a minute'.

This time I traced the voice as coming from one of the shabbiest creatures I have ever seen – patched and torn clothes, several days' growth of beard – but I knew, suddenly, that this must be Paddy's colleague, Sandy Randall. But it still seemed quite impossible that this extraordinary apparition could conceivably be an ex-*Times* correspondent; a polished and educated man, Sandy Randall.

Following the capture of the general on 26 April 1943, Bill Moss scribbled a brief entry into his diary describing the operation:

TUESDAY, 27 APRIL 1943

No time to write in full.

Anyhow, we made it! 10am Manoli, the General and I beside a stream just outside Anoyia. General washing in stream. Lovely day.

Last night we reached x rds at 8. 4 cars and bike came by. At 9.30 torch flashed that Gen's car coming. Paddy's 'Halt', starts talking, mad rush on all sides. Terrified face of chauffeur, he reaches for revolver, so I hit him with cosh. See Paddy and Manoli hauling out General, who struggles like mad, obviously thinking he's going to be killed. Chauffeur on ground being trussed up by George and Anthony.

I sit in driver's seat and I find engine running and car perfect. Look out of window and see group in centre of rd handcuffing Gen. in pool of torchlight. Then Gen is picked up bodily and jammed into back. Greeks very rough. See chauffeur bleeding. Micky's extraordinary display of hate. Everyone kissing everyone else! Then away. Car fine. Pass through three cars, plenty Germans on road. Paddy wearing General's hat, smoking. We pass Gen's villa at Kuosses. On to Heraklion. Thrill of driving through Market Square. Out of city east gate on to Retirio road.

Sentry with torch. We start climbing. Terrific elation of 'We've done it'.

Stop car opposite Anoyia. Paddy and George go on to dump car with letter. General talkative.

Manoli and I go off with General, Strati as guide. Long march. Gen quite cooperative. Reached mountains outside Anoyia hour before dawn. Down to river. Strati goes off for food and to deliver letter. General's leg bad – he speaks French. etc. 'All a sort of let's pretend.'

Operating in enemy territory was a highly risky business, with SOE teams facing the constant threat of capture and certain imprisonment and possible death. Major Ivor Porter and two other agents parachuted into Romania in December 1943, and the operation went wrong from the very beginning:

DECEMBER 1943

As soon as I had left the plane I realised that something was wrong. The mist was so thick that even the silk above me had lost its shape. I realised that R had almost certainly disobeyed his instructions. I made a turn, but could see no lights in any direction. I listened intently in the silence, which is always exaggerated when you have just left an aeroplane at 2,000 feet, but could hear nothing of the motor horn, which was to have sounded every few seconds. I took out my red torch to shine towards the ground, but as a black mass suddenly came up I put it quickly back into my pocket for fear this was the ground, but it was another thicker layer of mist which I passed through and before I reached the ground I knew we had been let down and all the time and trouble we had spent on the operation was now likely to come to nothing.

I developed some oscillation a few hundred feet from the ground but it was not much and I didn't trouble to turn, and so landed in a backward roll in a ploughed field. The skyline had come up a few seconds before I landed. It was the brow of a large field I had landed in.

Before I got up and unharnessed my parachute, I had smelt the earth which is always so good after a night drop. It was the first European earth I had smelt in many years. I felt in my pockets to check whether I had dropped anything and then rolled up my parachute. I flashed the red torch in all directions but had no answer. I blew my whistle and had no answer at first, but later got an answering whistle from Chas. I walked about fifteen paces towards him and put down my kit (I had taken off my flying suit) and used my whistle and torch until I saw his red light and then walked ten yards to meet him . . .

We sat down and reviewed the situation. As we had been dropped on the outward trip we should have been met by S and his friends, who would have carried green lamps. Our password would have been 'Caut pe Stefan' and theirs 'Stefan e Acasa'. They were to have had a car horn sounding at frequent intervals and would have prepared a hole for our gear and accommodation for us. There was no motor horn, there had been no ground signals as we came down and there was no answer to our whistles. We had to accept the situation as irregular to say the least and this was our conclusion before we had finished our first cigarette . . .

It was now about 0100 hours on 22nd. The first thing was to find S. Chas stayed with the kit. I made four recces. The first to the south-east brought me to the edge of our ploughed field, but no answer to my whistling. The second to the west and I reached the outskirts of a wood. Again no answer. The third to the north-west brought me again to the wood, which I followed to its edge. The fourth to the south parallel with the wood for a considerable distance and finally heard S's answering whistle. I returned to Chas and soon after I reached him S came up with his kit. He had landed in the wood and had had to cut his parachute free from the tree before looking for us. It was now nearly 3 o'clock.

We had heard cars and trains at some distance to the north and thought it possible that we had been dropped south of both road and railway, instead of between them. We heard dogs barking in the same direction . . .

Our first problem then, after camouflaging our kit, was how to orientate ourselves. Visibility at this time (0930 to 1000hrs) was about a hundred yards and we could see nothing to indicate our whereabouts. We could hear cars and an occasional train to the north and I was almost certain that we were south-west or south-east of our target.

The wood appeared to be communal because peasants began to arrive from the north and collect firewood. Owing to the urgency of orientating ourselves it was decided that S, who being Rumanian had least chance of arousing suspicion, should contact one of these peasants and try to find out where we were. S was away for about an hour and made a long reccy around the wood, but he was unable to speak to the peasants. By now the mist had lifted a little and we could see some trees and what appeared to [be] an east/west road to the north. We realised that to leave the wood would involve a certain risk but it had now become imperative to orientate ourselves. We decided to walk towards the road.

There was a village some four or five kilometres away . . . Chas now proposed that S should go to a small house on the brow of the hill and ask how far it was to Rosieri de Vede, but S was disinclined lest he should be associated with the plane which had been overhead the previous night. Still, we had to get this information although we realised a certain risk was involved. Chas and I had our foreign appearance against us, but I was also without adequate language, so Chas went down to the back garden of a little house on the outskirts of the village where we had seen a woman. The woman at first told him that Rosieri de Vede was thirty kilometres away and then, on second thoughts, fifteen. Chas returned and we set off back to the wood, passing several peasants on the way. One took particular interest in us and it appears later claimed a reward for having reported us to the gendarmerie. The woman got the reward . . .

On reaching the wood at about 12.30 we did a little more camouflaging of our kit, smoked a cigarette, and just after 1300 hours, when we were about to leave the north edge of the wood, we saw a group of men in gendarme uniform and civilian clothes, carrying rifles, coming from Plosca direction. We went to the west end of the wood and walked away towards our target hoping that they were not in fact after us, but they shouted, fired and told us to halt. We were unarmed and had no other alternative. We would not have got far in that open country if we had tried to run for it. Before they reached us we took off the kind of golf jacket which we were wearing and were arrested in uniform. When the gendarmes realised that we were unarmed, and English rather than Russian, the sergeant in charge of them apologised for arresting us, but pointed out that it was his duty to do so.

1943–44

I. The Battle of North Cape

Although the threat posed to Allied shipping by the German Navy had receded throughout 1943, they still had powerful vessels capable of playing havoc with Allied merchant shipping, notably the battleship *Tirpitz* and the battlecruisers *Scharnorst* and *Gneisenau*. The *Tirpitz* was attacked and damaged by Royal Navy midget submarines in September 1943, while the *Gneisenau* had been severely damaged by Royal Air Force raids after the Channel Dash and would play no meaningful part for the remainder of the war. This just left the *Scharnhorst*.

In December 1943, the Commander-in-Chief of the German Navy, Admiral Dönitz, decided to send the *Scharnhorst* out of her Norwegian harbour to intercept convoy JW55B, which was transporting supplies to Soviet Russia.

Although normally accompanied by a force of destroyers, the *Scharnhorst* had sent them away, as the commander of the German force, Admiral Erich Bey, said they could not cope with the severe weather conditions. Thus it was without an escort on 26 December that she encountered the British cruisers that were screening the convoy from any possible attack by German surface forces. This marked the start of what became known as the Battle of North Cape.

Alan Tyler was a Sub Lieutenant aboard the cruiser HMS *Norfolk*, which, along with HMS *Sheffield* and HMS *Belfast*, formed the covering Force 1 for the convoy threatened by the *Scharnhorst*. As the officer commanding one of the *Norfolk*'s 8-inch gun turrets, he had an excellent appreciation of the initial action, which he described in a letter to his parents:

WEDNESDAY, 29 DECEMBER 1943

We had been standing by for action all day as we always do when in the vicinity of some hundred miles of the German North Norwegian Naval Base of Altenfjord.

It had been known for some months that *Scharnhorst* was there with destroyers and other ships and every trip there was always the menace of her breaking loose on our convoys.

As usual, the Germans reckoned that Xmas was a good time to come out as we might be less prepared and have less ships ready (and there has been action with German Naval and/or Merchant Raiders in the last week of December every year of the war, and we have always been ready for them).

We learnt, early on the 26th, that she was at sea and our force, Vice Admiral Burnett in *Belfast* with *Sheffield* and us (*Norfolk*) went to action stations, ready for an encounter.

We were south of the convoy, between it and Norway and well north of the Arctic Circle, in the shortest week of the year.

Consequently the action was fought in a twilight and varying darkness all through.

It was 'piped' that we would go to action stations in 15 minutes' time when we heard she was about, and I got up a weird collection of gear to go into action with, as I thought we would have several hours' wait, if we ever saw her, so I prepared myself.

The turret temperature is about 40 degrees, and as it falls below freezing at night I put on my duffel coat, which is fawn in colour and reaches the knees and has a hood attached, over my oldest Reefer with polo necked sweater and warm clothes below. I also wore socks, stockings and leather sea boots and stayed warm throughout the action . . .

We had been standing by for action for three days previously, on watch four hours in every eight, and we were all pretty tired and dirty but bucked up to full efficiency when we knew there was something doing.

We had barely made our preparations when we received the report 'enemy in sight' from *Sheffield*, though for our honour's sake we claim to have seen it at the same time.

No doubt we did, but anyway we got off some half dozen rounds pretty soon and claimed, at least, one hit, announced on the news, with another probable.

This was very good and she pushed off to give us some time for dinner, soup and a lamb sandwich.

A couple of hours later, in the afternoon, when the 'blue of evening' or morning, was dying into a brightish night, she came in again and tried to get between us and the convoy.

We went straight towards her with our guns blazing as we poured in rapid salvoes.

This had been decided on previously as a plan of action. Attack is always the best method of defence against a stronger enemy and she turned and ran.

She was only showing us her stern as she ran away, instead of her broadside during the forenoon, which gave us only a very small target much harder to hit.

Consequently, although we fired a great many salvoes, we only claimed one hit in this action which headed her off.

It is possible she thought we were a battleship, as we must have seemed very frightening, coming towards her at 30 knots, with our guns flaming and our shots falling all round her.

It is astonishing what a drug and intoxicant action is. One barely noticed the shattering thud of recoils as the guns kept running back, and we did not feel or notice as their shells hit and fell around us.

It was all so exciting that everyone almost automatically did their jobs correctly with clear heads.

I am very proud of my turret's crew. Some had joined the ship barely a month ago and many were new to their jobs, but they all acted like veterans and we didn't miss a single salvo due to mistakes.

The whole ship worked together excellently which was why the shell damage was so soon controlled before it was able to spread and affect the ship's efficiency.

Scharnhorst, on turning from us, made off South towards home, in Norway, but destroyers headed her off and she didn't dare to dash through them.

She turned the only way open with us shepherding her along astern, just out of her sight, into the arms of Admiral Fraser, the C in C, coming up in the Home Fleet flagship *Duke of York*.

Several hours passed, during which time we had been repairing damage done to our turret by heavy seas. They had put out our lights, so that we looked a Wellsian Martian mine – steel machinery lit up by our emergency lighting, which is similar to Davy safety lamps, only they contain little electric bulbs shedding each their own little pool of light in a picturesque way.

About supper time, *Duke of York* opened up and she and *Scharnhorst* swapped salvoes for some time without much result.

Scharnhorst had as much armour as the *Duke of York* and suffered little damage.

This went on for a long time and 'S' looked like escaping while we had our evening corned beef stew, but destroyers had been detached to torpedo her.

They went in most gallantly, four of them, and scored three hits which crippled her, slowing her up and putting her steering gear and some turrets out of action.

Duke of York then smashed her up with steady fire from a safe range whilst the cruisers lit her up and spotted the shots falling for the *Duke of York*.

Finally C in C's Cruiser *Jamaica* went in to finish her off with final torpedoes.

We stood by to help but we did not need to as she sank about 19.30 GMT.

We went in quite close at the end, and could see survivors struggling in the water with boats and rafts as the great ship went quietly down.

She fought well but was defeated by boldness and superior strategy.

John McGregor was a leading seaman aboard the flagship of the Home
Fleet, the battleship HMS *Duke of York*, which was the largest British
ship at the battle and her weight of shell was important in winning the
encounter. Here he describes their welcome at the Home Fleet's base
at Scapa Flow on New Year's Day 1944:

TUESDAY, 18 JANUARY 1944

The C-in-C, Sir Bruce Fraser, had planned the action with very
great skill and we owe it to our Captain Hon. G. Russell for his
fine manoeuvring of the ship that we came out of it so well. Our
own Radar Division were sent for the next day by the Captain and
complimented on our part in the action and later in the day the C-
in-C congratulated the ship's company. It was a most impressive sight
as we returned to our anchorage at Scapa. The *Duke of York* led in
the Fleet flying two Battle Ensigns, followed by the cruiser *Jamaica*
and seven destroyers in line ahead. The other ships manned the rails
and cheered ship as we passed. It was perhaps just a show, but it did
feel good. We returned to Scapa on 1st Jan where we received our
Christmas mail and two days later our Christmas dinner.

Surgeon Lieutenant Dunlop was a medical officer aboard HMS
Sheffield, which was part of the 10th Cruiser Squadron at the Battle of
North Cape. He wrote back to his family about the action, and here
describes the aftermath of the battle and nature of naval warfare:

There were, as you say, only some 30 odd survivors – and I wouldn't
be surprised if she had nearly 2,000 men on board, and of course
it's the thought of those poor miserable wretches that makes the
whole thing really rather nauseating, especially when you know
what Arctic waters are like. We 'spliced the mainbrace' next day to
celebrate the action, but although naval rum (neat, in double tots)
is something whose effects have to be experienced to be believed,
I must admit that the edge was taken off one's enjoyment by the
personal tragedies behind it all.

If it had been like a football match after which one can
unreservedly rejoice in the well-deserved victory of one's own side

it would have been much nicer! But, of course, war is not like a football match, it is a grim business and it was either them or us; and, much more easily than they make out, it <u>might</u> have been us. If they had come on and fought the three cruisers fair and square in the early stages instead of turning away, they might easily have sunk the lot of us – and even if they hadn't done that they could probably have crippled us so that we couldn't maintain contact and then gone on either to demolish the convoy or to slink home unobserved and wait for a better opportunity. But, at the critical minute, the decision they made was (as it turned out) the wrong one, and from then on the odds were against them instead of in their favour – for the *Scharnhorst* is a very big ship and its own guns could pump out a considerably heavier weight of shells than all three of our cruisers simultaneously, and that was all she had to face in the initial stages. When brought to bay, as I've said, they fought extremely well, and against fairly heavy odds – for by the time the *Duke of York* came up our forces were quite definitely superior.

As our commander said afterwards when we heard the German broadcast version, it's a fundamental misconception of naval strategy to think that fighting well against superior forces is the be-all and end-all of the game. The <u>essential</u> thing in naval warfare is to make sure that you have got a superior force concentrated at the right place and the right time, and it is by no means easy; and I reckon that our organisation in the Admiralty deserves high praise for getting the whole thing to run like clockwork; and it's been working up to this for a long time now, of course. The crippling of the *Tirpitz* in September (by midget submarines, in a Northern Norwegian fjord) was an absolutely critical preliminary move – for she is probably more formidable than any single ship in our own Navy – and the provision of a tempting bait with suitably disposed covering forces, although in itself no mean feat of organisation, was only the last of many moves. And now that the last move has been successful I should imagine that our planners can sit back for a bit and contemplate the happy prospect of a pretty uninterrupted flow of material to Russia for several months to come, unless they spring some new surprise upon us – which is never impossible!

This encounter between capital ships in the icy waters of the Arctic was to be the last time that a major naval action was settled by naval gunfire alone in European waters. It was already something of an anachronism in an age of naval warfare increasingly dominated by naval aviation and the carrier air group.

2. Breakthrough in Italy

With the Italian capitulation and the Allied amphibious landings at Salerno, the German forces in Italy had undertaken a retreat northwards, where they resisted the Allied advance from successive defensive lines. The strongest of these was the Gustav Line, which stretched from Ortona on the Adriatic to the mouth of the River Garigliano on the Tyrrhenian Sea. One of the key positions on this line was the town of Cassino, dominated by the fortified mountain of Monte Cassino and its famous Benedictine monastery. Cassino controlled the Liri Valley, the main route through the mountains to Rome.

In order to outflank this strong defensive position, the Allied commanders decided to launch an amphibious landing at Anzio to the north of the Gustav Line, hoping to create a breakthrough using the US VI Corps. Preceding this, the Allied forces opposite the Gustav Line, British X Corps and US II Corps were to launch a major assault on the fortifications around Cassino itself to draw off German reserves at least if they could not break through the lines. The French Expeditionary Corps also attacked further inland.

E. Danger was a company clerk with the 5th Battalion Grenadier Guards, which was part of the 1st Division commanded by Major-General Penney, which provided the spearhead for the British part of the landing force, Task Force Peter. Here he records waiting offshore and the initial landings to the north of Anzio itself:

FRIDAY, 21 JANUARY 1944, AT SEA

We set sail in the morning and were able to have a better look at the Bay of Naples which certainly looked much better from the sea on a fine sunny morning. We passed quite close to Capri, mainly an extinct volcano with houses clustered in the crevices.

Once out at sea, the invasion fleet gathered itself together and a very imposing sight it looked. Two outer lines of LSTs and two inner lines of LSIs that seemed to stretch for miles, and all encircled by a Fleet escort. It was considered that we had little to fear from air attack and, indeed, we never saw a plane until after we had landed.

The day passed quietly enough with brews of tea at frequent intervals. We even brewed up on the troop deck and ate as much as we could safely eat. Fortunately the sea was calm or there might have been a different story. As night came, we were allowed no lights either above or below deck and in theory, we were not allowed to smoke although I think that most did. Although the atmosphere on the troop deck got a bit thick, no one was sick. We were supposed to land at 0700hrs and accordingly had our breakfast after reveille at 0400hrs.

During the day we were told that the landing was a joint Anglo–US effort and that the British element was to land north of Nettuno while the US element landed a bit further South at Anzio. The two were to link up and push towards Rome. Meanwhile 5 Army was continuing to push up the coast to try to link up with the invasion force and thus catch the Germans at Cassino in a trap.

There was to be 100 per cent air and naval support and also rocket ships to clear the beaches; these were LSTs fitted out with the equivalent of 500 3-inch mortars, fired in blocks of 30 at a time and designed to blast everything within range to smithereens. They did, however, require eight hours to re-load. These would clear the beaches and prepare the way for the Commandos [who] were to be first ashore; then the beach organisation; then ourselves and the tanks; and finally the guns and transport.

22 JANUARY 1944, ANZIO

At first light the ships were still in line with the balloons above them. We learnt that the initial landing had been successful, had been a complete surprise, and that there were no opposition. Presently we came within sight of land and dropped anchor about a mile offshore – it was evident that the landing was slower than had been anticipated because of a bad beach. As time went on the skipper suggested a brew up, and a brew up we had, and it was 0900hrs before we started towards the beach.

There were no aircraft about and very little gunfire although the cruisers were firing into the land. Presently we ran aground with a terrific crash which threw us all in a heap but fortunately no one was thrown overboard. It appeared that there was an unexpected sand bar, we found when we got the gangways down that the water would have been over our heads, so two smaller craft were called up and these ferried us to the shore – a somewhat ticklish operation which would have been even more ticklish if there had been heavy fire. As it was we did not even get our feet wet.

By this time the beach organisation was working like clockwork, tracks were marked, bulldozers were clearing roads, netting was being laid, signals were established, dumps for supplies marked out and a lengthy pier run out so that the LSTs could unload their vehicles. It was too shallow for the ships to get near enough to the beach for the vehicles to land straight off the ship.

We made our way off the beach with all haste and assembled in a wood. We had just started to dig in when we were moved about a mile and had to start all over again. Weighed down as we were this was hard going.

By evening our transport was unloaded and had caught up with us and we were able to have a hot meal without touching our rations. We slept where we were and very damp and chilly it was in the early morning.

Peter Lovett, who had already served throughout the North African campaign, and on Sicily and at the Salerno landings, was also present at Anzio, attached to 46th Royal Tank Regiment, which formed the armoured component of 1st Division:

SATURDAY, 22 JANUARY 1944, DAWN

A whole fleet at anchor a mile or two off the coast – a balloon floated from every boat, a wonderful sight. A mine floated past – corvettes pot at it and sink it. Initial assault seems to have gone well – seems to be a bit of a delay over landing us. Through field-glasses I could

see the beach from which a steep track made the same morning by
'bulldozers', rose up to wooded slopes. At the top of the track a
Scammell was waiting with winch ready to assist any vehicle that
failed to climb the steep sandy incline, Bofors guns were already
in position against expected dive-bombing, but not a plane did we
see. DUKWs (steel boats on six road-wheels, that can drive down
the beach and straight into the water) were plying to and fro down
the track and up to the sides of lighters to collect fuel, stores and
ammo, and blokes on the shore were already digging slit-trenches and
bivvy-holes. About midday we moved further in, ready to discharge
vehicles on to pontoons stretching to the beach, the water being too
deep (seven to nine feet) to permit an attempted wet landing. Then
the shelling began – German batteries got the range of the beach
and sent over air-bursts and shells, most of which whistled over and
landed in the water sending up a shower of spray, but some of them
were near misses, bursting with an ear-splitting crack near the boat;
if you were below on the tank-deck it seemed like being inside a
huge bell as shrapnel clanged against the hull. Later a plane dived
with lightning suddenness – machine-gun bullets spattered on the
deck and two bombs dropped in the woods above the beach. Our
boat had to have two attempts at ramming its keel over a sand-bar
to get up against the pontoons; every vehicle was preceded by a tank
which pulled and dragged it across the soft wet sand and up the
slope to the wood. A batch of German prisoners stood at the top of
the slope silently surveying the scene – tall youths in field-grey and
some wearing those grotesque tin hats. In the wood an MDS was
already up and signs pointing to concentration-areas were nailed on
road-side fences. A wonderfully good piece of organisation all of it.
Cruisers of the Navy stood some miles off-shore doing some heavy
shelling – every few minutes tongues of flame leapt from their huge
guns, tremendous explosions followed and shells went screaming
across the sky to cause some little trouble on the Appian Way. We
halted for the night about a mile and a half inland, and the work
of unloading boats went on all night.

Although the landings were initially unopposed, the Allies were cautious in their advance, which gave the Germans time to rush troops to the area and the first major counter-attack by the German Fourteenth Army was launched on the night of 3/4 February.

E. Danger wrote of the difficult days of early February, when German counter-offensives drove the Allied forces back towards the sea:

9 FEBRUARY 1944, ANZIO

I went back to the line after 24 hours' rest and found that Bn HQ had advanced slightly and was now in a disused quarry or gully. Here tents had been set up and a Command Post was in operation, reasonably safe from shelling. I set about looking for a trench and then went to the Command Post to do some work. An attack was expected and we had three days' rations in case of emergency. Sure enough, before long the forward companies reported that they were being attacked and as night wore on the situation became more and more critical. A call was sent for reinforcements but none was available. 1 and 3 companies were completely cut off; we were in wireless communication with the latter until the last. The signaller finally reported that the Germans were within a few yards and he was destroying his set.

4 Company gradually withdrew under pressure and were presently around Bn HQ with 2 Company on the right; they were isolated but kept going. Then it became clear that 4 Company had been overrun and the enemy was quite close to us. The situation was serious. We had one mortar with us and this fired to great effect for some time but eventually the Germans reached the edge of the quarry and started throwing down hand grenades. This cut us off from our rations and ammunition and from a small party who were defending the southern end of the gully. We hastily evacuated the quarry at the north end under cover of a smoke screen and took up positions on the eastern edge of the quarry. At daylight, Jerry could be seen entrenched about 50 yards from us. Here we sat for the whole long day while Jerry fired everything he had at us, including the kitchen sink.

10 FEBRUARY 1944, ANZIO

To make matters worse it started to rain and before long everyone was soaked. We were joined by a detachment of American Rangers who were first class, and quite fearless. As the night drew on we began to fear that we should be overrun if Jerry attacked in force. Just before dusk he put down a particularly heavy barrage and although nothing developed from this, we could see that he was moving towards the gully again; we were positioned on the edge of the gully to try to fight them off.

On the edge of the gully we were open to fire from every side and, what was worse, to every wind and in our sodden state it was freezing. We received orders to withdraw if we could and everything possible was piled on to a carrier which went away under cover of a smoke screen while we withdrew over the fields back to the embankment that we had left two days before. We had to abandon a good deal of kit.

It afterwards transpired that 20 or so of Bn HQ, a few American Rangers, our 2 Company and some N Staffs had been holding up two brigades of Germans. The N Staffs had been pretty badly knocked about and their Bn HQ was surrounded by Germans. While the line lasted we talked to them and they told us that their CO was down in a trench firing his rifle at the enemy.

11 FEBRUARY 1944, ANZIO

Back on the embankment, our position was a little less precarious as Jerry was now much nearer and in sight of us. However, his guns were still on the wrong side of the embankment and our dug outs were fairly safe although he sprinkled everything around and started sniping from the left. The only thing was to get into a dug out and trust to luck.

An unlucky shot killed our new CO (Lt. Col. Huntington) but fortunately our original second in command (Major, later Major-General, E. J. B. Nelson) who had been wounded earlier in the landing and evacuated to Naples, now arrived back and took command. It transpired afterwards that he had skipped Naples and found his way back as best he could.

That day was pretty grim and we were thankful to hear that we were to be relieved that evening. Part of the Bn was to remain until relief turned up and the remainder were to go back that night. The party left behind were relieved the following evening and we found that we had 400 men left out of our establishment of 811. Over 300 men were missing. However, we had held up three German divisions and enabled the bridgehead to be held, although things were still very critical.

Back on the Cassino front, another attempt was made to break through the defences during February. This time the troops involved came from the New Zealand II Corps and prior to their attack an aerial assault was made on the Benedictine monastery atop the mountain on 15 February. The bombing was not only politically controversial at the time, and remains so to this day, but also created a perfect defensive position for the German defenders. The Allied assault failed and another attempt was scheduled for a month later.

R. Blackford fought at Cassino as a signaller attached to the 23rd Field Regiment RA. He witnessed the bombing that pulverised the town on 15 March 1944 prior to the attack launched again by the New Zealand II Corps under Major-General Freyberg:

WEDNESDAY, 15 MARCH 1944

The big day – Cassino bombed for 3½ hrs then we had a go – one bomb-load . . . Jerry still very stubborn, what a fighter! . . . bombing officially described as 80% accurate, 10% poor, 10% very weak.

E. Smith was an officer with the 2nd Battalion 7th Gurkha Rifles, part of 4th Indian Division and New Zealand II Corps. He also took part in this, the third major battle for Cassino:

WEDNESDAY, 15 MARCH 1944

The attack begins – 08.30 bombing began and continued until 12.00, a few bombs on our position. New Zealanders reported to have captured Cassino town. Terrific battle, noise and smoke. Night came after fighter bombers had continued their work. Our artillery fired 17,000 shells during the night.

THURSDAY, 16 MARCH 1944

Learnt that all positions below Monastery had been more or less secured. Jerry very quiet – is something coming? Quite a few shells landed on our position. Papers arrived from home. More attacks at night. We were on minute's notice all night.

FRIDAY, 17 MARCH 1944

Quietish day. We received orders in case of emergency. Sun shining once more. A lot of activity. What a life!

SATURDAY, 18 MARCH 1944

Spent last night on a patrol without any real results. Day came. Suddenly had to move down into New Zealand battalion position in Cassino town. Reached there with mule party – terrible time before reaching HQ. About two to three hours sleep. Rumours of using us in an offensive role against the Monastery.

SUNDAY, 19 MARCH 1944

Our company told to move to attack point below Monastery in daylight. We went through Cassino. God help us. Reached the Castle – plenty of sniping. I went back to Brigade HQ during night. After a lot of discussion, our company was pulled back.

The failure of the New Zealand Corps to break through led to a reorganisation of the front, with the British Eighth Army moving into the area and taking over from the US Fifth Army, which had controlled operations up to this point. This reorganisation inevitably led to a lull in the pace of operations on the Cassino front, with no major attacks taking place till May. However, daily life on the front line was still arduous and dangerous.

One of the successes of the March battles had been the capture of the position known as the Castle, which played a major part in the daily routine of John Windeatt, who commanded 2nd Battalion The Sherwood Foresters, part of the British 1st Division:

March/April 1944

The Castle played a prominent part in the 36 Bde. existence as each Bn in turn did its stint in that sector. It stood on a precipitous rock 300ft above the town. The Germans on the Monastery feature looked straight down on to it. Other troops were a few hundred yards from the steep ridge of rock that led up to it. It had been decided that the Castle must be held at all costs as a jumping off place for the next attack, and the cost was heavy. At first it was garrisoned by two companies, but it was decided that it was as effective and much more economical, to hold it with as small a force as possible. Eventually it was held by two platoons at a time. The building itself consisted of a substantial tower, two thirds of it still standing, and a courtyard to the west facing the hillside. The whole was surrounded by a stone wall five feet thick and ten feet high. At the base of the tower was a well protected cellar in which one platoon at a time took shelter; there was another small cellar where the other platoon lay during regular shelling. There was no way of giving direct help to the garrison if it was attacked, but the Castle was ringed about by our own gun, mortar and MMG defensive fire tasks [pre-planned barrages on fixed positions]. The only access to the Castle for our own troops was up from the town by means of a precipitous ridge of rock which needed two hands to climb. To the north was a narrow gorge and beyond that again, a steep spur on which Bn HQ and two supporting companies clung precariously. Here the men lived in rough made hovels and holes protected by stone breastworks. The fourth company was in reserve half a mile to the north. Near Bn HQ was an old quarry which served as a dump, the nightly terminus for a column of jeeps and trailers loaded with rations, water, and ammunition. Everyone lay low during the day under constant artillery and mortar fire, but each night one of the two platoons in the Castle was relieved so that no platoon spent more than 48 hours there at a time, and supplies went up with each relief on the backs of Indian porters using Everest carriers. Between the Quarry and the Castle the Indian porters were protected by the anti-tank platoon of the Bn holding the Castle.

The perception of the monastery, originally destroyed in the bombing in mid-February, dominating the area comes through in a number of diaries covering the battle, notably that of John Williams of the 99th LAA Regiment RA:

APRIL 1944

The centuries old Benedictine Monastery, which stood at the top of the mountain, overlooked not only Cassino Town itself but also the complete Liri Valley. It was known that the Germans were using the Monastery as a vast OP and in fact had Troops in emplacements around the entire monastery as well.

The 3rd April, Kitty American Bombers [P40 Kittyhawk fighter-bombers] flew over every forty minutes, bombing Cassino and Monte Cassino. How could anyone live through it we thought? Jerry sent over a number of shells into our area. The 4th April brought lovely weather which stayed with us for a few days: there was more shelling last night including air bursts over Number Five site with 30 shells landing in Number Six Detachment area: thank god we had no casualties. My sites are well built into the ground and heavily sandbagged around the perimeter. The house in which I had my Tac HQ was constructed of very heavy large rocks and stones. In consequence the walls were very thick which afforded very good protection although a direct hit would be a different matter. R Troop had three casualties and one of their tractors hit, there is no doubt that it is grim here, War at its worst. We are firing hundreds of shells every day and every night targeting known German positions, German shellings seeking us out in return.

Cassino is in ruins, hardly a wall standing, Castle Hill shattered beyond recognition. Monte Cassino Abbey destroyed by a massive USA Flying Fortress attack and followed by the Kitty bombers. The ruins give even better protection to the German Troops offering 10 to 20 feet thickness of stone and masonry protection. With all our sites being under direct vision of the Germans in and around the Monastery all our maintenance has to be carried out at night. If rations and water are not delivered during the hours of darkness, we have to go without for another 24 hours.

I had three guns up with me and a further three guns further back at Horseshoe Bend, so I had to make trips sometimes in daylight, not funny coping with the 'Mad Mile'. Actually the distance is two miles and two furlongs and almost completely straight with the 'Double Dodgy' 500 yards of lane leading up to my sites, both of which are regularly shelled day and night. A prayer every time before I embark along this route, I knew that I would be targeted, as any vehicle negotiating the 'Mad Mile' became a cat and mouse condition. The Germans, estimating where we would arrive when their shells arrived, we in turn estimating their minds and either increasing the speed or slowing down or even going into reverse etc. zig zagging whenever possible, hoping to get in front of a shell or delay ourselves sufficiently so that the arriving shells were in front of us.

With Eighth Army having taken over the majority of the Cassino front another attack was planned for May and codenamed Operation *Diadem*. The aim was for the US Fifth and British Eighth Armies to launch coordinated attacks that would break through on a 20-mile front between Cassino and the sea, encircle the beleaguered town and monastery and push through the German defensive lines beyond. Once these lines had been broken, then the Allies could link up with the forces in the Anzio beachhead and push on to Rome.

Captain Cowles had risen from the ranks as a pre-war regular soldier and now served in the 2nd Regiment RHA, which provided support for the British 1st Armoured Division. Here he describes his unit's role during Operation *Diadem*, which launched on 11 May:

THURSDAY, 11 MAY 1944

Very quiet all day as everyone waited for the night attack. At 2300hrs tonight the big show started. As dusk fell the only sound coming from the OP area was the sound of the bag pipes from the Highland regiments getting ready for the attack and no doubt at the same time giving Jerry something to ponder on.

The fire plan consists of concentrations of half an hour followed by a barrage lasting four hours. The attack is on a grand scale with all nationalities taking part. The overall plan is for outflanking movements by the Poles in the hills to the north and the Free French in the hills to the south. The frontal attack in the centre is to be

made by the 4th Inf. Div. and the 8th Indian Div. with the 78 Inf.
Div. and the 6th Arm. Div. in reserve.

At exactly 11pm the whole world seemed to rise up and shake
itself. The noise of heavy guns and field guns firing was so rapid
it was like a machine gun firing. Looking back the whole horizon
was lit by flickering gun flashes. It seemed almost unbelievable that
each flicker was a gun hurling shells anything up to 80 lbs or so
through the air. I cannot help but feel a little sorry for the enemy as
I sit writing this with shells whistling overhead in rapid succession.
It seems like a solid arc of steel overhead. It must be unbelievably
terrifying to be at the receiving end of this tremendous weight of
shelling. Makes me think the army command are taking no chance
of this attack failing.

FRIDAY, 12 MAY 1944

The creeping barrage [slow-moving artillery fire designed to move
in front of advancing troops and suppress enemy defensive positions]
continued to move forward until 3.30am when we were told to
continue firing on one lift. Seems the infantry had been held up
and the barrage was getting too far ahead of them.

As dawn broke the infantry were across the Rapido River and on
their 1st objective 500–1,000 yards beyond the river. At this stage
the advance was halted by enemy fire and poor visibility due to the
morning mist and the smoke screen laid down. The enemy counter-
attacked a number of times and it looked as if the infantry would
have to withdraw but some Canadian tanks crossed the river and
gave the extra support needed to hold the bridgehead.

Throughout the day the 4th Div. and 8th Ind. Div. tried to make
progress but were held up by heavy enemy fire. The Bty. was very active
firing heavy concentrations. On the right the Poles had pushed forward
towards the Monastery but were counter-attacked and forced back.

Enemy shelling was most on the Rapido area but during the night a
105mm shell landed between two of the guns of Néry Troop. During
the firing 'I' Battery had a premature burst that killed two of the gun
crew and injured two. Eagle troop also had a premature which blew
off the muzzle brake but injured no-one – very lucky. The Bty. Cmdr.
was also lucky, a shell just missed him and failed to explode.

San Angelo was captured by the Ghurkas at 1830hrs but the Germans recaptured it at 2200hrs. On the left flank the French had made some progress.

The day finished with progress not as good as had been hoped but our position across the river is firmly established. The outcome of the battle is yet to be decided – I shall be very disappointed if we can't force a break-through.

SATURDAY, 13 MAY 1944

All day there was heavy fighting in all sectors. At 10am we fired another barrage under which 4 Div. managed to advance about 100 yards.

All day the enemy shelled and mortared the crossings over the river. The tanks of the Canadian Div. edged forward a little but were needing infantry support. Yesterday they reported knocking out 10 tanks or SPs and today they bagged another two SPs and one tank. In the south the French are doing very well indeed. Their native colonial troops from N. Africa are a fierce lot . . .

We ourselves again fired incessantly. In the afternoon we fired smoke for two hours to help the 4th Inf. Div. who were under heavy fire from the Monastery area.

Sitting outside during the morning there was again a 'carpet of steel' overhead as shells passed both ways although little came our way – the Germans had better targets than the 2 RHA.

The wireless referred to incessant air attacks. Personally I only saw one plane – our air OP. A tank officer related his experience. He was pushing forward in his tank when suddenly in a hollow came across a German machine-gun crew. They were so close he could not fire on them. He said he didn't know who was more frightened – them or him. However, the Germans beat him to it putting up their hands, so he took them prisoners instead of them taking him.

As night fell the firing continued although we eased up a little. At midnight orders were received that tomorrow we are to add fire support to the 38 Bde. who are to go through 4 Div. Flap on about packing in case we are ordered to move forward with them.

TUESDAY, 23 MAY 1944

Today was one of the most poignant I have experienced. The battle
to break through the Hitler Line started at 6am with the usual heavy
barrage. Following the barrage the Canadian infantry made a frontal
attack supported by tanks. On the radio rear line frequency we could
hear the tank commanders talking – the radio frequency being close
to ours. There was not a great deal happening for the first three
hours, the barrage moved forward according to plan and presumably
the infantry were following, then we were told to hold the barrage
on one line. On the tank frequency the drama ran its course. One
squadron leader reported that his tanks had been under heavy fire
for two hours. He had lost a number of tanks and the injured were
needing urgent attention. There were calls to one tank crew to go no
further as he was going into danger. Casualties and tank brew ups
continued to be reported, then a voice full of emotion I heard say
'Sunray has just been killed' (i.e. the tank commander). It seemed
weird listening to the radio conversations going on calmly whilst
the crews were in very great danger with tanks being knocked out.
Meanwhile we were sitting in comparative safety. Finally, because of
the casualties the tanks were ordered to withdraw. Now the trouble
really started as they pulled out, anti-tank guns and SP guns opened
up on them. The squadron leader who had reported his Sunray killed
went off the air – later from another tank we heard the message
that he had been hit and baled out. Soon there was only one tank
on the air. We could hear the tank commander on his intercom, in
a very young voice, giving his driver the directions to try and get
back without being hit.

At this stage the battle looked like being a complete fiasco but
quite suddenly at 5pm reports came through that the Germans were
destroying bridges and ammo dumps and were pulling out.

We were told that it is very likely the 2 RHA is to join a lorried
infantry brigade composed of Rifle Brigade units. Seems we are in
the fight to the end. *Ça ne faire rien. C'est la guerre . . .*

THURSDAY, 25 MAY 1944

I am desperately short of sleep and hope today to catch up but at 0500hrs I was awakened and told recce parties had to move out at 0615hrs. This meant a scrambled breakfast and hasty pack up of the jeep and we were away on time.

My jeep crew consists of L/Bdr. Hill, my signaller and Gr. Ford my driver and myself. We are self contained and always carry a few days rations, water and petrol. I have a small bivvie and there is a canvas sheet to make a shelter at the side of the jeep for the crew. Personal kit is to a minimum, any non essential stuff being carried in B echelon vehicles.

During the next 12 hours the journey was laborious. The track was packed with traffic trying to get forward and we just had to take our place and crawl along moving all the time through clouds of fine limestone dust. By mid afternoon we reached the Hitler Line proper. There certainly had been some battle. One area, through which we passed, was a large cornfield on the far boundary of which were two dug-in anti-tank guns, an 88mm and a 70mm. These two guns had dealt with our approaching tanks in a terrible manner. I counted 14 tanks knocked out in a small area – most of them useless Churchills with 2-pdr guns only. One Churchill had managed to outflank the 88mm and had put two 2-pdr shells through the steel turret. The Churchill was knocked out by another gun. There were many bodies around although some could not be seen because they were in the tall corn. Very upsetting to see a severed hand lying near the track. As we passed into the Hitler Line, there were signs that the Germans had taken a hammering. Dead Germans were in all manner of odd places. Two lay under a tree which a shell had hit. They were probably snipers. Most of the dead were in ditches. We were now well up with the advance – there were odd items of loot to pick up, particularly German small arms.

The Eighth Army had indeed broken through, with the monastery itself falling on 18 May to the men of Lieutenant-General Wladyslaw Anders Polish II Corps, while Eighth Army pushed XIII Corps beyond Cassino into the Liri Valley after another bloody attritional battle.

Unfortunately, the Liri acted as a funnel, and most of Eighth Army's transport immediately became stalled in an enormous traffic jam. In the mountains to the south, the French Expeditionary Corps also succeeded in breaking through. On the coast, US II Corps surged forward, driving on to link up with the US VI Corps at Anzio. The stalemate at Cassino had been broken and the front was fluid once more.

To the north at Anzio, the Allied forces had regrouped after the German attacks of February and were now able to launch Operation *Buffalo*, a drive towards Rome through the Alban Hills designed to coincide with the major effort by the British Eighth and US Fifth armies to the south. Peter Lovett, still attached to 46th RTR, describes this successful offensive:

THURSDAY, 25 MAY 1944

The long-awaited attack from the bridgehead commences tonight – God help Jerry, we think that onslaught will be tremendous. 8.30pm – a terrific artillery-barrage commences – reminds me of the memorable night of 23 October at El Alamein. The bridgehead being so small in comparison to most fields of battle, all the guns, American heavies, 4.5s, 25-pounders, are all barking out and roaring like closely-caged wild beasts – the din was hellish. In the still air of dusk heavy shells screamed and howled across the sky from the 6-inch guns of cruisers out in the bay. Life on the receiving end of that lot must be absolute hell . . .

28, 29 MAY 1944

The push has been overwhelming – Highways 6 and 7 already cut, Valmontone and Velletri captured, while the Fifth Army is around Frosinone. Again we find ourselves near the heavy artillery of the Scottish Horse – at intervals the 4.5s split your eardrums with salvos which go crashing on to German infantry and vehicles. We go forward (through a lovely scented pine-wood whose fragrance seemed to overwhelm the stink of cordite fumes) to service the wireless on a tank – get a grandstand view from a ridge of the present battlefield stretching towards the Alban Hills. Distant crashes and puffs of dust mark the fall of shells on enemy rear-guards, great mushrooms of smoke ascend from the poor little villages being pounded by the RAF, and away above Albano and Frascati billows of white smoke and dust envelop viaducts and bridges; the screen rises and fades away revealing great breaches in the stone structures as the Germans fight a delaying action by demolitions.

By the beginning of June, the German lines had been stretched to breaking point and the Allied troops pushed onwards towards Rome, with the American General Clark altering his axis of attack to focus on the city itself and allowing the German defenders to escape. This was not part of the original plan and remains controversial to this day. Peter Lovett again:

SATURDAY, 3 JUNE 1944

Albano captured. Big attack on our west flank 2 pm – half an hour's murderous hail of artillery from guns just behind us – shells come over the ridge 'whee . . . whee . . . whee . . . whee . . . whee . . . whee . . .' but you don't have to duck because they're ours! Listen to our squadron on the wireless in support of the infantry. Listening to a sort of running commentary on the action, which is what the tank-to-tank wireless communications seems like, grips you with a sort of aghast suspense. Sometimes a commander, a note of urgency in his voice, gives some rapid order, sometimes voices sound cool in the tightest of corners, references are made in a sort of jargon intelligible only to the men in the tanks. When orders are given to pump HE into houses or Spandau nests you cannot help visualising the fearful effect it will be having at the instant – just sudden violent death. One notes how the inviolable Red Cross is respected, German and British orderlies with Red Cross armbands and flags are allowed free passage among themselves and anywhere where there are wounded. Infantry casualties seem to be appalling . . .

An uncanny change has come over the battle-front – we drive slowly along this country road on a summer Sunday morning, all is peaceful, not an artillery shot disturbs the silence yesterday, continually shattered by the pounding of guns, no more enemy shell-bursts, no 'brrrrr . . . brrrr' of Spandau machine-guns – Jerry has pulled out over-night. Prisoners unkempt and dirty with battle relax in the backs of jeeps and lorries, wounded are still being brought down the road from yesterday's fighting. In parts the road is littered with debris – smashed farm-carts, two dead horses in the middle of the road – one had been run over by a tank – awful. Graves, German and British, are dotted by the way-side and at times the appalling stench of bodies arises from ditches and fields. If only people could see what a war really does mean. Looking across the plain towards Albano and Velletri which were yesterday peppered with shell-bursts, flashes from an occasional German gun and demolition-explosions, one is struck today by the dramatic peace which has swept across the scene – it is the peace of destruction and desertion. This afternoon we hear that advanced troops are now in Rome. We leaguer on a piece of high ground south of Rome and through field-glasses the buildings of the city are at long last visible.

Rome finally fell on 5 June 1944. The months of fighting for the Gustav Line devastated the area around Cassino. Patrick Burns served with the 160th Railway Construction Company and passed through Cassino following the end of the battle in June 1944. Here he eloquently describes the destruction wrought on the town by the successive battles:

SEPTEMBER 1944

On thro' Cassino. CASSINO – I guess this word had been a household word recently, and that much had been written about it and will be wrote about it in years to come. Cassino: never and I mean NEVER, have I seen such complete destruction, such appalling havoc and such awe inspiring desolation . . .

Blitzed areas of London, Bone docks repeatedly dive-bombed and machine gunned, demolished ports, stations, towns and villages in Africa, Sicily and Italy, such as; Agusta, Syracuse, Catania, Lentini, Messina, Foggia, Termoli and others: all that pales into insignificance in comparison with Cassino. Set at the foot of barren boulder-strewn Monte Cassino, on which is perched the famous Monastery; the town when seen from a distance looks like a mere continuation of the hill,

it is so pulverised. The approach to the town is a shell torn road thro'
acres of bomb craters as close as a cluster of mole-hills. Barbed wire and
slit trenches and dugouts, where men lived and fought like animals; and
died harder than any trapped wild beast. The hillside honeycombed with
caves and tunnels, that rocked with countless bombs; where men must
have gone mad, and been buried alive and crushed. When you enter the
'town' you are among piles of stinking rubble. All over is dead burnt out
stench. 'Wiped off the face of the earth.' 'Razed to the ground.' Such
phrases are seldom justified, here they are an understatement. Stormed
repeatedly, blasted by the very breath of hell, Cassino is only a name.
Like a scene from a dope-fiend's dream, with the shattered monastery
prostrate on the bleak hill top; tank turrets and guns poking from cellars
at crazy angles, broken weapons and ammo strewn about; all the place
thick with mines and booby traps, perhaps set by hands now dead to
trap the unwary living. Dust, heat, haze, smells and untold bodies under
the debris. Crumbling masonry and huge craters full of stagnant water
and other things . . . We pass through a dead town of the dead . . . and
somewhere you can almost picture the Prince of Darkness and all his
horrible satellites gibbering, gloating and dancing fiendishly; hysterical
with unholy glee at the folly and suffering of mankind . . . We see
not a tree with a green leaf on, not a tree clad in the glory of early
summer; only trees that have been stripped and torn by the awful blasts
stretching their broken arms upwards as if in mute appeal. Fields that
are scorched and churned by machines of war, and littered with burnt
out vehicles. The same fields that once grew crops to nourish man, and
where children romped and laughed.

All over is that indefinable sense of stillness and time holding its
breath, as if the very air has been sucked clear of sound and vitality.
Unconsciously we speak quietly, or a pitch higher, or laugh off key;
or keep quiet . . . Is it possible that men endured this? Yet when
the town was finally taken, the enemy had men to fight back, dazed,
desperately, hopelessly. Cassino — I've tried to describe, but I cannot.
It must be seen to be believed, but perhaps you would not believe it
then; but dismiss it as some wild impossible dream from which you
would wake shuddering.

Show me the man who says he has seen worse: <u>and I'll show you
a liar.</u>

3. Arakan and the Second Chindit Offensive

Early 1944 also saw the British attempt to take the offensive to the Japanese in Burma. Following the failure of the first Arakan offensive in 1943, when a British attempt to advance down to the port of Akyab had ended with a Japanese counter-attack, another offensive was made in January 1944. Two Indian divisions spearheaded the attack, supported by the British 36th and Indian 26th divisions in reserve. William Elliott served in 2nd Battalion East Lancashire Regiment, part of the 36th Division, and fought in the Arakan from January 1944 onwards. The British advance here was rapidly stopped by the Japanese Ha-Go offensive, launched on 6 February 1944, which the British managed to beat off after three weeks of heavy fighting. Here Elliott describes some of the problems of fighting in the Burmese jungle:

SATURDAY, 12 FEBRUARY 1944

It would be mid-afternoon on the 12th February when the baggage was finally packed and placed in position to the satisfaction of the mule-owners, and we began our trek, which, almost as soon as we left the camp, led us along a steep narrow mountain track, which widened in places, to some semblance of a road, but in the main was rough and difficult to walk on; yet, how easily those animals climbed, in spite of the 112 lbs load, so that after a time we found that by hanging on to the tail of a mule our progress was considerably easier, and the animals seemed not to mind the extra drag; as our journey continued, an odd man here and there would drop behind, finding the strain too much, and still we went on, up and up, until I began to think we would never stop climbing, – so this is the Arakan, I thought, precious little fighting we'll be able to do here, it's as much as we can do to walk! However, when we were nearing the summit, the whole column had slowed down, and we arrived at 26th Div. position, utterly exhausted, and greeted with the grinning faces of a company of Gurkhas, whose position 'B' Company was to occupy. From them we learned the lie of the land – where the water supply was, where we could wash, sleep, eat, find the medical people etc., and after a short time, our Gurkha friends bade us farewell, and happily began the downhill journey to base. And so we made our acquaintance with Goppe Pass.

That night, sentries were posted as we were now in enemy country. The Japs might be anywhere in the towering mountains that surrounded us, perhaps even now we had been observed, and they were planning to attack us. It was at this time that 7th Div. had been completely isolated by the enemy, and the famous battle of the Admin. Box [at Imphal–Kohima on the Indian border] was in progress somewhere between the Ngakyedauk Pass and where we now were, British and Indian troops were hammering the Jap, and forcing a corridor by which 7th Div. could escape. Nothing happened during the night, except that the air grew chill owing to the height of our position, and we were glad when daylight came, and the sun rose in the heavens with its life-giving warmth.

At the same time as the Fourteenth Army was launching the second Arakan offensive, Major-General Wingate was planning another operation by his Chindit forces, this time on a much larger scale. His second operation, codenamed *Thursday*, was to consist of 20,000 men in six brigades – with each brigade broken down into a series of columns of 500 or so men. This 'Special Force' was to seize vital airfields and disrupt the lines of communication to the rear of the Japanese forces.

N. Aylen served as a trooper in the 45th Reconnaissance Regiment during the operation and describes the daily routine of marching undertaken by a Chindit:

MARCH 1944

Each man carried rifle (or other weapon), ammunition, two or more grenades, two or more bren gun magazines, five days' rations, water bottle, groundsheet, blanket, spare clothing, washing kit, mess tin, chagal [leather or skin water bottle], and personal kit (if any) – total weight about 60lbs. In addition each man took his turn at carrying the section bren gun (24lbs). The first two or three miles along the road (which had progressed considerably during our stay in bivouac) was easy going except that our necks were almost dislocated by the weight of our packs. But presently we left the road, and took a track leading up to a steep gradient. Before long the track was littered with 'extras' with which many of us had burdened ourselves, but which we now found it was impossible to carry.

Throughout the march the usual rule was 'Move off at dawn – march for two hours – breakfast halt 8am – march till noon – midday halt till 3pm – march till sunset (about 6pm). Ten minutes halt was allowed each hour. After marching for ten minutes a man's shoulders would begin to ache from the weight of his pack. A little further along his feet would probably begin to feel sore from the extra weight carried. Then after an hour or two his sides would probably become chaffed from some item of equipment rubbing against them. Usually the pace was such that if a man dropped behind for any reason, he would be unable to catch up his section till the next halt. After a while a man would be able to think of nothing but the next halt and the relief it would bring to his aching body. At the end of each day we cooked our food (tea and bully stew, or soup and corned pork loaf if we carried American 'K' rations), made our beds, and took turn at guard duty.

Sometimes the nature of the country was such that we only covered a mile or two during the day's march. Where the track was impassable to a loaded mule, the loads were removed and carried by the men. Sometimes steps had to be cut, where the track was extra steep or slippery, before the column could get through. But in spite of the strain and hardships of the journey some of the men managed to retain their sense of humour. On one occasion as we toiled, aching, perspiring, and panting up a steep gradient, someone who had reach the top called out 'beautiful view from here, men'. It was indeed a beautiful view but few were in the mood to appreciate it. Stretching as far as the eye could see was ridge upon ridge of mountain. Those behind showed the results of our labour and those in front were still to conquer. The men's suggestions as to what to do with the view were predictable.

When marching with the column, any messages from front to rear were passed by word of mouth from one man to man, and sometimes the message was slightly contorted when it reached the other end. Once we passed up a message 'stop in front. Gap in column', and shortly afterwards we were mystified by someone who was sent back to find the 'Jap' in the column.

The allied air forces (RAF and USAAF) were now our only link with civilisation. We would signal our requirements and in due course the planes would appear overhead and drop the required supplies, or bomb and strafe an enemy target, or evacuate our wounded, as the case might be. We saw very little of the enemy air force, and our men seemed to be masters of the sky.

Five days after setting off on the expedition, we saw for the first time this link in operation. A clearing in the jungle had been selected, and presently the planes roared over our heads to inspect our signals, then turned round and roared over the selected clearing again, this time letting fall a cascade of bundles which were presently transformed into a stream of parachutes floating gently to earth. Some of the supplies, e.g. mule fodder, did not require a parachute, and fell with a resounding thud into the clearing.

On 23 March, Major-General Orde Wingate was killed in an air crash in Manipur, a town east of the Burmese border with India, leaving the Chindits without his dynamic leadership.

Wingate was and remains a controversial figure. Many distrusted his methods and approach. Pat O'Brien was an RAF liaison officer with 49 Column, 4/9th Battalion Gurkha Rifles, during the second Chindit operation and later compared Wingate to the man who took over his position, Major-General Joe Lentaigne:

It is impossible to imagine Wingate shedding a tear over a dead comrade. All generals will kill you, of course, that is part of their job and should be irrelevant to any comparisons between them; for that reason I can never see the point of Sassoon's bitter lines about the passing General on the mud fields of the Somme in that first World War:

> 'He's a cheery old card, grunted Harry to Jack,
> As they slogged up to Arras with rifle and pack . . .
> But he did for them both with his plan of attack.'

So what? Of course he would. As well criticise a butcher for a bloody apron, or a gambler for a losing bet. These things are included in the definition of his job. And if a general will probably kill you anyway in the end, then surely it is preferable he be a warm and friendly character in those last few days rather than Wingate, for example, an aloof and self-absorbed genius? Military commentators often say that fellow-feeling is misplaced in a Commander, such men must be cold and hard, but the fact is that friendliness inspires sympathy and sympathy might well have practical benefits in a desperate situation. In the early weeks after first joining Lentaigne's two battalions I often shared a drink with him in the evening, sitting under the hissing pressure lamp, drinking rum and listening to him and Masters as they told stories about India and the Army and the Gurkhas they had known as friends, and I would have done a lot for him. He met me on the street in Calcutta one day months after we got back, remembered me at once, called me by name and approached with a smile and outstretched hand. Wingate however looked at you like the ancient mariner, 'long grey beard and glittering eye', sensing you if at all not as a fellow human-being with a life and mind of your own but as a tool for him to wield in some God-given mission. Why risk your life for such an egocentric visionary? Or even do him a favour?

There was no doubt about the passionate enthusiasm he roused in many of the officers. They spoke of him with a sort of religious fervour. After that famous meeting at the cinema in Jhansi when he addressed us in his flat harsh voice, talking about the coming campaign, most of the officers came out with shining eyes, transformed into excited crusaders. They were so inspired by his personality that his actual words escaped scrutiny. A few however were not completely bewitched, were uneasy about some of his military ideas and said so. These were matters beyond my competence, the most junior subaltern knew far more about ground fighting than I did, but I did know something about air warfare and I thought he was talking fanciful nonsense on the subject of air support.

Major Ramsey served with the 7th Battalion Nigeria Regiment, part of the 3rd West African Brigade that formed 39 and 66 Columns during Operation *Thursday*. Here he records the aftermath of one of the hard-fought actions that characterised the expedition, the battle for Hill 60, in early August 1944:

SATURDAY, 5 AUGUST 1944

The hill was completely bare of any cover except for our friend the lone tree which was lacerated and naked, but still standing and still with some leaves at the top. The rest of the hill was pitted with bomb and shell craters, with about 20 Jap bodies lying about – terrific guts. One Jap officer with a Jap bayonet still through him etc. Another with a bayonet wound – a sloped hole – through the centre of his forehead.

4. Imphal and Kohima

The Japanese Ha-Go offensive that had stopped the British Arakan operation in its tracks was itself only a diversionary assault designed to camouflage their main offensive of early 1944, which was a strike towards the British Raj itself. Their target was the province of Assam in north-east India and their principal objectives were the towns of Imphal and Kohima. Called the U-Go offensive, it was launched on 6 March, with the Japanese Fifteenth Army crossing the Chindwin River on 8 March and pushing the Indian IV Corps back across the Imphal plain. However, the Japanese forces were at the end of extremely long supply chains and the longer the battle went on the more the initiative would pass to the British.

One of the key sectors of the battlefield was the town of Kohima, whose fall would permit a Japanese advance on Dimapur, isolating Imphal. The Japanese 31st Division advanced to take the town, which was only held by a light garrison of local troops.

H.F. Norman served with the 4th Battalion Royal West Kent Regiment, part of the Indian 161st Brigade, which was one of the few reserve units available at the start of the Japanese offensive. The West Kents were rushed to Kohima to support the units of the Assam Regiment and Assam Rifles that formed the main garrison of the town. In his diary, he relates the day-to-day events of the siege from his perspective on the ground:

WEDNESDAY, 5 APRIL 1944

Reveille (0515hrs). Washed and shaved (0530hrs). For breakfast (0545hrs) we had B &B, tea, porridge, two fried eggs, one sausage. We packed up all our kit and left this camp at 0645hrs in trucks, 'A' Coy. leading, then us behind (Coy HQ 13, 14 and 15 Platoons). When we arrived at the 43 milestone we got out of the trucks. The village of Kohima is on the 47 milestone. We then started climbing up past the Hospital for about one mile then we heard firing. We carried on for another mile and then we marched past 'A' Coy and took up positions which were then occupied by the IASC (Indian Army Service Corps) who were very 'shaky'. Ahead of us was a feature [very small hill] which we were told was occupied by one Coy. of Ghurkhas and one Coy. Assam Rifles. The Assam Rifles were firing two 3-inch mortars over the other side of the feature which they occupied on to the Japs and the latter retaliated by firing on to our feature. They fired about 20 bombs about five of them landing about 10 yards from us and another five yards. Cpl Webber was standing on the top of the pit and on telling him to come into the pit he jumped in and his feet had hardly touched the ground when a mortar bomb exploded one yard from where he had been standing and consequently two yards from our pit. We never had any tiffin, dinner or tea . . .

THURSDAY, 6 APRIL 1944

'Stood-To' (0545hrs – 0615hrs). For breakfast we had hard biscuits and ½ tin of blackcurrant jam which we scrounged from a 'basher'. We were mortared all day again today and had many narrow escapes. Cpl. Rees and Cpl. Webber's sections are right down the bottom of the feature with Cpl. Moxworthy's section, and Cpl. Beames' section is about 30 yards from the bottom, their trench being joined on to ours. (Ptn HQ) During the morning about 40 Assam Rifles came down off of their feature three or four times, but we drove them back again, firing at them but at 1400hrs 'the rot' set in and about 100 Assam Rifles and a few Ghurkhas came running from the feature, followed by their English officers. We thought that there was still one Coy. of West Yorks on there but about an hour later about 30 British lads came off of the feature. They told us that the feature was a convalescent depot and that they were all convalescing when the Japs attacked them. Poor devils: they certainly put up a 'good show'. We heard later that they were grenaded by the 'Jiffs' (Burmese turned traitor, who were trained by and fought for the Japs) and that nine out of ten Norfolk Regt. were killed. The Assam Rifles volunteered to take one Coy. back up with them, so 18 Platoon 'D' Coy. were brought forward and started climbing up the feature but were sniped at and came down again, and the whole of 'D' Coy went back 600 yards to their original feature. It was then noticed that the 'windy buggers' (the Assam Rifles and the few Ghurkhas) had left two 3-inch mortars intact with bombs behind so two small parties were sent up there and brought the lot back. A Jap reconnaissance plane circled over us at 1630hrs and a little later Capt. Watts came running around saying that it was vitally important to camouflage our pits and dig ourselves 'well in', as it was highly probable that we were going to be either shelled or dive-bombed . . .

FRIDAY, 7 APRIL 1944

Good Friday; The worst Good Friday I've ever spent. 'Stood-to' (0545hrs–0615hrs) to find that a Coy. of Japs (90 of them) had occupied the other half of our feature, so that 'C' Coy. were virtually surrounded and was in a space, 200 yds by 100 yds. 15 Platoon was in a position on the other side of the feature and was virtually 'out of the show'. We started dealing with them and at 1100hrs I was told to fire HE bombs on to the area occupied by the Japs. Sgt Tacon and myself went out into the open, 10 yds from our positions, without any cover from the few snipers on the feature in front of us or the Japs on our feature. I fired six HE bombs on to the target and then Sgt. Tacon left me to see if Capt. Watts wanted any more bombs fired. He left me there for 15 minutes and I must say that it wasn't pleasant, as I knew that either of the enemy could see me and shots were whizzing around everywhere, but I was lucky as I don't think that any were aimed at me. At 1145hrs Pte. Stirling had a bullet pass through the side of his neck, nothing serious and he was evacuated. For tiffin (1230hrs) we had hard biscuits and jam. At 1300hrs we were told that two platoons of 'D' Coy. were working their way around the other side of the feature and were going to encircle the Japs between us and them. By 1500hrs

the 'game was on'. There was plenty of firing and we set fire to the
bashers which the Japs and Jiffs were in, then the 'side-show' started.
They started running from the bashers and our lads fired everything
they had at them. I saw Jap bodies falling everywhere and piling up
all over the area. I was firing Ernie Thrussel's rifle and killed two Japs.
This lasted for about two hours and when the bashers burnt themselves
out we found approx 70 Jap bodies (12 Japs got away but they were
all wounded) and we searched the bodies for maps etc . . . We found
that there was quite a lot of milk tins had been opened and all the
dead Japs had milk smeared on their mouths so they were obviously
hungry. We were mortared again tonight and we were firing at the Japs
which we could see in the moonlight. There was no casualties in our
Coy. tonight. Battalion HQ where our wounded are lying was mortared
tonight and Capt. Watts was wounded again (twice in the arm) and
was evacuated to Battalion HQ much against his will.

The West Kents and other defenders of Kohima would spend the best
part of another fortnight fighting off Japanese attacks until Fourteenth
Army managed to push reinforcements through. By the night of 19/20
April, the Indian 161st Brigade had managed to establish a link with
the defenders and they were relieved, as the commanding officer of the
2nd Battalion The Manchester Regiment, Lieutenant-Colonel Rex
King-Clark, recorded in his diary:

WEDNESDAY, 19 APRIL 1944

Took some Naga [Burmese hill tribe who worked as scouts] round
to see mortars so that they can recognise them when out searching
for Japs.

The Country is extraordinary here. We're at 5,000 odd feet and
the hills above us go up to 7,500! They're higher still lower down
the Imphal Road.

Everywhere except immediately around Kohima is the most dense
jungle – all on precipitous slopes – particularly in the nullahs [steep,
narrow valleys].

Am acting as TCP [Traffic Control Person] Kohima for the relief
of the RWKs [Royal West Kents] by the Royal Berks, tomorrow.

THURSDAY, 20 APRIL 1944

All day at Kohima . . . at the foot of Garrison Hill doing TCP. Got all the Royal Berks in and the West Kents out. A hell of a job as there was no real organisation. Went into the garrison. Am about the first 2 Div Officer for having gone right in.

Harassing mortar fire at us all day. Just me, Birch and a couple of signallers and an excellent trooper from the Recce who just doesn't give a damn!

Two gunners were blown in half ten yards away from us . . . and their bodies stayed there all day.

Glad to be back. Same on tomorrow. Cross fingers!

FRIDAY, 21 APRIL 1944

Spent whole day at what is now known as Rex TCP – controlling relief of 1/1 Punjabs and Assam Regt by DLI [Durham Light Infantry] – went like a dream.

No shooting . . . carefully controlling traffic and preventing bunching.

Finished at 4.30pm.

Tank Waterhouse. DLI went in with the rest of the Bn.

The garrison have very long beards.

SATURDAY, 22 APRIL 1944

Up all day at Kohima again.

Some Mortar bombs landed on bank above us but weren't too bad.

Also troubled by some of our own smoke base ejection shells landing short which annoyed us.

A 'giant' tank of 149 Regt RAC went over the ridge and damn nearly pulled another one which tried to pull it out over too.

Bad show.

The hills drop away sheer from the road here everywhere.

David Lockhead . . . is a troop commander in 149. Very good too I believe.

Have the Kohima racket taped now.

Japs have guns on Merena Ridge. Their op. order (arty.) was captured off dead Jap BSM [Battery Sergeant Major].

By the end of May, the commander of the Japanese 31st Division at Kohima had realised that his supply position was untenable, and so ordered a retreat.

Captain Charles Satchell commanded the 45th Mule Company of the 17th Indian Division, a vital unit given the poor communications in north-east India. He recorded an attack on his unit during the closing days of the Battle of Imphal:

26 MAY 1944, IMPHAL

Tragic news, the column which went out was attacked by a battalion of Japs at 2am. Am waiting further news. Have asked to be allowed to go out but am told the battle is still raging there. It is on the edge of the village of Bishenpur. Feel quite worried.

27 MAY 1944, IMPHAL

Colonel sent me out to ascertain casualties. It's sixteen miles to Bishenpur. Left by jeep and got there in time to see two tanks and the company of Ghurkhas finish off the last two bunkers filled with the last eight Japs which attacked my column. Fell in the men, had a roll-call. This is a rotten moment. As I call out the name of anyone who was killed the men here keep on sobbing. At the end of the roll-call and investigation it's summed up: men killed 107: missing 38: wounded 26: animals 387 killed.

General is very concerned indeed. Tank commander says my men fought bravely, this was touching and proud news but couldn't offset the loss of some of my best men.

The stench of the men and the animals bodies is awful. Bulldozers are burying them, and collecting paybooks is sickening work. I have been sick twice but it's got to be done.

By 22 June, the siege of Imphal had finally been lifted and the road to Kohima reopened, and Japanese troops began to withdraw back into Burma. The invading Japanese had lost over 60,000 men in this disastrous operation, and Fourteenth Army was now in a position to go back into Burma in strength the following year.

5. D-Day

Despite the success in both Italy and Burma, the principal focus of Allied operations during June 1944 was most certainly on the long-awaited second front against the Germans in occupied Europe. For years, Allied planners had been preparing for the moment when the second front would be launched against the Germans in France, and by the summer of 1944 the time had come for Operation *Overlord*, the Allied invasion of Normandy. This was to be the largest amphibious operation in history, with *c*.155,000 men transported by air and sea to bridgeheads on the Normandy coast. Amphibious assaults are the most risky form of military assault and the planners and commanders were prepared for heavy casualties.

Under the overall command of US General Eisenhower, Allied ground forces under the command of General Bernard Montgomery were to be landed on five beaches along the Normandy coastline, codenamed: Utah, Omaha, Gold, Juno and Sword, while airborne forces protected the flanks and naval forces provided support off the coast. The invasion was originally scheduled for 5 June, but postponed for 24 hours due to bad weather.

Stan Hough of the LSI HMS *Princess Astrid* was now back in home waters and part of Force J, the Royal Navy force operating off Juno Beach on D-Day. Here he describes the scale of preparations leading up to the invasion itself:

FRIDAY, 2 JUNE 1944

D-Day, the day the landing will take place on Western Europe, is a matter of days now. The preparations are fantastic, and it seems nothing has been forgotten. Hundreds of Tank Landing Craft at full. All landing ships full of troops and in good working order. Lots of us, known as Landing Ships Infantry, including large Glen ships and Empire ships, Pre-war passenger liners, who carry two or three thousand troops each. Smaller ships such as ours carrying 300 troops each, will land troops on the beaches first, with the larger ferries and all kind of ships which did short runs to the Continent before the war. The security all over the South Coast is good, no civilians who do not live here allowed. Service men in the area not to go out of the 20-mile radius. All troops taking part are confined to barracks, or ships. No all night leave for the Navy. Hundreds of tugs just over from the US are here. Miles of pontoons, ready to be towed across. Dozens of concrete and brick floating jetties, which are going to be towed across to make a harbour. Large floating cranes which travel under their own power, armed with Oerlikon guns. Motor Launches and Motor Torpedo Boats, by the hundred. Queer ships that no one can guess what they are to be used for. Pontoons under their own power will take tanks, and all sorts of gangways for landing stores etc.

Around Southampton there are hundreds of thousands of troops, who can be moved in a few hours with full equipment. Thousands of tanks, lorries, etc. are lining the roads and filling the fields. It is impossible to get stores down here as all the store houses are full ready to be taken to Europe.

Planes fly over every day, mostly about 20 at a time, going over, bombing the beaches and returning. We have had two or three air raid warnings at night during the past week. German planes trying to take photos, but all ships possible make smoke, and fire AA guns, as well as shore batteries, manned by the Home Guard and the Army. The air raids are not a bother, apart from us having to get up in the middle of the night, although the smoke gets in one's eyes, and it is sometimes impossible to get below decks for above an hour at a time.

We hear ships in other ports are as many as here. Falmouth is a US base, and although smaller, is much the same as this one in the way of ships etc. Also Portland and New Haven. There are dozens of RN ships of all types in Portsmouth. Mail is taking eight days and more to come from north of London. We are not allowed to send telegrams or make private phone calls, and all letters have to go through the Censor on board and ashore.

As with the landings on Sicily, it had been decided to launch the main invasion of the Continent with an airborne operation to secure the flanks of the proposed bridgehead. An Anglo-American force of paratroopers and glider troops was assembled, consisting of the British 6th Airborne Division and the US 82nd and 101st Airborne Divisions. One of the most important tasks allotted to the British airborne units was the capture of the bridges over the River Orne and the Caen Canal, including the bridge at the village of Bénouville now known as Pegasus Bridge, in order to cut off German forces in the beachead from reinforcements elsewhere in France. In one of the first actions of D-Day, a force of glider-borne troops of the 2nd Battalion Oxfordshire and Buckinghamshire Light Infantry led by Major John Howard assaulted this key position. Amongst them was Denis Edwards:

TUESDAY, 6 JUNE 1944, D-DAY

As we drew level with the thickest of the flak and were beginning to make out, far down below, the coastline bathed in dim moonlight, there came the familiar 'Twang', a jerk, followed by almost total silence which, from past experience, told us that our glider had parted company from the towing bomber . . .

As we approached the coast we were ordered to keep quiet. Not a sound could be heard as the bombers flew onwards (to complete an inland bombing mission) and we seemed to be completely alone and momentarily in space. Then we were on our way down . . .

With our bodies taut, weapons tightly gripped, the Senior Pilot yelled 'Link Arms' and we knew that at any moment we would touch down. The time is now 0015hrs. We all held tight and braced ourselves for touchdown.

With the usual slight bump, a small jerk and a much heavier thump we knew that the glider had made contact with the ground – but only for a moment – it jerked again, shuddered, left the ground for a second or two, bumped over the rough ground again, and bounced forward at high speed like a Bucking Bronco.

For perhaps 40/50 yards we sped forward bouncing in our wooden seats as the vehicle lost contact with the ground, came down again with another heavy thump, a tug, and a jerk and, for a few moments at least, it seemed as if we were in for a comparatively smooth landing.

As that thought flashed through my mind the darkness suddenly filled with a stream of brilliant sparks as the glider probably lost its landing wheels and the underskids hit some stony ground. There quickly followed a sound like a giant sheet of cloth being viciously ripped apart, then a God Almighty crash like a clap of loud thunder and my body seemed to be moving in several different directions at the same time.

A few moments later the giant glider, skidding over the uneven ground, came to a juddering halt and I found myself perched at an uneven angle and peering into a misty bluey-greyish haze and, from somewhere out in endless space there zoomed towards me tracer-like streams of multi-coloured lights like a host of small shooting stars that moved at great speed towards my eyeballs – I was dazed and literally seeing stars . . .

The tall bridge superstructure seemed eerie as it appeared to shimmer in the pale moonlight. Already a few of the lads were up ahead and, not wishing to be alone in enemy occupied territory, I made haste to catch them up. The Company Commander (Major Howard) was already on the approach to the bridge and was standing there fully exposed. 'Come on boys – THIS IS IT' he roared as he waved us forward.

As we reached the bridge we let fly with rifles, hand grenades and light automatics whilst shouting as loudly as possible to put the wind up the Jerries and to boost our own morale.

The defenders were rushed and the bridge was captured, though in the process Denis Edwards's platoon commander, Lt. Den Brotheridge, was killed by German machine-gun fire, becoming the first Allied soldier to be killed on D-Day.

The assault phase of Operation *Overlord* was codenamed Operation *Neptune* and was the largest and most complex amphibious operation ever seen. Under the command of the resourceful Admiral Bertram Ramsay was an invasion force of 1,213 warships, including seven battleships and twenty-three cruisers, and 4,000 landing ships, and craft to transport the four Allied army corps to the five invasion beaches.

W. Cutler served aboard the Combined Operations headquarters ship HMS *Largs*, which served with the naval Force S off the coast of Sword Beach:

MONDA+Y, 5 JUNE 1944, 2130 HRS

At last, after many weeks of exercises, we are on our way towards making another epic in the history of the world. We are told we shall be storming the enemy bastions at approximately 0730hrs in the morning. What a task we have ahead of us, and what losses are we to suffer, in our endeavour to make a landing on enemy shores. All the force are going in fully knowing the task set us, and we will not fail. The minefields with their countless number of mines alone is a formidable job, and then we expect heavy opposition from the shore batteries. We are depending a great deal on the minesweepers, and the bombarding force.

Somewhere, submerged off the Normandy coast, we have a midget submarine, whose initial task is to pick out the most suitable beach for our landing force. Nothing has been heard from the sub. for two days so we do not yet know whether they have been successful. We have been delayed 24 hours, owing to bad weather, and it's not so good even now. This must have put the sub's crew in a terrible plight.

TUESDAY, 6 JUNE 1944, D-DAY

0100hrs Our progress is very satisfactory, nothing encountered up to pres. A heavy swell is running, and too much wind is blowing to be comfortable for our small craft. I see that one or two who were being towed have broken adrift, and are having to follow on under their own power.

0300hrs Airborne troops should have landed by now. Aircraft are continually going overhead, and they are meeting plenty of flak.

0400hrs Enemy coast line is in sight, and a great number of explosions are taking place. We are waiting for a signal to come from the midget sub. pointing the way to our beach (SWORD BEACH). This will be done by the sub. firing Verey lights in the direction we are to land. Signal received 0530hrs. We reached our objective, and assault craft were touched down ready to move in. Battleships, Monitors, Cruisers, Destroyers, etc. are pounding away at the enemy beaches. What a terrific amount of explosives are going over. Rocket ships are now moving up, goodness knows how any living thing can stand up to such a terrific battering.

0615hrs Destroyer *Svenner* torpedoed off our port quarter, and broke in two sunk in less than five minutes. Another torpedo narrowly missed us.

We managed to turn and the torpedo slid harmlessly by, missing our bow by a yard. These torpedoes must have been fired from shore.

0730hrs ZERO HOUR, Troops have landed on the beaches, the Marines are the first in, the assault followed up by the East Yorks. Bombarding force are still blazing away and shells are dropping just ahead of our troops, clearing the way.

One of those serving aboard the escorting destroyers on the morning of D-Day was Lieutenant John Pelly, on board the *Eglinton*, again part of Force S off Sword Beach. The destroyer he describes sinking below is probably *Svenner*, the same Norwegian destroyer mentioned in the diary of W. Cutler above:

TUESDAY, 6 JUNE 1944, D-DAY

We passed the endless landing craft, large and small, transports, landing craft carriers etc etc, all crammed with tanks and waving soldiers, 'thumbing it' back to England and finally took up our position in the lead. All night we slowly crossed the Channel with nothing happening and then as it grew light early on the morning of 6th June 1944 we saw ahead the coast of Normandy, and behind one sea of shipping.

Almost immediately the destroyer just to port of us went up – her bows and stern sticking right up and then sinking at once, while at the same time torpedoes were seen approaching from the port side and we went full ahead and avoided them. A few guns and mortars were now opening up, but they were soon forgotten about, when our attention was drawn to the terrible and accurate bombing of the beaches that had just started.

Fear – I remember that, just after seeing the destroyer so close to us go down and sensing that this was a very unpleasant welcome so early on, I felt a fear of uncertainty that I'd never before known – before it had just taken the usual form of excitement and an effort to appear calm in speech; but for a few seconds on this occasion I couldn't get a sound from my mouth. I remember that the doctor appeared on the bridge just then and I tried to tell him what was going on and nothing came out. How I envy the man who seems to have no fear and I've met quite a few like that.

All this time we were closing the beaches leading the other destroyers who were with us to carry out the initial in-shore bombardment of pillboxes and gun emplacement. After a while the one small minesweeper ahead turned back and we went on and on closing the beach – I expecting the ship to be mined at any minute – until but just over a mile away. The first bombing of the beaches was over and there seemed to be absolute quiet. Then at six thirty we opened up and so did the cruisers astern and the battleships behind them – and it was a great comfort to feel they were there. Our orders were to destroy anything that might be a gun or mortar site and we already knew of one or two. We had about two miles of sea front to deal with, including the village of Luc sur Mer, to the west of Courseilles. Most of the two miles of target area was houses and streets just beyond the beach. Finding hardly any opposition, and hardly any gunsights, the Captain chose his own targets and we were so close that we couldn't miss. Down came a water tower, the top of the gasworks went for six, any German who ran out of a house up the street had four four-inch shells overtaking him. In fact we had the time of our lives – all pointing out targets and shooting up anything that took or didn't take our fancy – like the green house that the captain thought to be an eyesore.

I just don't know what value our actual little port was – I think that it was pretty demoralising to the men billeted in the houses and it made a lot of noise, but there did not appear to be any organised enemy unit in our area.

However we had a grandstand view of the first landings at seven thirty as we ceased fire; we watched the bitter fighting and the masses of material being landed and the tanks getting ashore and fighting in the fields above the beaches. The rocket craft that completely obliterated areas of beach were among the many novelties and all day more and more ships arrived and quietly anchored. In fact as far as one could see it was ships.

We watched one or two ships get hit and sometimes sunk and yet we felt complete masters of the situation though I had awful qualms at times about the land fighting. I'll never forget the chaos and awful mess of landing craft returning out of control, full to almost sinking with a red mixture of blood, water and oil fuel with legs and heads sticking out. One or two came alongside and we hauled the wounded out, mostly Canadians and Marines, and placed them in their awful suffering along the Upper deck, doing what little we could. The wardroom was turned into a ward, so was the entire forehead messdeck – bottles of plasma tied up and hanging over nearly every man – the doctor and his assistants of stokers and stewards doing wonders.

The Navy was also running affairs on the beaches themselves, and Ken Oakley of 'Fox' RN Commando again found himself on an invasion beach controlling the flow of traffic, this time on Sword Beach:

Tuesday, 6 June 1944, D-Day

Reveille was early, approx. 0330hrs and the Beach Master, Lt. John Church, RNVR, and I boarded the LCA to run for our target Lion-Sur-Mer/Hermanville (code name Queen Red, Sword Sector) which was about five miles away. The sea was rough and several of the soldiers on board were sea sick, but as we ploughed along I could see that all around us were landing craft and warships of all shapes and sizes.

As I sighted the Plough formation of Stars ahead of us, the roar of the Naval Bombardment passed overhead and soon we heard the chatter of small arms fire directed at us. The LCA flotilla taking us to our target area were doing a great job by keeping us almost exactly on course.

Off to our Port Side an LCT(R) discharged a salvo of rockets in the direction of the Merville Battery we had been briefed about. We evaded all the small arms fire, but suddenly the dreaded steel stakes with mines or 56lb. shells attached, loomed ahead of us.

Daylight was with us now, and the cox'n of our LCA did very well to miss a shell attached to a stake on our starboard side, and then we heard the order, 'Down Ramp' and our time had come.

It was 0610hrs on 6/6/44 and the BM and I were quickly out of the craft and running up the sandy beach as mortar and machine-gun fire sped us on our way. At the high water mark we went to ground to take stock of the situation and get our bearings. John said we had landed almost exactly in our scheduled area, but as the mortar fire became more intense we wriggled deeper in the sand. My task was to protect and help the BM at all times, but when a stricken paratrooper cried out for help it was difficult to stay with the BM and ignore the cries. It seemed as if we were just outside the mortar fire pattern, and suddenly a DD [Duplex Drive, amphibious] tank loomed up behind us. The hatch opened, a voice called out 'Where is the fire coming from?' I answered, 'A couple of hundred yards to the right at 45°', 'OK' he said. The hatch banged closed, then bang, the shell screamed over our heads, it was no contest, the mortar fire ceased, the machine-gun fire subsided and just the occasional sniper shot rang out as we started to survey the beach.

More and more landing craft were beaching by now and we were kept busy persuading army personnel not to stay on the beach to brew their tea but go and chase those Germans who were still shelling us. The flail tanks and other 'funnies' had done a good job in clearing mines from the beach, and we were getting good exit lanes marked down leading to a good road.

Suddenly the shrill scream of bagpipes could be heard along the beach, and on looking to my right I saw a piper emerging from an LCT and following him came Lord Lovat, then the remainder of the Commando marched off as if they were on Horse Guards' parade ground, it was an incredible sight, I'll never forget it.

The 'funnies' referred to above were the specialised armour operated by the Royal Engineers and Major-General Percy Hobart's 79th Armoured Division. They were armoured vehicles specifically designed or altered to deal with 'Crocodile' tanks equipped with flame-throwers, specialised engineering tanks known as AVREs (Armoured Vehicle Royal Engineers), and 'flail' tanks for destroying minefields. Tim Wheway commanded a flail tank of 22nd Dragoon Guards:

TUESDAY, 6 JUNE 1944, D-DAY

0710hrs The DDs are floated, but owing to rough seas one by one they sink. We then realise it will depend on the flails to give the close support fire. We get into our tanks & seal down the hatches.

0720hrs The LCTs go full speed ahead & it is a race for the shore. We land at 0725hrs & the impact nearly shook the tanks through the doors. The flails stream out in 3ft of water, followed by the AVREs. We are met by terrific shell, mortar & 88 & 75 Ap & small arms fire at 300yds range. The LCT with our CO Col. Cox 5th ARE hit & the bangalores go up. Leading flail on the ship manages to get off, but Cpl. Brotherton is killed & crew wounded of the 2nd & also Col. Cox is killed. Several tanks are hit as the landing craft doors go down. Mines are sighted on top of the wooden beach obstacles. We go as far as possible in the water to be able to use our guns effectively & then open fire on concrete gun emplacements, houses & dug in infantry. Tanks are brewing up right & left. We then proceed flailing our gaps, but no mines are encountered so speed up & get within 50yds of our gapping places & open fire right into the slots of gun emplacements. (Lt. Boal & 4 Troop are on the extreme left flank and here the concrete gun emplacement with 88 mm guns was causing havoc to us further down the beach. Lt. Boal directed his gunner to fire the 75mm with HE at the apertures & with great accuracy a shell entered an aperture & demolished everything in the concrete emplacement. It saved our day, & many tanks & lives.) One flail tank (Cpl. Gazely) strikes a sunken obstacle with a mine on it & the bottom is blown in, Cpl. Snowhills sinks. Lt. Robertson's has a direct hit on the flails arms knocking them off. Lt. Allen has three 88mm AP straight through into the turret & all but Cpl. Pummell are killed. Wounded & burnt Pummell succeeds in getting into the sea & is picked up by an LCA. Cpl. Agnews tank has three AP through the engine & brews up. Tpr. Jennings is wounded in getting the driver's hatch undone. An 88 AP goes straight into the front of Sgt. Cochrane's tank killing the operator Tpr. Kemp & wounding

Sgt. Cochrane, Tpr. McKinnon. Some flails now start gapping & the East Yorks & the S. Lancs are now streaming up the beach covered by fire from the beach clearing flails. The AVREs follow the flails & the bridging AVREs dropped their bridges, the crews jump out to make them fast & in doing so are killed or wounded & the tanks receive direct hits & are brewed up. German soldiers rush from the houses shouting & firing as they come & soon the beach is strewn with the dead & wounded of our own & enemy troops. The beach clearance flails are now waiting for the 629 RE's to assist them in clearing the beach. Capt. Wheway & Lt. Sadler get out of their tanks & attempt to contact them. Shells & mortars are falling thick & fast but no one realises the danger of them until Tpr. Hogg is killed by his tank. A Lt. of 629 is eventually found & he states he is the only officer left & their casualties are so heavy they cannot assist us, so clearance flails proceed up the beach & commence gapping defences on the beach. Sgt. Turner & Cpl. Aird returned to the beach after having successfully made their gaps & flailed their laterals, small arms & shell fire is still intense & both Sgt. Turner & Cpl. Aird are killed by sniper bullets. After two hrs fierce fighting enemy resistance is wiped out & the surviving flails are back on the shore. We gather these between two houses where there are numerous weapon trenches & tunnels running under the houses & on searching these got 20 POWs, some from under the tanks.

Regular armour was also coming ashore on the beaches, amongst them the Sherman tanks of the Sherwood Rangers Yeomanry, who, as part of the 8th Armoured Brigade, supported the landings of the 50th (Northumbrian) Infantry Division on Gold Beach. The Reverend Leslie Skinner was attached to the regiment and recorded his brief observations at the time:

Tuesday, June 6 1944, D-Day

Up 0500hrs cold, wet, sea rough. 'Stand To' for 0700hrs. This is it. Land visible through mist by 0630hrs. Rain cleared. Running for Beach by 0700hrs under fire by 0710hrs. Beached 0725hrs. Lawrence Biddle/Bde. Major asked for volunteers unroll coconut matting at prow ship. I and three [or] four others volunteered, took places behind roll.

See nothing but good front cover. As beached hit mine. Man either side me wounded – one lost leg. I was blown backwards on to Bren carrier but OK.

Landing doors jammed. Gave morphine injections and rough dressings to injured men and helped put them in chain hatches. Ship's officer released doors and ramp. We rolled matting out. Water about six feet – sea rough – matting would not sink. Shellfire pretty hot. Infantry carriers/jeeps baling but left us to matting as tanks revved up. Washed aside but made it to beach though I had hell of pain in left side.

Chaos ashore. Germans firing everything they had. Road mined – great hole. Bulldozers unable to get through because mines. One tried – went up on mine.

Spent an hour with some engineers demolishing remains of some pillbox or whatever building it had been to make another exit from beach. Heavy work with pickaxe and chest hurting like hell. Finally got half-track into queue. Another standstill. Along line on foot, saw CO and A Sqdn waiting to get on faster and further. No RAMC landed as yet on our part beach. Some casualties. Got Sgt. Leades bring half-track back to beach, hull down behind sand dune. Start gathering wounded, mostly infantry. More as day went on from further down beach. No news yet of any Beach Dressing Station. Regt. clear now and moving well. By mid-day concerned to pass on wounded – to whom or what? Saw skipper of large LST waiting for evening tide to float him off. Persuaded him to take more seriously wounded when he left on rising tide. By 1430hrs hours got 43 on board – all carried by hand up 'Jacob's Ladder' and down near vertical companion ways to crew's quarters. Terribly tiring. Sent radio message requesting our Dr to examine these wounded, if possible before leaving. He came about 1530hrs. Saw them all. OK except one likely to die before reaching England.

Losses on D-Day were not as high as had been feared, though US troops suffered terrible casualties on Omaha Beach. Total casualties were in the region of 10,000, with 4,000 dead. By the end of D-Day, the Allies had secured all the beachheads and started to move inland.

❖

6. Operations in Normandy

The actual invasion itself was merely the first stage in a series of operations to consolidate the Allied position in Normandy, build up a suitable reserve of forces and break out.

One of the principal Allied objectives on the first day of the invasion was the city of Caen. Although initial attempts to take the city on the 6th failed, Montgomery persisted, launching a series of operations designed both to take the city and, he later argued, to wear down German armour reserves.

Major Burton was second in command of the 1/5th Battalion The Queen's Royal Regiment, part of the 7th Armoured Division that had come ashore as part of the follow-up formations to the initial invasion:

SUNDAY, 11 JUNE 1944

D5 and Sunday. During the day we got our orders for our first battle and a package of photographs of the ground we were to fight over. When we were briefed in England we were told that our task as a division was to break out of the bridgehead and make for Mont Pincon, a very high feature, half way between Aunay-sur-Odon and Conde-sur-Noireau. Stage 1 of this project was to advance and capture Villers Bocage a few miles north of Aunay. Up to date the invasion had gone well. All the beachheads had joined up and a bridgehead several miles deep had been formed. We had learnt from previous landings in this war and this time everyone pushed on inland as best he could. We hadn't got Caen – the Germans appreciated its value too much, but we were nearly there.

Then there was a bit of a salient in our line which bulged forward again towards Tilly. Between our right flank and the Americans the situation was rather vague. The Americans however had thrust forward rapidly and captured Caumont, the furthest point inland of all. The Germans had been slow to react to our landings and so far had brought up the 21 Pz & 12 SS Divisions against us in the Caen sector & Pz Lehr Division at Tilly.

The situation seemed favourable for a thrust by our 7 Armd. Div. We were therefore given the task of pushing forward & capturing or bypassing Tilly if possible & make a hole for the armour to go on to Villers Bocage.

Reconnaissances were carried out and contact was made with the 9 Worcesters of 56 Bde. who were opposite Tilly. They got into Tilly on this day but were counter-attacked out of it.

MONDAY, 12 JUNE 1944

1/5 Queens moved up to . . . about a mile north of Tilly, which was to be our jumping off place. 1/6 Queens was on the right. 1/5 Queens had a sqn of tanks under command and were supported by a battery of artillery. We started off on a two company front and advanced a few hundred yards when we contacted the enemy. They were dug-in in all the hedges, with their Spandaus & there seemed to be snipers everywhere. Behind there were carefully concealed tanks. They soon brought our advance to a halt. This was our first experience of 'Bocage' fighting. Bocage country was new to all of us. It consists of fields of all sizes and shapes, none very large, bounded by thick hedges usually with a bank and ditch as well. The hedges themselves besides the lower growing thorn & hazel etc are full of taller trees, oak, poplar & limes. This has the effect of making the country very enclosed. There are plenty of lanes but many of these are sunken & obstacles to tanks.

Anyhow, to an attacking force the enemy is completely unseen. Infantry get held up by machine gun fire & call up the tanks to help. When the tanks come up they get shot at by the concealed enemy tanks behind.

As a result of all this our advance was stopped and it became serious that the enemy was not going to fall back without making a stiff fight of it. The enemy were the Panzer Lehr Division, to whose fighting prowess 50 Div will bear witness. When this became obvious . . . the Corps Commd appreciated that the German left-flank was on the river Orne between Tilly and Caumont. Our battle was therefore called off and the whole Division was ordered to switch more to the west and try for Villers Bocage by another route.

However, as Laurie Phillips of the 1st Battalion The Rifle Brigade, now attached to the 7th Armoured Division, was to find, Villers Bocage was no easy target. As the British column advanced through the village, they were ambushed by the Tiger tanks of the 101st SS Heavy Panzer Battalion under its commander Michael Wittmann, in what was to become one of the most famous encounters of the Normandy campaign:

MONDAY, 12 JUNE 1944

Next morning we got on to the Caumont–Villers Bocage road, but after a while came to a prolonged halt, the loud noises ahead indicating that the head of the column had run into trouble. The CLY (County of London Yeomanry) were the leading armoured regiment, with our A Company and the anti-tank guns of 6 Platoon from our company under command. They motored down the road and into Villers Bocage without opposition, and were greeted by a cheering crowd of French people. The leading squadron drove straight through to occupy the high ground about one mile east, on the road to Caen. A Company and 6 Platoon followed on, but remained on the road for the time being; they were urged to close up, nose to tail, so that the following squadron of tanks could get into the village to protect the crossroads. The Colonel of the CLY went forward to the high ground to reconnoitre the position, as did all the officers of A Company, to pick out their positions before calling their platoons forward. Suddenly a Tiger tank emerged from the woods to the south of the road; he picked off the two rear tanks of the leading squadron and then drove down the hedge beside the road blowing up A Company's half-tracks and 6 Platoon's carriers one by one till he reached the centre of the village, where he disposed of the four tanks of the CLY's RHQ before turning back to rejoin his companions. Everything was chaos. The road was completely blocked with burning vehicles; the infantry, in a state of uncertainty because all their officers had gone forward, had no answer to the Tiger with only their small arms; one of the sergeants in 6 Platoon – 'Donkey' Bray – managed to get his 6-pounder unhooked and into action, and claimed to have hit an armoured car and a couple of half-tracks, but when his shots started bouncing off an approaching Tiger at point blank range, he decided that discretion was the better part of valour. A battalion of the Queens came up to defend the village, where quite a fierce little battle developed before the Germans were thrown out, but no one could reach the squadron on high ground, and their tanks were knocked out, and the survivors, together with those of A Company, were taken prisoner.

The CLY had 27 tanks knocked out and lost 14 officers and 86 men. A Company lost 80, including three officers killed; about 30 of them got back. About half of 6 Platoon got back, but Roger Butler, the platoon commander, was killed . . .

Meanwhile we had hastily taken up defensive positions near Amaye, a couple of miles west of Villers Bocage; the position was somewhat dicey, as the road back for several miles ran through German territory; to the north the Panzer Lehr Division were where we expected them, but to the south the 2nd Panzer Division had arrived undetected from beyond the Seine (as had the two companies of Tiger tanks which caused the initial chaos) and from time to time they were able to cut the road behind us. In the close Bocage country it was difficult to see what was happening; there was a tank gun firing so close to us that I thought it must be in the next field, so I gingerly went forward to have a look, but after crossing two fields I could still see nothing, although it still seemed very close. I decided it was not an immediate threat and beat a retreat. In the early evening the troops and tanks still in Villers withdrew to our perimeter, and we spent a somewhat restless night.

With the arrival of the British VIII Corps in Normandy, Montgomery tried again in late June. On 26 June he launched Operation *Epsom*, an attempt to cross the River Orne and encircle Caen from the south-west.

Trevor Greenwood was a corporal with the 9th Royal Tank Regiment, serving in Churchill tanks. His battalion landed in Normandy on D+16 as part of 31st Army Tank Brigade, moved inland and took part in Operation *Epsom* from 26 to 29 June:

D+19, Sunday, 25 June 1944

Moved to a new location last night: only about 3 miles nearer front, but we spent about four hours en route. Awkward route . . . probably for security. Conferences all day: all troop leaders doing little but study maps. Our first action is now imminent & everyone is more serious. A & B doing one attack . . . C another, & later in day.

We move out of harbour 7.0am Monday. I think we will have a hard task . . . Have spent all day trying to forget my jitters, but impossible. My stomach sinks to record low level when I think of facing barrage from Jerry 88s. Have seen their effect on a Sherman! Weather was bad too . . . rainy & gloomy. A really wretched day, all told. 2 letters from Jess! Wrote to J.

D+20, Monday, 26 June 1944

Yesterday, I had grave doubts as to whether this page would ever be written. I felt as though I had been condemned to death. But it is obvious that I have survived. We left harbour at 7.0am . . . for the front line, only about 3 miles away. Held up for an hour en route . . . slap in the middle of a concentration of our artillery. And they had just started a barrage. What pandemonium! The earth itself shook noticeably. Jerry must have had a hell of a time.

Village of Cheux had only been taken by our troops that morning, & there was much evidence of the battle. The stench of dead cows in adjoining fields was awful. Several human corpses along route . . . one, recognisable as a Jerry by torn bits of uniform, had been run over on the verge & tanks subsequently passed over his body. It was just a pulpy mass of bloody flesh & bones. No one appeared to be bothered by it. Our own troops were too busy 'digging in' against possible counter-attack to worry about dead bodies.

The village itself was a shambles . . . just a mass of gaunt looking walls & chimney pots, with a few remaining houses full of shell holes. Snipers were still busy in some of these houses. Kept my head down! Beyond village, everything was bustle and chaos. Enormous numbers of men & vehicles moving forward.

We took up our start position in a large field below crest of a hill: 5.0pm. Our infantry were in position too . . . some hundreds of them.

Had seen them on the way down. A sturdy looking crowd . . . mostly
Scotties . . . all smiling and cheerful. I think they were really glad to
have our support. They asked us to swipe hell out of Jerry!

Had previously received our orders & were thoroughly conversant
with plan of attack & ultimate objective. We also had a pretty good
idea of where enemy's main anti tank guns were, from previous
reconnaissance. Close to our zero hour, word came through that 60
Panthers had appeared within a few hundred yards of our line of
advance. Hell's bells! Poor little C squadron!

But very soon, & before we started, the Panthers advanced on our
position & were engaged by some fairly heavy stuff . . . 17-pounders,
I think. After about an hour, Jerry must have retired: he certainly
didn't get through! . . . & we commenced our delayed start at 6.15pm.
Infantry ahead . . . & rifles at the ready. Over the crest . . . towards
the woods where we knew there would be trouble. By 7.0pm the
battle was on. AT guns were firing like hell . . . & so were we. Very
soon, I saw one crew bale out, tank on fire. They crawled away in
the long corn, avoiding Jerry snipers & MG.

Advance proceeded: infantry kept 'going to ground' because of
Jerry's MGs. We sprayed those woods with Besa . . . tons of it . . . &
HE . . . & AP . . . & Smoke. Impossible to see AT guns in woods.
Could only fire at their 'flash'. Advance proceeded slowly: two or
three Jerry tanks appeared & were engaged: they disappeared. More
of ours were hit: some burning . . . crews baling out.

Found myself behaving rationally & quite calm. Was really terrified
just prior to 'going in'. Eventually we retired & waited . . . it seemed
hours to me. We were on the battlefield all the time. We should have
left, but stayed in case infantry required more assistance. Good job
we did. We had to advance a second time later on to help them out.
Awful business.

Jack Perman was a co-driver/wireless operator on the Shermans of
the 44th Royal Tank Regiment, part of 4th Armoured Brigade, and
also took part in Operation *Epsom*, defending positions along Hill
112 against the tanks and Panzergrenadiers of the 10th SS-Panzer
Division:

Thursday, 29 June 1944

The 29th June 1944 will stay in my memory for ever as one of the most horrible days of my life . . .

The slight elevation of ground known as Hill 112 (If, as I believe, it takes its name from a spot height in metres it is no more than 350, or so, feet above sea level) lies to the north of the large village of Evrecy. The 'hill' itself is almost exclusively occupied by acres of large open cornfield but all around it are thick belts of wood. For the purpose of the Odon Offensive these had been given separate code names 'Shepherds', 'Continental', 'Dorchester' etc.

The formation in which we were to advance to the attack was roughly an arrowhead one. Two 'Honeys' – the light tanks of the Regiment's Recce Troop – were to advance along with us on the right flank to assist us in any suitable capacity.

As during yesterday, the whole surrounding area was unusually silent. Our Artillery seemed to be firing from a great distance behind. The German shelling was very sporadic and did not trouble us at all, going well over when it did come. Of any infantry support there was no sign whatsoever and there seemed to be nothing in the air apart from a solitary 'Shufti' (spotter) plane in the far distance.

So when with the roar of our tank engines we started up and advanced over the brow of the high ground we seemed to be completely isolated and totally unconnected with any other part of the great war machine. However a Sqdn of tanks by itself is no unimpressive sight and with the score or so grey hulks moving at a good speed through the light coloured cornfield, a blue pennant flying from Teddy Foster's Aerial rod – his tank was somewhere towards the centre of this moving mass – we were quite a spectacle of armed might. Or so at least it would have seemed to be [to] a casual onlooker if there had been such a person, which of course, there was not, all onlookers being interested parties.

Our tank early developed clutch trouble and our Operator, Pete Spanner, transmitted a message to the Troop Leader 'Oboe Four Charlie, we are having trouble with our clutch, Oboe Four Charlie, Over'.

We had to transmit several times before Mr Cohen, the Troop Leader answered 'Oboe Four Charlie, Follow on as best you can, out'.

The first indication of any trouble was when Smudger signed rapidly over to the right and to my surprise and horror I saw the two Honeys a few hundred yards over from us were in flames.

The whole Sqdn drew to a halt with engines still running. A few seconds later a vicious sawing rushing sound was followed by a great fountain of earth as an AP tore into the ground a few yards ahead of our tank. Smudger swore rapidly between closed teeth. Despite the fact that the Schnapps had had a sustaining influence on him he was smoking rapidly cigarette after cigarette now. Dickie calmly but with a tremulous voice gave orders to Smudger to reverse slightly, guiding him into a hull down position whilst at the same time he directed our gunner, Georgie Boys, onto the target 'Back a bit left hand down Smudge – Traverse left Georgie, Steady On, disguised haystack.'

Whatever this disguised haystack was which had knocked out the two Honeys – camouflaged SP or tank or mobile 88 – it now received a terrific pounding from the whole Sqdn. AP, HE, angry red machine gun tracer all went flying over. 'Shall I have a go at him?' I asked fingering my Browning, which was now fully loaded. 'No' said Smudge curtly.

The firing died down as it became plain that the hidden gun was silenced, though whether knocked out or not we did not know. A request came over the air for a Cease Fire to allow the surviving crew members of the two Honeys to come back. Soon after, a few figures in overalls and berets ran across the cornfield towards us – the survivors. At the same time a request came over the air 'Could the Mike-Oboe [MO, Medical Officer] come up to one of our chaps who has been badly hit and is bleeding rather a lot.' Later a second message came over 'Regarding that request we made for the Mike-Oboe to come up – it is now too late'. I learnt later that the member of the Honey crew who had thus bled to death was my best friend for a long while in the Middle East and Southern Italy – R . . . He was a Honey driver and both his legs had been shot away.

A cautious advance a few hundred yards further forward was made and messages began to come over the air as the Sqdn began to engage different targets . . .

It was when we began moving forward again that further trouble developed. We had hardly moved 50 yards before there was a sudden shot and a great cloud of flame leaped up behind the turret of our leading tank, not very many yards ahead of us, enveloping the whole tank in a few seconds.

Before we had begun reversing properly a second tank went up in a terrible sheet of flame. Like black caterpillars on a cabbage leaf, the survivors of the crew appeared on the turret and leapt off. Again came a sudden pop like a cork being withdrawn from a bottle. Something glanced off the turret of a tank almost in front of us. I saw the commander throw up his arms and fall back into the turret. In front of the tank I could see the blackened features of two men that had baled out. One was reeling drunkenly away and his companion who seemed not so badly hurt put an arm round him and both staggered forward. It was too sickening to watch for long. I closed my eyes – I did not know what to pray – to pray for survival was foolish – but should I pray the end should be swift? When I opened my eyes again all in front seemed to be burning tanks. The MO's half-track had come up and he was knelt by the side of a tank that had halted, examining a badly wounded man. The Sqdn pulled back slowly and now halted in what was considered a hull-down position. Messages over the air were coming fast. The Colonel was enquiring – I heard Teddy Foster's reply and advice to us 'Now then remember this is your party'. Another tank went up in flames now, I could see the crew falling and throwing themselves out. We began pulling back once more.

The remnants of the Sqdn were still attempting to fire back where possible. The Germans seemed to be firing from a wood a long way over on the right to the South West of us but the horror of the situation was that we were stuck up there in the open and could not really make out where the firing was coming from.

One minute a tank would be a whole moving hulk of grey painted steel and next like a ball of paper thrown on the fire it would burst into flames.

That terrible billowing sheet of flames would leap out behind the turret and the tank would be engulfed in it.

The tank in front of us had gone up now, our turn would come next I suppose. Never in my whole life before had I experienced such abject terror. An AP shot tore past our suspension with a sawing roar, however by some miracle we seemed to have reversed at a terrific rate and were now climbing back down the other side of the hill. A few minutes later, shaken beyond description but otherwise quite sound we had taken up position with the other remnants of the Sqdn below the hill back practically at the point we had started from.

My memories of that desperate withdrawal are somewhat confused, besides the two Honeys that had been brewed at first I knew that at least five other tanks had gone up and a number of others had been knocked out without brewing, the plumes of smoke and exploding ammo from five burning tanks were still visible above the crest of the hill, but what the exact number that had been hit was I did not know. Who had been killed, who wounded and who survived? What would happen now, would we have to go back over that dreadful hill again? These and other questions turned over and over in my brain finding no solution. 'Why do you worry?' I asked myself 'When you came over you told yourself you didn't care what happened. You expected to run into something like this, now you've got it, aren't you still prepared to die?' To this I could find no answer. Wasn't the truth, that with every hour that had gone by I had found myself less ready to die?

We watched intently to frontward. A broken German army cart lay immediately in front. The plumes of smoke from the burning tanks still curled upwards. The smoke climbed rapidly upwards at first in a dense column that spread out and climbed more slowly with a bias to the right . . .

The watch to the front went on during the afternoon. I gradually grew more and more drowsy and utterly exhausted and slumped over my Browning and went to sleep. As I was dozing off I heard some of our crews start for the first time to discuss such news as had become available of the disaster. Up to then everyone had remained strangely taciturn.

I was awakened in the late afternoon by Smudger shaking me roughly and shouting 'Wake up kid! Some of our people are starting to go up again'. I unconsciously reached out for the trigger of my Browning which I had been caressing all morning and sent a stream of tracer over the head of Frank Lee the commander of the tank in front.

Although they had managed to hold off the German counter-attack, 44th RTR lost thirteen tanks with three damaged, nine men killed, twenty-seven wounded and nine missing.

This massed German counter-attack stopped *Epsom* in its tracks and further assaults on Caen were made throughout July. Massed aerial assaults flattened much of the medieval centre of the city with heavy loss of civilian life.

Major Peter Pettit commanded 481 Battery of the 116th Field Regiment, which, as part of the 59th Division, had landed in Normandy on 27 June and took part in one of the battles for Caen in early July, named Operation *Charnwood*. He found himself right in the front line:

FRIDAY, 7 JULY 1944

Sharp on time the fire plan opened up and within five minutes what must have been the enemy DF (defensive fire) task came down on Le Landel and all along the wall at the back of it where we were. John and I leaped into a one-man slit under the wall beside us & wished it was larger, things exploded all round and even head below ground could feel the blast, we were right in a stonk. After what seemed half an hour it stopped and we got out. Both cars seemed OK, I went to mine and found Milner lying by the front wheel untouched, beside him was the A tk Tp Cmd [Anti-Tank Troop Commander] hit in the leg. Inside the half track was T—, obviously dead from a piece through the side of the face but sitting up exactly as usual. Bdr (Bombardier) Malam slumped in his seat unconscious but breathing regularly, Chalk looking rather surprised with both hands covered in blood trying to help, and Holmes untouched (we discovered later two tiny bits just breaking the skin on temple and forearm). Told John to count us out for a bit, tried to bind up Chalk who was nearest, four stretcher bearers arrived and took over. Went to find John and CO but could not, more shells and bombs arrived but not so intense. Returned to half track and found they'd got them all out into a slit under the wall. Tried radio sets, could get no reading at all on the 19 though receiving well, the 22 set would not give a sign of life and the 18 set had a chunk clean through it. More shelling, John turned up and said no sign of CO and he was going back to vehicle park for news of him.

Charnwood saw the north of the city fall into British hands, while a further operation, *Goodwood*, succeeded in capturing the rest of the city by 19 July. Under pressure from a US advance to the west and further British attacks towards Falaise, the Germans began to withdraw southwards.

7. Breakout from Normandy

This German withdrawal was quickened with the break-out of the US forces in Operation *Cobra* in late July 1944, while British and Canadian troops launched a series of operations codenamed *Totalise* and *Tractable* between 7 and 14 August to secure the Caen–Falaise road and cut off the retreating German troops. The massed German columns also proved a tempting target for the numerous Allied fighter-bombers that controlled the skies over Normandy.

An informal diary of No. 263 Sqn RAF, who were equipped with Hawker Typhoons, reveals the destruction meted out on the retreating German columns by the aircraft of the RAF and other Allied air forces:

TUESDAY, 15 AUGUST 1944

(i) An armed recce of roads south and west of Lisieux. This yielded considerable joy and in the end we claimed three MT 'flamers' and a staff car destroyed.

(ii) A four a/c show by 'B' Flt. followed by

(iii) a four squadron attack on the woods east of Falaise where there are reported 150+ tanks.

We take four from each flight for this show and are the second sqdn. to attack. No results were observed, but the W/Cdr. reported flames from our part of the woods and a message was received from the Army later saying that the attack had been very successful.

(iv) More tanks were reported later heading east from Flers, and we went to look for them, but visibility and last minute changes in the bombline made conditions too uncertain for any attack, so the show was abandoned.

Friday, 18 August 1944

A great day for the 2nd TAF [Tactical Air Force] who are reputed to have destroyed 2,800 vehicles and about 300 tanks. 'A' Flight did its part and clobbered a few vehicles. F/O Proctor of 'B' Flight was hit in the radiator in an attack on a concentration of mot. and made a successful forced landing, it is believed, behind our lines.

Saturday, 19 August 1944

The weather dimmed later in the day and 'A' Flight only did one armed recce. With very little result, due to the fact that there was virtually nothing seen to prang. F/O Proc II [Proctor] arrived back after a night of wandering around in no man's land between the Frog & Jerry forces, however he was very little the worse for wear; splendid thing.

Sunday, 20 August 1944

In the morning 'B' Flight made an abortive Recce due to weather. Later we did what was supposed to be a show on some tanks inside our lines. The Cannocks, with due apology, clean forgot to put down the Red smoke, instead an armed recce was carried out when a lorry and a couple of bikes were stitched up by F/L Arkel's section. The CO's section saw a tank going like the clappers along a road and duly attacked. It disappeared into the nearest wood and they couldn't find it again.

Jack Perman of 44th RTR had survived the attritional warfare that had ground down so many armoured units outside Caen and now found himself part of the Allied forces attempting to close the Falaise gap:

WEDNESDAY, 16 AUGUST 1944

Someone has said that at this moment the Falaise pocket must be the hottest spot outside hell. Beautifully cloudless skies allow aerial hordes of planes to go over bombing and strafing the Germans from dawn till dusk. A crushing weight of artillery fire is being brought to bear on them from all angles, with the armoured vehicles available all pushing down to add to their discomfiture.

We who know what it means cannot help feeling an unrestrained sympathy for these Germans in their present plight. On the other hand we are exultant it is he, not us that is getting it and are happy to see this great victory of the weight of our machines over his.

Falaise is a <u>scientific</u> and <u>technical</u> victory, of more and in some cases better machines over fewer and in some cases inferior ones. Let there be no doubt about this, there is no question of the triumph of bravery or righteousness.

However there can be no doubt that the more fanatical and desperate of this foe are fighting and will fight tooth and claw to cut their way out.

We have seen that the fighting man is on the surface an inevitable pessimist. To him there is small difference in a desperate advance with heavy losses that leads to brilliant victory or merely failure.

No matter how important his attack may seem to those who follow the war on paper he can only feel that once again he must be ready to suffer death. Perhaps this is hard to realise for those who are just the necessary distance from the danger area to make their survival of the conflict a practical certainty, not a matter for conjecture, but it is, on the whole, true.

It is also true that some unimaginative ones go in not caring a hoot.

But the majority go in, believing on the surface that they are the ones destined for a mound of earth with wooden cross, or a trip back in an ambulance. Perhaps it is because somewhere underneath there is a lurking belief of hope that one day they will come through unscathed, that they force themselves to prepare for the worst. Or do they? It is hardly ever a subject for conversation among these men themselves so one can only conjecture . . .

We moved out in the morning and halted a while down a side road to cut foliage and camouflage up before moving on again. Soon afterwards we passed some whitewashed cottages that may have been on the outskirts of Falaise then we got onto the main Falaise–Argentan road. A long straight road flanked by tall trees that grow between cornfields. Along some stretches of the road the ditches were full of dead Germans, burnt out vehicles and abandoned guns lay in the cornfields.

We had a good run down this road. There were to be three bounds or limited objectives – stages on the advance 'Hop, Skip and Jump'.

The last seemed appropriate and as various wags ruminated that is what we might be expected to do when we got there . . .

The advance southward continued this morning. The Sqdn was given the job of advancing into a belt of orchard on sloping high ground.

We advanced cautiously into this and took up file positions behind a hedgerow. The ground sloped down to a small plain to the south terminated by further high ground and low cliffs in the distant background.

This was part of the very narrow gap between ourselves and the Americans around Argentan and the German armies cut off in the pocket were naturally doing all possible to escape eastwards through here. We were told to keep a sharp lookout. I could imagine fierce fanatics armed with bazookas in every hedgerow I looked at but these figures did not materialise.

Numbers of single vehicles attempting to dash eastwards were observed from time to time and soon the whole Sqdn was firing HE into them including ourselves. We could see these black toylike vehicles moving along then after they had been hit they would catch fire or stop dead. I have no doubt that they were packed with Germans and that we inflicted frightful carnage. Quite a few trucks were knocked out by our tanks.

Pte Sponner put on a brew in a nearby old tin shack. About mid morning the news came through that the Regiment had entered the village of Ronai, around which we had been operating and the Sqdn was called upon to move down into the village and beyond. The village was smoking in places and a litter of German equipment and personal belongings lay around in heaps everywhere. Several hundred prisoners had fallen in to our hands in this small village alone. Over the air prisoners were known as 'Cream'. Nobody knew why – it was a tradition from the desert.

Trevor Greenwood of 9th RTR was also involved in the fight to close the Falaise Gap, taking part in Operation *Tractable* on 14 August. However, the RAF heavy bombers dropped their loads short of the target, with tragic consequences:

D+69, MONDAY, 14 AUGUST 1944

Reached our area at 2.0pm, just as RAF four engined bombers commenced bombing wood 2,000 yds to our front. What a sight! Horrible: terrifying . . . & yet fascinating. The whole earth trembled: trees rocketed sky-high . . . enormous fountains of earth shot upwards: smoke – fire – death. God help the Germans in that wood! Hundreds of bombs rained down in the first few minutes. We were thrilled by the RAF. This was direct support for us with a vengeance. Every one of us felt more cheerful. Knowing too that our very heavy attack had commenced at 12.0 noon & that the end of this campaign may not be far off.

And then came tragedy: terrible, heartbreaking despair.

It was about 2.30pm. Many waves of bombers had unloaded their bombs where we wanted them . . . but suddenly a stick of bombs fell on a point about a mile to our rear. Was it Jerry? No! There were 2 or 3 dozen Lancasters over the spot: one of them must have dropped his bombs accidentally over our own lines . . . the damned fool! Hard luck on our lads, but an accident can't be helped.

More waves of bombers arrived, & most of these too dropped their bombs over our lines. The awful truth dawned: They were bombing the smoke laden area indicated by that first stick . . . even though it was 2 miles N. of their most northerly target.

Why couldn't they be stopped? We endured hell, even though we were fairly safe from the bombers. What a contrast with our former jubilation! Half an hour later, more bombers dropped their loads over another area . . . slightly west . . . in our lines. The destruction behind us was now becoming greater than that ahead. And so it went on . . . with our own bombs murdering our own men . . . & dropping nearer to us as the afternoon wore on. We put out yellow smoke flares in a frantic effort to save ourselves. I saw bomb doors opening as the planes approached . . . & expected to be blown to hell any moment. They were quite low . . . about 3 or 4 thousand feet. I saw 'Verey' lights being fired from the ground as signals to stop the bombing. I heard machine gunning in the air . . . & was afterwards told that Spitfires had been trying to divert the bombers. I heard later too that a little Auster went up to try & stop this ghastly blunder. But it went on. I didn't know then that there was no liaison between our ground forces & the bombers. I could only wonder, at the time, & my heart wept. So much depended upon today's action: the war even may be shortened by its success. It had been planned carefully & secretly . . . We had almost looked forward to it. And now . . . this thing.

And we could do nothing about it – nothing. But we **did** do something: we watched the clock & anxiously waited for 4 o'clock. But by then, our hearts & minds were torn with black despair. Even the blindest fool would know that such a fearful destruction must inevitably hinder, perhaps ruin, the day's action.

Only 77 of the 800 heavy bombers used by the RAF bombed short, but these resulted in over 400 Allied casualties, including 65 dead.

The Falaise gap was finally closed on 19 August, with the Germans losing thousands of guns, tanks, vehicles, horses and troops, mostly from Allied air attacks, and some 50,000 German prisoners were taken. The battle for Normandy was now over.

8. German 'Vengeance' Weapons

Following the invasion of Normandy, a wave of strange aircraft started to be seen over London and southern England. These weapons caused initial confusion amongst ARP workers such as Bill Regan of a heavy-duty rescue squad based on the Isle of Dogs. He recorded the initial attacks in his diary:

SUNDAY, 11 JUNE 1944

Alert 11.37pm. Gunfire immediately. One machine passed over from SE to SW as I got out. Searchlight held it, flying very low and fast. Every type of gun opened up, but it seemed unaffected. One pack of rockets from Rotherhithe surrounded it, but it just veered right as if from blast, and continued toward the city. Seconds later, the engine ceased, it dived, and immediately a terrific white flash was seen. After a lapse of about 6 seconds a big red flash, and a terrific explosion.

We congratulated the Ack-Ack to each other, and counted one plane down. Immediately, another came over, held by searchlights, and surrounded by shell-bursts; as before, right through it, over-head, and going towards Poplar, as I thought, Burdett Rd; as before, the engine cut out, it dived steeply, big white flash, pause, huge red flash, bang. We felt the blast distinctly. That's two planes, we said. They seemed to be small fast fighters, with an apparently outsize bombload. Just about here, Martin who had varnished his tonsils with his usual double scotches, got very talkative, and tried to bolster himself with loud talk. 'I'm with you lads, first to go out, I'll be there.' Etc etc. Before he could impress us, another one came over, passed, went silent, dropped, same white flash, pause – red flash, bang. I said to Alf Crawley, that the gunners were on form, three over, three down. Hardly credible.

We began to discuss the possibility of them being planes, as we could see flames coming from the tails of them, also a light in the nose. Some said rockets, as the flames did not seem to impede their progress.

These were indeed rockets, the German V1 (*Vergeltungswaffe 1 –* Vengeance Weapon 1), a form of cruise missile developed by German scientists. These weapons were launched against London and the south-east from bases in the Pas-de-Calais region of France and caused a resumption of the Blitz.

Gwyneth Thomas was an administrative sister at the Lewisham Hospital in south-east London and wrote of the initial attacks:

THURSDAY, 15 JUNE 1944

12 midnight, suddenly a plane dived, it seemed to come from nowhere. A load of incendiaries or bombs were dropped, then complete silence. It was all over in a moment; everyone thought it was a stray plane, but in 20 minutes the same thing happened again, and so it went on all through the night. Now it is 7.30am and still the guns are going, and the 'phantom' planes still come, unload and then silence. Several of the victims have been brought in here.

Some of the staff have managed to doze in between the attacks. Now I must go on duty.

2pm Three more rockets over during the morning; the last one came while four of us were in the dining room about to eat our dinner, when the warning went, and at the same time this terrific noise, then crash came all the glass that we left in the dining hall windows. I still do not know how we escaped, none of us had a scratch; the medical superintendent had a small cut; the block of houses just a stone's throw from my window have been very badly blasted. I have come off duty for a few hours to try to get a little sleep, but can see that this is impossible, the warning has gone again. Warnings through the night, little sleep.

By mid-June, more was known about these weapons, and countermeasures were developed to try and stop them. However, as they were small and flew fast they proved elusive targets for anti-aircraft weapons, as Miss Vere Hodgson, who lived in Notting Hill throughout the war, describes:

SUNDAY, 18 JUNE 1944

Well, these last three days have been one long air-raid alert and we have had very little sleep. In fact, I must get some sleep tonight if I am to work in the day, and so I have decided to come and bed down on the Sanctuary sofa. It is on the ground floor and I do not mind the guns. It is the shrapnel coming through my skylight that worries me and makes me hop out of bed to the door.

And these Robot raids go on after daybreak, which the old raids never did. I could hear the wretched things travelling overhead this morning at 6pm and later. They did not fall on us, but they fell on someone, and our guns barked out and spat and fussed until they had gone. They travel very quickly, but the one on Thursday night was very low over Kensington. In fact everyone of us was perfectly convinced it was exactly three inches above our roof!

It fell, however, in Wormwood Scrubs and did not damage anyone. But others have done a lot – and nothing is said on the wireless or the papers except Southern England. But that is us. And we are all fed-up . . .

I cannot remember all the events of the night, but I know we had very little sleep. I got out of bed from time to time and saw the rocket guns go up. I have a wide view of the sky over Camden Hill. No All Clear went, and we dozed off.

Nothing was mentioned on the wireless in the morning and we felt very injured, considering what a bad night we had had. The least we thought they could do would be to give it out and then we should have the sympathy of our friends. We all thought we had missed the All Clear. But not a bit of it. It did not go until nearly half past nine – as far as I can remember.

Then all through the day, on and off, we had Warnings and gun-fire. Mr Bendall brought back news that one Robot fell over the City and exploded in Tooley St.

On the Monday the line was damaged going from Liverpool St. Then one of the women in the Printing Works rang up to say at Eltham she had had a terrible night, and all the rumours pointed to Kent and those parts. She had had all her windows and doors blown out and could not come.

Then came the announcement on the wireless that the new Robot planes were coming over in large numbers, and we were to be classed as Southern England, so as not to let the Germans know where they had struck.

From June 1944, over 9,000 V1s were fired at England, mostly aiming for London, and they killed over 6,000 people on the ground, wounding nearly 18,000 more. One of those who had a lucky escape was Kenneth Holmes, who was a teenager in London:

SUNDAY, 23 JULY 1944

Today has been another day I shall not forget, during the night it was rather quiet, and during the morning there was a lull. About 2.30 this afternoon the warning sounded just as we were finishing lunch. About ten minutes after, I heard a 'Doodlebug' approaching, so I with my brother and his friend rushed outside to see it, as we usually do. We heard it for a few seconds and then the engine stopped, and the few people that were in the street scattered into shelters. We, thinking it would land in the distance, stood there waiting for the explosion when suddenly my brother's friend happened to look up and shouted 'Duck, quick, here it is!' and at the same time pointed up in the sky at our rear. I had one quick glance and saw it hurling down at a terrific speed. The three of us at once fell on the pavement and I could hear the swish of it as it came crashing down and the air vibrating. I was thinking I was going to be killed because I didn't know exactly where it was going to land and the rush of air as it hurtled down was terrific. There we were, lying on the pavement surrounded by 4 storey buildings, and I was dreading the explosion. Then it came and it was the loudest I've heard, or ever want to hear, my eardrums seemed to burst, the whole pavement appeared to rise . . . There was glass from the windows crashing all around us, out of the corner of my eye I saw my brother cover the back of his neck with his hands so I did the same. Pieces of glass fell on our backs but we escaped injury. When we stood up and looked around we could see nothing but glass on the ground and even where we had been lying.

In September, Kenneth Holmes recorded another entry in his diary:

SEPTEMBER 1944

As I was writing my Diary tonight 6.45pm there was a colossal explosion (certainly the loudest I've heard) which rocked the entire house and shook the windows violently, followed by a rumbling for a few seconds, and then a softer explosion. I at once thought that Hitler's threatened 'rocket bombardment' had begun, but as no other explosions followed I tried to get the idea from my head, then I thought 'It couldn't have been a Doodlebug because there were no sirens sounded and besides a flying bomb doesn't make a sound as loud as that', I also doubted if it was a Pick-A-Back plane because of the fact that there was no alert.

Well what else could it be? More like a gasometer had exploded? – or maybe a munitions dump? I tried to think it was one of these, but all the time at the back of my mind there was a doubt as I asked myself 'Is this the beginning of a new bombardment for London by Long-Range-Rockets!

However time will tell!

It was the V2, the first form of ballistic missile and the second and more powerful of Hitler's so-called 'vengeance' weapons to be used against London. The V2 continued to be aimed at London, as well as at Antwerp in Belgium, through to March 1945, with over 3,000 being launched. Civilian casualties from the V2 campaign amounted to 2,754 dead and 6,523 wounded in Great Britain alone.

1944–45

I. Operation *Market Garden*

Following the rapid advance through France, newly promoted Field Marshal Montgomery, aware that British manpower reserves were dwindling and keen to ensure a major role for British forces in the defeat of Germany, developed an uncharacteristically daring plan to get his troops across the River Rhine and into Germany using the recently created First Allied Airborne Army (comprising two British and three American airborne divisions) to capture vital bridges at Eindhoven, Nijmegen and Arnhem in the Netherlands, while the troops of the British Second Army would link up the airborne bridgeheads to create a corridor thrusting straight into Germany and outflanking the defences of the West Wall.

The US 101st and 82nd airborne divisions were to be responsible for Eindhoven and Nijmegen, while I British Airborne Corps, comprising the British 1st Airborne Division and the 1st Polish Parachute Brigade, would take the final position at Arnhem. The attack was launched on 17 September 1944, with the first wave of British airborne troops on the ground by 1400hrs. The British drop and landing zones were on heathland to the west of Arnhem around Wolfheze due to concerns over heavy flak near Arnhem itself and a lack of suitable landing areas for gliders. By the time the area had been secured by 1st Airlanding Brigade, and 1st Parachute Brigade was ready to march on Arnhem, it was already 3.40 p.m. and there were nearly eight miles to cover. The only unit that eventually managed to make it into Arnhem itself was 2nd Battalion the Parachute Regiment under Colonel John Frost, and they only managed to capture the northern end of the bridge. The ambitious operation went wrong right from the very start.

Major Blackwood served with 11th Battalion the Parachute Regiment, part of 4th Parachute Brigade, which landed in the second wave of British airborne drops on 18 September. The 11th Battalion was immediately taken away from 4th Brigade and sent to reinforce 1st Brigade's attack on Arnhem:

MONDAY, 18 SEPTEMBER 1944

I got my green light at 1410hrs, I gave the stick a final 'Hi-de-hi', and heard their yelp as I jumped.

My Sten, magazine-carrier with seven mags, respirator, and haversack were in a lashed bundle, attached to my harness by a cord. This was to give me a softer landing as fully-equipped I weighed 2½cwts. But my grip was not secure, and the jerk as the 'chute opened wrenched the whole issue from my arms, tore loose the cord, and I watched it crash to earth. This was serious, not only the loss of my weapon, but the loss of my 48 hrs rations, emergency rations, toilet kit and clean underclothing which the haversack contained. I marked where they fell: made a soft landing, and struggled out of harnessing, noticing (a) that my 'chute contained a modicum of bullet holes and (b) that a German machine gun was blasting away some 30 yards from me, inside the edge of a wood. However, my one concern was to recover my gear, so I plunged off in the direction of its fall. It was no use. The ground was covered with hundreds of parachutes: hundreds more were coming down; and waves of planes were sweeping in. Nor was the DZ [Drop Zone] a healthy place in which to linger. The German was ensconced in the woods which bordered the DZ on two sides, and was lacing the place with machine-gun and mortar fire. Men were coming down dead in the harness and others were hit before they could extricate themselves. With a curse of regret for the six bars of chocolate I had lost, I gathered some men about me and set off for the RV, by the autobahn, which ran E–W to the S at the DZ . . .

TUESDAY, 19 SEPTEMBER 1944

1300hrs. Message to say that our attack on the Arnhem Bridge had been beaten back and that German tanks had outflanked and surrounded us. Hastily we moved deeper into the town, and B Coy took up positions in houses overlooking a main crossroads. Our orders were brief – wait for the tanks, give them everything we had in the way of grenades, shoot up as many infantry as we could before we died.

The Reverend Menzies also dropped on the 18th, as he was attached to 4th Parachute Brigade. By this point in the battle, command and control was already breaking down due to the difficulties in communication and the fact that the divisional commander, Major-General Urquhart, had been cut off from his command by German troops:

MONDAY, 18 SEPTEMBER 1944

Flew from Coltsmore 'drome attached to 156 Bn, 4th Para Bde. Smooth flight until shrapnel over DZ; 'dropped' in afternoon. Firing all over DZ – much of bracken ablaze. Dragged considerable way by 'chute – cut myself free. Saw a beautiful 'white' hare panic-stricken, running to and fro not many yards away. Hopeless to look for my collapsible bicycle which was dropped from the 'plane. (But still had a camera lent me by 'Life' magazine.) The young French liaison officer (Yves H) in the stick never turned up at the Rendezvous, presumed killed descending or on the ground. He hoped to be the first Frenchman in Berlin. We marched off into the country, passing some German soldiers and Dutch Nazis in custody of Dutch Resistance men.

Nearer to Arnhem – then German counter-attack. We were thrust back. The Battalion split up. Colonel Dickie De Vaux and 2IC Major Ritson believed killed fighting the tanks. Buried some of our dead in a wood. Ended up at railway station (Wolfheze?) with (Doc) John Buck, the Medics (and Support Coy?). Firing all over the place: took a Pole's jeep and trailer loaded with wounded to try and find a Hospital. Drove down tracks into the forest; found civilian hospital – evacuated from Rotterdam – patients were in prefabs in the grounds. Hid jeep and trailer in undergrowth. Dutch doctors and nurses very friendly.

Helped (by handing out instruments) while the doctors performed some operations on the wounded.

On the ground, XXX Corps set off on the road up towards Nijmegen and Arnhem on the afternoon of 7 September, following a short artillery barrage. The advance was hampered by both the narrowness of the road, which was only a single highway, and the strength of the German resistance. The Guards Armoured Division spearheaded the advance, but following them was 8th Armoured Brigade, including the Sherwood Rangers Yeomanry.

The Reverend Leslie Skinner was still attached to the regiment and recorded its progress northwards:

Tuesday, 19 September 1944

Moved off 0600hrs into Holland and over canal – not so big as the Albert Canal at Geel.

Action and movement all day pushing steadily up the one road . . . only road possible in this country of dykes and canals as we move further into Holland.

Devil of a long convoy – Sherwood Rangers plus Squadron of Royals with Armoured Cars; plus Ack-Ack plus Battery of Essex Yeomanry; Company of KRRC [King's Royal Rifle Corps]; our Regimental Echelons and Recovery Unit, parts 552 Company RASC, and Field Ambulance and our Medical Aid sections – all making a column stretching along nearly seven miles of road. Squadron of tanks with some armoured cars and infantry up front, and at rear, with other 'fighting elements' scattered throughout the column. All making a hell of a target.

Shot up once or twice. Lost one or two vehicles but no men.

Leaguered up as were on road about 0200hrs to snatch some sleep.

Air raid again. Again lucky.

Wednesday, 20 September 1944

Annette's birthday.

Moved off with first light 0300hrs. On again all day as before, slowly and effectively.

Contact with US Paras. These Yanks good. Reached Grave by
1700hrs. Good tea and wash. Eindhoven had been tricky during
night. Bombed. All OK.

On over Grave Bridge and into woods south of Nijmegen arriving
in dark.

Fires burning in Nijmegen. Seemingly Boche still holds the bridges
over River Waal which is said to be 300 to 400 yards wide. No other
bridges over Waal for 25 miles either side. Germans still holding
paratroops down in city of Nijmegen.

The bridge over the River Waal at Nijmegen was cleared in a joint
attack by the US 82nd Airborne Division and the British Guards
Armoured Division, with the tanks of the Grenadier Guards finally
crossing the vital bridge on the evening of the 20th. The following day
the Guards, with the Irish Guards now leading the way, pushed on up
the road towards Arnhem.

Bill Kingsey was in the leading squadron of the advance and
describes the difficulties involved:

THURSDAY, 21 SEPTEMBER 1944

Later, my Squadron was given the task of going forward to Arnhem.
Consequently, we raced over the Nijmegen bridge and half way up the
road to that other famous bridge at Arnhem but we met with fierce
resistance from the German 88mm armoured-piercing shells directed
from their self-propelled guns. As we travelled along the elevated dyke
road, we were sitting ducks! The AP shells went through the tanks like
hot knives through butter. Of the 21 tanks in the Squadron, initially,
only a few were left, mobile and active. Our vehicle, 'MUNSTER',
managed to shelter in the lee of a farm-house. During darkness,
we took shelter in an orchard along with two others. On trying to
go forward at dawn, we found ourselves pinned down again by the
enemy's guns and the incessant mortar fire. We lived in the tank,
virtually, for three days until ordered to withdraw. As the air support
had failed to arrive, the Squadron (or what was left of it) could not
operate effectively. So near and yet so far!

By now, it was becoming quite clear to the advancing troops that the British Airborne's position at Arnhem was becoming increasingly tenuous.

Ivor Astley was an NCO with the 236th Anti-Tank Battery, part of the 43rd Wessex Division advancing with XXX Corps:

SEPTEMBER/OCTOBER 1944

It was becoming increasingly obvious that the airborne troops were in great difficulty. Every effort was made by the 2nd Army to establish contact. The ferocity of the nightly barrages was enough indication to us, and later the BBC bulletins were stressing the gravity of the position. The now famous 'corridor' was continually being closed and re-opened whilst the main bridge at Nijmegen was under fire from German heavy artillery. The Battery suffered casualties when the 'H' Troop reconnaissance jeep was crossing it. The driver was killed; the Troop Commander, Troop Sergeant and Artificer were injured. In addition to the shelling, the German fighters were doing their best to dive bomb this link with the island. The railway bridge could be crossed by jeep quite easily, but all heavy traffic had to cross the main bridge.

While we were still on the island, the railway bridge was blown up by German underwater swimmers (their equivalent of our frogmen). These specialist engineers were taken prisoner and were at Divisional HQ when I drove the Battery Commander there the next day. It became necessary for our food supplies to be brought by Duck [amphibious truck]. A pontoon bridge was built shortly afterwards.

In the town of Nijmegen itself, many of the Supply organisations had moved up. The supply position was considerably helped by the fact that a complete train-load of supplies for the German army had been found in the sidings there. Thus for a few days we were issued with German rations. Surprisingly we were issued with cigars!

At Arnhem itself the situation was rapidly becoming critical. The 2nd Battalion still held onto the bridge but were suffering heavy casualties, with Frost himself being seriously wounded on the 20th. Later that day resistance around the bridge collapsed, with most of 2nd Battalion becoming either casualties or prisoners of war.

Norman Dicken served with the 10th Battalion the Parachute Regiment and was involved in heavy fighting near the village of Wolfheze on the edge of the pocket around Oosterbeek, about 5km west of Arnhem, where most of the 1st Airborne Division withdrew after it failed to reach the bridge.

WEDNESDAY, 20 SEPTEMBER 1944

0730hrs. It was just about becoming light and I saw two Germans about 100 yards away. I prepared my Sten but then realised there was a line of Germans calling to each other so I lay down hoping they would pass me by. As I had my face in the earth I could only hear them. One of them stumbled over me and turned me over with his foot. I don't know why but I burst out laughing, he also started to laugh and a group gathered round. They gave me a drink of water and cleaned the blood from my face.

They were from the SS as some had the 'Hohenstaufen' cuff band while one had a 'Deutschland' one.

0800hrs. My captors wrapped a belt of MG42 ammo round my neck and gave me two ammo boxes and told me to come along with them. We headed towards Oosterbeek keeping to the woods, continually being engaged by British troops. In a clearing stacked with cut logs we were attacked by what I think were German multi barrelled mortars, but they didn't do much damage due to the sandy soil. They had a British first aid bag which they asked me to use on their wounded – I do recall they were impressed by the quality of our bandages but puzzled by the sulphanilamide powder.

1300hrs. We eventually came to a large sandy hollow with many wounded Airborne troops. I didn't see the water tower, but believe the hollow was below it, just off the Utrechtseweg which was about 300 yards away, down a sandy track.

1315hrs. We were formed up and told to take our helmets off. We joined the Utrechtseweg, which was narrow and overhung by trees, with a Vickers machine gun dug into the bank opposite facing in the direction of Renkum. There were about 70 of us mainly walking wounded marching towards Renkum. We passed a bullet holed Citroen car and some knocked out Renault tanks.

1430hrs. After about 2 miles we were fired upon from a gateway about 300 yards on our left.

All of us including our guards jumped into the roadside ditch. About three men were badly wounded in their chests. Another had a bullet shot through both cheeks without damaging his teeth. We refused to leave the ditch until the sentry with the machine gun was prevented from firing again. I believe the German Officer who was in charge went up to his position and shot him through the head.

By the 25th, it was clear to all that the position of the remainder of 1st Airborne Division was now untenable and the order was given to withdraw across the River Rhine. Major Blackwood was one of those still fighting in the final stages around Oosterbeek:

MONDAY, 25 SEPTEMBER 1944

Heavy rain. We snitched an umbrella from a ruined house and set it above the open space. Unmilitary, but useful.

A few score Dorsets got over the river in the night. Stout lads.

Our gunners called down a barrage of 2nd Army mediums to crush a threatened counter-attack. Some of the guns were firing short, and we got the full benefit. The whole earth quaked with the explosions; so did we. It was a study to hear the boys when later they crawled out and viewed the huge craters around our position.

In the afternoon the enemy drove in a tank and infantry attack in an attempt to split our position in two. There are few more terrifying noises than the whine and rattle of an approaching tank. I ordered part of my small force up over the hill to meet the attack, and myself went up the slope with one man and a Bren. (As I learned afterwards, the Spandau bird [German machine gunner] down by the railway gave me a burst as I went, and scored the ground just behind me).

From the crest of the ridge we could plainly see a Tiger in the valley below. He was moving slowly back and forth, shepherding his infantry across open ground covered by our fire. With my man and Bren I hared down the forward slope of the crest and dropped unharmed into a trench half way to the tank. Then we got cracking at the infantry as they rushed to the cover of the tank.

Once I thought we'd 'had' it. The Tiger stopped, and his great 88 gun slowly, very slowly moved round and faced us. For some reason he did not fire: and as soon as he traversed his turret again to move away, we up and had another whack at the Hun. Good shooting too. Something grimly humorous in seeing a frantically scurrying Hun legging it in vain with bullets kicking up the mud at his heels.

I saw the blast of a Spandau open up immediately across the valley. At the same instant I received a mighty blow on the right temple: and heard my companion scream. We fell back into the trench, bleeding like pigs; he from a smashed jaw. As laboriously we applied field dressings, crouching there in the mud and rain, the Tiger opened on us with his gun. The crack of passing shells, and the violent explosions made our eardrums bleed: and when for good measure he called down heavy mortar fire, the whole crest quivered and smoked.

It was almost an hour before we risked climbing out on to that exposed forward slope. Although I felt tired to death, result of not enough food or sleep, I covered the distance from trench to crest in an incredibly short time, expecting at every second a burst of bullets in my back. We swept over the fence at the ridge top, and plunged down into the gunners' command post as Jerry returned operation with his mortars.

And here I learned that the remnants of the 1st Airborne Div were that night to return across the Rhine. It was a bitter moment: but, with food and amm. exhausted, anti-tank guns all knocked out, and men dazed with nine days shelling and mortaring, there is no alternative.

The withdrawal took place that night, with 2,587 men escaping over the Lower Rhine, leaving about 1,600 seriously wounded behind with 204 medical personnel and chaplains.

Some of the wounded who managed to get out of the pocket ended up in 101 British General Hospital in Belgium, where they came under the care of Mary Morris:

5 OCTOBER 1944, 101 BGH

The patients are a lovely cheerful crowd – so delighted to be out of the ghastly horror of Arnhem and Nijmegen. Lt. Brian S— is in the first bed on the left inside the ward door. He has gunshot wounds of the stomach and is still on blood transfusions. The wound re-opened on the bumpy ambulance ride down here and he lost a great deal of blood. He is with the 1st Airborne Reconnaissance Squadron and landed in Arnhem on the 17th September. He is feeling a little better today but is obviously in a state of nervous shock – quick puffing of cigarettes and a great need to talk about the horror of what he calls 'The Cauldron'. Arnhem he tells me was a shambles, utter chaos, no communications and thousands of men from the 1st Airborne Division are dead. There was constant street fighting for eight days – houses burning and constant mortar 'stonking'. He was wounded after eight days of hell, no food just some fruit from the Dutch civilians – very little water and no sleep. Men were running around screaming, trying to find any escape. He was taken to a Dutch hospital behind the German lines. He had two abdominal operations performed by a German surgeon and he was well cared for by Dutch nurses. Brian will be alright physically once the wound has healed but I think it will be a long time before he gets over the shock of Arnhem. Connie tells me that he has to be constantly sedated at night to stop him screaming in terror. He is only 22 years old.

Sgt. Mullins also from the 1st Airborne has had an horrific experience, but seems to be recovering in an amazing way. He is I think just happy and surprised to be alive. He was crawling along in the street fighting in Arnhem, when he came face to face with a German self-propelled gun. He said 'I thought I was a gonner, but suddenly the anti-tank gunner, a big bloke leaned out, picked me up bodily and stuck me across the chassis beneath the barrel of the gun. The cheeky bastard then tracked back safely and my mates on either side of the road could not throw the "Gammon" bombs they had removed from their belts.' Later he said 'I was thrown on the side of the road where my mates picked me up and I was taken to the "First Aid Station"'.

Sgt. Mullins was 'patched up' as he put it and went back to the street fighting again. On the 8th day of Arnhem he 'copped this lot'. This 'lot' is an amputated left leg and gunshot wounds of the shoulder. He described that awful eighth day at Arnhem as chaotic fighting, groans and shrieks of pain, heavy gunfire – the dead lying all around us. The wounded screaming for water and stretcher bearers – machine guns everywhere – trapped between German infantry with mortars behind and half track tanks in front. It was also 'belting' rain and 'we had no sleep or much food for days'. This sergeant too was taken to the St. Elizabeth Hospital at Arnhem and from there has come down the line to us.

Overall, Operation *Market Garden* cost I Airborne Corps some 6,858 men, while the Second Army on the ground lost as many as 5,354. The two US divisions lost 3,664 men. High costs for an operation that ended in failure.

2. The Culmination of the Strategic Bomber Offensive

Although much of Air Chief Marshal Sir Arthur Harris's Bomber Command had been diverted to supporting the ground troops in Normandy in the summer of 1944, by the autumn he was able to return his force to what he considered to be its principal targets: the major cities of Germany.

Johnnie Byrne joined the RAF in 1942, qualifying as a wireless operator in October 1944, and was posted to No. 550 Squadron based at RAF Killingholme, Lincolnshire, where he flew on Lancasters. In his diary, he describes his first mission:

THURSDAY, 2 NOVEMBER 1944

We came back off leave this morning and last evening. That night F/Lt Morris & Crew were destined to take part in the bombing of Düsseldorf. The heaviest raid that city had had since the War. We flew with a Scotch Pilot and our own – F/Lt Shaw & F/Lt Morris.

Briefing was at 1345 hrs. There we learned that the 'Happy Valley' was our target that night.

We went out to dispersal and had our photographs taken outside our 'kite'. We incidentally were taking F-Fox on its 100th operational-sortie. The aircraft's name being 'Press-on-Regardless'.

We taxied out to the runway just after 1600hrs. The weather was exceptionally nice. Cloud about 9,000ft.

At last the moment had arrived. We turned into the main runway – a green was flashed from the ACP and with throttle pushed fully forward we raced into wind. I went into the astro dome, and a group of fellow air crews and ground staff officers waved 'good luck' to us. I replied with a proud 'thumbs-up', and then realised 'Would this be my last contact with England & home!' At this moment we seemed to have reached the end of the runway, and we were not as yet 'airborne'. We were carrying a full HE bomb load, and enough petrol for 8¼hrs in our tanks. But 'Jock' knew what he was doing. At the last moment, he pulled the 'stick' back. And the old 'Lancaster' shot straight into the sky: at this moment, another photograph was taken.

I settled down to do the job in hand now and I was rather hard worked during the next five or more hours. Oxygen, heating, lighting, listening watch to base and Bomber Command, frequent checks at the three gauges on the main electrical hand were a few of my duties.

We went out over Reading, Beachy Head on the South Coast, across the Channel and over now Liberated France.

I again went into the astrodome and could see in the coming darkness numerous other 'heavies' on either side of us – in the main bomber stream. Several Lancs were very near us, missing colliding by what seemed feet, Navigation lights were showing too.

At long last Germany was only minutes' flying time away: I now felt frightened. I wondered just how I would react to the coming flak, s'lights, fighters, etc.

But then at 1927hrs, we were attacking the Ruhr. S'lights were moderate and flak moderate. The target was now in view! A blazing inferno of many coloured lights. With flak bursting about 1,000ft below, and about 50 s'lights sweeping the skies in what seemed a useless attempt to cone our bombers. They didn't seem to have a clue.

I now remained in the astrodome on the lookout for fighters, but 'good-show' – 'no joy' in that respect.

Now the bombing run over Düsseldorf! I was almost shouting aloud, 'Cursing the Hun to do his damndest'. 'The filthy Hun'. 'How proud I was at that moment.' I remembered Manchester, I alone had a four-year debt to pay. Our bombardier from London wouldn't have much sympathy either! 'Let the Bastards die like the Rats they are!'

The Bombardier was giving his orders to his Captain 'Right a bit' – 'Steady' – 'Bombs-away'.

The time was exactly 1933½.

The kite lifted a little, now relieved of its heavy missiles of destruction. Then Jock took a firm hold – the stick was pushed forward and we dived straight out of Düsseldorf and the target area. With flak, fighter flares, s'lights all over the sky.

The target looked a wizard sight. The moon was fully visible, only a slight indication of cloud. On the ground far below I could just imagine the Hun confused and frightened to Hell as 851 heavy bombers blasted hell out of his heavily fortified town.

Fires were blazing everywhere, smoke could be seen, HEs exploding, 'Really a wizard show'. Red and green TIs and many more . . . grotesque sights.

The trip home was uneventful. I received a station weather forecast and visibility report for Base.

D/f. I was hellish <u>hot</u> and tired. We had been to the Continent and back in just under 6 hours!

At 2156hrs, we 'pancaked'.

Interrogation, Hot sweet coffee followed.

We then retired to the mess for eggs, beans, chips, sausage.

And later bed.

On 6 December, Johnnie Byrne missed a trip with his crew as he had an interview with the base commander about his commission. This proved to be a fateful interview:

THURSDAY, 7 DECEMBER 1944

The next morning whilst again waiting to see the base commander I read from a teleprinter foolscap that my crew were reported missing from last-night's operations.

The hand of fate proved that I had not to take my 11th trip with them. I came on a useless errand. But quite possibly my life was saved by a mere chance.

The W/Op., that took my place was Sgt. Bill Roberts, who was making his very first operation over Germany. The trip was very long and went into Germany for a long way.

The occasion of Johnnie Byrne's actual 11th operation was an emotional one for him, coming as it did with a different crew:

Friday, 15 December 1944

I was very pleased to be going on another op., I know now that I have really something to fly & fight for. No matter how long or dangerous the trip. My heart, body and soul are striving for one supreme purpose. That purpose being to avenge my crew. They were lost on their 11th op., I am the only member of that gallant team left: I will not fail in my duty. My life is given now to my job. I must and will have German blood. Imagine my pleasure as we approached the target area: the cloud has disappeared somewhat. And one could clearly see the fires burning on the deck: The red and green sky markers were now high over Ludwigshafen.

Tremendous flashes filled the sky all round us. Searchlight beams pin-pointed the darkness, and tried in vain to cone our 'beautiful' bombers. But we pressed onwards. Flak was moderate but barrage stuff. I went into the astro-dome to look for enemy fighters.

I was now counting the seconds as we came on to our actual bombing-run. 'Left, left' 'Right' 'Steady' 'Steady'. 'Bombs gone'.

A sigh of relief. The a/c, now rid of its bomb-load lifted skyward with an annoying jerk.

My feelings at this moment would be very hard for me to explain. I cursed the Hun, and inwardly wept for my crew. I was with another crew, new to me. But 19,500ft over this German city I called the Jerry so much shit!! I sincerely hoped our bombs would smash his wicked filthy skull clean open: I have no mercy; my heart is cold now; I am only out for revenge!

Johnnie Byrne was only spared for a short time; he was lost when his aircraft was shot down during the raid on Dresden on 13 February 1945. He was only 20.

The raid on Dresden is one of the most controversial actions of the RAF during the Second World War. From 13 to 15 February 1945, the heavy bombers of the RAF bombed the town by night, while US aircraft returned in daylight, with the anti-aircraft defences largely overwhelmed. The intensity of the bombing and the age of the buildings led to a firestorm that, along with poor German ARP precautions, combined to cause a high death toll on the ground.

Flying Officer Robert Wannop was a pilot with No. 90 Squadron, one of the Lancaster units that took part in the raid on the night of 13/14 February:

13/14 FEBRUARY 1945

Ten days elapsed before we did another trip and then it was the most memorable of my tour. Dresden. The town had never before been bombed. But now, due to the Russian advance, it required our attention. I understand that large areas of the place consisted of timber buildings and judging by the load we carried I should say it was correct. Namely 1 x 4,000lb and five 750lb incendiaries.

The Squadron was in the second wave so by the time we arrived the fires were well under way. As we approached the glow could be seen – 50 miles away. The target area was almost like day. Down below – 19,000 feet – the town was simply a mass of flames – a pool of fire – it was awe inspiring – breath-taking – I had never before – nor never again will see such a sight. Searchlights flickered aimlessly around – even their usual brilliance lost by the blazing inferno. Around us we could see other Lancasters – it was light enough to formate had we wished. Even vapour trails were plainly visible, an unusual phenomenon at night. The opposition was negligible – like taking candy from a baby. We saw one night fighter as we left the area but he wasn't interested in us – which was a good thing.

It was a long trip home, the monotony broken occasionally by a few bursts of 'flak' as we approached too near a defended area. As we flew over Ostend we saw an unusual light shooting rapidly up into the heavens: curving slowly out across the Channel in the direction of London – a V2.

The bombing campaign continued right till the end of the war, with the last raid on Berlin taking place on the night of 21/22 April. Kenneth Holmes, who lived in London during both the Blitz and the later V1 and V2 attacks, wrote of it:

> The last RAF bombs to fall on Berlin were dropped, appropriately enough, by two men from Southern England – the area which suffered most at the hands of the Luftwaffe. Said the navigator 'If we had known that this was the RAF's last bombing attack on Berlin we should have made a show of it. But we didn't and I pressed the button and down the bombs went just like that'!
>
> Berlin has been bombed 282 times by British and American aircraft operating from British bases – 264 of the attacks by British bombers. Since the first raid on the night of August 25, 1940, Bomber Command has unloaded on Berlin 45,386 tons of high explosives and incendiaries. Fortresses and Liberators (American) dropped another 22,940 tons – making a total of 68,326 tons. At the end of the RAF's Battle of Berlin, 326 important factories had been destroyed or damaged. Also 20 Government departments, seven gasworks and three power plants were put out of action.
>
> We living in Southern England cannot help but feel pity for the Berliners when we hear that 'our bombers were out over Berlin again last night'.

Out of a total number of aircrew of 125,000 who served with Bomber Command during the Second World War, 55,573 died, some 44 per cent.

3. Operations in North-West Europe

On the ground in north-west Europe, the Allied armies were confronting growing German resistance as, in what came to be known as the 'miracle of the west', the German front stabilised following their headlong retreat from France. Conversely, the Allied chains of logistics and communications became increasingly extended due to the problem of supplying their front-line forces from the damaged French ports.

The welcome received by the advancing troops was often ecstatic, as Trevor Greenwood of 9th RTR found when he entered Brussels in October 1944:

D+122, FRIDAY, 6 OCTOBER 1944

A long day on the transporter. Route:- Douai and then into Belgium – Rumes, Tournai, Ath, Enghien, Brussels – harbour about six miles east of Brussels on aerodrome. We crossed the border at 11.0am – and there was an immediate difference in the appearance of our surroundings. Firstly, the 'Tricolour' was superseded by the Black Yellow Red of the Belgian flag . . . Practically every house was adorned with some evidence of the national colours. And then, the homes of the people – neater, tidier, more modern. The air of dilapidation, so evident in France, was far less noticeable.

The people everywhere gave us a grand welcome. There seemed to be no end to the showers of fruit, including peaches, grapes, tomatoes, pears, apples. Our vehicles were littered with the stuff. Passing through Tournai, I saw an ice-cream vendor on the roadside selling 'wafers'! At Tournai too the trams were running as well as the railways. It is a large town, and seemed to have suffered little material damage.

Our journey into Belgium was an interesting experience. I felt that, here, we were really welcome . . . But at Brussels! It is difficult to describe the scene. It may have been a royal procession so great was the acclamation. We passed through some of the principal streets of the city at a time when there were many business people about – 6.0pm . . . and what a contrast with France! Here there were well-dressed civilians, fine shops, cleanliness, order – and intelligent looking people. And the girls! There were so many – so clean – healthy – fine looking. What a sight for our lads!!! The city was a blaze of colour: every shop, every house, every window carried a flag. And many civilians too were wearing colours.

Our convoy was a very large one – and attracted great crowds.

And once again we were bombarded with fruit and flowers – on a greater scale than ever. One lady handed me a huge bouquet of dahlias – beautiful flowers: she had bought them specially! Perhaps it is strange for grimy and coarse looking soldiers to be given flowers in this manner – but maybe it was the only way these people could demonstrate what was in their hearts. The German occupation – four weary years – has caused indescribable misery and depression amongst the majority of the population. And now their gratitude knows no bounds.

There can be no doubt that the Germans have left behind memories which will remain, perhaps for ever, in the mind of the Belgian people. They have learned to hate – really hate . . .

However, the fighting itself was becoming harder as the German border grew closer. Following the failure of Operation *Market Garden*, British and Canadian troops were involved in bitter fighting in the Scheldt estuary in an attempt to open the port of Antwerp for shipping, while other forces became embroiled in the attempt to break through the outer defences of Hitler's West Wall, the Siegfried Line.

Reverend Leslie Skinner was still accompanying the Sherwood Rangers Yeomanry as they assaulted Siegfried Line positions in November 1944 during Operation *Clipper*:

SATURDAY, 18 NOVEMBER 1944

During night very little sleep. Artillery changed to barrage at 0300. At 0500 whole area suddenly illuminated by 'artificial moonlight' produced by battery of searchlights which was most effective. Breaching party of Lothians and Border Horse moved forward with 'Flails' making a gap in minefield, special Churchill tanks of R. Engineers laid bridge over railway tracks, and our tanks moved forward with flame-throwers in support. One of the flails, mission accomplished, reversed out of the way into an orchard only itself to go up on a mine and have suspension off.

A and B squadrons, each supporting an American battalion, set to work on the pillboxes of Siegfried Line, firing at the observation slits so that the defenders had to close them, enabling the infantry and sappers to move up and lay explosive charges. One by one the pillboxes were reduced.

By mid-day A Squadron had taken Prummern. Squadron Leader's tank went up on mine becoming a 'write off' but none of crew seriously injured.

At same time B Squadron group had gained their objective with some infantry losses, knocked out four pillboxes, and 350 prisoners had been taken.

The German counter-attack in the Ardennes in December 1944/January 1945 brought a halt to Allied offensive operations until February, when British and Canadian forces began the process of forcing the German lines back beyond the River Rhine in a series of offensives codenamed *Veritable* and *Blockbuster*.

By March 1945, the British 21st Army Group was poised for a major crossing of the River Rhine into Germany. Operation *Plunder* was launched on the night of 23/24 March, with two divisions crossing under the cover of darkness. The following day a massive airborne operation, Operation *Varsity*, preceded the main British advance.

E. Mallpress served as a tank driver with 44th RTR, part of the 4th Armoured Brigade, and was crewing an amphibious DD tank in this operation:

MARCH 1945

So on 21 March we 'swam' the tanks across the Maas for the last time and lined up for loading on a long line of tank transporters. On 22 March at dawn we moved off riding where we could, back into Germany and to a forest near Xanten which we reached about midnight. At 1100hrs the following day, the 23rd, the weather being so fine, we were told the crossing had been retimed for that night. As far as we were concerned it was a waiting time, all commanders were absent at briefing meetings until later that night when a tremendous barrage was opened, the noise reinforced by RAF bombing of the far bank. Tension rose as we took up station and David and I gripped our seats very hard. Away to our right we saw a number of CDL [Canal

Defence Light] tanks, their lights shining over the river.

I have often been asked if I was scared, and the simple answer had been that I was, very. But there were other factors which I, and certainly the men I had anything to do with, had to cope. We learnt to be sensible and not do silly things – for instance we were very careful where we walked, and we did not pick up odd-looking things on the ground. The main thing, though, was our aim to remain calm – I won't say unconcerned – and the conscious effort which actually became easier with use – was not to act or show that we were afraid. By 1945 many men in the regiment had fought in the battles in North Africa and Italy, not to mention Normandy, and I found that their behaviour, their calmness and philosophical acceptance, not to mention their humour was a wonderful example to me. I can only remember two cases of men's nerves breaking; in both cases they had fought in many theatres of war and I simply never saw them again – in one case his discharge under the Python scheme [repatriation to the UK for long-serving British troops] was just about due and he wrote one or two letters to me when he got home.

So we moved off in two columns to the water's edge, down a metal-mesh ramp prepared by the REs, and we were soon conscious of being water-borne. The engine's revolutions increased; the tank rocked a bit – I listened to orders and information passed to and fro on the radio; I heard the operator announcing that they were sinking but were all right. Minutes passed and eventually the tank rose up the bank and we assembled in an area earmarked for us. We dismounted quickly and in no time the canvas was collapsed and we were ready for action. A later declaration by Col. Hopkinson was to assert that we were the first tanks across the Rhine 'and let no-one dispute it'. For the record we were in the seventh tank across.

We could not hope that our landing would be unopposed and I remember a good deal of noise as we moved off. What followed, however, we were unprepared for and the memory never fades. Hundreds of planes and gliders appeared from the west and what seemed like thousands of paratroopers filled the sky – it was a truly unforgettable sight. Casualties there were and I recall my shock when I first saw ranks of the dead laid out by the road as we passed.

Gunfire continued till nightfall and the sky was criss-crossed by lines of red tracer. A heavy, but mercifully short, barrage of artillery landed shells amongst us and our supporting infantry from the 53rd Welsh Division – shells fired by our own RHA who were very vociferously and quickly stopped.

Gunner John White of the 25th Field Regiment RA was also present at the crossing of the Rhine and recorded his impressions of the sheer scale of the event:

Saturday, 24 March 1945

The operation was going well and according to plan. Two crossings of the Rhine had been effected by the Commandos and 15th Scottish and bridgeheads established on East side of Rhine. The weather was still glorious with brilliant sunshine, very hot and more like summer than spring. There was a slight haze in the air caused by the bombers and gun firing.

We witnessed a marvellous and inspiring sight when at 10 o'clock the first troop-carrying planes (Dakotas) arrived streaming across the sky in their hundreds with fighter escorts. It was too hazy to see the actual landings from here, but to see the planes coming in from all directions, to be later followed by gliders, one plane trailing two gliders. These come in very low and frequently flew immediately over our heads. This went on until 1 o'clock during which time the 7th Airborne Army, 19th US Airborne were landed.

After dinner Liberators went roaring overhead just skimming the treetops, with supplies for these troops. The bomb doors were already open and the cylinders containing supplies could be clearly seen all ready to be released.

News of the afternoon was officially announced over the wireless at 1 o'clock. Things were going well and our guns were not called upon for support today and the enemy was now getting out of range. The heavies and medium did a little firing during the day and night. Preliminary orders received that we were to move across the Rhine tomorrow.

25/26 March 1945

Recce position left at 8 o'clock this morning to establish gun positions over the Rhine. The rest of the battery got packed up as far as possible but still remaining in action pending orders to move. Weather still fair and hot, but slightly cloudy.

Time of move kept being postponed and it was not until 4 past midnight that we eventually left. It was a clear moonlit night and we slowly moved along the congested roads towards the Rhine.

There was some enemy air activity and a lot of our Ack-Ack going up. Jerry was trying to bomb the bridges but our Ack-Ack was so intense that he was having no success. It was a very slow journey, the roads being congested with vehicles, and it was 0215hrs when we passed over the Rhine. It was a good bridge built on boats floating on the water and the crossing was made without incident. We continued at a slow pace to our RV which we reached at 6 o'clock in the morning after remaining stationary on the road for several hours.

4. The Reconquest of Burma

Following the successful defence of Kohima and Imphal, the British Fourteenth Army under General Sir William Slim followed up the Japanese retreat. Slim developed a plan to push on into the central Burmese plain to safeguard the supply routes to China, capture Mandalay and inflict a further defeat on the Japanese armies. By the beginning of December, the British forces had pushed up to the River Chindwin, and Slim altered his plan, sending XXXIII Corps to attack Mandalay while IV Corps would head south to the key town of Meiktila, cutting the road from Rangoon to Mandalay. By early February, Slim's men were ready to cross the Irrawaddy.

William Farrow was a company intelligence officer with the 1st Battalion 11th Sikh Regiment, part of the 7th Indian Division, and took part in the opposed crossing of the Irrawaddy:

WEDNESDAY, 14 FEBRUARY 1945

As dawn broke the battery of mountain artillery (3.7-inch guns) who were with us managed to get off some good shots in the area of the Red Pagoda. We could see numbers of Japs and JIFs on the other bank quite plainly.

On several occasions during the morning we were greatly saddened to see a number of assault boats drifting past our position, some empty but many contained dead officers and men of the South Lancashire Regiment and Royal Engineers. These were some of the heavy casualties sustained at the main crossing at Nyaungu, six miles north of our position. Main problem was engine malfunction with the result that number of boats just drifted out of control downstream and past Japanese entrenched positions on far bank. We were able to collect several of these badly shot up boats and the bodies were moved back to Myitche.

The crossing of the Irrawaddy at Nyaungu was the longest opposed river crossing attempted in any theatre of the Second World War. The river at this point was over 2,000 yards wide and fairly fast flowing. The south bank consisted of paddy fields, devoid of cover, only a few feet above flood level. The roads serving the area were deep rutted, and every vehicle raised a great column of dust clearly visible from the south bank. Added to this, on the night of the crossing there was a strong wind and the water was 'lumpy'.

Our abortive attempt to cross the previous night must have drawn enemy attention away from the main crossing further north. I return to Bn HQ at Taungbansu. Air strike goes into Pagan using VCP (Visual Control Post) complete with RAF officer and wireless operator in their own jeep. We are sending fighting patrol over to Pagan tonight. Message from Brigadier Crowther that we will get across somehow and supported by General Messervy with 'Throw your heart over and your body will surely follow'.

THURSDAY, 15 FEBRUARY 1945

Early in the morning we were surprised to see two men on the opposite bank carrying a white flag. They were of the Indian National Army, sometimes called JIFs, and they crossed to our position by country boat. They reported that the Japanese who had been with them on the far bank had moved north, leaving a company of the INA to hold Pagan. It was obvious that our fighting patrol which had gone across to Pagan the night before had been most successful as the INA company wanted to surrender!

Jim Merrick immediately volunteered to take B Company across the river. Only three country boats were available and the local boatmen nowhere to be found. Jim took over one of his platoons in the first wave and the INA filled up the boats and brought them back to us. Their weapons were laid down in dumps on the far bank as Jim and his platoon took up defensive positions. We gradually got his other two platoons over, but found that we officers had to do much of the rowing as our men had no experience and very little idea. Not much rowing down in the Punjab! By evening both A and B Companies plus Bn HQ were established in Pagan and dug in for any counter-attack. The remainder of the Battalion, less C Company, were to join us the next morning plus the mountain battery.

By 28 February, IV Corps had reached Meiktila, with the town falling on 3 March. Realising the significance of the British breakthrough, the Japanese resolved to take back Meiktila and launched a series of desperate assaults on the town. William Farrow recorded an example of these attacks in a diary entry in mid-March:

THURSDAY, 15 MARCH 1945

Extremely heavy night attack on A Company positions in Tetma village area. Japanese Captain led the first assault waving his sword. He was shot and got caught in the wire, where he stayed shouting and crying for most of the night. When he was approached at dawn he pulled a pin from a grenade and committed hara-kiri.

It was found during these Japanese assaults that it took several hits to stop these fanatical infantrymen. Sometimes it was almost as if they were wearing some form of protective clothing and even the odd head wound, showing brain, still found them much alive and thereby dangerous.

During the body count the next morning Japanese sergeant major was discovered and made prisoner. Although wounded he was able to give us some information when interrogated. Apparently this column was supposed to cut us off in a hook towards the river where it was to join the main Japanese thrust up to the bridgehead.

Another who was active in the defence of Meiktila was 'Dobbie'

Dobbins, a Spitfire pilot of No. 607 Squadron, who was grounded at the time and could only be involved in the defence in an infantry role:

MARCH 1945

It was like this all the time & after a few days, the boys took the Spits to Meiktila & operated against the Japs from there. The main reason was, that the airstrip of ours was becoming one sea of mud, & kites could not land or take off a couple of days after the kites were operating from Meiktila.

I remember one night, just after our spit was serviceable, and the boys were operating on it again, we were all called out about 11pm, & informed that the Japs were closing in on us. They were only a few miles away, & they were expected about 12.30 that night, we were split up into parties of four & given a certain area to watch.

All around the strip there was dense jungle, no matter which way one turned a solid mass of jungle confronted us. The Japs had everything in their favour, for we wouldn't know how strong they were out there in the jungle.

The majority of us only had a knife, & a revolver that contained six bullets . . . I remember crouching in a ditch with three other guys, & was I scared. Every twig that cracked appeared as though there were hundreds of Japs out there, & as it was a pitch-black night, you couldn't tell friend from foe till you were about three yards apart. I found myself perspiring like a guy who had run for quite a while, & now, again, I found my heart pumping that fast, that I thought anyone would be able to hear it. The jungle started to begin just about 20 yds from where we crouched, & my eyes played more tricks with me than I ever want them to do again.

About 11.30pm we heard sounds of firing in the jungle, there was pistol, rifle, & machine-gun fire, but owing to the stillness of the night, I couldn't place whether it was a hundred yards or a mile away. I can remember though, my heart stopped for a time, & I thought of all the folks at home. I thought of everything & everybody I knew & I prayed that I wouldn't funk when the Japs appeared out of the black mass of night.

After a quarter of an hour the firing ceased, & about 12.30 we were startled by a guy creeping along past us. I was just about to let fly,

when I thought it may be one of our boys, so I hissed a challenge, &
it was bloody quickly returned. WHEW! It turned out that this bod
had been looking for us to tell us to go back & report, & on report
we were told that the Japs had retreated, & that we could go to bed,
but we must sleep fully dressed & with our arms strapped to us. I
never slept a wink that night, what with the smell of death around,
& what with the wind blowing through the trees I was a bundle of
nerves the next morning.

XXXIII Corps captured Mandalay on 20 March and pushed
southwards to link up with the defenders of Meiktila. By the end of
the month, the Japanese had abandoned their attempts to retake the
town, and the road to Rangoon lay open for Slim's victorious forces.
Bob Court flew into Meiktila in the aftermath of the battle in his role
as a fitter with the ground crew of 'C' Flight, the Casualty Evacuation
Unit of No. 194 Squadron. He recorded the scene that met him in
his diary:

MAY 1945, MEIKTILA

By the end of April the front had advanced well forward, Meiktila
was secure after the siege so General Slim decided that his HQ would
be better sited in Meiktila. Accordingly, on April 28th we were up
at 05.00, breakfasted, struck the tents, and loaded the gharries for
those who would be travelling by road. By 13.30 all was ready for
departure and they were sent on their way.

Frank recorded in his diary that they arrived at the ferry crossing
of the Irrawaddy at 18.30 in the evening where, after crossing over,
they bedded down to spend the night under the stars, quite where
he did not know but it may have been Pakokku.

Next day they journeyed on to reach Meiktila at 11.45 after a quite
exhilarating trip. After settling in they all had a swim in the lake to
refresh themselves. Later we learnt that Jap bodies kept coming to
the surface from the lake. This was also the source of our drinking
water but we were assured that after due processing it was quite safe
to drink! We are still here!

I myself flew down to Meiktila from Monywa with F/O Kimber. I remember flying over the area and seeing the devastation below and thinking how glad I was that I was in the Air Force and not the Army. We landed on a small strip and the first thing we saw were three or four Japanese soldiers in threadbare clothes and quite severely wounded lying on the ground in the blazing sunshine. One, with a bad throat wound, was pleading for water and I felt quite sorry for him at the time. We had no water that we could give him so he just had to suffer. Another with a filthy, bloodstained bandage around an eye and head wound which was infested with maggots, not a pretty sight.

5. The End in Italy

The troops of the Fourteenth Army in Burma referred to themselves as the 'Forgotten Army' whose exploits were largely ignored by the British press, whose interest lay with the force in north-west Europe. Those men still fighting in Italy had also seen the focus of Allied attention and publicity shift away from them following the fall of Rome and the launching of the invasion of Normandy in June 1944. The invasion of southern France in Operation *Dragoon* in August saw a further transfer of resources. However, fighting continued as the British Eighth and US Fifth armies pushed up the Italian peninsula, being confronted by a series of fixed German defensive lines, the most formidable of which was the Gothic Line. This was not one simple line, but a series of positions that would have to be taken one by one. The Allies launched their assault on 25 August, breaking through the first line of defences with relative ease and, after a month of hard fighting, the strongest defensive position in Italy had been taken.

Captain Cowles of the 2nd Regiment RHA was still operating in support of the 1st Armoured Division and recorded the assault on the Gothic Line proper:

THURSDAY, 7 SEPTEMBER 1944

Still the battle rages. It is now very certain we have struck the Gothic Line and that the earlier defensive line we passed through was just a very good piece of bluff that completely foxed our higher command.

His concentration of guns for the first time for many years equals our own. Our infantry casualties have been high – yesterday the Sherwood Foresters lost 70 men including nine officers. Our own position was much better, the guns not being shelled at all. Of the OPs we lost one signaller and another slightly injured, also one jeep was hit. All the OPs say that they have never before been under such heavy fire – they seem a little shaken.

Yesterday's gains by the 56 Div. on our left were all lost during the day. Seems a major attack will have to be developed to break this line. Already we have started to build up an ammunition dump.

Today, again, we fired almost without a break. It rained during the afternoon making ammunition replenishment difficult. Somehow we managed to get through the day but I have never known such a mad rush in the Command Post before – made worse by having so many new reinforcements to cope with.

FRIDAY, 8 SEPTEMBER 1944

The artillery battle goes on but the infantry have settled down in their slit trenches and are sitting down taking it. How miserable it must be to be in the infantry. No matter what praise is given to the Navy, the tanks crews, the REs and the RAF, the infantry have by a long way the hardest, most unpleasant and dangerous job in the war. They do not receive half enough praise and certainly not a quarter of the financial reward they merit. I am very grateful I did not apply for an infantry commission when in England with the AA.

I wonder what the high command will do about the present situation. It looks very obvious that a full-scale attack will be necessary and casualties are bound to be very heavy indeed. Perhaps they will decide to wait until the Russians coming from the East and the Americans from the West force the Germans to pull out. The prospect of the 1st Arm. Div. swanning through to Vienna diminishes daily.

Following the hard-fought capture of the Gothic Line by the end of September, there was a pause in operations caused by the onset of winter and the resulting dreadful weather conditions in the mountains of central Italy. The Allied forces did not resume the offensive until spring 1945 when, reinforced by the newly arrived Brazilian Expeditionary Force, they attacked through Lombardy, capturing Bologna and advancing to the banks of the River Po.

Norman Cox served with the 16/5th Lancers, part of the 6th Armoured Division, and recorded his squadron's experiences in the final advance:

MONDAY, 9 APRIL 1945

We were up before dawn and at once moved from close harbour into a more scattered harbour, and then got working on cooking some breakfast. As we boiled the 'char' and fried the bacon some Jerry planes came over and there was an exciting interlude, plenty of AA fire going up. Almost immediately after this the order came through that we were moving immediately. We gulped down our char, hurriedly packed our 'grub' and kit on the back of the tanks and got mounted. I was still clutching my mess-tin in which I had 15 or 20 rashers of bacon which I had been frying, and we shared these between us and quickly swallowed them just as they were, then off we went. I was going into action for the first time, so I wondered a bit what it would be like. The 17th/21st Lancers are ahead of us, but we are leading the Squadron of the 16th/5th. The position is that the infantry have not been able to clear the hills of enemy, but we are going to take the risk and try and break through. We moved forward a bit, then stopped in a grove of figs. We could see the pass in front of us and around us were slit trenches in which were American infantrymen. They were being shelled badly and were suffering casualties. Enemy aircraft were overhead, too, though they didn't trouble us a lot. After a bit we moved forward again. The 17th/21st ahead of us had run into trouble and already many of their tanks were knocked out, several of them burning fiercely. The 17th/21st had suffered such heavy casualties that we were to take over the lead from them. We crossed over a nullah [stream], and enemy guns in the hills were engaging us. Lt. Bull, our troop leader, came on the air and told us to move round a bit as we were in his line of fire as he wanted to engage a target. We tried to back into the nullah but couldn't, so we decided to turn right round. We had half-turned when there was a colossal explosion. For a moment everything went black and indistinct, then we got the order to 'bale out'. It appeared that we had been hit by a mortar, which had smashed our front sprocket, ripped our right track off, and put us right out of action. An immobilised tank is a sitting target for enemy guns, hence the order to evacuate. We dived out, and took cover in a meagre clump of bushes. Within a few yards of us were two or three burnt out tanks of 17th/21st, but we were the first 16th/5th tank to be knocked out. As we lay in the bushes shells were bursting around us and it was decided we must get back to the nullah, where there would be a certain amount of cover. Our orders were that we must remain near our tank. We nipped across to the nullah where we found two or three half-dug slit trenches, and got in these. Shells were bursting very near, but all fell just short of our position. We were also being sniped by the enemy, and if we approached the tank or showed ourselves unduly, rifle bullets came whistling by our ears . . .

SUNDAY, 22 APRIL 1945

We were awoken at 3.0am with orders to move at 5.0am. We loaded up in the pitch darkness, and were on the road by dawn, passing through Argenta, the much battered down town which guarded the Argenta gap. We passed a 'fleet' of ducks as we drew out. We went some way up Route 16, then turned left along the dusty Div. Axis. The roads were very full. We harboured in a field of clover (much is grown round here as a fodder crop), and pitched our tent, only to get orders to move on again after dinner. Rumours are thick and fast, such as 'Berlin has fallen', 'Ferrara' has fallen, etc. – all false. Lots of Jerry anti-personnel mines lying in the ditches near us.

We struck our tent again and were soon on our way again, but it was stop-start-stop-start all the way. A freak storm with bags of dust blew up from the east, and a little, but not much, rain. On our left were the terraced dykes beyond which flowed the river Reno. We passed several burning farms which were an aftermath of our flame throwers, some of which we saw in harbour . . .

MONDAY, 23 APRIL 1945

This had been a really big day for the regiment. They had had Jerry absolutely on the run, and much enemy kit and thousands of prisoners have been taken. The Lothians have reached the Po, and large enemy forces are encircled . . .

WEDNESDAY, 25 APRIL 1945

Crossings over the Po have been made by both 5th and 8th Armies. The Brigadier came today and congratulated the regt. on the part they played in the recent battle. It has been a busy day for me with office work. The tanks are liable to move any time to cross the Po.

With the crossing of the Po, the last major barrier before the Alps had been breached and the German position in Italy collapsed. Captain John Ross, who had been operating in northern Italy as part of SOE, found himself negotiating with the retreating German troops:

TUESDAY, 1 MAY 1945

Allies near. 100s of German prisoners. Agordino free. Bombing of Bolzano and massacre of Huns on PnA [Ponte nelle Alpi] road. Electric light off. Down in evening to find electric light in Vezzano – no luck. Allies fighting at PnA but I had little news . . .

WEDNESDAY, 2 MAY 1945

Contact at Bolzano. Held *parliamentario* with 29 Panzer Grenadiers (I drove in a horse drawn buggy with the American Capt. to meet the Germans as they wanted to pass through our area undisturbed and without fighting, back towards Germany. An arrogant lot of young officers who told me that we would soon be fighting together against the Russians. I said that they could go on knowing that they would not get far as bridges higher up were destroyed). Shooting. To Belluno. British. Americans. SS fighting above Bolzano di Belluno and tried to get Americans to help – up with tanks and armoured cars – called back from Gioz (the end of the war was announced on their radio). Giannis house.

The surrender of all German forces in Italy came into effect on 2 May 1945.

6. The Liberation of Belsen

As Allied troops pushed further west into Germany they began to encounter the most horrific legacy of the Nazi regime, the concentration camps. The most significant camp found by the British was that at Bergen-Belsen, which was entered by units of the 11th Armoured Division on 15 April 1945.

The camp, situated near the town of Celle in Lower Saxony, had originally been set up to house Soviet prisoners of war, but in April 1943 part of it had been handed over to the SS, who began to use it as a detention camp for Jews. Throughout 1944 and 1945 the population of the camp swelled as prisoners from the east were marched westwards, away from the advancing Russians. Belsen was not an extermination camp, but the lack of food and high levels of overcrowding led to outbreaks of disease, notably typhus, which decimated the camp's population.

Robert Daniell was the commanding officer of 13th (HAC) RHA and may have been the first British soldier to enter Belsen, crashing through the front gate in his armoured vehicle. He recorded his experiences following the war:

THURSDAY, 12 APRIL 1945

About 10am one brilliantly fine morning in April, 1945, Brigadier Roscoe Harvey commanding the 29th Armoured Brigade, and myself with a few tanks, arrived at the entrance of what appeared to be a small heavily wired-in camp. Through an archway of dead laurel leaves, a guard of obviously terrified Romanian soldiers appeared, their officer was so frightened, he literally was unable to stand . . .

Firstly I went over to have a look at a few cattle trucks on a siding nearby, finding them still containing 20 or 30 dead men and women, the nature of this camp hidden away in the woods was immediately apparent. Scattering the dejected looking guard, I drove into the camp where a few well-built brick buildings surrounded a small square. Panic stricken groups of Waffen-SS, a few girls, clerks and one or two elderly German soldiers milled around, all in total and absolute silence. A most unpleasant and brutal looking officer, unshaven and in shirtsleeves, I found in what appeared to be the HQ office, feverishly packing a vast pile of records into a small car. He proved to be Col. von Kramer, subsequently hanged.

Clearing the house, I instructed them to sit down in front of my tank, whilst they were doing this, I noticed a German SS soldier come out of a rather larger building, carefully locking the door after him. I immediately walked over and kicked the door open. Inside a sight revealed itself that daunted even a battle-experienced man like myself. Inside there were tiers of bunks each containing one and sometimes even three completely naked human beings, the stench was appalling. Many of the inmates were obviously dead, some of those on the lower bunks had drowned in the excreta and blood flowing down on to them. It was a truly terrible sight, quite obviously they had received no food or medical attention for sometime yet outside were lusty young SS officers fit and well, milling around.

There was nothing I personally could do, so I set off down a grassy slope towards three or four large black huts, passing on my way, a huge trench filled with moderately fresh naked bodies of men and women, maybe a thousand or two. Reaching the first hut I flung open the doors. At my feet I saw four or five small children sitting on the body of a woman, who had crawled out to the door before she died. They were playing a game with different lengths of straw. Flinging the doors wide open I beckoned them to come out. The other huts housed a similar ghastly collection. As I left I walked straight into a smartly dressed woman SS officer with a large Alsatian on a lead. This latter proved to be the most hated member of the SS in the camp, Erma Grease [Irma Grese]. She was wont to loose her Alsatian on the children and others tearing them to pieces whilst yet alive. She promptly turned and disappeared. Over by the wired perimeter, I heard occasional revolver shots and on approaching, I saw two young Waffen-SS busily engaged in causing the dying throes of the numerous inmates who lay spread-eagled on the barbwire, even more painful by kicking their legs apart and shooting them, men and women in the groin.

I was appalled and when they [the SS] turned their attention to me, I was pleased to put an end to them. All this had taken time and I knew that I must get back to Roscoe Harvey and tell him what

I had seen. Hurrying back up the slope, I came across a German soldier, who semi-paralysed with fear, led me round to the back of the huts. Here were quite obvious lethal gas ovens, several still full of corpses, huge incinerators, piles of decaying corpses and mountains of rags, which I am sure were the clothes they had stripped off their victims. I have no doubt all these unfortunate inmates were perfectly harmless Jews, many of them had been rich and intelligent citizens of the Reich.

I think that for quite a long time no food or fuel had been delivered at the camp, so the commandant, Colonel Kramer, had just left them to die of slow starvation, and various diseases. This was all the more ghastly as Belsen Camp was situated in part of the most fertile farmland in Germany, abounding in cabbages, potatoes, beans and wheat, yet not a cartload was delivered to the camp, or a single pig or chicken. Roscoe Harvey asked me how many of the thousand or so inmates I thought would recover with good medical care. I replied maybe six or a dozen.

I had had enough. Never will I forget what I had seen that day and never never will I forgive the race, who produced men capable of such cold blooded misery and death to the thousands who were driven into Belsen Camp.

The immediate priority for the British was to treat those who had survived. Typhus was rife throughout the camp, while the malnourished prisoners were unable to digest British rations. Accordingly, a number of medical students from London hospitals were enlisted to assist with the relief effort. Among them was David Bradford, a medical student from St Bartholomew's Hospital, who arrived in early May. He describes the situation he found in the camp:

THURSDAY, 3 MAY 1945

We were up at 7.30, had breakfast and Dr. Micklejohn of UNRRA [United Nations Relief and Rehabilitation Administration] – who is our new chief, told us of our work and warned us how awful and filthy it would be. We set off in three three-ton lorries for Camp 1 – 1½ miles away. When we arrived de-lousing powder was sprayed into our clothes, and our hair, and we were each allotted to one of the huts. I had hut 14. I went down there to see what it was like. How can I describe it? It was about as long as a tennis court, but about 12 feet narrower. Up one end was a separate compartment, and about 10 three-tier bunks. All these were filled with men – sometimes two in each, and in two rows along the middle of the hut and along the sides of the hut were crammed on top of each other, other men – everybody being in various degrees of starvation and typhus. All had severe diarrhoea, and the floor, blankets and clothes were covered in weeks of filth and vomit, etc. etc. The smell cannot be described, but may be imagined. About 50 people were able to walk about, but only 10 were capable of carrying food from the *Kirche* [*sic*] (Cookhouse). 450 people were supposed to live in this place, but about 600 merely slept there and wandered around the camp and countryside during the day. There must have been 250 very ill there. First of all I found that there was one lad of 21 (a Pole who was in Cracow University) could speak English quite well. He was Fritz, and was very useful. He told me the situation and then I had a look round. Four people were lying dead, and I had them dragged out. Immediately, the others scrambled for their clothes and blankets. Nobody bothered to cover them up when they died. They were just left in their rows as they died and those next door took no notice and lay on top of them. Each hut had a block leader who was a kind of Führer over the hut. Mine was down with Typhus, and had a deputy who I sent to the cookhouse 200 yards away. Some filthy soup was brought to them and I ladled it out so that each had some. Many were too weak to eat, and had to be helped, so it took a long time to get round. I had to smoke most of the time, as the stench was overpowering. I was able to get some biscuits in the afternoon, which went down well, and also one cigarette per man. These of course were very popular. Twice a day, a large lorry and trailer comes round with guards and about 60 German POWs who load up the dead from each hut. By the time it has got round, it is full completely. About 600 die a day. Just behind my hut is a large grave with 800 dead.

Peter Horsey of St Thomas' Hospital also volunteered to help in the relief work, and recorded the harrowing scenes he encountered in the camp:

MONDAY, 14 MAY 1945

Shortly after midnight there was a frightful scream somewhere outside. Then a series of shrieks. Went out to see what it all was, and found a group of people standing round a woman who was flinging herself about on the ground outside K2 and making all the noise. Picked her up and told her to shut up (in German) and then tried to find out the cause. They took me into K2, but it was pitch dark. So came back and fetched candle. On returning they took me to a bed on the far side of the room and said 'Kaput.' Of all the things I shall forget in Belsen, that bed will not be among them. On it was what had been a woman. She was naked and lying in filth, and she was scarcely more than a skin-covered skeleton. To me she looked as though she had been dead for ages, but she was still warm. The woman who had been making all the noise was her sister, and she slept in the same bed. There was nothing I could do, so I left after finding another bed for her sister.

Due to the typhus epidemic, the whole camp was burned to the ground on 21 May, with the occupants being removed to a nearby location. When the camp was overrun, it contained over 50,000 prisoners and some 10,000 unburied corpses.

7. VE Day

With the crossing of the Rhine, the Allies had breached the last major German defensive line. Their armies began to spread rapidly over the Reich, the Americans heading into southern Germany, whilst the British went north. The British Second Army, aiming for the cities of Bremen and Hamburg, reached Osnabrück on 4 April and the River Elbe by the 19th. Here they stopped, as it was the agreed dividing line between Allied and Soviet occupation zones. The British now turned northwards towards the Baltic coast, from where they proceeded to liberate Denmark and Norway. The German capital, Berlin, finally fell to the advancing Red Army on 2 May, while Hamburg fell to the British on 3 May. Following the death of Adolf Hitler, the surrender of all German forces in Europe became effective on 8 May, Victory in Europe (VE) Day.

Mary Morris was still serving with the 101 British General Hospital in Belgium when she heard the news of the surrender:

7 MAY 1945, 101 BGH

There is tremendous excitement here to-day. Germany has surrendered unconditionally and we are all waiting breathlessly for Mr. Churchill to announce the end of war in Europe. How dramatic that speech will be. Have just been watching the Belgian people in the street below this window. They are running about and talking to each other excitedly in little groups. There are flags flying from every window and church bells are ringing. The last 'All Clear' has just died down mournfully in the distance. This is a great day for them also. It is such a short time ago since the Gestapo patrolled along the streets where the flags are now flying so gaily. Wish 'M' were here with me. We could go out in the country, walk through fields and sit down quietly and try to realise fully how much this means – no more waste of life – no more casualties, no more horror and destruction. How wonderful to think of walking through the streets of London with the lights shining everywhere, to look into the dark depths of the Thames and to realise that the dark days of the 'blitz', the V1 and V2 are really over.

We must not forget the war with Japan of course. Wonder if 'M' and I will be posted to SEAC [South East Asia Command].

At sea, the U-boats were active right till the end of the war, and Allied convoys were still escorted by warships, such as the destroyer HMS *Hesperus*, on which Charles Matthews served. Here he records their experience of the end of the war and the sinking of *U242*, the last U-boat to be sunk in the war:

TUESDAY, 8 MAY 1945

The 8th turns out to be a beautiful day and we proudly dress ship with ensigns at yardarms and masthead. At 1500 hrs Churchill speaks to announce the end of the war at midnight. The wireless broadcasts the celebrations from London, dear old Liverpool, and cities the length and breadth of the British Isles: we are still yearning to be ashore and taking part but still have to follow this convoy. Things brighten up a bit after 1830 hrs when we 'Splice the Mainbrace'.

During the evening of this great day the King makes a speech (at 2100 hrs) and we intend to have our own celebrations. We are lined up in line abreast at the rear of the convoy and after the King's speech intend to go through the lines of the merchantmen at full speed firing everything we have got. I'd got two Verey pistols and was going to fire red and green shells. It was to be rockets, starshells, the lot in honour of the Mercantile Mariners.

We had 16 escorts with the convoy. The King's speech was broadcast to the ship over loudspeakers and as he was speaking we got a U-boat contact. His voice was lost in the roar of explosives. The greatest day in English history, everyone ashore wild with joy but just another contact for us, another evening, another convoy.

We make several attacks when oil and air bubbles come to the surface from the wreckage. We pull this inboard and find that we have got German rubber dinghies and interior woodwork of a German U-boat. We have had the honour of killing the last U-boat of the war. He was probably trying to have the honour of sinking the last British ship.

The end of the war in Europe was perhaps felt most strongly by those who had been occupied by the Nazi regime. Iris Bullen had seen the fall of the Channel Islands to the Germans in June 1940, now she was able to witness their liberation by British forces:

WEDNESDAY, 9 MAY 1945

Truly this is the greatest day of our lives for most of us in these Islands, Wireless Sets sprung up from everywhere and we heard Mr Churchill's speech. Our emotion was overwhelmed when he mentioned the dear Channel Islands would be freed today. After the speech just after 3 pm we all put our Union Jacks up and other flags of the Allies. Anyone who has not had the experience that we have had under occupation can not realise what it meant to hoist our beloved flag once again. For five years we have had our patriotism suppressed, we could only show our faith in the future by our acts and forbearance. The evening I walked to town and back with some friends we expected the fleet to arrive today but were disappointed but we enjoyed ourselves immensely and thought it wonderful to be free and without 10 o'clock curfew; we arrived home about 11.30pm. It was wonderful to see the electric on once again and no black outs.

On Wednesday May 9th I left at 1.30pm with the children in a little handcart en route for town. We went to the end of Victoria pier and there saw some Germans packing up. What a glorious sight for us who have been under their domination for so long. We waited a long time expecting some of our Tommies to land for there were some big ships just outside in the Rounds. Little boats were up and down, and we had the joy of seeing some of our Jack Tars, they had a great reception. We were just making off for home when someone called out there was a boat coming in. We raced along to the middle pier to welcome them. What a reception!! They were simply mobbed and could hardly move. We heard there were six Jersey men on board, so all who had their relatives in the Forces were eagerly looking if they could spot one. I saw a touching scene of a mother who found her son; we all cried, it was a touching episode. We had a good time shaking hands with the Tommies and cheering; we could barely move with the crowd. Eventually we arrived back home past 11pm very tired.

Surgeon Lieutenant Dunlop was by now on HMS *Norfolk* and he recorded the reception awaiting King Haakon's return to Norway at the beginning of June 1945 in a letter home:

WEDNESDAY, 13 JUNE 1945

The little boats started to come out to meet our ships some 18 hours or more before we were due in Oslo, i.e. as we approached the southernmost tip of the country – a cold, miserable wet evening that was too, and they must have been waiting there five miles out to sea for the better part of the whole day, just on the off chance of our passing that way; and that gave one some indication of his popularity; but it was nothing to the procession of boats that met us when we entered the fjord next morning. Almost every boat in Oslo and the whole neighbourhood must have been out that day – hundreds of them, literally – decked with flags from stem to stern, many of them decorated too with flowers and shrubs (as is their attractive custom), and all of them crammed with people – some even of the larger pleasure steamers so full that they listed alarmingly as we passed and the passengers all thronged to one side; and the antics of the one-man canoes were no less fantastic as they got caught up in our wake! Why there weren't some bad accidents is a bit of a mystery to me, but somehow we passed through the throng without any serious incident, and those that could keep up with us followed along; bands playing in the pleasure steamers as well as on our quarterdeck (often drowned by the rather less musical, but no less cheerful, sound of foghorns and sirens blowing off in every direction); the flags waving frantically and the cheering wild.

It was truly an amazing sight. The King and the Royal party were on our quarterdeck acknowledging the cheers (the Crown Prince's little son of eight so exhausted after five or six hours of the excitement that all he could do was to lean against the guard rails and let his hanky flutter). I can't imagine quite such a demonstration coming from any other nation (even our own), and – as someone remarked to me in humorous understatement – 'I think one might almost be justified in concluding that the monarchy in Norway is a fairly popular institution.'

Although the war had ended, for many there was still heartache and dislocation. The advancing Soviet forces had compelled the German authorities to evacuate many of the prisoner of war camps in the east, forcing the prisoners on long westward marches, often in bitter winter conditions. One who suffered in such a march was Howard Bates, who had been in Stalag VIII A in Görlitz, now in modern Poland. The camp was evacuated from mid-February onwards, and the column later encountered the advancing Soviet troops with fatal consequences:

FEBRUARY 1945

The greying darkness of the pre-dawn hour was slightly lightened by the whiteness of the deep snow. Our struggling column moved off from the station along the path next to the wall of the Fabriek on our right and a deep furrow and the railway line on our left. The road through the village was further to the right and came in at an angle, through the edge of the forest, to the rail crossing not far ahead. Apart from the distant rumble of guns, the silence of the hour was only broken by the muffled, slushing of our footsteps in the snow and the low murmur of our voices. Suddenly, the start, chaotic havoc of the vicious crackle of Tommy guns and the blast of 20mm cannon burst around us as shell and bullet scythed down the line of our column. I was about six chaps from the front and my reaction was instantaneous.

I dived into the deep snow beside the path and gouged my way down into the frozen ground, finding a small hollow behind a fir tree in which to shelter. There were two Russian tanks, half hidden in the trees, with a group of infantry sitting on them. Ominous and threatening, they kept a steady stream of bullets and shells spraying up and down our position and I was quite sure that this was the end for all of us. Time stood still and the firing seemed to go on interminably as I apprehensively waited for the Russians to come over and finish us off. Les Bowles and Jack Roberts were lying close by and Les asked if I was OK. I whispered back to him, 'Keep quiet – Just lie doggo'. Fortunately, apart from the first burst of shooting, which caught us all by surprise, most of the shells were going over our heads or hitting the railway bank behind us. Quite a lot of splinters and ricocheting bullets were flying around and it would have been fatal to have raised our heads or move away. Away to my left I could hear the groans of the wounded and dying men and I wondered how many there were and who they were. After an agonising age, the firing stopped and silence, apart from the groans of the wounded, settled over the scene once more. No one moved as we waited, with bated breath, for more shooting but, finally, the tension broke as the two tanks' engines thundered into life and, the rumble of their tracks indicated that they were moving away up the road to Oberleschen.

Then they were gone! Our guards sprang to life and shouted for all of us to follow them across the railway line and make for the forest on the other side. Through the deep ditch, alongside the line, breaking through the ice into knee-deep water, then up, over and away, the fellows fled. Some six or seven of us, however, hung back in order to assess the situation before blundering into any more Russian patrols. One of our guards was a Pole who had been dragooned into the German forces and he accompanied us when we crept into the small hut at the railway crossing. Time passed and just as we had decided that it was quite safe to move on, we saw, from the window, a patrol of 'Ruskies' coming back down the line towards the village. We told 'our Pole' to drop his rifle and to crawl out and start talking Polish to explain who he was and who we were. He was, I am sure, far more terrified than we were as being in a German uniform was inviting a bullet. Anyway, he crept out, closely followed by us with our hands held high above our heads and poured out a torrent of Polish. The Russians had Mongolian features and their attitude was totally hostile. They thrust their Tommy guns into our stomachs, shouting and pushing us around while the poor old Pole kept talking. Slowly they relaxed as the Pole answered their questions and they understood that we were British POW (*Anglichani*). I do not know whether they were the patrol which had shot us up earlier but, as they marched us back to the village, we showed them the bodies of our friends still lying in the snow. We were taken to the first house in the village and put under guard. Fortunately our Pole, with whom we were now on equal terms, stayed with us and helped to organise a rescue party to go out and bring in our wounded and the dead friends. The slate-grey, gloomy, snow-laden day drew to a dismal, devastating close.

8. The End in the Far East

The war in Europe may have finished, but operations were still ongoing in the Far East. Slim's Fourteenth Army in Burma had launched an attack on Rangoon at the beginning of May, Operation *Dracula*, with airborne landings and a naval assault securing the city in the face of very limited Japanese resistance. The main Japanese force had by this stage abandoned the city and withdrawn across the Sittang River. There was still a degree of mopping up to do and David Upson, who served with the Burma Naval Reserve and had been forced out to India during the occupation of Burma, wrote of encountering Japanese naval forces in the Rangoon River:

WEDNESDAY, 16 MAY 1945

On the morning of 16th May at 5.30am we heard firing so we started up and slowly proceeded upstream. I was at the Bofors. While proceeding upstream, Campbell No. 3 and myself No. 2, he the layer and I the trainer practised on water Hyacinths floating down the river, so when we came to a bend in the river, we tried to see if we could train on the first water Hyacinth that came around the bend, by this time 7 a.m. we had forgotten about the Japs (the battle begins). Well, instead of water Hyacinths three Jap boats came straight into my gun sights, for a few seconds I was startled and could not do anything at the shock of seeing the boats so close, the next thing our ship swung hard over to port to give them a broadside, as we were turning the Japs opened fire at us, two shells went through our bow and got stuck just above our ammo locker, I swung the gun around and as the boats were in my sights again Campbell shouted 'open fire', our first burst was 8 rounds of 40mm HE. The next minute the first Jap boat was ablaze, we started to shout at the top of our voices with joy, we swung to the next boat which ML367 was already firing upon, our next shot was single straight to the middle of the fuel drums they were carrying, she also blazed up, as each boat caught fire it headed for the bank, thank God they did not try to ram us with their burning boats. The last boat's engines were still running, a few Japs got ashore from the second boat, the 3rd boat was shattered by a direct hit from a 3-pdr, one of the Japs climbed up a tree and ML367 shot him and half the tree down with a 3-pdr round, the action lasted about 18 minutes all told. Two out of the three Jap boats had sunk but one drifted into a small choung, the men from this boat got ashore into a big group of bushes, the villagers tried to round them up but failed as the Japs were shooting at them, so we told the villagers to clear themselves from the area, and we mortared the Japs with 3-inch mortar shell.

There still were a number of pockets of major Japanese resistance as well, notably the 28th Army to the west of the River Sittang and the remains of the 15th and 33rd Armies in the Shan. Although their ability to conduct offensive operations was negligible, they still remained a threat and were subject to constant attention by the aircraft of the RAF. 'Dobbie' Dobbins was by now restored to flight duties and describes a typical operation during this period:

17 JUNE 1945: OFFENSIVE RECCE OF THE SITTANG

At last the War was starting with a swing, for the Army had observed the Japs crossing the Sittang in boats, & we had been asked to go & knock hell out of as many boats as possible. I went over with a guy called Andy (F/O Andrews), & we hugged the deck all the way so that the Japs couldn't see us coming. I sure enjoyed that trip, for as soon as we hit the banks of the Sittang, we pulled up like bats out of hell & gave a quick look round for any boats. Andy saw two up river & I saw three down river, so we split up & went to give the boats a bit of lead.

Unless you have flown, you will never know the thrill of going past your objective at 1,000ft, turning over on your side & peeling straight for the target.

I switched my gun sight on, & turned my 'fire & safe' unit to 'fire'. As I straightened out in the dive, I placed my bead on the boats, & when I was about 400ft, I opened up with cannons. What a wizard sight, there were bags of explosions, & bits of boats blew up everywhere, I went in twice, & gave a couple of bursts on each dive. I know that I made a mess of them, for two sank, & the other was blown to hell, so I went & joined Andy higher up. In all, we pranged about nine boats, four boats were sunk, & the other five that were moored on the bank were knocked to hell.

We were the last patrol, & after we had used all our cannon & machine-gun bullets, we returned to base, time, 7.00pm. When we got back it was pretty dark, but we got down OK & after giving the IO & the ALO [Army Liaison Officer] all the gen, we returned to the billets for a well-earned dinner.

The Royal Navy was increasingly active in the Far East following the surrender of Germany and the British Pacific Fleet was formed in

November 1944 with Admiral Sir Bruce Fraser as its commander in chief. This was the largest fleet ever assembled by the Royal Navy and its role was controversial, with senior American commanders not keen on having a British presence in what they considered an American theatre.

The fleet was based around the carriers *Indomitable*, *Victorious*, *Indefatigable* and *Illustrious*, supported by the battleships *King George V* and *Howe*, five cruisers and fourteen destroyers. It joined the US Fifth Fleet in March 1945. The Americans were preparing for Operation *Iceberg*, the invasion of Okinawa in the Ryukyu Islands, the first assault on Japanese home territory. The British Pacific Fleet was to protect the flank of the invasion and prevent the Japanese from moving aircraft across from the islands of Sakishima Gunto to the south of Okinawa itself.

Ken Morris served as a leading sick berth attendant in the aircraft carrier HMS *Illustrious* and recorded his memories of events during this period after the war:

APRIL 1945

We were glad to get away from Leyte in the end, and sailed north again to about the latitude of Formosa (now Taiwan), 25 degrees North. From this area our aircraft started a series of attacks against Japanese airfields in the Ryukyu Islands, Sakishima Gunto and the Ishigaki. The Americans were planning to capture Okinawa to the north east but, as part of the plan, the British were to try to neutralise the airfields in the Ryukyus and prevent the Japanese attacking the American invasion forces off Okinawa. This involved bombing the airstrips continuously and to enable us to remain in the area more or less all the time, we availed ourselves of the Fleet Train. This was a fleet of auxiliary supply ships which would meet us at some quiet rendezvous away from the combat zone and re-stock us with ammunition, food and other supplies. Thus, the need for us to sail all the way back to Sydney, some 5,000 miles to the south and then return, was avoided: we saved time and fuel.

On one day, I counted six other ships 'plugged-in' to us whilst sailing along, one at each corner and one each side of us. Destroyers would also bring us mail from home – which only took 17 days to reach us – and for which we rewarded them by sending back – along the lines between us – nets of fresh bread from our bakery. If the lines sagged, however, and the nets drooped into the sea, we got wet mail and the destroyer men got soggy bread. We dried out our letters on the hotplate in the mess!

Although this was a good idea from the Allies' point of view, it meant that we spent even more time at sea, which was hazardous for us all, and more so for the aircrews.

Another of the reasons that the Americans were not keen to have the British Pacific Fleet was the lack of an adequate Fleet Train, despite Ken Morris's comments above. The resupply elements accompanying the British Pacific Fleet were improvised and inadequate and the Americans feared that they would end up having to shoulder the principal logistical burden. Ken Morris goes on to describe the attacks suffered by the British Pacific Fleet:

APRIL 1945

By this late stage of the War, the Japanese had started using *kamikaze* ('Floating Chrysanthemums') or suicide planes against the Allied shipping. Their pilots were fanatical young men imbued with the *Bushido* ideal that it was honourable to give their lives for their Emperor and country, and to delight in doing so. These suicide attacks, often *en masse*, caused considerable damage, but were a desperate measure.

In turn, HMS *Victorious*, *Indomitable*, *Indefatigable* and *Illustrious* were hit by this type of attack, fortunately without great damage, although *Indefatigable* had a number of casualties and damage to her flight deck which put her out of action for a few hours. The fact that the British carriers had armoured flight decks enabled them to withstand bomb bursts better than the American carriers, which had wooden ones, usually well soaked in oil from the aircraft. A bomb would cut through a wooden deck and explode inside the ship, causing severe damage and fire and, quite often, withdrawal of the carrier to a dockyard for repairs . . .

Aircraft carriers were, of course, a prime target and while at sea we were always under the threat of attack by bomb or torpedo, but we were well protected by being at the centre of the fleet, sometimes with a battleship or two on our flanks, cruisers outside of them, and then a screen of destroyers in an outer circle on the horizon. With their radar the destroyers could pick up incoming aircraft or ships and the concentration of anti-aircraft fire-power and fighter plane cover from the carrier(s) usually dealt with any air attack. The destroyers, too, had their ASDIC (or sonar detection gear) which, hopefully, would pick up enemy submarines. Ships' gunners, in having to deal with suicide planes, were naturally a bit 'trigger-happy' and as well as the *Euryalus* putting two shells into us, we also shot down a Seafire fighter from one of the other carriers. He was following a Japanese plane over the fleet and, despite warnings to keep away, carried on into our anti-aircraft barrage. Sadly these things do happen in wartime.

The invasion of the island of Okinawa provoked a major response from the Japanese, who launched ten massed *kamikaze* attacks against the fleet, striking the carriers *Formidable*, *Indefatigable* and *Victorious* between 6 April and 29 May. In all, 1,465 aircraft made attacks on the carriers.

Edward Lipman was a seaman torpedoman in the destroyer HMS *Ulster*, part of the 25th Destroyer Flotilla, and he describes being under Japanese aerial attack:

MARCH/APRIL 1945

As we moved along towards the 'Okinawa' Coast ships moved into their battle stations, forming a ring around the *Anson* and *King George V* who were being used for bait.

Then came aircraft carriers, cruisers and destroyers. Our position was Aft-forward. The cruising speed was 25 knots, except for the aircraft carriers when turning into the wind for planes to take off. Then all hell broke loose. It is something I'll never forget. From my new action station I only saw what was going on sometimes. The sky had black dots all over it from the AA guns from the big boys, battle wagons, cruisers and carriers and *kamikaze* planes were crashing onto the decks trying to stop our planes from taking off. The Japs threw everything they had at us.

We kept this up for about three days, then pulled out to go and meet up with the tankers and ammo ships, form up and back into it again. We being on the out side of the ring we didn't cop it as much as the big boys did, we were mostly on the look-out for subs which the Japs still had a few of in that area.

There was an American aircraft carrier who got the worst of it. Eight *kamikaze* planes landed on top and inside of her, she never sank so the Yanks towed her into a cove and left her there till the fighting was all over . . .

It was around 7 in the morning on April Fools Day, we had been at battle stations for a couple of days and when you are like this the cooks make sandwiches and bring them around, I rang Doug M— and the other ST in No 2 boiler room and Nobby Clark who was in the Engine room and had just asked Doug if he had any news of what was going on, thought he might have been up, I'd just hung up the phone when I heard a loud explosion and the ship lifted up into the air and dropped straight down again. All the lights went out and emergency ones came on, steam pipes were going off everywhere.

We knew we'd been hit so I tried to get Doug but the phone was dead. The stokers shut down the boiler and waited to see what would happen. Next, a head came through the air lock and told us to get on deck quickly and when we got up on deck we found out what had happened. The first thing we saw was a bit of the bow and stern hanging onto the davits where once the cutter (skipper's whale boat) had been. Then we found out only two got out of the boiler room, PO Stoker and a young lad stoker, but the steam had got to him and he passed on about an hour later, how they had got out we don't know . . .

Four including Doug didn't make it.

The *Ulster* was towed back to Sydney for repairs, while the remainder of the British Pacific Fleet left the waters around Okinawa on 25 May 1945. This battle proved to be its last major action, and indeed the last for the Royal Navy in the Second World War. The fleet rejoined the Americans in June and fought on through till the end of the war in August, with

Seafires of HMS *Indefatigable* destroying eight Zeros on 15 August in what was to be the last fighter combat of the Second World War.

The previous day Japan surrendered, the result of the earlier atomic attacks on Hiroshima and Nagasaki. Canon Rupert Godfrey had been captured by the Japanese on Java in March 1942 and was held at the mining camp Fukuoka 12 at the time of the first atomic explosion at Hiroshima:

AUGUST 1945

Of this of course we had no knowledge nor did they ever tell us but on August 7th, the day after the first bomb fell on Hiroshima, we the British officers were lined up in three rows facing the Camp Commandant and harangued to the effect that we had all been complaining about short rations. He threatened us, through the interpreter, with death if any further complaints were made. Then followed a vicious beating up by all the goons with their heavy sticks. We were made to go down on the ground in the 'press-up' position while they went between the lines beating every man's back with all the ferocity of which they were capable. We carried the weals around for days. That was not the sort of thing one forgets in a hurry.

Next day, August 8th, we were back at work again in the fields. About mid-day in the glorious sunlight we looked up and there high above us like a shoal of silvery fish was a perfect formation of about 200 American bombers far beyond the reach of ack-ack heading purposefully (and presumably) for Nagasaki. It was a wonderful sight. And as we watched we saw masses of tinfoil being dropped from them as they went. We had no knowledge that this was all to do with radar. The guards said nothing and back we went to the camp, when the day's work was over, as though nothing unusual had happened. (The bomb was dropped on Nagasaki on August 9th.)

9. VJ Day

The dropping of the atomic bombs on Hiroshima and Nagasaki in August 1945 quickly brought the war in the Far East to a conclusion.

Emperor Hirohito announced the Japanese surrender in a radio broadcast to the nation on 14 August. Victory over Japan (VJ) Day was proclaimed on 15 August, although the Instrument of Surrender was not signed until 2 September 1945. The formal capitulation of all Japanese armed forces in South East Asia, including those in Burma, finally took place at Singapore on 12 September 1945. British troops landed in Malaya and reoccupied Singapore and Hong Kong, beginning the task of restoring order following the Japanese withdrawal.

Audrey Deacon served as a cipher officer in the WRNS (Women's Royal Naval Service) based at HMS *Fledgling*, an FAA (Fleet Air Arm) base near Stafford, and recorded her reaction to the dropping of the bombs and the announcement of the Japanese surrender:

AUGUST 1945

The main news today is that the first atomic bomb has been dropped, on a Japanese town of about 300,000 inhabitants, *Hiroshima*. It has not been possible to see what damage has been done, on account of the thick cloud of dust covering the area; but the force of the bomb is calculated as 2,000 that of the 10,000 [pound] *high explosive* bomb, which is the largest yet used. The new bomb is based on the power liberated by splitting the atom; and it is said that this source of power will be able to be used for commercial and industrial purposes after further research. The research carried out up to now, by British and US scientists, has been going on throughout the war and has cost £500,000,000 [actual cost $2 billion]. It was not decided to use the new weapon until after Japan had rejected the Potsdam offer of peace . . .

A second atomic bomb has been dropped – on Nagasaki. At 1300hrs today we heard the first news of Japan's reported offer to surrender – provided that the position of the Emperor will not be affected by so doing. There was, up to 2100hrs, no confirmation from any Allied government – apart from a Russian announcement that the Russian ambassador, who had not had time to leave, had been received by the Japanese Government, but the offer has been announced by the Japanese Domei news agency. As usual with these things, it is more than one can truly realise. It takes a little while to change one's whole perspective.

The atomic bomb has made a tremendous sensation. One feels more than ever that another war could mean the end of the human race. Germany was also working on the same theory – but fortunately hadn't got far enough to make use of it on us. It is said that the principle is so well known that all nations will be able to make use of it, and there is talk of control. Churchill, before going out of office, drafted a statement, and President Truman has spoken, about the potentialities for good and evil of the discovery.

TUESDAY, 14 AUGUST 1945

Throughout the weekend there were rumours, and denials of rumours, that Japan had surrendered. We listened to every news bulletin: my Wren even brought her wireless to the office so that we shouldn't miss anything. By this evening we were half inclined to think that perhaps they weren't going to surrender after all. However, one had hardly settled down in bed when there were shouts and whistlings and what not: I looked out of my door to see what was happening and was greeted by a dustbin lid *rolling* along the corridor. The surrender had been announced at midnight by Mr Attlee. We all got up and went out; the ship's bell was rung – to such an extent that the Dutch fire-party rushed out looking for the fire! We had been preparing a bonfire for VJ day itself, but someone set light to it now, and it began to blaze. It was a wonderful bonfire. There was an effigy of Tojo (or Hirohito?) which was duly burned. The wardroom piano was carried out on to the grass, and we sang songs, English and Dutch, and vaguely rushed round the fire for an hour or so. A barrel of beer was broached; and we retired to the wardroom for drinks. Then out to the bonfire again – and then rounding up the Wrens and checking them into the cabins. It was quite a job, and we didn't get back to our beds until about 0330hrs. Fortunately the Captain decided that there was to be Sunday routine today (Wednesday) – I spent a few minutes in the office, and that was all. We had a service, on the lines of the VE service, and then the day was our own . . .

I should have said that we 'spliced the main brace' this evening – my first taste of rum, which I didn't like much. Strictly speaking, WRNS personnel are not entitled – but one doesn't win a war every day. I had only half a tot, and had to disguise that with orange juice in order to drink it.

I just can't really comprehend that the war is over. Six years is a long time, and all our ideas have been focused one way, so it's very hard to take in the fact. The Chinese have had eight years of war – it must be even more wonderful for them.

Lieutenant John Pelly was with the British Pacific Fleet aboard the destroyer HMS *Tyrian* and describes the liberation of Hong Kong and the repatriation of the first British prisoners of war from the island of Formosa (now Taiwan):

AUGUST/SEPTEMBER 1945

So on August 15th we sailed arriving in a few days at Manus in the Admiralty Islands – then on up through the Philippines to Leyte, which was most impressive – all these hundreds of high islands covered with forests and jungle. But, except for fuelling, we didn't stop, going straight on up to Hong Kong to relieve it on 30th Aug.

We were in company with *Anson*, two cruisers, an aircraft carrier and two other destroyers. It was a very interesting incident – the frightful chaos and destruction, the Jap flags still flying, the very green colour, the very impressive height of Hong Kong itself, the tops of the mounts covered with cloud.

The larger ships landed men and there was a certain amount of trouble ashore with looting etc. After a day or two we were sent at full speed to Subic Bay in the Philippines to collect mail. A day or two after our return to Hong Kong we sailed for Kiirun in Formosa [Taiwan]. The object was to remove the surviving prisoners of war. We sailed into Kiirun and I have never seen a place so badly bombed with every building apparently down and sunk ships all over the harbour. And there on the jetty were fully armed Japanese.

All the time we were there (7–11th September) we felt most uncomfortable as there was nothing definite and we were a force of two cruisers and two destroyers in contrast to 300,000 fully armed Japanese. However nothing very untoward happened and we cleared the jetty for the arrival of a hospital ship. Various doctors went inland to the camp and eventually the improvised hospital train arrived bearing its grim cargo. I just can't describe the scene – a boiling hot humid day with the sun beating down, the frightful smell of rotting human flesh and the lack of any breeze. The train was brought alongside the ship and the surviving prisoners of war were carried aboard . . . too weak to lift a fleshless arm, let alone smile or usually even open their eyes. It was the most ghastly sight and made one realise just how inhuman the Jap has become. Apparently the camp was too indescribably sordid and thousands of men had died or been executed.

I talked to a lot of the Stanley Camp (HK) people in the hospital ship and they were better off, though horribly emaciated and weak – there they were mostly civilian prisoners.

The end of the war was a time of reflection for William Elliott. At the time of the Japanese surrender, his unit, the 2nd Battalion East Lancashire Regiment, was in India, having been pulled out of the line in May 1945 following the capture of Mandalay. He looked back on the course of the war in the Far East from his initial baptism of fire in the Arakan campaign in early 1944:

AUGUST 1945

I remembered those who had come out with us full of life and the spirit of adventure, who now for ever rested in the spoil of this land, this same soil remained, in spite of the devastation of battle, almost untouched, and in a little while the scars which blemished the land would be healed by the incessant process of nature, and the ravages of man would be forgotten, the great forests would sleep once more in deep silence, a silence enhanced rather than broken, by the song of birds, the chattering of the monkey, the cry of the leopard, the rustle of the snake, the buzz of insects, or the trumpeting of the elusive elephant, and lulled by the ripple of the leisurely stream in its meandering to the mighty Irrawaddy or the broad Sittang.

It was a solemn moment when one, for the first time since this hazardous adventure was embarked upon, could begin to reflect calmly, this was the Exodus, the closing of a chapter of our lives, never again would we be called upon to endure the perils of the jungle and to live so dangerously from day to day, nor should we again look

forward eagerly to the first glimpse of the 'Lado Road' – the road
which was built at such expense in lives and labour to link with the
more famous 'Burma Road' to China.

My mind went back to my first picture of Burma, the pack-mules,
the strenuous ascent of Goppe pass which opened up the magnificent
sight of Ngachydgauk [Ngakyedauk] where then the 5th and 7th
Divisions were making history in a brilliant manner. Then the second
trip, the grounding at devastated Myitkyina, from where we began our
last and longest campaign – how long ago it all seemed now, the long
weary marches under the pitiless sun, when the sweat from our bodies
soaked through our battle-dress and dried on the surface, leaving only
a white salt deposit, while from our heads it ran into our eyes, stinging
and blinding, coursed down our cheeks and was licked from our lips
by parched tongues, which thereby became even drier, our blistered
and bleeding feet, legs stiffened by marching so that when, after a
halt, we had great difficulty in getting into stride again, our rifles and
Tommy guns weighed on our shoulders and the slings bit into our
flesh and our packs seemed to be boring a way into our backs until
they became a living, painful part of us; climbing mile upon mile of
rough tortuous mountain-track, pressing through deep, evil-smelling
mud and, passing vile, stagnant mosquito-ridden pools the stench
of which sometimes overpowered us, fording swift-flowing chaungs,
with the water often breast high, and then continuing our march with
sodden clothes which clung to our legs and slowed us down while
our boots squelched at every step until we began to wonder whether
the coolness of the water on our burning feet and perspiring bodies
had been worth the discomfort which inevitably followed, for the sun
seemed to double its heat and our feet were more readily blistered
– how we longed for the iced-drinks of Poona and dreamed of long
copious draughts of iced-beer such as we knew in Durban, or the
Knickerbocker Glories of Bombay, only to come down to earth and sip
two or three drops of tepid brackish water from our bottles, which for
a short time would ease the harsh dryness of our mouths and throats
– I can taste now the soap-flavoured tea we often drank when water
was too scarce to allow us to rinse our cups after shaving.

Gone were the days and nights of strain and concentration, the
breathless, cautious advance along the narrow jungle track when at

every step one expected to hear the high crack of a Jap rifle or a sudden burst of machine-gun fire which was the signal to take cover behind the nearest tree and hope the marksman didn't see one over his sights – we were always momentarily helpless, not knowing whether he might be behind or before us concealed in the branches of some adjacent tree or lurking in a fox-hole, it was impossible to locate him where in the depth of the jungle a shot might come from any side and in any direction; then the nights of a hastily dug trench, perhaps barely deep enough to afford us anything like adequate protection, in which we stood behind a Bren gun and peered intently into the blackness of the undergrowth for perhaps two or even four long hours, startled by the slightest sound, the stirring of leaves or the stealthy movement of some small creature in its haunts, and many times, when the moon came up yellow and large, its light here and there filtering through the leaves of the trees played tricks with our eyes, persuading us that shadowy human figures were moving in the darkness around us, while we ourselves seemed to be bathed in silvery radiance; on such nights the romantic 'moon over Burma' held no enchantment for us and we were thankful when our spell of guard duty came to an end and we could crawl under our blankets and mosquito nets to fall into a dreamless sleep until aroused for 'stand to' before dawn, when we would stand shivering and only half awake in the cold morning air, listening as the fading night sounds gave way to the activities of day and the sun rose swiftly over the trees bringing fresh life to our chilled bodies and causing us to ignore the fact that within the space of five hours the heat would be appalling and we should be praying for the cool of the evening.

There was so much to call forth from the recesses of the mind, half forgotten incidents, tragic, humorous, kindly, vulgar, brave; movements of fear and despair, and the ever present heaviness of heart on waking each morning to face another weary day. Most of us, I am sure, latterly began to feel that the war would never end, our loved ones and our country seemed to be in another world, long past and almost unreal, only the jungle was real, the unending struggle and purposeless existence, it was something to marvel throughout, yet the spirit that prevailed was probably the very essence of our success and without doubt is one fact which can never be forgotten.

Conclusion

During the course of the Second World War, some 55 million people perished. Soviet Russia suffered most of all, with as many as 6.3 million military and 17 million civilian deaths, while in Great Britain there were 305,800 killed and missing among its armed forces and a further 60,600 civilian dead.

These losses were not spread evenly over the armed forces of Great Britain. Members of the flight crew of Bomber Command, such as Johnnie Byrne, paid a heavy price for the aerial campaign over Germany and occupied Europe. They made up nearly 20 per cent of all British fatalities, though only just over 2 per cent of the total combatants. Likewise, some regiments saw considerably more service than others. The Sherwood Rangers Yeomanry, to whom the Reverend Leslie Skinner was attached throughout the campaign of 1944–45 in north-west Europe, began the war as a mounted cavalry unit in Palestine before converting to armour and serving successively throughout the campaigns in the Western Desert and Tunisia. It was then summoned back to England and went ashore in the first wave at D-Day, fighting on till the end of the war, amassing a grand total of 30 battle honours while suffering 827 casualties. These examples illustrate how extreme the situation was for those shipped around the world to fight and sometimes die in conditions and climates of which they had no previous experience.

The men and women who lived through these events were often reticent about them when they returned home. The reasons for their silence are myriad: an effort to forget traumatic episodes, protect their loved ones from the grim realities of war or simply out of a desire to move on from their life in the armed forces and concentrate on the civilian world that needed rebuilding. The first many families knew of such wartime experiences was through the discovery of a notebook, diary or collection of letters that had been left untended for years. These documents, thousands of which are held in the Department of Documents at the Imperial War Museum, have formed the basis of this study and cast new light upon the lives of those at war from 1939 through to 1945.

Glossary

A tk Tp Cmd	Anti-Tank Troop Commander
AA/Ack-Ack	Anti-Aircraft
ADC	Aide-de-Camp
ADS	Advanced Dressing Station
ALO	Army Liaison Officer
ARP	Air Raid Precautions
AWOL	Absent Without Leave
Bde.	Brigade
BEF	British Expeditionary Force
BGS	Brigadier General Staff
BSM	Battery Sergeant Major
CDL	Canal Defence Light, searchlight tank
CF	Chaplain to the Forces
CGS	Chief of the General Staff
chagal	leather or skin water bottle
CinC	Commander-in-Chief
COS	Chief of Staff
DCGS	Deputy Chief of the General Staff
DCM	Distinguished Conduct Medal
DD	Duplex Drive, amphibious tank
DF	Defensive Fire
DS	Director Station
Duck/DUKW	amphibious truck
DY	dockyard
DZ	Drop Zone
EA	Enemy Aircraft

Echelon	the troops who man the rear area, with supply dumps, cooks, etc.
FAA	Fleet Air Arm
F/O	Flying Officer
GHQ	General Headquarters
GP	General Purpose
griff	rumour
GRO	General Routine Order
HA	High Angle
HE	High Explosive
IFF	Identification Friend or Foe
IO	Intelligence Officer
Ities	derogatory term used during the period to describe Italians
Japs	derogatory term used during the period to describe the Japanese
Jerry	derogatory term used during the period to describe Germans
KRRC	King's Royal Rifle Corps
LAA	Light Anti-Aircraft, gun or regiment
LCA	Landing Craft Assault
LCG	Landing Craft Gun
LCVP	Landing Craft Vehicle Personnel
LMG	Light Machine Gun
LSI	Landing Ship Infantry
LST	Landing Ship Tank
MDS	Main Dressing Station
MO	Medical Officer
MT	Motor Transport
MTB	Motor Torpedo Boat
Naga	Burmese hill tribe who worked as scouts
NCO	Non-Commissioned Officer
nullah	steep, narrow valley
Oerlikon	20 mm Swiss-made anti-aircraft gun
Pick-A-Back	air-launched V1 missile
P/O	Pilot Officer

Python scheme	Scheme for repatriation to the UK for long-serving British troops
Pz Lehr Division	Panzer Demonstration Division
QMG	Quartermaster General
RA	Royal Artillery
RAAF	Royal Australian Air Force
RAF	Royal Air Force
RAMC	Royal Army Medical Corps
RAOC	Royal Army Ordnance Corps
RASC	Royal Army Service Corps
RCAF	Royal Canadian Air Force
RE	Royal Engineers
RHA	Royal Horse Artillery
RN	Royal Navy
RSM	Regimental Sergeant Major
SAMC	South African Medical Corps
SEAC	South East Asia Command
TAF	Tactical Air Force
TBD	Torpedo Boat Destroyer
TCP	Traffic Control Person
TI	Torpedo Instructor
the Blue	the desert
TT	teetotal
UNRRA	United Nations Relief and Rehabilitation Administration
Wops	derogatory term used during the period to describe Italians
WRNS	Women's Royal Naval Service

Acknowledgements

Within the Imperial War Museum, I am indebted to Roderick Suddaby, the keeper of the Department of Documents, and all his staff, with particular thanks to Sabrina Rowlatt, Simon Offord and Emma Goodrum. I would also like to thank Abbie Ratcliffe, publishing and licensing manager at the museum, who has overseen the whole project, and Nick Hewitt, historian at the museum, who checked the manuscript for historical accuracy and pointed out a number of instances where it could be improved.

At Mainstream Publishing, I would like to thank Iain MacGregor, who conceived the whole project in the first place, and also Deborah Warner, who has edited the book with great skill and efficiency.

I would like to thank Jenny Snyman for all her hard work in transcribing the documents that form the most important part of this study.

For providing board, lodging and great company while I was researching the book in London, I would like to thank Will and Elmarie Brown, Jamie and Rachel Cowper, and Gareth and Willow Robinson.

Finally, I would like to thank my wife Jo for all her help, encouragement and editorial skills.

Any errors in this book are entirely the responsibility of the author.

The extracts in this book all come from the collection of the Department of Documents in the Imperial War Museum. In all cases, I am grateful to the Trustees of the Imperial War Museum for allowing me access to these materials and to the following for granting permission to use the various documents.

Mr A. Abbott for the papers of Lieutenant S.S. Abbott (89/15/1); Mrs Astley for the papers of I.D. Astley (99/16/1); Mrs M.J. Aylen for the papers of N.P. Aylen (80/49/1); Mr L.A. Bains for the papers of L.A. Bains (88/57/1); Mr E.D. Barnes for the papers of Mrs G.E. Barnes (99/25/1); Mrs E. Bates for the papers of H.J. Bates (03/57/1); Mrs L.E. Bethell for the papers of Flight Lieutenant R.A. Bethell (05/04/1); Mrs V. Billings for the papers of A.R. Billings (PP/MCR/121); Mr H. Bolland for the papers of Group Captain G.A. Bolland (02/34/1); Mrs D.M. Bradford for the papers of Dr D.C. Bradford (86/7/1); Mrs C. Buckley for the papers of Miss P.M. Briggs (82/24/1); Mrs V. Brooks for the papers of J.E. Brooks (84/13/1); Mrs M. Brundle for the papers of K.A. Brundle (99/50/1); Mrs K. Strickland for the papers of P. Burns (08/47/1); Mrs A. Burton for the papers of Major B.E.L. Burton (94/8/1); Mr J. Johnson for the papers of Pilot Officer J.R. Byrne (04/24/1); Mrs B. Sherriff for the papers of Sub Lieutenant J.E.N. Carter (Con Shelf and 92/45/1); Mr R. Macleod for the papers of Miss M. Charlton (88/13/2); Mrs J.V. Clark for the papers of D. Clark (99/16/1); Mr J. Clark for the papers of J.W. Clark (07/76/1); Mr P.R. Court for the papers of P.R. Court (98/30/1); Mr H. Crawford for the papers of W.M. Crawford (92/27/1); Mr W. Cutler for the papers of W. Cutler (89/3/1); Mr W. de Segundo for the papers of Brigadier R.B.T. Daniell (67/429/1-2); Mr N.H. Dicken for the papers of N.H. Dicken (05/47/1); Mrs J. Parker for the papers of Surgeon Lieutenant J.C.H. Dunlop (82/13/1); the Right Honourable Sir Robin Dunn for the papers of Sir Robin Dunn (94/41/1); Mr R.C. Wilkin for the papers of Vice Admiral Sir Alistair Ewing (DS/MISC/31); Lieutenant Colonel W.L. Farrow for the papers of Lieutenant Colonel W.L. Farrow (95/33/1); Mr R.J. Fayers for the papers of Flying Officer R.J. Fayers (PP/MCR/268 & 88/22/2A); Mrs A. Blaydon for the papers of H.G. Fisher (01/13/1); Mrs D.

Francis for the papers of Lieutenant H.B. Francis (08/23/1); Mr M.J. Gould for the papers of C.A. Gould (02/56/1); Mr E.G. Blunden for the papers of Captain J.S. Gray (97/29/2); Mr R.K. Green for the papers of J.K. Green (98/35/1); Mr B. Greenwood and Mrs J. Schroder for the papers of R.T. Greenwood (95/19/1); Mr W.K. Handley for the papers of Pilot Officer W.K. Handley (96/16/1); Mr G.A.W. Heppell MC for the papers of Lieutenant G.A.W. Heppell (03/20/1); Mrs B. Hicks for the papers of A.J.R. Hicks (06/42/1); Mrs V. Bowater for the papers of Miss V. Hodgson (Con Shelf); Miss L. Holmes for the papers of K.A. Holmes (P129); Dr P.J. Horsey for the papers of Dr P.J. Horsey (Con Shelf); Mr S.W. Hough for the papers of S.W. Hough (98/1/1); Mrs P.J. Preese for the papers of Air Commodore N.C. Hyde (88/14/4 & 4A); Mr R. Innes-Ker for the papers of W.M. Innes-Ker (84/45/1); the Kemsing Heritage Centre for the papers of the village of Kemsing (Misc 262 (3569)); Mr R. King-Clark for the papers of Lieutenant Colonel R. King-Clark (83/10/1); Mrs C. Knight for the papers of A.W.C. Knight (07/23/1); for the papers of Lieutenant W.K. Laing (Con Shelf); Mr E.G. Laker for the papers of E.G. Laker (85/18/1); Mr P. Lambert and Mr K. Lambert for the papers of W. Lambert (04/02/2001); Mrs M. Ling for the papers of Major D.C. Ling (90/25/1); Mr P. Matthews for the papers of C.L.R. Matthews (08/59/1); Mr P. Mayfield for the papers of the Venerable Guy Mayfield (06/12/1); Mrs M. Woodman for the papers of R.G. Meadows (05/63/1); Professor G. Abramson for the papers of Lieutenant Colonel L. Melzer (07/27/1); Mr K. Morris for the papers of K. Morris (03/14/1); Mrs N.A.L. Wheeler for the papers of A.W.M. Mowbray (95/32/1); Mr M. Newey for the papers of M. Newey (90/4/1); Mrs G. Emberson for the papers of Canon R. Nicholls (06/27/1); the Crown for the papers of No. 73 Squadron RAF (Misc 102 (1598)); Mrs W.A. Stokes for the papers of N.A. Paine (89/3/1); Mr G. Parkinson for the papers of J.E. Parkinson (99/61/1); Mrs J. Pelly for the papers of Lieutenant J.G. Pelly (91/15/2); Mr C. Pettit for the papers of Major P. Pettit (07/86/1); Mr I. Porter for the papers of Major I.F. Porter (05/76/1); Mrs E. Potts for the papers of A. Potts (06/50/1); the Reverend G. Deave for the papers of Admiral Sir Manley Power (P87); Mrs B. Anslow for the papers of Miss B.C. Redwood (73/67/1); Mrs A. Regan-Atherton for the papers of W.B. Regan (Con Shelf & 88/10/1); Mr B. Richardson for the papers of C. Richardson (85/6/1); Mrs J. Anderson for the papers of Mrs E.J. Riddell (92/25/1); Dr J.H. Ross for the papers of Captain J.H. Ross (06/18/1); Mr G. Sear for the papers of G. Sear (91/17/1); Mrs W. Shackleton and Woodfield Publishing for the papers of Flight Lieutenant G. Shackleton (03/34/1); Mrs A. Conway for the papers of the Reverend L.F. Skinner (01/13/1); Miss J. Smith for the papers of Brigadier E.D. Smith (93/39/1); Mr H. Speakman for the papers of H. Speakman (91/17/1); Mrs O.V. Ascroft for the papers of Miss F.M. Speed (86/45/2); Mrs C. Strother Smith for the papers of Captain N.C. Strother Smith (97/1/1); Mrs Margaret Clark for the papers of G.B. Thompson (99/3/1); Mr W.G. Peto for the papers of Captain D.H.H. Turner (01/04/1); Lieutenant Commander A.J.L. Tyler for the papers of Lieutenant Commander A.J.L. Tyler (96/56/1); Mr A. Gardner for the papers of D. Upson (08/59/1); Mr J. Wakefield for the papers of H.E. Wakefield (06/125/1); Mr R.J.B. Walker for the papers of Lieutenant R.J.B. Walker (04/31/1); Mrs Jean Holland for the papers of Major H.F. Wheway (05/27/1); Mr P. White for the papers of J.Y. White (90/6/1); Mr B. Whitehouse, librarian of Southwell Minster Historic Chapter Library, on behalf of the Dean and Chapter of Southwell for the papers of H. Wiles (06/99/1); Mrs W.M. Jones for the papers of Captain J.E. Williams (03/02/1); Mrs H. Wilson for the papers of Lieutenant J.N. Wilson (P470); Mrs N. Windeatt for the papers of Lieutenant Colonel J.K. Windeatt (90/20/1); Mrs E. Kup for the papers of Pilot Officer D.H. Wissler (91/41/1); Mrs H.J. Wright for the papers of K.R. Wyse (03/33/1).

Every effort has been made to trace copyright holders, and the author and the Imperial War Museum would be grateful for any information which might help to trace those whose identities or addresses are not currently known. Should the copyright holders of the following collections come forward, the author will happily acknowledge them in future editions.

The papers of Lieutenant Colonel O.A. Archdale (78/52/1); the papers of Major E.M. Barrett (05/05/1); the papers of J.W. Beaumont (83/36/1); the papers of J.H. Beazley (85/34/1); the papers of R. Blackford (06/41/1); the papers of Major J.E. Blackwood (81/16/1); the papers of Captain G.C. Blundell (90/38/1); the papers of Mrs I.M. Bullen (P324); the papers of R.A. Butler (P449); the papers of Major J. Caneri (08/08/1); the papers of Lieutenant D.J. Carnegie (95/15/1 & Con Shelf); the papers of Dr S.P.W. Chave (79/27/1); the papers of B.R. Christy (99/49/1); the papers of Captain A.B. Clements (67/343/1); the papers of Captain B.R. Cowles (93/6/1); the papers of Captain F. Cox (88/4/1); the papers of N.A. Cox (99/48/1); the papers of R.L. Crimp (96/50/1 & PP/MCR/245); the papers of E.P. Danger (82/37/1); the papers of Mrs A.D. Deacon (89/17/1); the papers of H.J. Dibbens (80/30/1); the papers of N. Dobbins (83/41/1); the papers of Reverend G.P. Druitt (96/38/1); the papers of W. Edgley (94/32/1); the papers of D.E. Edwards (78/68/1); the papers of W.N. Elliott (P146); the papers of C.J. Fairrie (04/02/1); the papers of Flight Lieutenant C.S.C. Flick (83/28/1); the papers of Lieutenant M. Roger Freer (P382); the papers of Canon R.C.R. Godfrey (97/33/1); the papers of Lieutenant D.G.F. Gudgeon (85/8/1); the papers of G. Hall (PP/MCR/340); the papers of D.A. Hibbit (89/3/1); the papers of Squadron Leader D.S. Hill (05/58/1); the papers of Captain H.M. Jones (91/16/1); the papers of Captain T. Kerr (75/99/2); the papers of W. Kingsley (P424); the papers of T. Kitching (86/67/1); the papers of Lieutenant H.G. Knowles (92/4/1); the papers of W.J. Leaney (84/45/1); the papers of E.N.W. Lipman (94/32/1); the papers of P.J. Lovett (95/12/1); the papers of E.P. Mallpress (06/99/1); the papers of J. McGregor (06/127/1); the papers of C. Meadows (91/14/1); the papers of Reverend Captain A.C.V.

Menzies (67/373/1); the papers of Mrs M. Morris (80/38/1); the papers of Major W.S. Moss (05/74/1); the papers of Dr A.N.L. Munby (87/25/1); the papers of J. Nicholls (79/53/1); the papers of No. 263 Squadron RAF (Miscellaneous 3732) ; the papers of H.F. Norman (81/16/1); the papers of Squadron Leader T.P. O'Brien (84/21/1); the papers of K.G. Oakley (96/22/1); the papers of Group Captain C.B. Owen (85/16/1); the papers of E.W. Parry (86/35/1); the papers of A.J. Perman (08/85/4); the papers of K.L. Phillips (06/02/3); the papers of Captain M.J. Pleydell (90/25/1); the papers of Major A.A.K. Pope (99/18/1); the papers of E.G. Porter (82/32/1); the papers of W.A. Quinney (Con Shelf & 92/31/1); the papers of Major I.F.R. Ramsey (99/21/1); the papers of R.S. Raymond (P325 & PP/MCR/94); the papers of Lieutenant J.A. Richardson (87/58/1); the papers of Captain C. Satchell (P461); the papers of Mrs E.M. Simon (05/14/1); the papers of Miss B. Skea (79/32/1); the papers of Lieutenant Commander B.W. Smith (85/44/1); the papers of Rear Admiral O.H.M. St J. Steiner (PP/MCR/336); the papers of Miss G. Thomas (90/30/1); the papers of Major R.G.S. Tolson (05/44/1); the papers of G. Treadaway (89/5/1); the papers of H.E. Venn (92/27/1); the papers of Flying Officer R.E. Wannop (80/30/1); the papers of H.L. White (01/04/1); the papers of Captain V.A. Wight-Boycott (96/59/6); the papers of Captain R.A. Wilding (86/35/1); the papers of K. Wilson (67/12/1); the papers of S.M.S. Woodcock (87/36/1).

The Imperial War Museum

The Imperial War Museum is the national museum of the experiences of people who have lived, fought and died in conflicts involving Britain and the Commonwealth since 1914.

The Imperial War Museum is the museum of everyone's story: the history of modern war and people's experience of war and wartime life in Britain and the Commonwealth. It is an educational and historical institution responsible for archives, collections and sites of outstanding national importance.

The museum's five branches include the award-winning Imperial War Museum London; the Second World War cruiser HMS *Belfast*; the Churchill Museum and Cabinet War Rooms, housed in Churchill's secret headquarters below Whitehall; Imperial War Museum Duxford, a world-renowned aviation and heritage complex; and Imperial War Museum North.

IMPERIAL WAR MUSEUM LONDON

This London branch of the Imperial War Museum houses exhibits ranging from tanks and aircraft to photographs and personal letters; they include film and sound recordings, and some of the twentieth century's best-known paintings. Visitors can explore six floors of exhibitions and displays, including a permanent exhibition dedicated to the Holocaust and a changing programme of special temporary exhibitions.

CHURCHILL MUSEUM AND CABINET WAR ROOMS
The Cabinet War Rooms were the secret underground HQ used by Winston Churchill and his staff during the Second World War. The rooms now house the world's first major museum recording and illustrating the life and achievements of Churchill through extensive original material and cutting-edge computer technology.

HMS BELFAST
Europe's last surviving big-gun armoured warship from the Second World War. HMS *Belfast* was launched in 1938 and played a leading part in the Battle of North Cape and the Normandy landings. Today this huge and complex warship provides a unique insight into naval history and the harsh, dangerous conditions which her crew endured.

IMPERIAL WAR MUSEUM DUXFORD
This historic heritage complex has a unique collection of some 200 aircraft, including biplanes, Spitfires, Concorde and Gulf War jets. It is also home to the American Air Museum and one of the finest collections of tanks, military vehicles and artillery in Britain. Throughout the year visitors can experience a wonderful range of events from world-class air shows to Flying Proms.

IMPERIAL WAR MUSEUM NORTH
Opened to visitors on 5 July 2002, IWM North is one of the most talked-about new museums in the country. It is on the banks of the Manchester Ship Canal in Trafford, in a spectacular award-winning building designed by Daniel Libeskind. Created to give northern audiences access to the national collections, IWM North focuses on how war shapes lives.

IMPERIAL WAR MUSEUM COLLECTIONS
The Imperial War Museum has an incomparable collection covering all aspects of twentieth and twenty-first century conflict involving Britain and the Commonwealth. The collections include works of art and posters, film and video, photographs, oral history recordings, objects ranging from aircraft to toy bears, a huge range of documents, maps, diaries and letters, and a national reference library.

www.iwm.org.uk